DISCARD

Bernstein

A BIOGRAPHY

Revised & Updated

Bernstein

A BIOGRAPHY

Revised & Updated

———

JOAN PEYSER

———

Billboard Books

———

An imprint of Watson-Guptill Publications

NEW YORK

Senior Editor: Bob Nirkind
Production Manager: Ellen Greene
Cover and book design: Derek Bacchus

First published in 1998 by Billboard Books,
An imprint of Watson-Guptill Publications,
A division of BPI Communications, Inc.
1515 Broadway, New York, NY 10036

Library of Congress Cataloging-in-Publication Data
Peyser, Joan.
Bernstein: a biography, revised and updated /Joan Peyser.
p.   cm.
Includes index.
ISBN 0-8230-8259-8
1. Bernstein, Leonard, 1918–1990.
2. Musicians—United States—Biography.
I. Title.
ML410.B566P5 1998
780'.92—dc21
[B]   98–22551
                                                   CIP
                                                   MN

Manufactured in the United States of America

First Printing, 1998

1 2 3 4 5 6 7 8 9 / 06 05 04 03 02 01 99 98

First publication of this book was by Beech Tree Books/
William Morrow and Company, Inc., 1987.

To Sarah, Eric, and Leah Seligman
and
To Hannah Elizabeth Parks

Acknowledgments

OF THE MANY PEOPLE who have assisted me with their recollections of Leonard Bernstein, I first want to thank those closest to him: Jennie, his mother; Shirley, his sister; Burton, his brother; and his children: Jamie, Alex, and Nina. They gave me interviews ranging from lively telephone conversations to long and probing face-to-face sessions. I also sought out Bernstein's colleagues and friends, especially David Diamond, the distinguished American composer who has been close to Bernstein for almost fifty years. Diamond not only lent me all the letters Bernstein had sent him over this period, he gave me hours of his time.

Others who have contributed to this biography include George Abbott, James Aliferis, Alison Ames, Arnold Arnstein, George Avakian, Milton Babbitt, Julius Baker, Stefan Bauer-Mengelberg, Arthur Berger, Eric Binder, Suzanne Bloch, Arthur Bloom, Daniel Brewbaker, Florence Brooks-Dunay, Leonard Burkat, Schuyler Chapin, Marc Cogley, Philip Conole, Frank Corsaro, Thomas Cothran, Lester Cowan, Oliver Daniel, Arthur Davis, Lenore DeKoven, John de Lancie, Maria DePasquale, Irene Diamond, James Dixon, John Dunlop, Martin Eshelman, William Fertik, Beatrice Fields, Verna Fine, Lukas Foss, Morris Golde, Albert Goltzer, Eric Gordon, Jack Gottlieb, Morton Gottlieb, Morton Gould, John Gruen, Philip Hart, Hans Heinsheimer, Will Holzman, Al Howard, Edys Merrill Hunter, Miles Kastendieck, Peter Kazaras, Rabbi Israel Kazis, Larry Kert, Leon Kirchner, Irving Kolodin, Louis Krasner, Harry Kraut, Herman Krawitz, Robert Lantz, Arthur Laurents, Vera Lawrence, Richard Leacock, Gary Lemko, Janice Levit, Peter Lieberson, Seymour Lipkin, Joseph Machlis, John McClure, Gerald Marx, Gay Mehegan, Edna Ocko Meyers, Vera Michaelson, Thomas Mowrey, Peter Munves, David Oppenheim, Maurice Peress, Shirley Gabis Perle, Vincent Persichetti, Earl Price, Harvey Probber, Douglas Pugh, Matthew

Raimondi, Phillip Ramey, Sid Ramin, Azaria Rapoport, Faith Reed, Regina Resnick, Halina Rodzinski, Ann Ronell, Friede Rothe, Gunther Schuller, William Schuman, Marian Seldes, Harold Shapero, Nicolas Slonimsky, Harry Smyles, Stephen Sondheim, Jonathan Sternberg, Howard Taubman, Michael Tilson Thomas, Charles Turner, William van Gerven, Stephen Wadsworth, Jane Wilson, Paul Wittke, and Mildred Spiegel Zucker. I am grateful to all of them.

Certain sources are quoted frequently in the text. They are numbered in the following way:

1   Burton Bernstein, Family Matters (New York: Summit Books, 1982).
2   Leonard Bernstein, Findings (New York: Simon and Schuster, 1982).
3   Peter Rosen, Reflections, a film (United States Information Agency, 1978).
4   Dimitri Mitropoulos, A Correspondence with Katy Katsoyanis: 1930–1960 (New York: Martin Dale, 1973).
5   John Gruen, The Private World of Leonard Bernstein (New York: Viking Press, 1968).
6   Herbert Russcol and Margalit Banai, Philharmonic (New York: Coward, McCann and Geoghegen, 1971).
7   "On the Town," The Dramatists Guild Quarterly, Vol. 18, No. 2 (1971).

A note of thanks is also in order to Mark Rosenstein, a Manhattan-based music-theater buff, who generously sent me little-known information on Bernstein's Broadway shows.

Bernstein's own voice comes through in this book not only in his personal letters, in remarks made to me over a period of three years, and in excerpts from his own writings, it can also be heard in idiosyncratic color and remarkable detail through those quotations taken from the transcript of Reflections, the USIA film. Bernstein has not only given me permission to make use of this rich material, in November 1986 he updated it. I am grateful to him for that, as I am for his permission to quote from his letters and from Findings, the Simon and Schuster book that contains his poetry and prose.

Friends, not all of them in music, also played a major role. Throughout the period of my research Joseph Wershba, a producer of

CBS's *60 Minutes*, sent me out-of-print books on Bernstein and on those people whose lives had intersected his. Playwright Myrna Lamb listened virtually every night to the discoveries I had made during the day and offered her own striking insights. City College and New York University Professor Richard Goldstone not only conversed with me on a wide variety of aesthetic matters, he opened the door to his old friends who were among Bernstein's major collaborators on Broadway. Novelist Lucille Kallen and conductor Liza Redfield were equally helpful in opening doors; theirs led to Bernstein's associates from his earliest adult years, people whom he had not seen for decades.

Stanley H. Brown, writer and editor, gave me the benefit of his intelligence and editorial skills. He shaped and polished the manuscript; without him the book would be considerably less than it is.

James Landis, my editor, whose imprint, Beech Tree Books, is publishing this biography, left me entirely on my own until I gave him the completed work. Then he sprang into rapid, effective action.

Kami, Monica, and Tony, my daughters and son, nourished me in the best possible ways. My love and appreciation know no bounds.

Joan Peyser, January 1987

Nothing in my professional experience is more exciting than the process of interpreting a complicated life. Because my specialty is music, the lives I explore are those of composers—the prime creators in an art which requires a maker, a performer, and a listener.

I prefer to write about living composers because I can learn from the subject himself what he wants me to know, and because I have access to source material—teachers, relatives, childhood friends, and more current colleagues who are rarely available after his death. Finally there is another benefit: if I write something egregiously wrong, the person at the center of the study is there to challenge it. If there is no challenge, the reader can reasonably assume that the life story I have told is true.

There are, however, some negative consequences that come with this choice. Many who love Bernstein believe that to analyze is to dissect and to dissect is to destroy. They expressed anger with my biography. Others, professionals in music with vested economic interests in him, thought that the revelation of his dark side would interfere with the image they had done so much to promote, and ultimately reduce the money he was bringing in. They expressed outrage with my biography.

The late Leon Edel, the highly respected author of a five-volume biography of Henry James, and a colleague of mine in the English Department at New York University, spoke with me some months after *Bernstein: A Biography* first appeared. "I told you," he said, "that you could not write a *real* biography of a living person." Confused, I answered, "That is exactly what I did." "Ah, yes," Edel went on. "But just look at the response."

The response was a small price for me to pay for the pleasure of fitting together the intricate pieces of this particular jigsaw puzzle. In the end, when each of the pieces is placed where it belongs, it forms with the others the picture of a man virtually everyone recognizes as Bernstein. That this is true is attested to by the new edition you now hold in your hands. Scheduled to coincide with the 80th anniversary of the birth of America's most extraordinary musician, it contains an afterword and some never-before used photographs contributed by Frank Driggs, the noted archivist and the man at the center of my life.

For this handsome book, I express my profound gratitude to Alison Hagge, its editor; Ellen Greene, its production manager; Derek Bacchus, its designer; and to Bob Nirkind, the intelligent and gifted man who is orchestrating the acquisition and stunning republication of all of my biographical works.

Joan Peyser, April 1998

Introduction

ON DECEMBER 12, 1985, Leonard Bernstein visited the Juilliard School, America's foremost conservatory, to conduct a master class. The plan was for him to guide five student conductors ranging in age from twenty-one to twenty-seven through parts of Mahler's Symphony No. 7 and Copland's Symphony No. 3, both of which they had observed Bernstein rehearsing with the New York Philharmonic a few weeks before.

Bernstein seemed to captivate everyone there with his combination serious-slang-hip-jive talk. Seated on a table, legs dangling, he cheered on the first conductor with "At-a-boy, baby," and "Go for it." Then he got on the podium himself and conducted a few measures. After arbitrarily deciding that "Go for it" was the opposite of "Reach for it," but that both were "equally Mahlerian ways," he said, "Sometimes I went for it, sometimes I reached for it, but each time they knew what I wanted." Indeed they did. What the session revealed above everything else was Bernstein's nontechnical, gut approach to his craft. He never seemed to prepare a gesture, never told anyone how to cue. When Bernstein looks up into the heavens, with right hand extended, fingers spread open in the air, musicians underneath him anywhere in the world hold that tone under seemingly impossible circumstances until his right hand sweeps them on to whatever comes next. Whether control like this is teachable is open to question.

Bernstein extended the Juilliard rehearsal beyond the allotted time. Afterward, at a cocktail reception in the president's office, he held forth at the head of a coffee table surrounded by the five young conductors, some faculty, and me. The conversation touched on his experiences at Boston Latin, the school he had attended from the seventh through the twelfth grade. Bernstein said it offered "absolutely no music at all" and added that whatever he was today, he had achieved completely on his own. That simply is not true. Bernstein was the piano soloist with the school orchestra and sang in the glee club year after year.

Then he began to attack Sam Bernstein, his father, painting him as uncultivated in general as Boston Latin was uncultivated in music. "My childhood," he said, "was one of complete poverty. The only year my father made money was 1931 and that was because he picked up the New England franchise for a permanent wave machine. Then he bought the Newton house. Can you imagine," he said with incredulity, "a man whose only dream was to own his own house?" When someone mentioned a country house, Bernstein said with impatience, "He bought that the same year he bought the Newton house. After that there was only poverty again."

This is Bernstein making myths. Mark Twain once remarked that the older he got, the more vivid the recollection of things that had not happened. Regarding this particular conversation, Bernstein's primary purpose was to convince those at the table of his heroic transcendence of his lowly origins, symbolized by his beauty-supply-dealer father. But the facts, like those about Boston Latin, are at odds with what he said. Sam Bernstein was a successful businessman who owned not only two houses but two family cars. For years there was a succession of maids, and, for a time, a butler-chauffeur. In addition to these clear examples of the Bernstein family affluence in the 1930s, there was Leonard's Harvard education.

This firstborn son never could accept the fact that your father is bigger than you, stronger than you, knows more than you. Bernstein has tried to make that reality go away by creating a legend that his father played no role in his career, but the monologue at Juilliard suggests he still has not convinced himself of his father's insignificance.

A few months earlier, in concerts on May 21 and 23, 1985, at the Vienna State Opera, Bernstein had conducted the Vienna Philharmonic in the third acts of *Siegfried* and *Die Walküre*. It was the first time he had conducted either work. The Vienna State Opera orchestra is the Vienna Philharmonic, which explains the genesis of a particularly interesting quid pro quo.

The Vienna State Opera had agreed to present Bernstein's *A Quiet Place & Trouble in Tahiti* during its Spring 1986 season only if he would

conduct the Wagner evening the year before. It was natural for
Bernstein to want the Vienna State Opera to perform his only opera
and most recent work; he needed an opera company outside of the three
that had commissioned the piece, to give it a certain legitimacy.
According to several members of Bernstein's staff, the exchange was
exacted as "a kind of penance from him." Because it was the first time
he had ever conducted the music of Wagner, a notorious anti-Semite,
in Vienna, Hitler's intellectual home for several years and the city where
the population of Jews had fallen from two hundred thousand before
World War II to two thousand after it, Bernstein was confronted with
feelings he said he did not completely understand. As he had done in
the past, he chose to try to understand them in public on television. The
first step was to make a videotape for himself to see if his reflections on
Wagner could make an effective television show. Although he had no
title in mind, he stated his subtitle on the tape: "What's a nice Jewish
boy like you doing in a place like this playing racist music?"

Bernstein planned the program around an imaginary visit to
Sigmund Freud, the pioneer of psychoanalysis. Through the description of his conflicts, he thought he could illuminate his theme: "How
can such a first-rate genius be such a third-rate man?" Bernstein was
using Wagner here, but any number of other artists could have served
this theme as well.

The tape starts with Bernstein in front of Freud's house at 19
Berggasse dressed in a brown velvet suit, wearing sunglasses, smoking
a cigarette.

"This is Vienna," he says, "only a short walk away from the opera
house where I've been conducting ... and this is the birthplace and cradle of psychoanalysis. Freud," he continues, "had an incredible intellect,
a Faustian sense of inquiry," while Wagner "was a man about whom
more words were written than any man of his era, more than about anyone other than Mohammed or Jesus, even more than Napoleon."

Bernstein goes on to speak of Wagner's treatment of "unabashed
sibling incest on both a conscious and unconscious level," of Siegfried's
"spontaneous identification of his bride-to-be with his mother," and
he describes *Tristan and Isolde*, which he recorded in 1981 in Munich,
as "the painfully slow laying open of the unconscious." Wagner, he
says, "was a sublime genius ... so prophetic, so profoundly understanding

of the human condition." At the same time, Bernstein adds, he "was the most disagreeable, intolerable megalomaniac. There are moments when I want to close the book and I hear myself saying 'Richard Wagner, I hate you. But I hate you on my knees.' Can you help me resolve that one, Dr. Freud?"

Bernstein notes that even in "the most sympathetic and apparently accurate biography, Wagner emerges as a fairly monstrous kind of person, inconsistent and ambitious, a perfect egomaniac, a revolutionary when it suited him, a bourgeois" at other times, "an irrational anti-Semite and a man interested in everything as long as these directly contributed to and profited himself and his art, and only insofar as they did."

In trying to locate the source of Wagner's egomania, Bernstein says, "Some of us grow up more successfully than others. I have the feeling that Wagner never grew up in this sense, that he retained all his life that infantile feeling of being the center of the universe."

Bernstein went to Freud's house and focused on Wagner to deal with himself. He knows that the characteristics he here ascribes to Wagner—from unabashed sibling incest to sometime revolutionary to the feeling of being the center of the universe—are ones that have haunted him throughout his life. In fact, in this videotape, he never really asks Freud for help. Instead, he instructs him in a variety of ways that where there is genius, allowances must be made. He has himself at least as much as Wagner in mind, for he answers his original question of why he is there conducting Wagner with "I'm not nice."

But, like his remarks about Boston Latin, and his description of his father's poverty, that is not the truth, at least it is not the whole truth. The whole truth is that he made a deal: He would conduct Wagner in Vienna in order to have his only opera presented there, in the home of Mozart and Beethoven. It may be that in Bernstein's scheme of values the making of that deal renders him not nice. But in this supposed uncensored catharsis, he does not tell Freud all of the facts.

On the tape Bernstein says that the key to Wagner can be found in the third act of *Siegfried*. "Here he deals with his problem," Bernstein says, "which is the father figure. How can one hear Siegfried say, 'All my life an old man has stood in my way,' and not understand the importance of his father in his life?"

Bernstein goes on to mention that Wagner was his mother's ninth child and that Ludwig Geyer, a lodger in the house, married her only six months after Richard was born. He quotes from some of the books he leafs through that note that Geyer was a Jew. Speculating that Wagner's suspicions of his Jewish origins lay underneath his profound self-hatred, Bernstein says, "The aroma of father fixation is too strong in both the life and art of Wagner. It simply won't go away."

In closing Bernstein explains that he is going into all of these personal areas, probing the complexities of the life, "because it could make a big difference in the way we hear Wagner."

The reasons for going into the personal areas of Bernstein's life, for probing its complexities in this book, are the same: It can make a big difference in the way we hear Bernstein as well as the way we assess his achievements. One cannot claim, after all, that through his own music, Bernstein has expanded the boundaries of musical thought in our own time. Nor can one say he crystallized a style associated with an era immediately past, as some other composers in history have done. What Bernstein did above everything else was prove to the world that an American, and one who had not studied abroad, could be not only well trained but also a remarkable and exciting musician.

No musician of the twentieth century has ranged so far. Bernstein has written books, appeared on television in programs he wrote himself, lectured at universities, and performed as a pianist in public until recent years. As a composer, he has created chamber music, symphonies, and opera, as well as music for voice, film, dance, and Broadway. As a conductor he has given countless memorable performances. Moreover his interpretations of the Haydn masses, the Brahms Symphony No. 1, the Second, Seventh, and Ninth Mahler symphonies, and Stravinsky's *Le Sacre du Printemps* reveal him not only as a figure of magnetic power but as one whose musicianship is so profound that it transcends the limits of any one tradition.

Adulation for him is now everywhere. It not only informs the tone of reviews in New York, it embraces him in Europe. In April 1986, the Vienna State Opera presented *A Quiet Place & Trouble in Tahiti.* In May Bernstein conducted one of the six concerts in the Barbican Bernstein Festival, with Queen Elizabeth II and Prince Philip present. The following month François Mitterrand awarded him the Legion of Honor in Paris. And in 1987 Bernstein received the Siemens prize, the most prestigious music award in Germany.

The purpose of this book is to try to find out why Bernstein is the way he is, why he made the choices he did, and why, with his fame and wealth, his later years have been characterized by frustration and despair.

Bernstein is a complicated man ridden with stresses and tensions that have survived many years of psychoanalysis. He started his career as a composer of classical music but found his greatest creative success on Broadway. As a conductor, he refused to demean himself by getting into the pit of a Broadway house. Instead he has limited himself entirely to the so-called classical repertory. As a composer, Bernstein is most renowned for *West Side Story*, a fact that causes him anguish, for he would prefer to enter the pantheon with a symphony or a grand opera. But as one of Mozart's highest achievements was *The Magic Flute*, a work for the popular theater of the day, so *West Side Story* may one day possess those particular credentials Bernstein has coveted all his life.

Approaching seventy, Bernstein continues at a frenetic pace, conducting, lecturing, proselytizing, composing. When Bernstein received the Lifetime Achievement Award of the National Academy of Recording Arts and Sciences in 1985, he said that he felt that his life and work were still ahead of him. In a story that appeared on the front page of *USA Today*, August 4, 1986, Bernstein was quoted as saying, "I was diagnosed as having emphysema in my mid-20s, and I've been smoking for decades. I was told that if I didn't stop, I'd be dead by age 25. Then they said I'd be dead by age 45. And 55. Well, I beat the rap. I smoke, I drink, I stay up all night and screw around. I'm over-committed on all fronts."

Bernstein's recollection of these various prognoses should be seen through the same prism as his description of his father as poor and of Boston Latin as offering no music. All of it serves to dramatize his success at defying and transcending confining authority. Those who suffer from emphysema cannot climb even a few steps. They certainly could not survive years of chain-smoking or the physical stress of a conducting career. Bernstein not only smokes several packs a day, drinks inordinate amounts of scotch whisky, and is sexually promiscuous, but he displays his excesses to prove he is above all the laws of nature, for he prevails, apparently healthy and fit. Metaphorically shaking his fist at

God, Bernstein comes out on top. It is no accident that a cover story in *The New York Times Magazine* on August 31, 1986, was entitled "Bernstein Triumphant."

Samuel Johnson warned that a biographer may be tempted to invent or conceal. Concerning Bernstein, there is no temptation to invent. His real life is rich enough. There is, however, some temptation to conceal, for Bernstein is right; there are aspects of Wagner in him, canyons of darkness as well as shafts of brilliant light. A biographer can ignore neither.

The crevices of character have to be explored as fully as the peaks of achievement to understand why Bernstein lived the life he did, and why, against a setting of deepening despair, he continues to be driven by the need to create what fulfills his criteria for a great work of art. It is hoped that this portrait will shed light not only on Bernstein, the most famous musician of our time, but also on music in the United States during the last fifty years.

One day in the mid-1950s, after Leonard Bernstein had conducted a concert at Tanglewood, Sam Bernstein, his father, told a reporter, "Every genius had a handicap; Lenny had a father."

Sam Bernstein was wrong. He was no handicap. In fact he behaved in a way that was conducive to his son's establishing his great

1922
Jennie, Louis ("Lenny"), and Sam. "From the beginning, he was special."

career. Throughout history there have been musical geniuses who have felt harsh resistance from their fathers. Gentle support appears to induce indolence, while the father who insults, degrades, humiliates his son appears to stimulate the aggression necessary for the combat inherent in a life in the arts.

In the eighteenth century Handel had such a father; in the nineteenth Schumann did. But in the twentieth, where rebellion has characterized so much of the tone of the art itself, the negative father is almost the rule. Varèse's father locked the piano, covered the instrument with a shroud, and threw away the key. Boulez had a father almost as intransigent. Encouraging his son to enter engineering, he put every possible obstacle in his musical path. Stravinsky's father, a bass singer, sent his son to law school. It was only after the elder Stravinsky died that Igor left law to study composition.

Sam Bernstein had even more reason than most to fight his son's choice of career. In 1908 at sixteen Sam had fled from his family in the Ukraine for a better life in the United States. At home he had known Jews as musicians only as *klezmers*, strolling players who performed for weddings and bar mitzvahs in exchange for a few kopecks, some food, or a night's lodging. Sam Bernstein refused to believe that he had gone through three weeks in the filthy steerage of a ship, hard work at the Fulton Fish Market in New York, menial chores in a Hartford, Connecticut, barbershop, and an aggressive career building a beauty supply business in Boston so that his firstborn son could spend his days playing piano "under a palm tree in some cocktail lounge."

Sam would often tell Leonard that it was all right if "you were a Koussevitzky, a Toscanini, a Rachmaninoff, but how many of these people are there around anyhow?" He did not have the slightest idea of the size of his son's talent. Well into the years of Leonard's success, he would ask his son's friends and colleagues, "Do you think he has something in him? Do you think this success can last?" Such an attitude is not unique. Stravinsky's mother chided her son for not "recognizing his betters, like Scriabin," and she did not hear *Le Sacre du Printemps*, one of the pathbreaking works of the century, until its twenty-fifth anniversary performance, a year before she died. Even then she told friends she did not expect to like it, that he did not write "her kind of music."

But every artist needs support from somewhere. Stravinsky's came from a cousin. Bernstein was more fortunate: He had the unqualified love of his sister, Shirley, and his mother, Jennie.

Jennie Bernstein had suffered the same kind of hard early life as Sam. She came to the United States at eight, and began to work full time in a factory at twelve. Jennie's mother, Pearl Resnick, wanted her daughter to marry Sam. He was smart, ambitious, religious, and had already shown a talent for making money. At first Jennie resisted his attentions. But she changed her mind when Sam was drafted during World War I and she thought he would have to fight in the war. When he returned home a few days later, discharged because of bad eyesight, she was so pleased to see him that she married him. They rented a small apartment in Mattapan, an economically depressed suburb of Boston.

Good marriages are rarely built on such moments. Sam and Jennie's was particularly bad. Visitors to their home in the 1930s remark on the constant fighting, the absence of mutual consideration, the joylessness between the couple. Because the tone of the marriage was angry from the start, Jennie left Sam to be with her mother in nearby Lawrence when it came time to give birth to their first child.

When the boy was born on August 25, 1918, Sam was still at home in Mattapan. Jennie's mother, a strong-willed woman, insisted he be named Louis, like her brother, for their father. Because Jennie and Sam preferred Leonard, that is what they called him. So the boy, during his first five years, did not know his legal name. When he first attended kindergarten, the teacher asked "Louis Bernstein" to stand up. Recalling the incident recently, Bernstein said he had looked around the room for a boy with the same last name as his. But the teacher kept pointing at him. When he returned home and asked his mother about what had happened, she admitted his real name was Louis. From then until he turned sixteen, when he applied for his first driver's license and changed his name legally, all of Bernstein's report cards and official documents bore the name "Louis."

On hearing this story from Bernstein, someone suggested that the early confusion surrounding his name may well account for a life that he himself has characterized as schizophrenic. He is, after all, known to be torn between composing and conducting, between art music and pop, between hetero- and homosexuality. Could these profound conflicts be traced to an identity crisis in his formative years?

This remark was delivered as something of a joke, but Bernstein appropriated the diagnosis. Weeks later, on his sixty-fifth birthday, which was being celebrated in his "hometown" of Lawrence, Massachusetts, he told a stadium audience of about twelve thousand people that his real name had been Louis, that he had always been called Lenny, and that the early confusion accounted for his schizophrenic ways.

Now in her eighties, Bernstein's mother speaks of him with adoration and pride: "Scratch any part of him and he oozes with talent. Where do you get a musician who could also write the Harvard lectures? In his apartment there are walls of books. He reads the Talmud, reads everything you can imagine. There are thousands of books on psychiatry alone.

"Leonard is a great musician. He is a Renaissance man. To write a book about him is like writing a book on Einstein."

Her son's birth provided Jennie with a ray of hope in the midst of her unhappiness with Sam. And her attentions to the infant Lenny increased when it became apparent that his health was frail. "From the beginning," his brother, Burton, writes, "he was special. Asthmatic, sensitive, intelligent, he left a deep impression on everyone, whether because of his chronic wheezing or because of his unmistakable precocity. Jennie knew she had an unusual child: 'When he was a sickly little boy and he'd turn blue from asthma, Sam and I were scared to death,' she has said. 'Every time he had an attack, we thought he was going to die. I would be up all night with steam kettles and hot towels, helping him to breathe. If Lenny so much as sneezed, we would turn pale with worry.... But sickly or not, Lenny was such a brilliant boy—always the leader of his gang, always the best in school.' "[1]

Bernstein's own memories of his leadership days do not extend back to grammar school, which he remembers with some pain. He says he was not only thin and sickly but terrified of anti-Semitic neighborhood gangs. However, he recalls that he changed virtually overnight when an aunt, in the process of a divorce, left an old upright piano in the Bernstein house. The aunt, Clara, was Sam's sister, a woman the older Bernstein could not abide. Throughout her life he called her "crazy Clara," and she became a favorite of the son, who claims her singing could shatter glass.

It was Leonard's discovery of the piano that he credits with transforming him from a frail nobody into a powerful human being, capable of conquering the world. Jennie says she was aware of her son's connection to music long before Aunt Clara's piano arrived: "When he was a little toddler creeping around on the floor and he heard music, he would stop on a dime and cry. We rented part of a summer house when he was almost two. We didn't have access to the living room but there was a piano in it and whenever someone played it, Lenny would press his ear to the wall.

"Lenny always had colds and had to stay inside. When he was about four or five he would play an imaginary piano on his windowsill. When he finally got a piano, he did what he now says he did: made love to it all the time."

There were other musical experiences as well, though hardly those of a Schoenberg or Stravinsky. In fact it is the absence of the kind of musical education and experience that every young European goes through and the plethora of idiosyncratic American ones that account for the freshness and vitality of Bernstein's music at its best.

By the late 1920s, the Bernsteins did own a phonograph but the only music Bernstein remembers coming from it was "Barney Google" and "Oh, by Jingo," the hit songs of the day. On his aunt's piano, he started to reconstruct the popular melodies in his head. "Blue Skies" was one of them. But he asked his parents for lessons and began to study with a neighbor's daughter, Frieda Karp, who charged a dollar a lesson. She gave him such beginning pieces as "On to Victory" and "The Mountain Belle." Bernstein says it was then he began to thrive, put on weight, and make friends with his schoolmates.

Leonard learned to read music quickly and before long was playing far better than Frieda Karp, who soon married and moved to California. At twelve, Leonard moved on to the New England Conservatory of Music, where he was assigned to Susan Williams, who charged three dollars an hour. That move enraged Sam. He interpreted it correctly: His son was serious about music. It was then that the real fighting began; Leonard was thirteen years old.

From that point on, Sam's "Stop that damn piano" was counterpoint to Jennie's quiet encouragement. If Jennie had searched for a way to express her rage at her domineering husband, she could not have found a more constructive one than encouraging her gifted son to go on. "Lenny always played at night," Jennie Bernstein says. "Of course it disturbed his father's sleep. But I would listen way into the night. I couldn't ever get him into bed. Whenever he composed—and he started composing when he was about twelve—he would ask me, 'Do you like this ending or that one?' He always wanted an audience. In those years I was his audience."

In 1927, when Leonard was nine, Sam changed his affiliation from an Orthodox synagogue to the Conservative Congregation Mishkan Tefilah. Years later he recalled his son being affected not only by the cantor, Iszo C. Glickstein, but by the synagogue's ritual music. Both, he said, brought his son to tears. According to Burton Bernstein, the rabbi, H. H. Rubenovitz, delivered his sermons not only in English but in Oxford-accented English. Sam has said that for a time Lenny's ambition was to become a rabbi. It is likely that his somewhat affected, orotund speech was modeled on Rubenovitz. It is precise and contains a broad *a* combined with a hard *r*. It owes little to his father's locution—Sam never lost his heavy Yiddish accent—and almost nothing to his mother's Boston sound. Lenny, who recalls wanting to be a rabbi, once gave Rubenovitz a curious gift. At an anniversary party for the rabbi, he took a melody from the High Holy Day music he says he had heard his father sing in the shower, and played it in the style of Mozart, Chopin, and Gershwin. It is hard to believe the rabbi could have appreciated this secular treatment of the sacred music.

Sam Bernstein devoted his free time to reading the Talmud; his father and grandfather had been talmudic scholars. But he was also a skillful businessman and made many astute decisions. The year before his son discovered the piano, the year he shifted to Mishkan Tefilah, Sam discovered a product called the Fredericks permanent wave machine and outbid his Boston competitors for the New England franchise. Suddenly Sam had real money in the bank and a great deal of credit everywhere. He often described the event as "the American dream coming through."

Throughout the latter half of the 1920s, every advance in Sam's business was translated into more comfortable housing. In 1927, the best of these years, when Lenny was nine and Shirley four, the Bernsteins moved to a house in Roxbury where brother and sister would no longer share a room. Still, they were thrown together a great deal, huddling for comfort when Sam and Jennie fought bitterly. In the early years, Lenny and Shirley played four-hand piano; still later Shirley performed in his shows. The connection between brother and sister transcended virtually all other family ties. They protected each other from the wrath of their parents, and since Burtie, the younger brother, was so much younger, they pretended he was their son.

In the 1930s, the years of the Great Depression, the Bernsteins continued to prosper. Sam's business was literally "hair." A completely bald man, he specialized in toupees and permanents. Sam built a red brick house on Park Avenue in Newton and left Roxbury. He also built a summer house in nearby Sharon, a community south of Boston that was a favorite of middle-class Jews. He bought a Packard sedan for himself, a Plymouth roadster with a rumble seat for his wife, and he supported a succession of maids and a West Indian butler-chauffeur. In 1931 he even bought a Chickering grand piano for his son.

For a man who claimed he was against music for his son, there were subtle signs of cooperation. When his synagogue had a benefit—a Boston Pops concert—Sam invited Lenny to join him. Then fourteen, the boy had never been to a public concert before. A few months later a business associate gave Sam two tickets for a Rachmaninoff concert. Again the father invited the son. At the Pops concert Ravel's *Boléro* was played. According to friends Sam hummed the melody for years, and Lenny saved to buy the score. As for the Rachmaninoff concert, the pianist played a late Beethoven sonata, opening a whole new world of art to the teenager.

In 1916, Arnold Schoenberg established the Society for Private Musical Performances in Vienna. Anton Webern and Alban Berg were both members. What made the society somewhat bizarre were the regulations determined by Schoenberg. Each member had to come to each performance armed not only with an identification card but with an accompanying photograph so that no hostile outsider could possibly slip into the hall. The insiders were those who understood the new musical language; the outsiders were those conservatives who did not.

Ten years later in a Boston suburb, Lenny Bernstein and his best friend, Eddie Ryack, established a club of their own that had at its center a similar purpose: the establishment of a new language that would separate insiders from older outsiders. The language was Rybernian and it came from a country, Rybernia, ruled over by Bernstein and Ryack. The name obviously was a combination of their own. Lenny's sister, Shirley, was a charter member. Later Burtie entered the fold. Only the most privileged of friends were allowed into the club's secrets and today, when its members meet, the language invariably turns Rybernian.

One day at Eddie Ryack's, Lenny was teaching him to play "Goodnight, Sweetheart" in the key of C. Ryack was having trouble. Also seated at the piano was Eddie's friend, Sid Ramin. When Ramin played the passage and asked, "You mean like this?" a friendship began. Lenny started to teach Ramin piano and, in a businesslike manner, charged Sid a dollar a lesson. Ramin, one of the most talented and successful orchestrators today, says Bernstein was his only teacher.

"We would play four-handed arrangements of 'St. Louis Blues,' 'I've Told Every little Star,' 'I Hear Music,' and 'Carioca,'" Ramin said recently. "I remember him being so taken with *Rhapsody in Blue*. Lenny saved money to buy the music and then learned it immediately. He would sight-read it, transposing all the parts simultaneously. When Lenny visited me he would sit right down and play songs like 'The Thrill Is Gone,' reading every piece of sheet music on the piano and never making a mistake."

The kind of music Sid's mother kept on her piano was the kind on many pianos in those days. It was the kind to which Bernstein had also been exposed on trips to relatives in Hartford, where a wind-up phonograph played Frank Munn singing "I Want to Go Back to Michigan," Frank Crumit singing "I Wish That I'd Been Born in Borneo," and Rosa Ponselle performing arias. Bernstein has described Hartford as an "aesthetic experience."

Ramin and Bernstein were inseparable as adolescents. "We shared a love of music," Ramin explains. "We also had a laboratory where we did scientific experiments. They involved distilling alcohol. We would get rubbing alcohol from Burtie's nurse, because she used it on the baby. We'd put it on a Bunsen burner, heat it, and as the alcohol went up the glass tubing all steamed up, we'd cover the flask with a cold towel and produce pure alcohol. We thought it was a great experiment. We never even considered drinking it. When Lenny grabbed the flask he would said, 'It's hotsky-totsky,' or something like that.

"Lenny's father," Ramin went on, "was vice president of the synagogue and a very well-read man. He was stern, a harsh disciplinarian. There were violent arguments between father and mother. The father was a successful businessman but there was no love between husband and wife. Just lots of friction. Lenny's mother was very easy-going and very loving of Lenny all the time.

"They had a summer house. When I was there, he and I would share a room. Shirley would be asleep in her room and we would creep into it and hold her finger for a time." Lenny had heard that if you held the finger of a sleeping person, that person would recount his or her dreams. According to Ramin, Shirley remained silent.

When Sid was not at Sharon, he would receive letters or cards from Lenny. "For a long time he wanted to buy the sheet music for Ravel's *Boléro*. Then I received a card with only these words: 'I bought *Boléro*.'"

Sid and Lenny double-dated. "Lenny was very grand. He would bow and kiss the girl's hand. He did it straight, without mocking. We talked a lot about sex. We would walk through Franklin Park looking for condoms. Lenny would attach funny notes to discarded mattresses we saw. Once Lenny and I were walking down the street and someone was playing the piano. The person couldn't get it right. Suddenly Lenny bounded up the steps, onto the porch, and through the window. A girl was sitting on a piano bench. He shoved her aside, sat down, and played it. 'That's the way it should go,' he said. Then he disappeared."

Bernstein was unremitting in his intolerance of musical mistakes. His sister was one of his earliest students—and victims. Here are Shirley's own words: "The bond between us really started when we were singing opera together. I was nine or ten, Lenny fourteen or fifteen. He took scores out of the public library and the screaming went on into the wee hours of the night. It was terribly exciting. We were creating music. We played four-handed symphonies and I sang my lungs out. My voice fell an octave from singing wrong.

"Lenny taught me to sight-read quickly," Shirley Bernstein goes on. "How? He hit me if I did it wrong. He also taught me how to get through a piece, how to fake it, how to play the harmonies with the left hand while keeping the melody going with the right. I started to take

piano lessons with someone else but after a few years I stopped. By then
Lenny was playing concertos and it was too silly for me to go on. I
remember my mother being relieved when I let it go."

At fifteen, Bernstein played the Grieg Piano Concerto; at college,
he played with the Massachusetts State Symphony under the auspices
of the Works Progress Administration. But between his early adolescence and his Harvard days a number of powerful forces intervened.
Sex was certainly one of them. Bernstein, quoted in his brother's memoirs, recalls his first impulses coming about the time that Burtie was
born: "I was crazed with curiosity. I would look up 'childbirth' in the
Jewish encyclopedia, the only encyclopedia we had at the time, but
there wasn't much to learn from that." He still managed in a small way
to get into the act. He had been studying alliteration that week and
when the infant arrived, he suggested "Burton" because it was allitera-
tive with Bernstein.

From earliest times Leonard got his way. Friends recall he even got
his way with the various maids in the house; riding in the rumble seat
with them, his hands seemed always to be up under their skirts. It was
around the time of his puberty that Lenny discovered music theater as
well as sex. In Sharon, at fourteen, he put on a grotesque production of
Carmen. Written in collaboration with Dana Schnittkind, a classmate, it
was an Americanized version with the boys playing girls and vice versa.
Burton quotes his brother:

> In our innocence it just seemed terribly funny that Dana
> Schnittkind, who already had a dark, heavy beard, should play
> Micaëla, that tender, loving creature, and that I, out of sheer
> ego, should play Carmen, and that my girlfriend at the
> moment, Beatrice Gordon, should play Don José. As I recall,
> Rose Schwartz played the bullfighter, Escamillo. Since most
> of the people we could find for the chorus were girls, we had
> what turned out to be an all-male chorus sung by females, cos-
> tumed as little old men wearing yarmulkes. We borrowed
> evening gowns from Mrs. Finn, and the wigs were supplied
> by none other than the Samuel Bernstein Hair Company. I
> played the piano, except when I was onstage as Carmen; then
> Ruth Potash played. [1]

According to observers, Lenny stole the show when, to the music of the "Seguidilla," he swayed his hips and sang:

> *You think my lips are tender, eh?*
> *You think my waist is slender, eh?*

"The score was much simplified," Bernstein went on, "with lots of cuts, and our version of the libretto was full of private jokes and allusions to Sharon." Admission cost twenty-five cents, and the show was a great success.

Two summers later, calling themselves the Sharon Community Players, the group raised the admission to one dollar, with profits going to charity, for a production of *The Mikado*. This time there was no shift of sexes. Lenny played Nanki-Poo, Shirley Yum-Yum. *The Mikado* led to the next season's even more professional *H.M.S. Pinafore*, with the family maid as Buttercup. *Carmen*, *The Mikado*, and *Pinafore* were highlights.

But the center of his musical life in his early teens was jazz. Bernstein's own participation in jazz combos was always minimal. Even in his youth he stood out too much as a personality to blend in with delicate ensemble work. But his identification with the idiom was critical. As a teenager Bernstein achieved popularity, even a certain notoriety, by playing what was then called jazz at parties. Often he did not take off his top coat. He could stand rather than sit at the piano, with his coat open, then move to the next party and play again.

But along with the frenetic social life, he continued to take piano lessons. Soon he knew he would have to leave Susan Williams. He went for an audition with Heinrich Gebhard, Boston's foremost music teacher, but because the twenty-five dollar fee was prohibitive and because he really was not yet ready for Gebhard, Bernstein began lessons with Gebhard's assistant, Helen Coates, from Rockford, Illinois. Although he had studied four years by that time, he had received no instruction in harmony or theory, had not been taught anything about tonality, the underlying structure of most of the music in the repertory. According to Coates, he had at least sensed it on his own and invented his own terminology for it. Helen Coates, about the same age as Jennie Bernstein, was as loving as Bernstein's mother and even more giving, if that was possible. She permitted the one-hour lessons, for which she charged six dollars, to extend to three hours or more. She listened to

him discourse on philosophy and warmly received his own compositions. By the time he turned sixteen, Bernstein moved on to Gebhard.

Leonard's talent surprised everyone, even Sam. On cruises to
Florida and the Caribbean, Sam brought along his son, who entertained
the passengers at the piano. His *pièce de résistance* was to play a popular
melody in the style of Mozart, Chopin, and Gershwin, adapting it in
much the same way he had the High Holy Day music for Rabbi
Rubenovitz. In 1934 Sam went even further: He paid out three hundred
dollars a week to radio station WBZ for thirteen weeks of quarter-hour
programs called *Avol Presents Leonard Bernstein at the Piano.* Avol was a
cosmetic preparation Sam was selling at the time. Lenny would play the
"light classics" such as "Malagueña."

Even so, on the surface the relationship between father and son was
combative. Friends use a stronger word: hate. But if that hate had not
contained love (indifference was not an issue here), Sam Bernstein
would not have lent Lenny wigs for *Carmen,* would not have invited
him to concerts, would not have brought him along on cruises, nor
would Lenny have played on Sam's radio show.

In high school Leonard devoted an essay to his father. It began,
"My father is a very complicated human being. A man of irregular
temperament and unusual convictions, he is a rare combination of
the shrewd businessman and the ardent religionist. It is rare that one
finds such a combination. In my father's case, I attribute whatever
degree of material success he has attained to this very suboccupation:
religious activity."

The essay ends, "Because of his diligent study, his work has
flourished materially, and he is a leader in his field—living proof that
the wise man combines the spiritual and material in order to ensure a
sound life." [2]

If, throughout the essay, the reader substitutes the word "artistic"
whenever "religious" or "spiritual" appears, one has the credo of
Leonard Bernstein's own life.

Although Leonard rebelled against Sam in choosing a career in music, he followed his father's lead in balancing art, as Sam did the Talmud, with the acquisition of money. To say Bernstein adopted materialistic values is not to suggest he did anything mean. Rather it is to emphasize that by doing virtually everything in music

About 1935

"At eighteen, Bernstein pretended that Mildred was Myra Hess, the English pianist, and he was the legendary Josef Hofmann."

and by doing it all very well, he became what can be called the first industrialist in the field, supporting a number of employees as his father had. Bernstein did not do this by attracting a wealthy patron, marrying a rich woman, or investing on Wall Street. He did it by working hard in music: by composing, conducting, recording, playing piano, writing books, appearing on television delivering his own ideas, and composing several first-rate Broadway musicals that produced a number of pop hits. There is nothing pejorative in this. More than two hundred years ago Alexander Hamilton applauded his fellow Americans who "took on extra employment as a resource for multiplying their acquisitions or their enjoyment." Who is to say this should not be done through art?

In the late 1950s Sam, whose English was haphazard at best, told a reporter that "Lenny was never an infant pedigree." A musical prodigy the boy was not; there were no available musical outlets for him when he was young. But his superior intelligence was obvious from the start.

Soon after Leonard was born, the Bernsteins moved from Mattapan to an apartment in Allston, not a particularly good neighborhood. Burton Bernstein writes that Sam's stinting on the family budget and his late hours at the office brought about a separation even more serious than before. Again there was a reconciliation. Such unhappiness did not often precipitate divorce among middle-class couples in those days.

The Bernsteins were continually on the move. Within a six-year period, beginning in 1925, they moved five times within the town of Roxbury. Each move, an improvement on the last, was to a different street: Abbotsford, Crawford, Brookledge, Schuyler, and Pleasanton. Throughout this period, Leonard attended the W. L. Garrison Grammar School. When he was ready to enter the seventh grade, Sam and Jennie moved to Newton, where their firstborn could enter Boston Latin School. This meant paying tuition because Newton is not part of Boston. But his children's education was paramount to Sam, and by the late 1920s, the cost presented no real difficulty to him.

Whatever the cost, it was well worth it to have his son at Boston Latin. Founded in 1635, with an alumni roster that included Cotton Mather, Samuel Adams, John Hancock, Ralph Waldo Emerson, George Santayana, and Bernard Berenson, it provided an exacting, classical education. Even the physical surroundings nourished the concept of academic excellence. Set on the wide Avenue Louis Pasteur, the three-story classical building had as its neighbors Simmons College, Harvard Medical School, the Boston Museum of Fine Arts, the Isabella Stewart Gardner Museum, the Wentworth Institute of Technology, and at least half a dozen other institutions that contributed to Boston's view of itself as "the Hub of the Universe." Boston Latin was an institution where students called their teachers masters, where they stood when they were addressed by the faculty, and where "approbation" and "approbation with distinction" were the equivalent of honors and high honors. At Latin, where misdemeanor marks, detention after school, and "censures" were the costs of undesirable conduct, suits and ties were required. Most important was the idea that the students take their place in an "aristocracy" based not on inherited wealth or family lineage but on their own mental prowess. Boston Latin, from its beginnings, was conceived as a ladder for upward mobility.

In his autobiography, *In Search of History*, Theodore H. White, who had graduated from the school a year before Bernstein, wrote, "In my day, the Latin School was a cruel school…. Absolutely anyone was free to enter. And the school was free to fail and expel absolutely anyone who did not meet its standards. It accepted students without discrimination, and it flunked them…."

In the 1930s the school was one of the most academically demanding in the United States. Students faced three hours of homework every night and examinations in every subject every week. Latin went from the seventh through the twelfth grades. Sixty-five percent of the boys admitted were expected to fail and be sent back to ordinary schools. Bernstein's graduation year, 1935, was the school's tercentenary.

Students took six years of Latin, four years of French, and two or three of German or Greek; Leonard chose German. The school also required a standard curriculum: history, English, mathematics, and so forth. According to his parents, Lenny did virtually no homework. According to his teachers, he invariably stood near the top of the class. Lenny also attended Hebrew school every afternoon after class. Records from the Mishkan Tefilah school show he graduated as an honor student in 1931, the year of his bar mitzvah.

Invariably, he attracted considerable attention. Philip Marson, a legendary English teacher at Boston Latin, said some years ago that Bernstein, "as a kid, was always gracious, very much alive, so much so that I can remember thirty years later where he sat in my class. First seat in the second row. *Hamlet* and *Macbeth* set him afire. He was tremendously absorbed. A great reader, he loved Milton, Browning, and Shelley. He ate up Untermeyer's *Anthology of Modern Poetry*."

Under the quotation "Tis the Tone That Makes the Music," Lenny's yearbook entry reads, "Modern Prize, 1929–30; Special Reading Prize, 1929–30; Classical Prize, 1932–33; French Club, 1934–35; Physics Club, 1934–35; Glee Club, 1929–30–31–33–34–35; School Orchestra, 1931–32–33; Soloist with the School Orchestra, 1933–34–35; co-author of 1935 Class Song, 1935." The hiatus in his glee club activity that occurred in 1932 was probably the result of his voice change; Leonard was then fourteen years old. As for the other co-author of the 1935 class song, that was Lawrence Ebb who worked with Lenny as a collaborator on the lyrics. Here are some of them:

> *Worthy servants of the state:*
> *Pioneers have gone before us,*
> *They are ours to emulate....*

Conversations with classmates reveal that in addition to a stunning facility for sight-reading, simultaneous transposition, and other unteachable techniques, there was another less definable instinct. Leonard Burkat, a fellow student and an oboist in the school orchestra, says that Lenny amazed the conductor by playing waltzes in the Viennese style, holding the second beat slightly. When asked where he had learned to do that, Bernstein said he didn't know he was doing it. Burkat introduced his friend to Stravinsky's *Petrouchka* in the tenth grade and the fourteen-year-old boy, without missing a beat, read through the piano part.

There are other musicians who possess musical facility that may be comparable to this. Lukas Foss is one of them. But few have the personality—a combination of charm, electricity, and aggression—that instantly attracts audiences, money, and fame. Sid Ramin, a member of a club, the Maccabees, recalls that when Lenny was fourteen, he came to address the members. "Everyone was flabbergasted," Ramin says. "People were mesmerized. Even when he was a kid, I knew he'd be someone great."

About that time—his early teens—Lenny swam and played tennis, though he still enjoyed music. It was then he put on his own *Carmen* at

Singer's Inn in Sharon. He also enjoyed female impersonation without music. At the end of his high school days, he played the female lead in Le Cercle Français's production of Molièrés *Le Médecin Malgré Lui.* According to the club's notes, he played the role with "*une grande vocabulaire et une longue langue.*"

Four-hand piano with his sister or other close friends provided the basis for his personal relationships. One such friend was Mildred Spiegel—now Mrs. Mildred S. Zucker—who first heard him play at an assembly in the auditorium at the Roxbury Memorial High School. "There was a big bunch of kids around him, just listening," she remembers. "He was playing *Malagueña* and *Rhapsody in Blue.* He was just like the Pied Piper. Everyone stood around listening. There was something about it—wild and lots of expression. I had studied piano since I was very young but I couldn't play like this.…"

"Then he took to coming by my house to play, usually after going to temple on a Saturday. Oh, the strings he broke on that piano, playing as he did. He really hadn't had any good teachers up to then. It was shortly after that he studied under Helen Coates and Heinrich Gebhard, who was the best teacher in Boston. I had been studying under Gebhard for some time. Lenny would come to the house and ask me to play for him. His own playing was somewhat undisciplined and he would ask how I managed to develop such a technique, and he wanted to know how I practiced. I'd show him, setting up a metronome and going through a piece carefully.

"But the things he could do! He would come in and sit down at the piano and play any music that happened to be there, sight-reading as fast as if he'd been playing it for years. Then he got so he'd go to the library and show up with an armload of strange music, and he'd play it through the same way."

The friendship with Mildred Spiegel lasted until Lenny went to New York, in his early twenties. "But it was just a musical friendship," she emphasizes. "We were close friends and he was like a member of the family. He would come in, throw his arms around my mother, and kiss her. But it didn't mean anything. He wasn't a prospective son-in-law or a potential one. It's just that Lenny is very demonstrative. We went to lots of concerts and recitals together. I remember one night in Symphony Hall. We were sitting up very high and Koussevitzky had just done a beautiful job of conducting something very difficult. There was a great ovation, people standing and cheering, and Lenny just sat there clapping very softly. 'What's the matter, didn't you like it?' I asked him. And he said, 'I'm so jealous....'"

In October 1937, Bernstein gave Mildred a program that read, "The State Symphony Orchestra, Alexander Thiede, conductor, announces Leonard Bernstein (Artist-Pupil of Heinrich Gebhard), Soloist, in the Ravel Piano Concerto at Sanders Theater, Cambridge." In her copy, Bernstein had crossed out "State" and replaced it with "Boston," changed the conductor's name to "Serge Koussevitzky," and started to change the theater name to "Symphony Hall" but had stopped after "Symph" and written "Oh! I can't go on," apparently in embarrassment at his presumption.

"He could get so stirred up by music," she says. "Once we went to a Chopin program at Jordan Hall and when we came out he made me dance a mazurka with him down the street to the Huntington Avenue subway station." For her twentieth and twenty-first birthdays, he composed short piano pieces for her.

W. H. Auden wrote, "We are all of us actors who cannot be anything until we have pretended to be it." On January 5, 1936, for a concert to be held in the Boston Public Library in which Bernstein was to accompany a baritone, violinist, and cellist, he wrote this note to Mildred: "Myra Dear—Will you please turn pages for me at this darn lecture? I'll call you up next Saturday. Josef (Lenny)." At eighteen, Bernstein pretended that Mildred was Myra Hess, the English pianist, and he was the legendary Josef Hofmann.

Friends in the Brookline, Massachusetts, area remember Lenny and Mildred as a very popular couple, invited to all the parties. One of their memorable routines was Mildred doing a burlesque imitation of a singer in an aria from *Traviata* with Lenny playing the piano part and improvising the tenor with his right hand. Often they played four-hand piano singing a jazzed-up Bernstein version of Gilbert and Sullivan; a variation of this was Mildred playing while Lenny screamed nonsense words to go with the music. But there were also serious composition efforts connected to his friendship with Mildred. These included a pianoforte trio for violin, cello, and piano, performed at Harvard in 1937 with Mildred Spiegel at the piano; *Music for Two Pianos*, played by

Bernstein and Spiegel in a recital at Gebhard's studio in Brookline in 1938; a piano sonata, dedicated to Gebhard, completed in 1938; and *Music for the Dance*, dedicated "to Mildred," who performed it along with Bernstein's two-piano piece at the recital in Gebhard's studio.

Harvard did not bring with it striking changes in Leonard's life. Boston Latin had prepared him well and he continued to do a minimum of work with remarkably good results; he graduated cum laude. Ramin remembers that when Lenny was about to enter Harvard, in the fall of 1935, he said he would assume a more "snooty" manner, broadening his *a* to achieve that effect. But the critical characteristics remained intact. Bernstein continued to party, making music all the way. He went into his freshman year without a real romance and came out of his senior year in the same state. He entered Harvard with the piano as his major area of concentration and graduated still thinking of himself as a pianist.

What made the difference for Bernstein at Harvard was the men he met there. Two became more than friends in the sense they altered his life: the composer Aaron Copland and the conductor Dimitri Mitropoulos. But Bernstein also came into contact with younger, gifted American composers who were even then enjoying good careers or else were on the brink of success. Among these were David Diamond, William Schuman, Marc Blitzstein, Irving Fine, and Harold Shapero.

Diamond recalled that he first met Bernstein at a 1939 Boston Symphony concert at Carnegie Hall. "Blitzstein and Copland had told me there was this extraordinary pianist at Harvard. Even Mitropoulos told me there was this 'genius-boy' there. The word was out. Everyone was taken with him. No wonder! Lenny in the thirties was unbelievable. There was immense joy in his music-making. Lenny will always be a re-creator for me. He didn't just play a lot of jazz; he played reductions at the piano of all the masters. Reinterpreting was his forte. The question I have always asked myself was why, with Lenny so gifted, he didn't end up with Nadia Boulanger [the renowned French composition teacher]. She would have turned him into the most famous man in the world overnight."

It is not as though Bernstein didn't covet fame, even then. His remark about his jealousy of Koussevitzky testifies to that. But going abroad to study held no appeal at all. Bernstein had spent so little of his life immersed in the masters of the past that he could not have felt the inferiority that many American musicians feel when confronted with their European counterparts. Growing up loving *Rhapsody in Blue*, producing *The Mikado*, and parodying *Carmen* does not lead, in one's young adulthood, to holding the descendants of Bach or Rameau in awe.

It was not only a matter of indifference to a European heritage. Bernstein resisted all discipline. High school friends recall that he would drive around in his mother's car—he was the only student in his class who would drive to school—and if he landed at their houses late at night, he would make himself comfortable and stay until daylight. He also avoided pedagogic demands. All his instruction in music came from classes in schools. With the exception of piano lessons, Bernstein never studied privately. Unlike most young people planning a career in music, he never submitted to the teachings of a composer, a conductor, or a theoretician.

At Harvard Bernstein followed the pattern he had established at Boston Latin: brilliant and undisciplined. The lowest mark he received there was a C+ from A. Tillman Merritt in counterpoint. Merritt, his tutor at Eliot House, told people he was the only professor who had given the young man the grade he deserved.

Walter Piston, the distinguished American composer who then held the Walter Bigelow Rosen Chair in Music at Harvard, taught composition and theory. "There wasn't much to teach him," Piston has said. "He knew most of it by instinct." In Bernstein's junior year, Piston assigned the members of his class a fugue built around a theme of their own choosing. Lenny arrived late with his; he cut classes with abandon. When he did arrive with his fugue, it was based on a theme from a Saint-Saens Cello Concerto, a lengthy, lyrical melody. Harold Shapero, then a freshman, was in the same class. He says that Piston criticized it, saying it was inappropriate for a fugal treatment. "Lenny," Shapero remembers, "banged his hand on the table and said, 'Well, *I* like it.'"

Piston told colleagues of this incident, adding that he could never figure out whether Lenny was pulling his leg or trying, in a pioneering musical spirit, to do the genuinely impossible. Piston said he did not think Bernstein would become a good composer, adding that as far as school experiences were concerned, he was always so busy with outside activities that he did not give adequate time to assignments. "He was always putting on a show or something."

Bernstein *was* always putting on a show or something. Early in his freshman year he tried out as accompanist for the Harvard Glee Club. Irving Fine was the regular accompanist and two freshmen were tested for a job as Fine's assistant. Lenny got the job but was soon fired for being late to rehearsal. Director George Woodworth chose William Austin to succeed him. Austin, his co-contender, is now professor of music at Cornell.

This was not Bernstein's first disappointment. During his high school years he entered a competition sponsored by the piano firm of Mason and Hamlin and played Bach's English Suite in A Minor. The winner was Edna Ida Itkin, who went on to become a music teacher in Boston.

But he was resilient and enormously gifted. Irving Fine knew that. In addition to being the club's accompanist, Fine also played piano for the old movies resurrected and exhibited by the Harvard Film Society. Overburdened with work, he asked Lenny to do that job for him. Sitting in the dark theater, Bernstein would watch the film and play music he felt appropriate. Soon the society's posters would read, "The Harvard Film Society Presents *Potemkin* [this in small type] with LEONARD BERNSTEIN AT THE PIANO." Later, writing in a music journal, Fine referred to Bernstein's "extraordinary memory and his flair for improvisation … almost legendary at college. I remember with great nostalgia his appearance as piano accompanist at a series of historical films. The Battleship *Potemkin* rode at anchor to the accompaniment of Copland's *Piano Variations* [and] excerpts from *Petrouchka*...."

Always a skilled writer of prose, Bernstein began to write music criticism for both the *Harvard Advocate*, where he was music editor, and *Modern Music*, an influential journal published in New York devoted to contemporary music. When Bernstein met the editor at a party in Manhattan, she invited him to cover all new music introduced by the Boston Symphony. Bernstein was a tough critic. Here he is in the *Advocate*, covering a pianist, Vera Carson, who gave a concert of demanding new music that included his own favorite Copland *Variations*: "She played without the slightest conception of the rhythms or tempi … with a butcher's lack of sensitivity, with the tone of a Woolworth xylophone, the half-heartedness of a professor in his twenty-fourth year of reading the same lectures. I felt, after a minute of it, that I must leave or scream."

Again in the *Advocate* on a Boston Symphony performance conducted by the same Koussevitzky of whom he had said, "I'm so jealous," Bernstein wrote:

> By and large it was the traditional Boston Symphony Orchestra offering: magnificent precision, the unbreakable tradition of wrong notes in the French horn department, the phenomenon (in the Vivaldi) of seeing woodwinds blown and not hearing them, the remarkable industry of the percussion boys, Our Director's most individualistic conception of tempi—all the things we have come to know and love. One innovation, however: Dr. Koussevitzky has added a tenth bull fiddle, so that the Scherzo of Beethoven's Fifth had something of Fate in it after all.

In *Modern Music*, Bernstein assessed Prokofiev's First Piano Concerto with the composer playing:

> Truthfully, it is not a good piece.... Its one real tune is worked to death (especially ... since it was always in D Flat), it lacks continuity and it sounded like the student work that it is. When it was over you asked "Why?"

One of the most consistent aspects of Bernstein's personality is his refusal to be intimidated by those on whom he depends. It started with his rebellion against his father. It continued with resistance to teachers, particularly those who either did not believe in him or failed to back up their belief in tangible ways. Here is Bernstein on the Symphony No. 1 by Walter Piston, published in *Modern Music* while Bernstein was still in Harvard. In this review, even the compliments are backhanded:

> Adverse criticisms were profuse and diverse; some thought the Largo unduly long and uninteresting; others thought that the work lacked emotional appeal. Whatever the case ... no one would deny the expert handling of the orchestra, the innovations of instrumental color, the never-failing good taste, the

masterly proportioning of the structure, and the fine lyric sense which Mr. Piston has not often betrayed in the past.

William Schuman fared considerably better than Piston; his Symphony No. 2 elicited a favorable Bernstein review in *Modern Music*. This was the first work by Schuman that Koussevitzky conducted, and he programmed it for February 1938. Schuman recalls that Harvard sent him a letter inviting him to stay in the Alumni Suite at Eliot House and informing him that two students would meet him at the train.

The students were Bernstein and another Eliot House inhabitant. "That evening," Schuman recalls, "Lenny said he wanted to see the score and then asked if he could keep it overnight, I told him I needed it at ten A.M. in time for the rehearsal. But in the morning he was nowhere to be found. I went to his room, found him sleeping soundly, and shook his shoulders until he started to move. Then, with a wide yawn, with his eyes still closed, he said, 'You like Sibelius.' The work was hissed by the Boston audiences but Lenny and a few students, up in a balcony, yelled bravo."

Schuman says he remembers Bernstein and his sister singing Gilbert and Sullivan at a mad pace at a café, the Amalfi, near Symphony Hall: "At the time Lenny was just another Harvard kid but I knew he was a star and I mean that in the real sense of the word. I am not speaking of charisma. One simply had an innate feeling that here was a person of absolutely extraordinary ability and that whatever he wanted to accomplish he would."

At Harvard one of Bernstein's favorite occupations was to participate in a kind of open house attended by intellectual students and teachers and presided over by the late David Prall, professor of philosophy. Prall was a homosexual who enjoyed the company of bright, articulate young men and he was sufficiently drawn to Bernstein to give him his own upright piano. It was in Prall's rooms that Bernstein heard for the first time the Hornbostel collection of recordings of Asian, African, and other non-European music. Erich Moritz von Hornbostel had been director of the Berlin Phonogramm-Archiv from 1906 until 1933, when he was dismissed because his mother was Jewish. The material he collected opened new worlds of sound for many composers and many of the exotic themes, strange rhythms, and new harmonies, particularly those from Far Eastern sources, turned up in Bernstein's incidental music composed for a production of Aristophanes' *The Birds* presented by the Classical Club in Bernstein's senior year. Bernstein also conducted the chorus and orchestra. The *Harvard Crimson* liked it, noting that the show was the "nearest thing to Barnum and Bailey minus elephants."

Six weeks later, on May 27, 1939, in Sanders Theater, Bernstein staged, directed, and played piano in Marc Blitzstein's then famous *The Cradle Will Rock*, with Prall as one of the sponsors. The work, a bitter, satirical piece, presents a plea for unionism through the conventions of popular music and idiomatic American speech. The approach, although fresh, was certainly in the air in those days. The Depression, coupled with the power of radio, encouraged an anti-elitist attitude that was picked up by people in all of the arts. Kurt Weill's *Johnny Johnson* and Copland's *Second Hurricane*, both similar in concept, were written about the same time. This was 1936; Robert Sherwood was working on *Abe Lincoln in Illinois*, John Steinbeck on *Tortilla Flat*, and Ben Shahn on a mural for a garment workers' resettlement project in Roosevelt, New Jersey.

Cradle's premiere in 1937 attracted big talent. John Houseman was producer and Orson Welles director. The sponsor was the Works Progress Administration, a federal agency that provided employment for the jobless. The play was set in a fictitious city, Steeltown, U.S.A., but just before it was scheduled to open, steelworkers actually went on strike. The libretto, which made heroes of steelworkers and black-guards of capitalists, would have appeared to be the federal government's point of view if presented with WPA funds. Three days before the premiere, the performance was canceled. Houseman and Welles appealed the ruling but President Roosevelt himself called the director of the Federal Theater Project to say the show could not go on.

The audience arrived on opening night to find the doors of Manhattan's Maxine Elliott Theater closed. Another theater was found. Welles and Houseman called the musicians' union and were told that its members could not appear in the pit; they could, however, be onstage, for that would be a "recital." The actors' union said its performers could not appear onstage but could buy tickets and sit in the audience. Jean Rosenthal, who later became famous as a lighting designer, found an upright piano and a truck to haul it. She, Welles, and Houseman boarded the truck while the actors started the march up Sixth Avenue with Howard da Silva, who played the protagonist, leading the way. The audience followed them to the Venice Theater, picking up a band of stragglers as they paraded through Times Square.

When the lights at the Venice Theater went down and the curtain went up, Blitzstein was sitting in his shirtsleeves alone at a piano. He planned to take all the roles himself but as he began the Moll's song, the cast member whose solo it was began to sing it from the balcony. When Blitzstein started the Gent's song, the same thing happened. One by one the cues were picked up by actors and actresses who had joined in the mile-long walk and were sitting all over the house. Mister Mister, Junior Mister, almost all the characters were there. Blitzstein remarked that the audience resembled spectators at a tennis match, looking from left to right as each member of the cast rose to sing. It was, Archibald MacLeish wrote, "the most exciting evening of theater this New York generation has seen."

It was also a hard act to follow, yet that is exactly what Bernstein chose to do in his senior year at Harvard. He took Blitzstein's role playing the piano, performing the entire score by memory, and directing the action. Shirley, then only fifteen, took on the part of the whore in such a remarkable way that some in the audience speak of her performance today. Bernstein outdid himself. A Cambridge city councilman, Michael Sullivan, agitated for the police to prosecute the backers of this "indecent show," but the Boston papers were unanimous in their raves. Politics and aesthetics converged. Bernstein, like Blitzstein, had embraced the Left and the music-theater principles appropriate to that philosophy: The use of the vernacular in words and music was realized in 1936 in *The Cradle Will Rock* and in the operas Bernstein composed in his own later years.

On hearing about the production, Blitzstein is reported to have wondered who this presumptuous young man was who had put it together in only ten days. He attended a second performance one week later and, stunned by the professionalism he saw, he and Bernstein formed a friendship that lasted almost three decades, until Blitzstein's death at the hands of sailors in a bar in Martinique.

Bernstein associated with Blitzstein and other committed leftists as a matter of course. A cadre of Harvard students had symbolically linked arms with the many intellectuals and artists who had been turning to Marxism. Blitzstein was one of these artists, and Bernstein, already sympathetic to the ideology, was tugged further along the way by Blitzstein's militant convictions.

In his freshman year, Bernstein lived at Wigglesworth, a dormitory on the Harvard campus. At the end of the year, outgoing freshmen were invited to apply to an off-campus house of their choice. The houses had special identities. Lowell House attracted musicians; Eliot House drew artists, as well as intellectuals and homosexuals. Bernstein applied to Eliot House and was accepted. During his sophomore and junior years he lived in Room G-41 with one roommate, Norman Brisson, who had also attended Boston Latin. Brisson was not only bright, he worked hard and graduated not cum laude like Lenny but *magna* cum laude. The two did not get along. "He used to call me a reactionary and a fascist—me, a Jew," Brisson has said.

Midway through his junior year, Lenny told Norman that his father was having financial troubles and that he would have to cut down on expenses. Brisson, the practical roommate, arranged for them to move to a suite that would accommodate a third student. That student was Alfred Eisner, a New Yorker who had recently transferred from the University of Wisconsin.

Eisner, a depressed young intellectual, active in Harvard's Communist party cell, became Bernstein's close friend. After graduation, Eisner went to work in Hollywood as a screenwriter for MGM for fifty dollars a week. He died of cancer at twenty-three. Later Bernstein included a memorial composition dedicated to him in his own *Seven Anniversaries.*

Brisson reports that Bernstein was profoundly unhappy during his last year. At graduation Eisner was headed for his job with MGM, Brisson for a post with General Motors in Detroit. "Lenny was worried because he still didn't know exactly what he was going to do," according to Brisson. "He asked me what I thought he ought to do and I suggested he get a job as leader of a dance band. We haven't been friendly since." Brisson says he was half serious, that he was convinced there wasn't any great depth to Bernstein.

It is true that Bernstein had no place to go on his graduation from Harvard. What he did have was a particular notion of the essence of American music. In his bachelor's thesis he writes of the variety of "racial codes," citing the New England colonists' hymns as one of the more important ones. But he concludes that the most important phenomenon in twentieth-century music in the United States is the one that is known as jazz. "Through the incredible popularity of this art, Negro music has finally shown itself to be the really universal basis of American composition."

In discussing the movement of this raw material into the realm of art, Bernstein concentrates on George Gershwin. In what appears to be an unsettling faculty for seeing into the future, he discusses Gershwin in much the same manner as contemporary American critics discuss Bernstein today:

> That this Negro scale is inevitably limited to diatonic music* has resulted in the fact that only such conservative composers as Gershwin were able to make unqualified use of it.... He has left music none of which is dull, much of which is mediocre, and some of which is imaginative, skillful and beautiful. There is rightly much controversy as to its lasting value....
>
> Gershwin did not try to reconcile a "modern" idiom with the diatonic Negro scale. He simply remained steeped in nineteenth-century methods and made the most of them.... The important point is that Gershwin's music *was* the result of all his musical experience; but that experience was limited to the older music—an inevitability, since that kind of music tied up so much better with the material he had to use. [2]

In 1983, when he was asked exactly what he had been doing on the day Gershwin died, Bernstein replied, "I adored Gershwin. I went ape over *Porgy and Bess*. In the summer of 1937, after my sophomore year at Harvard I was a counselor at a camp in upstate New York. I taught swimming and music and had a bunk filled with spoiled New York brats.

---

* *The diatonic scale was the Western world's primary scale until the end of the nineteenth century. The seven white notes on the piano between one C and the next are such a scale.*

When Parents' Weekend arrived, the director told me that I was to play during lunch on Sunday. I decided I would not do that. It would be a noisy group and I could imagine the noise of silver and china and the clatter of people.

"But Sunday morning when I awakened, I heard that Gershwin had died. I decided I would play, after all. There was this terrible clatter at lunch. Then I went to the piano and played a chord to get the group's attention. I told them Gershwin had died and that I would play one of his pieces for them and wanted no applause afterwards. I played the Prelude No. 2 and there was absolute silence—a heavy silence. That was the first time I realized the power of music. As I walked off I felt I *was* Gershwin, not that I was there in Heaven, but that I was Gershwin and had composed that piece."

After telling the story Bernstein started to cough, and continued for more than ten minutes. He said he was embarrassed by his inability to stop and that the fit was "an emotional reaction to your question about Gershwin."

In 1983, when the Institute for Studies in American Music published a monograph consisting of articles and reviews from Minna Lederman's *Modern Music, The New York Times* interviewed Lederman. Still active and articulate in her eighties, she prided herself on the fact that during her long tenure at the magazine she

1946

Walter Damrosch, Paul Whiteman, and Leonard Bernstein in New York for the premiere of the movie Rhapsody in Blue. *Twenty-two years earlier "Gershwin had tried to enter the world of 'high art' with* Rhapsody in Blue" *conducted by Whiteman at Aeolian Hall.*

had never published an article by or about Gershwin. Hers was a serious journal, she said, and Gershwin "was so popular; the attention he received was ridiculous."

The emphasis on intellect over emotion, on abstraction over representation, has had wide-ranging consequences for twentieth-century art. Stravinsky, an incisively intelligent man, knew, by the 1930s, that he could become more famous by pretending to be a literary intellectual than by being the musical genius he was. To that end he used ghostwriters, not only for his *Autobiography* and the essays, but also for *The Poetics of Music*, the Charles Eliot Norton Lectures he delivered at Harvard in the fall of 1939. According to his amanuensis, Robert Craft, Stravinsky wrote only fifteen hundred of the final thirty thousand words. The ghostwriter here was Pierre Souvchinsky, Parisian *éminence grise*, who, honored to be used in this way, gracefully accepted anonymity.

Gershwin suffered under the intellectual bias of the time. A few years before he died, he asked Arnold Schoenberg for composition lessons. Schoenberg agreed. It is impossible to know the exact nature of the lessons, but, after Gershwin's death, Schoenberg wrote the following words about the man who had composed "'S Wonderful" and "Fascinating Rhythm": "…he is an artist and a composer; he expressed musical ideas; and they were new, as is the way in which he expressed them."

Before approaching Schoenberg, Gershwin had tried to enter the world of "high art" with *Rhapsody in Blue* and the Concerto in F. While there is much that is remarkable here—fresh and inventive melodies in profusion—the pieces themselves falter because of inherent structural weaknesses. It is in the songs that Gershwin left his greatest legacy. But because they were imbedded in Broadway shows with chorus lines and show-business hoopla, the critical establishment disregarded them. Schoenberg knew better. He told friends that his greatest wish was to write tunes like Tchaikovsky's that people would whistle while leaving the hall. He knew that at least in this regard Gershwin would transcend him.

One can trace the influence of intellect on music by examining the elevated status that science began to hold at the beginning of the twentieth century. Apparently desirous of being treated with the same respect as an Einstein or a Niels Bohr, artists, especially composers, adopted a scientific lexicon. By the 1960s, it would have been difficult for an outsider to enter a university classroom and know whether the chalk marks on the blackboard were those of a physicist's equation or a composer's serial chart. From a philosophical point of view, the change is understandable. Serial music is to tonality what Einsteinian physics is to Newtonian gravity: The center of each has disappeared. But while science appears to progress toward truth, the same cannot be said of art. In the more than sixty years since the emergence of twelve-tone music, little of it can be said to have pleased most listeners.

Gershwin was not alone in his ambition to cross the line into this more respectable world. Mel Powell, who built a considerable reputation as a jazz pianist in Benny Goodman's band, abandoned the dance band after World War II to study composition with Paul Hindemith, the German composer, at Yale. He went on to teach music theory at Yale and, in 1969, became dean of music at the California Institute of the Arts.

In a recent letter, Powell discussed the dichotomy between art and pop in the United States:

> What is "serious" about serious music ("classical" in the pop parlance) is essentially European. What Babbitt does, what I do, what others in our field do, is, in this sense not distinguishable from what our European colleagues do. Of course there are idiosyncratic accents, "dialects," so to speak, *ad hominem* distinctions, etc., but generically the underpinnings of a formal "high" musical art belong to the European heritage.
>
> I believe that a socio-psycho-cultural taxonomist can make out a good case for the presence of a special nostalgia, encoded in the genes of many Americans, that secretly longs for the "forbidden" (that is, aristocratic) palaces and chapels of Europe's past. And this links to a familiar American self-perception as the "outsider," the "barbarian," etc., which in turn can generate an American view of quintessentially "American" items—the pop idiom, jazz, etc.—as inescapably vulgar.
>
> Europeans catch onto this very readily. They know how to take advantage of it, since even today we'll celebrate tenth-rate Europeans and ignore first-rate Americans.

In the 1930s and 1940s, the attitude Powell now deplores appears to have been virtually the rule. William Schuman followed this route: In his teens he led his own New York band, Billy Schuman and the Alamo Society Orchestra. In the 1930s, he composed dozens of pop songs in collaboration with Frank Loesser. Yet he, too, made the shift from pop to art, and in 1938 he received the ultimate blessing: Koussevitzky conducted one of his works with the Boston Symphony Orchestra. In 1945, Schuman became president of the Juilliard School, a post he held until 1962 when he became president of Lincoln Center.

Milton Babbitt, the leading advocate of serialism in the United States after World War II, has a strong pop background. In 1946 he composed a sophisticated musical that was to star Mary Martin on Broadway. But the show never opened, and Babbitt cultivated an academic career. Now retired and a MacArthur Fellow, he held a chair in music at Princeton for many years.

Just as American English is among the youngest of the Western languages, American jazz-based pop is among the youngest and freshest of musical idioms. While it is true that Babbitt, Schuman, and Powell felt its seductive power, other factors came into play that moved them in the direction of their European antecedents.

With Bernstein it was different. Even the presence of the European masters in the United States—Nadia Boulanger in Boston, Hindemith at Yale, and Schoenberg and Stravinsky in California—did not affect him, because his own background in music had begun so late and his family tie to European culture was so fragile that he never totally annihilated jazz from his creative life. In fact it can be heard in everything he did. Still there was always the implicit value judgment that art music was morally superior to unadulterated pop.

Bernstein's inclination toward art is not difficult to explain. For one thing, although he was not overwhelmed by it, he was subject to the idea that high art had a special cachet. For another he was, like Babbitt, Schuman, and Powell, too intellectually restless to devote himself to the challenges the popular idiom then provided. Finally he would have had the battle of his life with his father, for if concert music presented a problem for Sam, the American counterpart of the Russian-Jewish *klezmer* would have been intolerable.

No. Regarding the dichotomy of pop and art, Bernstein followed

Gershwin's route and tried to become a so-called serious artist. A sonata for violin and piano composed in 1940, performed by the composer and Raphael Hillyer in Cambridge, and *Four Studies for Two Clarinets, Two Bassoons, and Piano*, performed and broadcast in 1940 at a League of Composers Concert in Philadelphia, testify to the route he had chosen at this time. Like Gershwin he wanted a place in history and this meant making "art," not just delighting listeners. For this reason he wrote about Gershwin as he did in his undergraduate thesis, rejecting him as a conscious model and choosing instead Aaron Copland, then being performed by Koussevitzky and the Boston Symphony Orchestra. Copland possessed still another advantage over Gershwin as a model: He was alive and therefore capable not only of guiding Bernstein in his art but helping him in his career. Bernstein was not the only American who looked on Copland as a father figure. Copland was probably the single most important influence on American art music in the second third of this century.

Despite the wide-open intervals that give his music a Western American flavor, what Copland passed on to his disciples was a decidedly European outlook. For as early as his twenty-first year, he had taken what little money he could raise and gone to Paris to study under Nadia Boulanger. She made a point of not inhibiting the musical personality of any of her students. That is why the American sound could come through. She did something else; she introduced Copland to Koussevitzky, a thoroughgoing European, with rigid ideas about an artist's ways.

During the early 1920s, the Russian conductor directed the pathbreaking "Concerts Koussevitzky" in Paris. It was there he presented world premieres of Honegger's *Pacific 231* and Prokofiev's *Sept, Ils Sont Sept*. In the spring of 1924, when Koussevitzky was completing his last season in Paris and planning to take over the Boston Symphony in the fall, Boulanger brought Copland to his house. Prokofiev was also there. Copland sat down at the piano and played through *Cortège Macabre*, at that time his only orchestral work. Koussevitzky said he would program it during his first season in Boston. He also commissioned Copland to write a work for organ and orchestra that Boulanger would play. By introducing Koussevitzky to Copland, the legendary French teacher set up a conduit between the Russian maestro and a small army of

American composers, because Copland was generous with his influence. In fact, it was after Copland heard Schuman's Symphony No. 2 on *Everybody's Music*, a CBS Sunday afternoon broadcast for which he himself served as host, that he suggested to Schuman that he send Koussevitzky the score. That led to Koussevitzky's first performance of a Schuman work. It also brought Schuman to Harvard's Eliot House, where he met Bernstein.

In the 1920s Copland was a primary influence in American music through the League of Composers, an organization devoted to new American works. From 1927 to 1937, he taught at the New School for Social Research in New York. Throughout this period he wrote for the journal *Modern Music*, which was an offshoot of the League. From 1928 to 1931, along with the composer Roger Sessions, he supervised the Copland-Sessions Concerts at which twentieth-century European and American works were played.

However influential Copland was at the time, another composer, Roy Harris, held center stage. Born in Oklahoma, he had grown up in California and studied with the American composer Arthur Farwell. In 1926 Harris followed Copland's example and went to Paris to study with Boulanger. When he returned in 1929, Koussevitzky began to conduct Harris's works with the same fervor with which he had promoted Copland. In *The Musical Quarterly*, a musicological journal with an international readership, an article by Farwell hailed Harris as an authentic American genius. Bernstein met Harris in 1938. Despite Harris's renown, Bernstein was not drawn to him. In Copland he found far deeper ties. Like Bernstein, Copland came from a Russian-Jewish background; his family name had been Kaplan. Like Bernstein, Copland was urban; he'd been born and raised in Brooklyn. Like Bernstein, Copland was left-wing politically. Like Bernstein, Copland was homosexual. Copland's homosexuality was less ambiguous than Bernstein's and for years Bernstein's connections to women, his quasi-romantic entanglements with them, irritated the older man, who called him—among friends—PH, for "phony homosexual."

In the fall of 1937, Bernstein was already an admirer of Copland's music. He had mastered the *Piano Variations* and played them everywhere. He called them "my trademark" and said he especially enjoyed upsetting parties with the work, that he could be relied on to empty any room in Boston within minutes of sitting down at the piano and start-ing it. Bernstein envisioned Copland as "a cross between Walt Whitman and an Old Testament prophet." Taken to a dance recital in New York, he found himself sitting next to a man whom he later described as odd-looking, "a pair of glasses resting on his great hooked nose and a mouth filled with teeth flashing a wide grin...."

Invited after a recital to Copland's birthday party that same night, November 14, Bernstein commandeered the piano and swept through the *Piano Variations.* Then he continued to play for hours. Copland was captivated; he even said he wished he could play his own music like that. A lifelong friendship had begun.

"Whenever I came to New York," Bernstein recalled in an article celebrating Copland's seventieth birthday,

> I went to Aaron's. I would arrive in the morning and we'd breakfast at his hotel, then wander around and sometimes go to a concert. And all during those years I would bring my own music for his criticism. I remember that I was writing a violin sonata during those Harvard days, and a two-piano piece, and a four-hand piece, and a string quartet. I even completed a trio. I would show Aaron the bits and pieces, and he would say, "All that has to go.... This is just pure Scriabin. You've got to get that out of your head and start fresh.... This is good; these two bars are good. Take these two bars and start from there." And in these sessions he taught me a tremendous amount about taste, style, and consistency in music.... Through his critical analyses of whatever I happened to be working on at the moment, Aaron became the closest thing to a composition teacher I ever had.
>
> We of course played other music than mine at these ses-sions. We played his. Not while he was composing it, though; Aaron was very jealous of the music he was working on and would never show anything before it reached its reasonably final form. But then would come that glorious day when he would pull something out and we would play it, four hands, from the score. I learned such works as *Billy the Kid* and *An Outdoor Overture*—later the *Piano Sonata,* and the *Third*

Symphony—that way before they were ever performed publicly, and the scores to *Quiet City*, *Of Mice and Men*, and *Our Town*, before Hollywood got them. *El Salón México* had already been composed—and first performed by Carlos Chávez in Mexico City a few months before I met Aaron—but the published transcription was made by me. [2]

Copland brought Bernstein to Boosey and Hawkes, the music publisher, where Hans Heinsheimer, the director of publications, agreed to pay him twenty-five dollars for a piano transcription of the orchestral work. Bernstein's name remains on the score today.

One of the Harvard musicians with whom Bernstein made contact through Copland was Harold Shapero, whose reputation as a composer of art music was to surpass Bernstein's own in the 1940s. Recalling how they met, Shapero says, "I sent Copland a woodwind piece and Copland told Bernstein to look me up. I was living near him in Newton Center and we became friends." Shapero says that he and Irving Fine were generally grouped together as Boston composers who looked to Stravinsky, while Bernstein, even as an undergraduate, appeared to be concentrating on the ballet. "He was writing scores for Sokolow," Shapero recalls. Anna Sokolow was a young dancer on whom Bernstein says he "had a great crush." It was at a Sokolow recital that he first met Copland.

In the spring of 1939, Bernstein's last semester at Harvard, Copland went to Cambridge for the Harvard Classical Club's production of Aristophanes' *The Birds*, for which Bernstein had composed incidental music. But it was not on the music Copland remarked. This was Bernstein's first experience at the helm of even a small orchestra and Copland suggested that conducting be his field.

As it turned out, Bernstein's conducting career served Copland well. A few years later, in 1941, Bernstein produced, virtually by himself, Copland's *Second Hurricane* at the New England Conservatory's Jordan Hall. The event was sparsely attended; there had been virtually no publicity. According to filmmaker Ricky Leacock, it was a "gorgeous performance. Koussevitzky was there. Afterwards several of us met with Lenny and conspired to move the whole thing to Sanders Theater. There the performances were well attended. Lenny had hocked a girlfriend's emerald ring to raise the money to rent the theater."

Bernstein was almost invariably remiss in fulfilling his part of any implied bargain where women were concerned. Even so, throughout his life women were willing to do more than contribute emerald rings to be in his luminescent presence. Moreover, he seems always to have lived up to his part of a bargain when it came to professional relationships. However much he profited from Copland's musical advice, however much he drew from Copland's music itself, he more than repaid his mentor. According to David Diamond, "Lenny helped Aaron more than the other way around. He performed *Billy the Kid*, *Appalachian Spring*, *El Salón México*, the Piano Sonata, film scores, and more. He conducted Copland more than he did any of us."

That is a valuable gift. Harold Shapero says, "To have a performance under Bernstein is to have a truly great pleasure. He is so musical he will do anything you ever hoped to be done with a work." Bernstein's conducting and playing of Copland's works surely helped move him into the position of preeminence that had been occupied by Harris.

The winter before Bernstein sat next to Copland in the balcony at the Anna Sokolow recital, he met Dimitri Mitropoulos. That was in January 1937, Bernstein's sophomore year at Harvard. According to Bernstein's college friends, Mitropoulos intoxicated Leonard with his extraordinary memory, fanatic devotion to music, power in front of an orchestra, and sheer physical presence. This last attribute Copland never enjoyed. When Bernstein referred to Copland's "great hooked nose and mouth filled with teeth," he was telling the reader precisely what he saw. In the 1930s and 1940s, before having work done on his mouth, Copland confided to friends that he believed all his relationships with young men came from their wish to use him professionally. He said he knew he was an ugly man. Not so Mitropoulos.

In 1984 Jennie Bernstein attributed her son's Career to the influence of the Greek conductor: "I wanted him to be a great pianist. That was my dream for him. When he met Mitropoulos all that changed. I remember the meeting very well. Mitropoulos was visiting Harvard on a Friday night. You know how Jewish mothers cook and bake on Fridays. But Lenny said, 'You must come back to school with me to meet Mitropoulos. He wants to meet me and it has been arranged.' Well.

One, two, three, in my housedress we went. Lenny and I were very close. I was nineteen when I married and I grew up with him. I went to concerts with him when he was in high school. At college of course that stopped. But I would still cook and bake and bring food to him."

Jennie Bernstein appears never to have turned her son down. She gave him her own Plymouth roadster, lent him her maid for *Pinafore*, and, on this particular cold Friday night, put a fur coat on top of her housedress to meet Mitropoulos at Harvard.

Mitropoulos, then forty-one, was a remarkable-looking man with a great hairless dome of a head and power emanating from every pore. A Greek friend, Katy Katsoyanis, has written that he possessed "so much physical strength that he could drive a nail into the wall with his finger, and his hand was so steady he could draw an absolutely straight line on paper."

In school, at the Athens Odeion, Mitropoulos had studied piano and composition and played in the percussion section of the school orchestra. He started composing when he was sixteen, studied one year in Berlin under Busoni, and until he took his first permanent post as music director of an American orchestra in 1938, he continued to compose: thirteen works for piano, eleven songs, two pieces for orchestra, some chamber music works, one opera, and incidental music to Sophocles' *Electra* and Euripides' *Hippolytus*. From 1924 to 1935 Mitropoulos was permanent conductor of the Greek Orchestra, during which time he also toured Europe and the United States. Mitropoulos made his first guest appearance here in 1936 with the Boston Symphony Orchestra. He was unknown in this country then and Bernstein did not attend the event. But in 1937 when he appeared again, there was considerable excitement in musical circles, for his U.S. debut had been an unqualified triumph. The Greek Society at Harvard arranged a reception and Leonidas B. Demeter, a Harvard student of Greek extraction, invited Bernstein and asked him to play. Bernstein, his mother in tow, played part of a piece he was composing and Chopin's Nocturne in F-sharp Major. Mitropoulos was impressed enough to invite him to attend rehearsals the following week.

That was the week before examinations, but Bernstein did not let that stand in his way. For the first rehearsal he took a seat in the back row, and when Mitropoulos entered and saw him, he gestured for the young man to move to the front. He even handed him his own score to follow. After another rehearsal Mitropoulos invited the Harvard sophomore to lunch. At lunch he offered him an oyster from his own fork. The move thrilled Bernstein, who reported it to anyone willing to listen. The exchange of the oyster was, at the very least, a sensually stimulating gesture for giver and receiver. It also probably reflected some ambiguity on Bernstein's part concerning his Jewish heritage since oysters are *trayf*—unclean, unkosher, therefore forbidden. During the lunch Mitropoulos told him that he exuded greatness, even genius. Bernstein has said that at this he felt faint.

Bernstein attended Mitropoulos's concert and heard him conduct Ravel's *Rapsodie Espagnole* and Schumann's Second Symphony. The conductor was called back repeatedly. The audience stamped its feet; women threw flowers on the stage. The orchestra cheered and beat their instruments. The dressing room was packed, but as soon as Bernstein entered, Mitropoulos beckoned to him. Taking him into the bathroom to ensure privacy, he told the nineteen-year-old musician that he should work very hard and not allow friends to spoil him with flattery. With that he gave Bernstein an inscribed photograph and said that although he was off to Europe, he would not only write but even send him some of his own scores.

Spring and summer passed and Mitropoulos sent no word. Bernstein met Copland in the fall and was busy composing a ballet for Sokolow, playing piano in public, trying to keep up with his academic work. But Mitropoulos was still on his mind, and he kept the photograph on his desk. When, in the fall of 1937, he read that Mitropoulos was to be a guest conductor in Minneapolis, Bernstein sent him a letter there. Mitropoulos responded by wiring two hundred dollars so that Bernstein could spend the Christmas holiday with him. The spartan Mitropoulos, at his own choosing, was living in inelegant quarters in a university dormitory and put Bernstein in the room next to his own.

In 1959 Sam Bernstein identified that visit as the turning point of his son's career. "He came back and said, 'Papa, I'm going to make music my life.' Mr. Mitropoulos had said he would give him a job with the Minneapolis Symphony as soon as he graduated from college."

But as Mitropoulos had disappointed Bernstein by not writing the year before, so he disappointed him again for there was no further word from him. As Eisner was packing for Hollywood, Brisson preparing for Detroit, Bernstein faced an unplanned summer and an altogether undetermined future. The Minneapolis visit had taken place during his junior year. If he had not counted on the post under Mitropoulos, he would surely have made other plans for his entrance into the real world.

Mitropoulos's promise evaporated. Still, rejection rarely stops adoration. Rather it tends to goad it. Although Bernstein went on to study under other great conductors, the essence of his style is that of Mitropoulos.

Recently, with all his mentor-conductors dead, Bernstein said:

> The influence of Mitropoulos on my life, on my conducting life, is enormous and usually greatly underrated or not known at all, because ordinarily the two great conductors with whom I studied are the ones who receive the credit for whatever conducting prowess I have; namely, Serge Koussevitzky and Fritz Reiner.... But long before I met either of them, I had met Dimitri Mitropoulos ... and watching him conduct those two weeks of rehearsals and concerts with the Boston Symphony laid some kind of conductorial passion and groundwork in my psyche which I wasn't even aware of until many years later. I remember every piece he did. All ... I do is proof enough of the force of that influence. The C-sharp Minor Quartet of Beethoven, played by all the strings of the Boston Symphony (and most recently the Vienna Philharmonic); the *Rapsodie Espagnole* of Ravel; the Ravel Piano Concerto in G, which I have played hundreds of times, conducting from the piano as he did; the Schumann Second Symphony, which I've conducted hundreds of times ... these pieces that Mitropoulos played, nobody will ever forget who played them or who attended them. [3]

Bernstein drew from Mitropoulos not only in his choice of some repertory but also in more personal ways. James Dixon, the conductor of the Quad Cities Symphony, whom Mitropoulos later supported in ways he never supported Bernstein, says, "Bernstein's mannerisms, the dramatic approach, the personal connection to music, the kind of trance he goes into—all that stems from Mitropoulos." People who knew both Mitropoulos and Bernstein add that the younger man adopted the older man's habit of stripping to the waist in the presence of visitors backstage and of inviting privileged young disciples into the bathroom of the Green Room to facilitate a private talk.

More than that, Mitropoulos demonstrated that a homosexual could be a conductor. According to Ned Rorem, in those days that was far from the rule. "The conductor," says Rorem, "had to be an absolute monarch. Musicians in the orchestra were there for the money and were concerned about union fees, chicks, and poker. The average musician didn't want to be under the baton of some fairy." Nowadays, of course, all that has changed. But when Bernstein was a young man, Mitropoulos was the only exception.

"[David] Diamond," Rorem recalls, "introduced me to Mitropoulos. Between the introduction and our first date, I lost my lover of many years and was devastated. Still I kept the appointment with Mitropoulos and told him as soon as I arrived that I would have difficulty concentrating because I was in a state of such despair. Mitropoulos replied, 'If only I could suffer this way and roll at the feet of the one I love.' "

According to Oliver Daniel, who is writing a biography of Mitropoulos, the Greek conductor was interested "in all attractive young male musicians and Bernstein was an attractive personality." But Mitropoulos seems to have needed a less abrasive person, one whose ambition was not as awesome, for he finally found just such a person in James Dixon, to whom he left his entire estate.

The summer of his sophomore year, when Bernstein played Gershwin's Prelude No. 2 for a group of children and their parents, he was the music counselor at Camp Onota in the Berkshires. One of the highlights of the season was a production of *The Pirates of Penzance*. He had had good preparation for this show. After all, he

FRANK DRIGGS

1939

"Reiner ... opened up the orchestral score ... and asked Bernstein to identify and then play it.... When Bernstein first looked at the score, he saw a tune in the woodwinds he had learned to recognize in grammar school with these words:
What clatters on the roof,
with quick impatient hoof?
I think it must be Santa Claus,
Dear old Santa Claus.

had produced Gilbert and Sullivan as an adolescent at Singer's Inn in Sharon, Massachusetts. To help Lenny with his *Pirates*, the camp brought in an outsider, a young man from the Bronx, Adolph Green, to play the role of The Pirate King.

Burton Bernstein tells the story in his memoir:

> Lenny and Adolph became instant friends, each of them entranced by each other's sense of humor and knowledge of music. Green's musicality was, and is, extraordinary because he never received formal musical training. He is capable of performing—a cappella and with every orchestral instrument outrageously imitated—just about any symphonic work, classical or modern, down to its last cymbal crash. At Camp Onota, he passed Lenny's rigorous testing on obscure-themes identification, and an enduring friendship and collaboration was born. When Lenny invited Green to Sharon, they would sit around the house for hours, quizzing each other on, say, Beethoven's Scherzi and inventing brilliant musical parodies while Sam stewed and paced. "Who is that nut?" he'd say to the equally bemused Jennie. "I want him out of my house." [1]

The friendship grew in Bernstein's senior year and when he graduated, finding himself without a job, he decided to go to New York and spend the summer there with Green. Green had a large circle of acquaintances and he let everyone know he and a friend needed an apartment with a piano.

One of his acquaintances was Edna Ocko, the editor of the *Theater Arts Committee Magazine* (*TAC*), founded to aid the Spanish Republican side in the Civil War. In 1937 Ocko was in the Soviet Union reviewing the Bolshoi Ballet for dance magazines in New York. On her return she became dance critic for *Cue* and such left-wing publications as *Masses and Mainstream*, *New Masses*, and *TAC*. The *TAC* office was in Times Square and one day Green dropped in to tell Ocko of his apartment-with-a-piano search. Her sister-in-law, Beatrice Fields, had just such an apartment at 63 East Ninth Street and she, her husband, and her son would be away all of July and August. An appointment was made for Bernstein and Green to meet Ocko at the apartment.

"Bernstein was handsome and brash," Ocko recalls. "He fell in love with the Steinway grand and ran his fingers over the keyboard. I asked him what he played and he answered by playing the piano transcription that he had prepared of *El Salón México*. I had heard the orchestral version and I was very impressed. They had no money but neither did my sister-in-law so we agreed on a very small sum—fifty dollars a month for July and August."

Bernstein and Green invited Julian Claman, a friend of Green's, and they shared this apartment near Wanamaker's department store. Bernstein recalls it being hot and airless and even the piano did not help much.

Although he had gotten letters of recommendation from such powerful figures in the music world as Copland, Schuman, and Blitzstein, Bernstein could not find a job in New York. He was not a member of the American Federation of Musicians; to get a union card you had to be a resident for six months. He talked to many people, including Davidson Taylor of the Columbia Broadcasting System, all of whom said there was nothing available.

During this period there were constant rumors of war in Europe. The Depression was still hanging on, and Sam's weekly allowance of twenty-five dollars, although generous for the time, did not go a long way with Leonard. Recalling those days, Bernstein has said:

> I spent a lot of time with Adolph Green and his friends who had just incorporated themselves into a little satirical nightclub group called the Revuers. They were just starting out in a Greenwich Village nightclub called the Village Vanguard. I used to spend almost every night there watching them and sometimes playing for them, just for fun, and they became my dearest friends: Green, Betty Comden, Judy Holliday, Alvin Hammer, and John Frank. At the end of the summer, having failed to find a job, I went home to Massachusetts with my tail between my legs. [3]

At the end of the summer, Beatrice Fields returned to East Ninth Street with her husband and son to find an apartment that looked like a mad orgy had taken place. Eight weeks of dirty linen were in the bathtub, dirty dishes were everywhere, and among the bills unpaid to this day was one for the telephone that exceeded a month's rent and another for the August rental. Bernstein felt entitled to anything he could get. He behaved like an errant god.

Bernstein returned to Boston. "I had just turned 21," he says.

> Here I was, twenty-one, and a graduate of Harvard, and I couldn't find a job. That was a big sense of defeat. And there I was on September first, sitting in Sharon, Massachusetts, where we had our funny little summer house, and the news of Hitler marching into Poland broke, which further depressed me, and I realized the jig was up and we were in for something. That something turned out to be World War II. [3]

While Bernstein was sitting in his Sharon house, the telephone rang and it was his high school friend, the Boston Latin School orchestra's oboist, Leonard Burkat. Burkat told him he had been at the Boston harbor meeting friends who were coming from Greece and that Mitropoulos was also on the same boat. Mutual friends introduced Burkat to Mitropoulos, and the conductor said that he had known a young man at Harvard with a name remarkably similar to his own. Burkat said he and Bernstein were friends and the conductor asked what the young man was doing now. When Burkat said not a thing, Mitropoulos told him to tell Bernstein that he would be at the Commodore Hotel in New York for about a week. Mitropoulos was then on his way to begin the season as music director of the Minneapolis Symphony.

Bernstein lost no time getting to New York. He had no money saved from his father's allowances. In fact he had spent his last four dollars on a clarinet in a New York pawnshop. So he called a friend, Robert Lubell, and persuaded him to drive him down to New York.

At the Commodore he rang Mitropoulos's room. According to Bernstein's own account of the meeting:

> There he was and he said, "Well, what has happened to you?" and I said, "Well, what's happened to me is that I've finished Harvard. I've had a marvelous education. I've had great

teachers. I've studied the piano all along with Helen Coates and Heinrich Gebhard and I'm playing pretty well. I write music. But I can't find a job. I've been here in New York all summer....What shall I do?" I asked Dimitri.

And Dimitri said, "I know what you should do. You must be a conductor." I said, "Conductor? Me? A conductor?" I mean for me a conductor was a tiny little figure … seen from very far away who was so glamorous and so inaccessible and special, conducting a hundred men, that it never occurred to me that I could be such a thing. Well, he said I should be such a thing. And I said, "Fine, well, how does one become one?" He said, "You study." I said, "Where do you study conducting?" He said, "There's the Juilliard School," which was then up on Claremont Avenue, uptown New York, "and there is a marvelous man called Albert Stoessel who teaches conducting there. Perhaps you can get into his class." [3]

Bernstein called Juilliard but was told that all Stoessel's classes were filled. Then he went back to Mitropoulos, who said he had just heard that Fritz Reiner had begun to form a class for conductors at the Curtis Institute in Philadelphia. Bernstein called Curtis and learned that because Reiner had been delayed in Europe with conducting assignments, his class was not yet filled. It would begin in October.

With borrowed money, Bernstein bought two miniature scores: Beethoven's Symphony No. 7 and Rimsky-Korsakov's *Scheherazade*. He studied them, he says,

because I had never really studied orchestral scores from the point of view of conducting them.... There was an audition in late September. I went down to Philadelphia with a tremendous case of hay fever. I could barely see out of my eyes. I was coughing and sneezing and there was this very gruff, tough man called Fritz Reiner, who sort of grunted and said hmmm. And he took a big score and put in on the piano, opening it to the middle—he wouldn't let me see the title. [3]

Reiner spent no time in conversation with Bernstein. He opened up the orchestral score, put it on the piano's music stand, and asked Bernstein to identify and then play it. To read an orchestra score is like reading at the same time fifteen lines of type, some of which are in different languages. When Bernstein first looked at the score, he saw a tune in the woodwinds he had learned to recognize in grammar school with these words:

> *What clatter on the roof,*
> *with quick impatient hoof?*
> *I think it must be Santa Claus,*
> *Dear old Santa Claus.*

From that piece of doggerel, Bernstein knew at once that it was Brahms's *Academic Festival* Overture. "I was a good sight-reader," Bernstein says. "He was quite impressed that I could play all of that. In short I was admitted to his class."

So Bernstein, a Harvard intellectual, a left-wing activist, a musician who counted among his friends Copland, Blitzstein, Schuman, and Mitropoulos, an enthusiast of cabaret music who loved spending nights in a club in New York, turned his back on all of that for almost two years. Embarking on a program in a conservatory dedicated to the cultivation of instrumental technique, he took up residence in the city where Benjamin Franklin had founded *The Saturday Evening Post* in 1789.

The name Curtis derives from Mary Curtis Bok, the daughter of Cyrus Curtis, who purchased the *Post* in 1896. Curtis turned the failing weekly newspaper into the first great popular national magazine. He hired George Horace Lorimer as editor.

Aside from having his pulse on precisely what America was interested in, Lorimer was the first editor to offer substantial advances to authors and lured them away from other media. The *Post* became the most successful magazine in the United States.

When Cyrus Curtis died in 1933, he created a trust and left the controlling stock to his daughter Mary and her two brothers. One brother died; the other was pleasant and ineffectual. Mary, the surviving brother, and the board of directors were all figureheads. Lorimer, who had been named chief executive officer, genuinely believed that the Curtis company would live forever, shaping the country as it prospered. The company's headquarters, looking like a national monument, was in Philadelphia on Independence Square in an imposing building near Independence Hall and the Liberty Bell. Mary Curtis's first husband, Edward W. Bok, a philanthropist and high executive with the company, died in 1930. Mary Bok was not interested in the Curtis Publishing Company.

Her consuming interest was music. From her earliest adult years, she had left the running of the business to Lorimer and the board, but the business provided her with a great deal of money. In 1924 she used some of it to establish the Curtis Institute of Music, endowing it then with $12.5 million. She founded an advisory council made up of such impressive figures as Josef Hofmann, Willem Mengelberg, Leopold Stokowski, and Ossip Gabrilówitsch as well as her father and husband. But she was the guiding light. It is therefore not surprising that the conservatory came to symbolize the Main Line families who ran Philadelphia and much else. It was extremely conservative, extremely proper, with everything done in the best tradition. And the emphasis was placed on virtuosity. Hofmann himself was director from 1934 to 1938.

That was the climate in which Bernstein found himself in the fall of 1939. Because the *Post* was violently isolationist, passionately opposed to Roosevelt, strongly supportive of Herbert Hoover, big business, and the mores of the 1920s, so was the Curtis Institute. Here was Bernstein, a cocky Jewish kid, who called his teachers by their first names. (He once even called Reiner "Fritz." The conductor reacted by calling him "Mr. Bernstein.") Immediately Bernstein was made to understand that at Curtis, in this elegant nineteenth-century mansion with its Oriental rugs, ancestral portraits, and delicate antiques, he was a foreigner who didn't belong. It was generally known that Mary Curtis Bok despised him—her favorites had been Gian Carlo Menotti and Samuel Barber—and that Bernstein could never be admitted into the high ranks of social life there. Bernstein was a leftist and therefore represented ideas allied to atheism, Communist Russia, and all the forces the Philadelphia magnates believed were out to destroy civilized values. The city was a center of anti-intellectualism and rarely was there any activity at the University of Pennsylvania that corresponded to the political or social stimulation at such universities as Harvard and Columbia.

Besides his encounters with social and cultural problems, Bernstein faced difficulty at Curtis with the piano. Auditioning to study with

Rudolf Serkin, who was away on a concert tour, Bernstein was heard by a group of judges that included Isabella Vengerova, a strong link to a great tradition of pianists. She had studied with Theodore Leschetizky. Bernstein says he "hacked his way through" a Bach prelude and fugue. After the audition, Vengerova, who had been teaching at Curtis since its inception, was the only one to say he had potential as a pianist. The panel turned Bernstein down for Serkin, and Vengerova accepted him for herself.

In those days there was no formal diploma program. A student went through the requisite training and received a diploma when the faculty decided to give it to him. There was no such thing as the accrediting of music schools. Work done in one conservatory was not transferable to another.

Bernstein was an outstanding pupil. Records show he excelled in all his subjects: score reading, theory, piano, conducting. Spending hours at the piano held little appeal for him and during the years he was at Curtis he became increasingly attracted to the conducting of a large orchestra.

Not that he often had the chance. Each week at a chamber music concert, students were permitted to conduct. But it was much more difficult for them to lead the Curtis symphony; that was considered Reiner's own. From time to time, however, the orchestra would visit the elegant home of philanthropist and amateur flutist Walter Wolf. If Stokowski—or another celebrated conductor—disappointed the host and failed to appear, the youthful Bernstein would invariably take over the podium.

The only photograph of Bernstein at Curtis today is with his graduating class of June 1941. It hangs on the third floor with pictures of other classes. For the school's fiftieth anniversary, Bernstein was the keynote speaker.

Noting that he had arrived at Curtis in September 1939, the year in which World War II began, he said:

> It was like walking into an alien land. The school at that
> time was a fairly accurate reflection of the isolationist attitude
> that gripped so large a part of our country. The motto was:
> Avoid entanglements. Curtis was an island of musical enter-

prise; there seemed to be no one with whom I could share my Audenesque feelings, at least not among the students. Those first few months were lonely and agonizing.

... I was not a smash hit with the student body. As you can imagine, they regarded me as a Harvard smart aleck, an intellectual big shot, a snob, a show-off. I know this to be true because they later told me so. Well, maybe they had a point; but the fact remains that I was the only university type around, and we may all have overreacted. After all, not one of them had gone to college; some were still in short pants; others had entered the school in short pants years before, and were still totally immersed in hammering out the Etude in thirds faster than the nearest competitor; or perhaps it was a Paganini Caprice, or a Puccini aria. In any case, interdisciplinary it was not. Philosophy, history, aesthetics — all irrelevant. The school seemed to me like a virtuoso factory, turning out identical virtuosi like sausages. I exaggerate, of course; but that's how it *seemed* to me in September, 1939.

... My only real friends, those first few months, were faculty members — and some members of the staff.... But among the students, no friends. On the contrary I had enemies, official enemies. There was actually a secret anti-Bernstein club ... their names engraved on my brain. Not too many, perhaps half a dozen, who believed, beyond the gripe that I was a Harvard snob, that I was also a fake, especially in my ability to sight-read orchestral scores. They were convinced that I had secretly prepared them and then passed them off as sight-reading. Alas. The word spread, the tension mounted.

Then came the astonishing climax. A colleague of mine in Reiner's class went out and bought a gun, plus bullets with my name on them. This highly disturbed young man, who shall remain nameless, was having terrible trouble memorizing his scores for the merciless Reiner who, as you may know, could stop you at any point in the music and paralyze you with the question "What is the second clarinet playing in this bar?" Well, all this became too much for my colleague, who decided that I was Reiner's favorite, that he was being discriminated against, and that he would therefore clear up the whole situation by shooting not only me, but Reiner *and* Randall Thompson as well.* But he made the fatal mistake of announcing his intentions to Randall, laying his gun on the table, *literally*. Randall cleverly soothed him, called the police, and had the poor boy carted away, back to his hometown.[2]

Bernstein concluded his remarks by saying that this event had turned the situation around and that "foes became friends."

Bernstein's recollections of his Curtis days have an element of revisionism. In his statement that the institute was isolationist, he implies that he was not. And yet the facts are different. In 1940 when Roosevelt was supporting the defense efforts of the British through the Lend-Lease program, many Americans were accusing him of leading us into war. This was the period of the military and political alliance between Hitler and Stalin, undertaken by both for the most cynical of reasons. Stalin was happy to see the Nazis overrun the British and French at this time and assumed that when the Germans were through, their own forces would be spent. The American Communists, defending the position of the Soviet Union, claimed that the Russians had allied themselves with the Germans in self-defense, that if they had not done so, the Allies and the Germans would have combined their forces and ganged up against them. Thus the American Communists found themselves siding with the Russians and Germans and against the English. Because of these special alliances, the left was as isolationist as the right; the left was anti-Roosevelt, some of its members even joining forces with the America First Committee, the principal isolationist group.

In the winter of 1940, Bernstein's first year at Curtis, he was living in a small ugly room without a bath over Lessin's delicatessen. One day while he was hanging around the store, Shirley Gabis, a beautiful, dark-haired Jewish girl, came in. Later married to the composer George Perle, she had not only the same name as Bernstein's sister but the same kind of looks. For a young man feeling isolated and depressed, such an echo of the past must have been at the least comforting.

"We met," Shirley Gabis Perle says, "during Lenny's first winter in

---

* *Thompson, a composer and a former Harvard professor, had been engaged in 1939 as the director of Curtis.*

Philadelphia. Curtis is in Rittenhouse Square and the kids on scholar-ships are placed all around the area in private homes and rooming hous-es. Lenny lived in 406 South Twenty-second Street, a rooming house owned by a Mrs. Ules. One evening I walked into Lessin's and there was one lone person there. He was doing an imitation for Mr. Lessin of Roosevelt's famous 'I hate war' speech, mocking it, as so many comedi-ans were doing then. He also mimicked Mrs. Roosevelt and Fala. He was incredibly good-looking and exuded vitality.

"We began to see each other all the time. He used to hang out at the Delancey Pharmacy where you could get a tuna fish on toast for fif-teen cents and read *The New Yorker* for nothing. I was in high school and a passionate music lover. My mother made a congenial environ-ment. There was always a great deal of food and we had a Fischer grand. My grandfather had been a dealer in phonograph records and equip-ment and we still had shelves of pop music from the 1920s. Lenny would tear through the songs at the piano singing at the top of his lungs. I remember we went to jam sessions on Sansore Street when Billy Krechmer was on clarinet and Mickey House on piano.

"My parents were divorced. On Sundays my father would visit and complain about all the Bohemians in the apartment. I remember Lenny sitting at the other end of the couch where my father sat rigid. It was the only time I saw Lenny intimidated."

Not only did Bernstein find a new Shirley, in Shirley's father he seems to have found another Sam. Shirley Gabis Perle characterizes her youthful relationship with Bernstein as one in which each was "involved" with the other, qualifying that by saying, "Things were not then the way they are today." Indeed, however "involved" they were, it is unlikely that the connection was that of lovers in the traditional sense of the word. Shirley was sixteen and a high school junior when the twenty-one-year-old Harvard graduate entered her life.

"I remember," she recalls, "Lenny coming over with *Billy the Kid*, a photocopied, accordion-pleated score. After we played it four-hands he unfolded the score all the way down the three flights of stairs. That was the same day he stamped his foot so hard on the floor while he was play-ing the Copland *Variations* that the chandelier fell in the apartment below. My mother got a letter from the landlord saying that this was the last straw and that we would have to move. We did."

Eugene Istomin, the pianist, was then fourteen and also a constant visitor to the Gabis house. "Lenny adored playing," according to Shirley Gabis Perle, "but he was up against stiff competition. Istomin was incredible. Lenny played Copland's *Variations*. Preparing for a concert at Curtis, he played Ravel's *Tombeau de Couperin*. We both played a four-hand Hindemith sonata and together we heard Horowitz's recording of the Rachmaninoff Third. I remember Lenny's father coming to the house and telling my mother he didn't know why Lenny wanted to be a musician when he could make a hundred dollars a week with free room and board by working for him in the beauty supply business."

Lenny and Shirley attended musical events together in Philadelphia. Shirley recalls, "Lenny adored Mitropoulos." They went to the world premiere of Schoenberg's Violin Concerto with Louis Krasner playing. They saw their first *La Bohéme* together. "I remember," she says, "Lenny saying, 'And how's by you?' at the end of the first act. We were so overwhelmed by it. I also recall his analyzing a movement of a Beethoven sonata for my mother. He loved to teach even then."

Herschel and Janice Levit, long devoted to Renée Longy Miquelle, a teacher at Curtis, were a Jewish couple who befriended Bernstein during that first winter in Philadelphia. In February 1940, Miquelle told the Levits she wanted them to meet one of the students. "She brought in this skinny little kid," Janice Levit says, "and it was love at first sight.

"Our apartment," she says, "was on the first floor of one of the small houses on South Twenty-second Street, just a few doors from his. The only bathtub he had in 406 was the one in the hallway and it was always stopped up. The first thing he said when he walked into our place was 'Can I only take a bath here?' We had a woman who cleaned. One day, when we weren't in, Lenny came by and told her he was there to take a bath. She accepted it without question and that was that. In addition to taking baths at our house, he was always eating there. I remember him knocking at our window one morning with a package of bacon asking if he could come in for breakfast."

Curtis gave its students scholarships that covered tuition—room and board were paid by parents—as well as a grand piano in each one's room. "Lenny had a Steinway," Janice Levit says. "My husband and I were very poor and we bought an upright for twenty dollars. We had it tuned beautifully one day when we knew he was coming to play. He came in with his score to *El Salón México* and as soon as he started he said, 'This is perfect because it sounds exactly like a barroom piano.' We were devastated. After he finished, the piano was totally out of tune."

She remembers Copland and Diamond visiting Bernstein in Philadelphia. "It wasn't surprising," she says. "His conversation was fantastic. He read a great deal then. He was very brash, very full of confidence. He did everything so naturally. I don't remember him composing in those days. He seemed to be busy with conducting and piano and although he was a remarkable pianist—I remember him playing Brahms's Intermezzi, which he had never seen before, as though he had been performing them for years—he did not get on with Vengerova. She was a tyrant and he loathed her. Recently I have heard him say that he appreciates her today."

However combative the relationship between Vengerova and Bernstein may have been, she thought Bernstein a marvelous pianist. She never gave him less than an A and once gave him an A+. There is no doubt that Bernstein could have had a distinguished career as a concert pianist if his temperament had been different.

BER**N**STEIN

5

During the 1930s Koussevitzky promoted American works by performing them with the Boston Symphony. In New York, small chamber ensembles devoted themselves to new American music. The League of Composers, the Copland-Sessions concerts, the Pan-American Association were just a few of the groups that might

© WHITESTONE PHOTO/HEINZ H. WEISSENSTEIN

"… at the end of a Koussevitzky concert … Bernstein had confessed he was 'so jealous.'"

have welcomed a Bernstein score.

During the summer of 1939, when Davidson Taylor of CBS radio turned him down for a job, Bernstein had little to do during the day. He composed sketches for a movement which eventually became part of *Jeremiah*, his First Symphony. He based it on the Book of Lamentations, scored it for soprano and orchestra, and dedicated it "to My Father." Yet when chance intervened and Mitropoulos beckoned him to New York, Bernstein dropped the work for more than two years to make conducting his first priority. Curtis did offer composition. Rosario Scalero, who had taught Barber and Menotti, was still there. But Bernstein ignored him and chose conducting and piano as his double major.

Despite the efforts of Koussevitzky in Boston, the small ensembles in New York, and Davidson Taylor and CBS, little recognition or reward was to be found in composition. In December 1937, the year before he met Bernstein, Copland, as president of the newly formed Composers' Alliance, issued a statement in *Modern Music* that held that "the American composer of serious music is about to proclaim a new principle for the right to make a living composing." The articulation of such a modest demand indicates how bad things were. For a Young Turk like Bernstein, physical and sexual in the extreme, the isolated, sedentary, unpaid act of composition offered little in the way of immediate gratification. Conducting, on the other hand, meant applause and adoring crowds pushing in for just a look or a touch. Whatever spotlight Schuman, Harris, or Copland enjoyed, it could not compare to the one then reserved for such exotic figures as Stokowski, Toscanini, and Koussevitzky, the great conductors on the American scene when Bernstein came of age. It was at the end of a Koussevitzky concert at Symphony Hall, not a Copland premiere at a league event, that Bernstein had confessed he was "so jealous."

In the late spring of Bernstein's first year at Curtis, 1940, he read that Koussevitzky was starting a music school at Tanglewood, the Massachusetts summer home of the Boston Symphony since 1936. A part of the Berkshire Music Center, the school would offer conducting courses taught by Koussevitzky himself. Bernstein applied.

I got letters of recommendation from Aaron Copland and

this time from Fritz Reiner, from Roy Harris whom I had met, from William Schuman, and so on. And I came to Boston that spring, was admitted to the sanctum sanctorum of Symphony Hall, which was Koussevitzky's greenroom, armed with those letters, and we talked a minute or two. And so, there I was sitting in the presence of the great Koussevitzky, trembling and white, and suddenly Koussevitzky said, "But of course I vill take you in my class." It was just like that. A great shock. A wonderful shock. [3]

It was a wonderful shock that came at precisely the right moment in Bernstein's life. The career he had hoped for through Mitropoulos never came about. David Diamond recently characterized Mitropoulos in a letter as possessing "distortions of character which were not only ambivalences but also the opposites of the 'saintliness' for which he was primarily known." Whatever Mitropoulos may have felt for Bernstein, his ambivalence certainly set the tone. He had first promised Bernstein a post as his "assistant" in Minneapolis for the 1939–1940 season, then again for 1940–1941, the year after Bernstein came to Curtis. On this promise, too, he reneged. In April 1940, Mitropoulos sent Bernstein this telegram: "Don't leave your class for next season. Some real difficulties here because of my engagement in New York and one month of orchestra tour and some guest conductors. Am very awfully sorry, Dimitri."

Devastated, Bernstein sent a letter to Diamond in which he said that the prospect of the next year in Minneapolis had been "the one, single motive" of his activity in Philadelphia and that "every move, every note studied, person loved, hope ignored, was a direct preparation for next year. From the scores I chose to study to the sexual life which I have abandoned—all."

Unable to conceive that his deeply felt connection to Mitropoulos had ended, Bernstein wrote Diamond that perhaps he still could go to Minneapolis as a staff pianist or, failing that, could assume the post of assistant conductor in 1941–1942, after graduation from Curtis. "One must have faith," he wrote, "to be able to make these efforts at adjustment."

Later Mitropoulos did send a letter, attributing the difficulty now *not* to guest conductors, *not* to touring or an engagement in New York, but to union problems. In response to a letter Diamond wrote him about his own interpretation of Mitropoulos's behavior, Bernstein replied, "DM is no false promiser. He has an integrity that is *sans pareil.*"

By June even Bernstein knew something was wrong. In a letter to Diamond he said he had waited for a promised call that never came and of the strange silence "which is difficult for me to understand. It cannot be that the thing is over. I wrote asking Why and as yet have had no answer."

In 1938, after Bernstein's visit to Minneapolis and after Mitropoulos received the appointment as conductor of the Minneapolis Symphony, Mitropoulos had written to Katy Katsoyanis:

> Here is why America is better. There is everywhere an encouraging breath—for work, for morality. When they see you as a god, an apostle, a leader, you feel the need to be as pure as possible before people who are ready to adore you, to follow you, to respond to you. All these things seem childish in Europe. Here, even the gangsters have some glory, some idealism in them, and are a thousand times more interesting than the European blasés.... [4]

But in 1940 an uncharacteristic stream of letters to Katsoyanis revealed a different attitude. His relationship to America was now characterized by despair. This represented a significant change from his feelings of only a few years before. Almost certainly, the Greek conductor was deeply pained by the series of tragedies that befell Greece—the 1935 destruction of the republic that he himself had fought to install by a repressive dictatorship, and then the invasion by Italy and then Germany. During June, the month that Bernstein sat paralyzed waiting for a call, here is what Mitropoulos was writing to Katsoyanis:

> I am alone, completely alone, practically locked up in my room reading books and scores. If I manage to survive this time, then I'll never be in danger again of needing the company of any human being. It is the hardest test I've ever had in my life. I've explained to you that since I haven't been able, up to

now, to relate spiritually with any American being, this means that it will never happen to me. I came to this country at too mature an age, and it is now quite impossible for me to link myself completely with the environment and with the people. Most of all, the absence of romanticism, of warmth, makes me feel more alone than if I chose to be alone in a warm environment. Maybe you'll be amazed at what I write here, after all I had told you in person about my impression of this country and its people. I've discovered that, up to now, most of the time I colored them with my imagination and saw them as I wanted them to be, but as, unfortunately, they are not.

...I'm writing you today with a very heavy heart. France has fallen, Paris even, into the hands of the barbarians! I've stopped believing in anything. I doubt that there's any humanity left! My God, why, at such a time, is there no one near me to give me courage, but only cold-blooded Americans who still think it is not their business to get involved in European events. I'm disgusted with all of them, and, to tell you the truth, I wish with all my heart that they'll taste the sweetness of Hitlerian influence in their country. There's selfishness everywhere; all is well as long as America in not affected. They're intoxicated with *comfort* and nothing else interests them. The ambition of every one of my musicians is to buy a car. The students are signing petitions to keep America *out of the war!* This is the daily motto...."[4]

Mitropoulos apparently did not understand the ethnic diversity of the United States or the effect of that diversity on public opinion toward Europe and its politics. Nor was he in a mood to deepen his tie to Bernstein, a young American who liked comfort and cars and expressed the Communist party line by ridiculing Roosevelt's inclination to involve America in war.

In late June 1940 Bernstein went to New York to work on a television project with the Revuers. The Berkshire Music Center was prepared to cover all tuition costs for him and pay for half his room and board so the fee for the Revuers job would make up the difference. In the context of the void he felt because of the treatment from

Mitropoulos, Koussevitzky's loving care was all the more appreciated.

Koussevitzky had started to work toward a school attached to the Boston Symphony as early as 1929. By the time it came about in 1940, there could be no doubt that the festival was his own. He chose the faculty, supervised the selection of students, seemed constantly to survey the grounds. His faculty was remarkable: Copland and Paul Hindemith for composition; Herbert Graf and Boris Goldovsky for opera; G. Wallace Woodworth, chairman of Harvard's Department of Music, and Hugh Ross, director of the Schola Cantorum, for chorus; Olin Downes, music critic of *The New York Times*, for music history; and members of the Boston Symphony, including all the first-desk men, for instrumental instruction.

Koussevitzky taught two conducting classes. One was large, about thirty students. Here he dispensed information on technique and interpretation. The other was small, about five students. To this group he gave his special attention. For the most part he used phonograph records—a relatively recent innovation—so the student could conduct while he advised. He hired a ballet master to help his students be graceful on the podium and had the room covered with mirrors so they could see themselves. Each day the class would begin with the students pirouetting and posturing. Finally Koussevitzky allowed them to conduct the student orchestra.

Despite Bernstein's refusal to pirouette and posture, he and Koussevitzky "became instant friends. Almost a father-son relationship," Bernstein says.

> He became like a surrogate father to me. He had no children of his own and I had a father whom I loved very much but who was not for this musical thing at all....
>
> And so I found another father: first Mitropoulos, then Reiner, and now Koussevitzky; but the Koussevitzky relationship was very special, very warm, and there was something about his being Russian that was terribly moving and close to me. I didn't know Russian and I had not met many Russians but my parents had been born in Russia, although they were quite young children when they came over to this country. But I sensed something ethnologically and demographically and

intuitively close. In short we became loving friends and student-teacher. [3]

In one way Koussevitzky was different from Bernstein's own father.
The conductor, who had been born a Jew and converted while still in
Russia in order to further his career, advised Bernstein to play down his
religion and in 1942 even suggested he change his name. "Leonard S.
Burns" was the name he picked out for his student. The *S* was to stand
for Bernstein's father's name, perhaps as a kind of compensation for the
deep insult the name change would have been to Sam and to his heritage. But other aspects of Koussevitzky's morality did mirror those of
Sam. At Tanglewood he often lectured on good and bad. A conductor
was a teacher in the community with social responsibility. "You must
conduct your lives in such a way," Koussevitzky is reported to have said,
"that when you come out on the stage to lead your orchestra, you can
truthfully say to yourself: 'Yes, I have the right to appear before these
lovers of good music. They can watch me without shame. I have the
right because my life and work are clean.'"

Like Curtis, Tanglewood offered composition classes; Copland and
Hindemith divided the students. Lukas Foss, who, with Bernstein, went
from Curtis to Tanglewood, studied composition with Scalero and conducting with Reiner while he was in Philadelphia and composition with
Hindemith and conducting with Koussevitzky in the Berkshires.
Bernstein did not take any composition courses at either of the schools.
In 1985 he explained, "It never occurred to me to study composition.
Whatever I wrote I took to Aaron. Aaron was my guide. That is very
different than having someone who assigns you. I showed Dimitri some
of my scores, too. He thought I was quite talented but also that they
could be improved. I showed what I did to people I was in awe of. That
seemed to be as much a study of composition as I could take."

At Tanglewood Bernstein invested his energy in conducting and
Koussevitzky. Koussevitzky responded to the student with the same
intensity with which Bernstein had reacted to him. According to Olga
Koussevitzky, the conductor's third wife, "Bernstein and Koussevitzky
had much in common, in their approach to music and in their leadership. And they were both outgoing men. Dr. Koussevitzky felt that
Bernstein justified his belief in a young American.... He thought of him

as a born conductor. He came to regard him almost as a son. He addressed Bernstein as Lenyushka and Bernstein addressed him as Serge Alexandrovitch."

During July and August of 1940, Bernstein lived in Room 57 of the Cranwell Jesuit School in Lenox, Massachusetts, used in the summers by the Tanglewood students. His fellow conducting students were Richard Bales, later the conductor of the National Gallery Orchestra in Washington, Thor Johnson, later the music director of the Cincinnati Symphony, Gaylord Browne, who did not go on to a conducting career, and Lukas Foss. His roommates included the pianist-composer Harold Shapero from his Harvard days, clarinetist David Glazer, violist Raphael Hillyer, and cellist Jesse Ehrlich. All of them have gone on to musical careers. Then it was a manic group and one contemporary describes them as a "bunch of hyperactive kids. Their room was by far the noisiest at Tanglewood." Shapero for his composition class wrote a work for clarinet, cello, and violin that he called *Room 57*.

The opening concert led off with the student body in a newly commissioned work: Randall Thompson's *Alleluia*, under the direction of Woodworth, the head of the Harvard Glee Club who had fired Bernstein as the club's accompanist. Even if this connection was a negative one, there must have been some exhilaration in being on familiar terms with both conductor and composer of a public event. Everything about Tanglewood suited Bernstein.

Burton Bernstein quotes his brother's first letter home:

Dearest folks: I have never seen such a beautiful setup in my life. I've been conducting the orchestra every morning, & I'm playing my first concert tomorrow night. Kouss gave me the hardest and longest number of all—the Second Symphony of Randall Thompson—30 minutes long—a modern American work—as my first performance. And Kouss is so pleased with my work. He likes me & works very hard with me in our private sessions. He is the most marvelous man—a beautiful spirit that never lags or fails—that inspires me terrifically. And he told me he is convinced that I have a wonderful gift, & he is already making me a *great* conductor. (I actually rode in his car with him today!) He has wonderful teaching ability, which I never expected—& is very hard to please—so that when he says he is pleased I know it means something. I am so thrilled—have never been more happy & satisfied. The orchestra likes me very much, best of all the conductors, & responds so beautifully in rehearsal. Of course the concert tomorrow night (Shabbas, yet!) will tell whether I can keep my head in performance. We've been working very hard—you're always going mad here—no time to think how tired you are or how little you slept last night—the inspiration of this Center is terrific enough to keep you going with no sleep at all. I'm so excited about tomorrow night—I wish you could all be there—it's so important to me—& Kouss is banking on it to convince him that he's right—if it goes well, there's no telling what may happen....

Bernstein ends the letter with a plea: "Please come up—I think I'll be conducting every Friday night & rehearsing every morning—please come up—All my love, Lenny." [1]

The big advantage of Tanglewood over Curtis was student access to an orchestra. At Curtis there was a student orchestra but that was for Reiner alone. On occasion he relinquished the podium; once Bernstein conducted Brahms' A-major Serenade. But in general the students in the class—Foss, Max Goberman, Walter Hendl, Ezra Rochlin, and Bernstein—would take turns playing the piano while a fellow student conducted, so except for those occasions at Walter Wolf's house, Bernstein had little opportunity to test what he had learned.

At Tanglewood, Bernstein often found himself conducting the student orchestra. Those around at the time report that Koussevitzky would stand at the side with an uninterrupted, beatific grin. The high point of Bernstein's first season at Tanglewood was his conducting Stravinsky's *L'Histoire du Soldat* with his own jokes about Tanglewood inserted, a little like the days at Singer's Inn. The major question that faced Bernstein that summer was whether he should return to Curtis at all. Koussevitzky was almost pathologically jealous. The conductor Seymour Lipkin says that in 1946, he fell completely out of favor with Koussevitzky because he took the summer to study with George Szell.

Koussevitzky had been promising Bernstein an orchestra of his own

one day. Bernstein did not want to risk losing that prospect by returning to Reiner for another year. But he had good reason to be cautious
about turning his back on Curtis. For one thing Koussevitzky had a reputation for breaking promises, which is documented in the biography
by Moses Smith. For another Bernstein had already been devastated
waiting for Mitropoulos to come through. Finally Bernstein was always
well aware of the value of Reiner's instruction and the standards Reiner
held his students to. For advice Bernstein consulted Randall
Thompson, who said he should return to Curtis, not only because he
was on scholarship there and consequently obligated to the Institute,
but also because Reiner had worked hard with him. Reiner had
expressed irritation to his colleagues at Bernstein's refusal to attend to
his schooling. But he also gave him what was probably the only A of
Reiner's teaching career.

So, in September 1940, Bernstein returned to Curtis for his second
year. He says:

> I finished my two-year course with Reiner, which was a
> whole other kettle of fish. I mean Reiner's way of teaching was
> tyrannical in the extreme. He demanded total knowledge. You
> had no right to step up on the podium unless you knew every-
> thing about what every member of the orchestra had to do. And
> if you didn't, God pity you. But Reiner and I also finally became
> good friends. It was hard going because he was not basically a
> friendly man, being so demanding and severe. Whereas
> Koussevitzky's way of teaching was inspirational. He demand-
> ed, of course, knowledge and high standards of capability and
> commitment but his method of teaching was more in terms of
> emotion and "it must be varm like the sun come up in the
> morning and the crescendo must be" you know, whereas Reiner
> would say: "What is the second clarinet playing at this
> moment?" He'd stop you and you'd think: "Is there a second
> clarinet playing? I really don't know. Do you mean transposed
> or the way it is in the score?" And you'd freeze up. It was a scary
> way of teaching and Koussy's way was the opposite. It was invit-
> ing and warm and embracing and very beautiful. But I'm not
> trying to make Koussevitzky's way of teaching any better. I'm

not putting down Reiner's method. On the contrary, Reiner is responsible for my own very high standards. [3]

Bernstein's standards may have come from Reiner, his cape and theatricality from Koussevitzky, but his essence derives from Mitropoulos and that was apparent from the start. One area in which he came into conflict with both Reiner and Koussevitzky was his wish to conduct without a baton—as Mitropoulos did. Both men objected strenuously but they both gave in. Burton Bernstein's description of his brother as the Great Persuader receives confirmation again. Not only had Jennie lent him her car and her maid. Not only was Sam now supporting him in these postgraduate years in a field he himself abhorred and at a time when his business was in trouble. But Reiner and Koussevitzky let him have his way in this crucial matter of working without a stick. Something about the use of his hands must have excited Bernstein. He told his teachers what he believed to be true: that the conducting movements he made with his hands were more related to those at the piano than anything he could ever do with a baton. Years later Olga Koussevitzky said, "Dr. Koussevitzky was worried about it. He sat for hours looking at his own hands. Then he extended the index fingers and waved them a little. Finally he smiled. He found that the index fingers do exactly what a baton does. So he allowed Bernstein to conduct without a baton."

Returning to Philadelphia, nourished by his exhilarating summer, Bernstein was brasher than ever. Instead of going back to Mrs. Ules's room, he rented a spacious one-room apartment in a tall, red-brick building with an elevator that was easily visible from the big bay windows at Curtis. Here, at 1922 Walnut, he not only could take a bath but entertain Copland and Diamond in style. The year was happier in many ways. His friendship with Renée Miquelle grew and he attended the monthly meetings of her Twentieth Century Music Club where she discoursed on Stefan Wolpe and Hindemith's *Mathis der Maler.* The friendship with Shirley Gabis flourished. They attended Stokowski's youth concerts. Once Bernstein persuaded her to go with him to Stokowski's house and ring his bell. Stokowski appeared on the second-floor balcony and, in soft, carefully measured words, greeted them but did not invite them in. To bring the meeting to a quick close he intoned,

"And thank you for coming." Bernstein, under his breath and in mock-Stokowski style, formally replied, "And fuck you."

During Koussevitzky's 1940–1941 season, he brought the Boston Symphony to Philadelphia. Bernstein asked Shirley to join him at the concert. Recalling that event, she remarked on the transformation she saw when Bernstein faced his Russian mentor: "Lenny was five years older than I. I was sixteen, going on seventeen. I had to finish my algebra homework before my mother would let me leave the house. When Lenny took me backstage to meet Koussevitzky, he suddenly became a little boy. He looked to me not like the Harvard graduate he was, but as he might have appeared if I were many years older than he."

Bernstein may have assumed a childlike demeanor in front of Koussevitzky in 1940 but that did not last for long. Within a short time he was calling the Russian maestro Serge Alexandrovitch—not Maestro, or Père, or even Dr. Koussevitzky. Bernstein was never intimidated for long by any father, his own or others, and in the case of Koussevitzky, the tables started turning almost immediately. For Bernstein possessed talents and skills that were beyond Koussevitzky's. Bernstein was a phenomenal score reader. Bernstein possessed an uncanny musical memory. Bernstein's capacity for articulating the most complex of rhythms dazzled observers from his earliest conducting days.

Leonard Burkat, whose career took him from high school oboist to the position of artistic administrator of the Boston Symphony, describes Koussevitzky as "a great man with all the terrors that offend those who know how they got into the limelight."

Koussevitzky, who had started his career with no financial resources but a fine talent for the double bass, got into the limelight by marrying one of the wealthiest women in Russia. Natalie Koussevitzky contributed generously to her husband's budding career as a conductor. She gave him the money to hire musicians so that he could train, and then gave him more to buy the orchestras. His decision to shift from virtuoso on the double bass to conductor was made when he was in his thirties, and his musical training suffered. Moses Smith claims that Koussevitzky could not read a score with any facility and was unable to memorize music. Also that he could not keep time. All of this becomes credible when one learns that he hired Nicolas Slonimsky, a nephew of

Vengerova's and the now-legendary music dictionary author, to play piano reductions of new pieces for him so he could be familiar with them before he faced the musicians at the first rehearsal. As late as his first performance of Stravinsky's *Le Sacre du Printemps*, Slonimsky had to prepare a simplified score so that Koussevitzky could get through it. Bernstein's gifts in all of these areas must have awed the older man and given Bernstein the power that he was never able to enjoy with Reiner or with Mitropoulos.

During his second year at Curtis, Bernstein continued his studies with Reiner and Vengerova. Curtis had a booking office for its student talent that was run by Tod Perry, who later became the manager of the Boston Symphony. Perry booked Bernstein on some piano dates. Because he didn't own a tailcoat, Perry lent him his own. It was years before Bernstein bought formal attire. Apart from the fact that he had little money, he must have viewed white tie and tails as a symbol of a degenerate capitalist society's musical mores. Even after two years at Curtis, his left-wing convictions remained intact. Almost immediately after graduation, he rushed into a production by the Harvard Student Union of Aristophanes' *The Peace*. Bernstein composed incidental music and conducted the performance on two evenings in Harvard's Sanders Theater. This was May 1941. The Communist party line was still anti-war. In June, Germany invaded Russia.

In an undated letter, Bernstein charted events for his Philadelphia Shirley:

> Hello, you Galatea, Time out (two minutes) from orches-trating music for a Harvard production of *The Peace* by Aristophanes (a new headache I've contracted). My hand is numb from writing score; and to make matters worse, I bruised my metacarpal(!) playing baseball this afternoon. All of which makes it good for concerti playing the 25th, to say nothing of Scriabin playing the 17th. And conducting *The Peace* music for the 23rd and 24th. Life, dear one, is hectic plus. I really need your steadying hand on mine now. It's amazing to look back and see that it really was a steadying hand. Phenomenal effect for an adolescent Galatea to have: But then, you're you.

Of course Bill has told you of our Atlantic City escapade

(mostly gabbing with Curtisites). [Bernstein had celebrated his graduation with Copland and the cellist William Saputelli in the New Jersey resort town.] And now you're doing Algebra and going to Ivy Balls ... and putting your hair up and down according to your escort, and eating *chez* Saputelli—and I've left your mind. See? I told you so.

But make an effort anyway, and write me all—a bright moment of letter opening in the middle of bustle. And darling, take care of yourself. All my love to split with Rae [Shirley's mother], Lenny.

Isn't it daring to produce *The Peace* at a time like this? I love it—the music is good, too.

Ricky Leacock recalls, "The Harvard Student Union was a pink organization. The work had been totally rewritten. It was an antiwar piece with many allusions to the war effort. The left was antiwar and Lenny was influenced by the left. He was preparing for a piano performance of Beethoven concerti in Chicago at the time and between the rehearsals for *Peace*, which was scored for four trombones, piano, and percussion, he would hammer out the Beethoven standing up. People came to the theater to boo but everybody loved it. They just laughed their heads off. It was a wonderful production." On May 27, again from Newton, Bernstein wrote to Shirley.

Sweets, It's all over and I breathe again. *Quel* week! The Greek show brought down the house both nights and my score was universally beloved. But at the price of awakening on Concerti day with a fine feverish cold. Hence the concerti were under par, but very exciting, good reviews too. Vital, vastly impressive etc. But it could have been perfect but for that damned fever.

Now I'm home nursing this lovely cold. Sort of good-for-nothing and let down. No trip for me, I think. I'll spend the money on records, racquets and phonographs. God, it's good to be home.

When do you graduate? Or do you?

Miquelle came for the concert. In fact, she's dropping

around this afternoon, as one might expect.

Nothing now til Tanglewood; and I plan to go up within a week to look at hice [the plural of "house"] and see Kouss. Will you be up this summer? I think I'll write an orchestral piece.

Have you read Henry James? Read "The Turn of the Screw," one of the stories in a book called *The Two Magics*.

Write soon—Love—Lenny.

He was looking for a place to live that would be an improvement over his 1940 Room 57 and when he learned that Copland rented a house, he wrote and asked him if he could stay there: "Is it really impossible to live in your house? You don't work anyway during those six weeks. And think of the fun: We're all feeling rather antidormitory...." Copland found the strength to say no but Bernstein apparently was at his house most of the time anyway. Rosamond Bernlet, one of Copland's good friends, says that whenever she telephoned, Copland would whisper, "There are guests in the house," as if to say, "There are *mice* in the kitchen."

Koussevitzky's class in 1941 consisted of Foss, Bernstein, Thor Johnson, Walter Hendl, Richard Korn, and Robert Whitney. Bernstein continued his pattern of making friends not from among the students but the faculty. One alumnus remembers him sitting at a table in a restaurant with Copland, Hindemith, and the concert pianist Jesús María Sanromá. One would tap a rhythm with his right hand and start another with his left. The next would add two more rhythms and so on until there were eight rhythms going at the same time, each with its own profile but all working together.

At Tanglewood Bernstein kept in touch with Shirley.

Dear Gabe, abe: I'm limp. I've just written Alvin Ross [a Philadelphia painter]. *Quel* effort! I just took off the morning and cancelled everything at Tanglewood, & stayed home, & wrote letters. Otherwise, impossible. Life here is hectic—but hectic. Tremendous success in conducting the last two weeks. I did William Schuman's *American Festival* Overture and it knocked everyone for a bingo. Really brought it down. And last week, I did Lambert's *Rio Grande* with chorus etc. *Très* brilliant,

& terrific hit.* This week I'm stuck with the Brahms B Flat Concerto, but it's only interregnum of rest. Ain't you never coming up?

God, I pity you in Philly! I'd perish, personally. You, of course, are of hardier stock.

I got my questionnaire.

Love to Rae—and let's hear—Love, Lenny.

The questionnaire to which Bernstein referred was the first sent to him by his draft board. By this time Germany had invaded Russia, and the Communist party line switched to support of the war effort. Many Communists and other leftists went into the army. But Bernstein stayed out: His long-standing asthma got him a deferment. David Diamond remembers Sam Bernstein's joy. In Yiddish he cried out, "Thanks be to God my son won't have to go to war."

Here is Bernstein on these events:

I was instantly turned down by the draft board for asthma and marked 4-F, which enabled me to continue my studies at Curtis and Tanglewood. For which I was sort of grateful. On the other hand it was a bit depressing not to be able to take part in this war, but I felt: I don't like wars at all. And as a matter of fact it seems to me that one of the marks of the continuing Neanderthalism of our breed of humankind is the fact that we have not eliminated the stupidity of war from our way of life. We don't seem to be able to live with each other in peace after all these centuries.

It just seems beyond belief, but this war seemed different. It seemed *necessary.* In the first place, we were totally on the defensive, and secondly, there was the whole Nazi threat, not only to all of Europe and all the world, but beyond that in a

---

*Rio Grande *is a big work for piano, chorus, and orchestra that is shot through with jazz. Immediately after the last rehearsal on the day of the performance, the actress Tallulah Bankhead, appearing in summer stock in the area, introduced herself to Bernstein, complimenting him on his back muscles. She was not alone. Over the years Bernstein's open rehearsals attracted scores of adoring fans who were mesmerized by his back muscles as seen through T-shirts or nothing at all. On this occasion the actress invited him to dine, assuring him he would be back in time for the performance. At 8 P.M. the conductor had had several drinks but no food. He fled back to Tanglewood in Bankhead's limousine, stopping only to change his clothes. For years this was his only publicly noted incident with racy connotations involving a woman. That Bernstein, the day afterward, did not include it in his letter to Shirley Gabis indicates some consideration for her feelings.*

more personal sense to me as an American and a Jew. And naturally we were all deeply concerned; and so I was a little disappointed at being rejected by the draft board. [3]

There may be some revisionism here. Musician friends of Bernstein's who were called into the army recall his initial reaction to their news was "What a waste!" If Bernstein's dominant feeling had been anything other than "What a waste," he could have volunteered for noncombatant activity, entertained the troops, or found some other way to participate in the war he claims disappointment at being rejected for as an American and a Jew.

No. The army and Bernstein were ill matched. Even if he had passed his physical, his homosexuality and his refusal to accept even a modicum of discipline would have produced a disastrous military career. Bernstein's commitment to peace at virtually any price, his ambition, his determination to be available for the career opportunity the moment it presented itself, made his deferment welcome. Although publicly he had deplored his inability to serve in the armed forces and has cited these efforts to volunteer, he has never commented on his limited civilian role. While thousands of performers entertained in combat zones and others worked in defense industries, Bernstein appears to have registered only as an air raid warden. That and the playing of some boogie-woogie at Fort Dix in New Jersey seem to have been the extent of his activity in World War II.

The summer of 1941 found Bernstein's relations

still focused on fathers. At Tanglewood he spent most of his time in Copland's house. After the season, Koussevitzky persuaded him to stick close to Boston. Here is Bernstein on those days:

I still could not get a job because I wasn't in the union.

1943
Artur Rodzinski: "... I finally asked God whom I shall take and God said,
'Take Bernstein.'"

I wasn't even in the Boston union because the Boston Symphony was the last holdout, the last nonunion orchestra in the United States. If I ever wanted to work with the Boston Symphony, which I had hoped to be able to do because Koussevitzky was now my mentor and Boston was my home-town, I couldn't belong to the union because it was the opposite of the way it is now…. Then, holding a union card was a disadvantage. So Koussevitzky said to me, "Why don't you stay in Boston and sort of be an assistant. I mean when I need you to play scores over or give me advice on new pieces which I don't understand now. Of course modern music is becoming so crazy and you young people understand it but I don't. Stay around in Boston and I'll pay you a little sum every once in a while to keep you going." And I thought it was a pretty good idea, although it wasn't a way of life. I mean, there was no modus vivendi attached to it. [3]

Sam Bernstein also wanted his son to stay close to home. In the late 1950s he spoke about those days: "Lenny was very depressed and didn't know what to do. I offered to take him into business with me at $100 a week and free room and board. But he wanted music. So I got him a studio on Huntington Avenue and had a piano put in it for him."

The studio, at the corner of Gainsborough and Huntington, was a stone's throw from Symphony Hall, Jordan Hall, the Opera House and the New England Conservatory of Music.

"I sent printed announcements all over the place," Lenny goes on,

that I was now going to give piano lessons and I thought that would help me support myself. No one came—I think one— I got one pupil from Worcester whose name was Bernie—and he used to drive in once a week. And he was my only pupil. Nobody else applied. And there I was—stuck up in my little garret on Huntington Avenue. I wrote music and I did see Koussevitzky from time to time but it was quite rare. He was very busy. [3]

Bernstein wrote Shirley Gabis:

I'm still in the throes of that two-weeks-ago cold. It won't go. I give it all kinds of subtle hints, but it won't leave. Sort of the way I refused to be moved out of your house at 1:30 am. It's a mad life, mainly because while I'm supposedly lounging and resting and loafing, I fall into bed exhausted every night. We're selling our Newton house, rebuilding our Sharon, and are planning to live there permanently. [Mimicking his father:] So is gradually involving all kinds picking art, fixtures and rugs and stuff and continual drives out there to see the house is going right, etc.

I'm so tired today I could scream. I can do nothing but sleep, get up to answer the phone, & sleep again. "C'est comme la vie a Philadelphie." Very dull: Very very dull. Very very dull.

The emergence of the cold-wave permanent made Sam Bernstein's Fredericks machine obsolete. His business difficulties, which forced him to sell his beloved Newton house, may have contributed to his own son's sense of failure. The depression manifested itself by Leonard's sleeping around the clock. A trip to New York to see Mitropoulos and to attend the wedding of Adolph Green to the wealthy and beautiful Elizabeth Reitel provided a welcome relief. In his letter to Shirley Gabis, Bernstein told her where he could be found in New York if she happened to be there that weekend.

During the fall of 1941 Bernstein did whatever he could to relieve the monotony and make some money. He undertook to arrange, direct, and perform in a series of musical programs for Boston's Institute of Modern Art, now known as the Institute of Contemporary Art. It was here he gave a two-piano recital with Harold Shapero—Stravinsky's *Concerto for Two Solo Pianos*, a four-hand sonata by Bernstein, and some Mozart—that Shapero has characterized as a "lively, chic, intellectual event." It was also during this time that he staged and conducted Copland's *Second Hurricane*, first at Jordan Hall, then at Sanders Theater using children from settlement houses in the cast. In the evenings Bernstein sometimes played piano in a little nightclub in Boston's Fensgate Hotel. One night the actor Paul Lukas, then appearing in *Watch on the Rhine*, saw him and said he would get Bernstein a screen test. But it was just talk. In a letter to Diamond, Bernstein complained of Lukas's "hollowness."

Once Koussevitzky asked Bernstein to take over the orchestra while he was away and to rehearse some Brahms. Instead Bernstein got the parts to Bartók's *Music for Strings, Percussion, and Celesta*, a work that had been composed less than five years before. He not only conducted it, he saw to it that someone recorded it and then sent this secret recording to his musician friends. Composer Vincent Persichetti, living in Philadelphia, got hold of one. He says he played it "twice every hour of a six-or seven-hour day." Persichetti adds that even then "Bernstein could get into a piece and shape it. He could do that with any kind of twentieth century music. As for the rest, it was better than all right."

On one occasion, success seemed to be within Bernstein's grasp. Koussevitzky told him, "I have this new piano concerto by Carlos Chávez, the Mexican composer. How would you like to play the piano part with the Boston Symphony?" Bernstein says that he thought:

> What excitement! Here at last is a debut with the Boston Symphony, not as a conductor but as a pianist. And so I learned that bloody thing. It took three months. Very difficult, and a severe, dissonant piece. At the end of it, when I was ready to play with the Boston Symphony, I was informed I couldn't because by now I had a union card. I had had to have one to do little gigs and jobs around Boston and that disentitled me to work with the Boston Symphony, which was still a nonunion orchestra. So that fell through. In short, another depressing winter in Boston. [3]

Bernstein was not the only musician who suffered because the Boston Symphony was not yet unionized. The serious troubles began in the summer of 1940 when James C. Petrillo, the president of the American Federation of Musicians, announced that the union had taken the Boston Symphony off the radio and got its recording contract canceled. Petrillo made it impossible for any soloists or conductors belonging to the American Guild of Musical Artists (AGMA) to perform with the Boston Symphony. During the 1941–1942 season, when Bernstein was teaching Bernie in his Huntington Avenue studio, the soloists and guest conductors whose appearances with the orchestra were canceled included Efrem Zimbalist, Joseph Szigeti, Howard Hanson, Bruno Walter, and Carlos Chávez, who was scheduled to conduct his own concerto. By that time Koussevitzky believed in the necessity of signing with the union, but he could not persuade the board. Its chairman, Ernest B. Dane, remained intransigent. In April 1942 Dane died, leaving nothing to the orchestra.

The trustees proceeded slowly, and Koussevitzky grew impatient. His irritation increased when he learned that the trustees had canceled the performances of the Boston Symphony at the Berkshire Festival for the summer of 1942 because of the war. Always a practical man, Koussevitzky started negotiations with the New York Philharmonic. The New York orchestra had been experiencing something of a letdown under the English conductor John Barbirolli, who had taken over after Toscanini left in 1937. Barbirolli was being eased out. To get Koussevitzky to make a commitment, the New York Philharmonic board went so far as to promise that it would create a summer school along the lines of Tanglewood.

Throughout this period, Koussevitzky's own problems precluded his taking care of Bernstein. So, with literally nothing else to do, Bernstein joined Comden, Green, and Judy Holliday with their show *My Dear Public*, written by Irving Caesar and Gerald Marx. It opened in Philadelphia in December 1941. But Bernstein had been hanging out with the cast even at its Boston tryout, and, as usual, he played piano at a cast party. Irving Caesar, who had written "Swanee" with Gershwin, told Bernstein that he reminded him of Gershwin and that he thought Bernstein was a genius. Caesar promised he would get him a job.

During the following spring Bernstein went back to work on *Jeremiah* and completed his Sonata for Clarinet, which he had begun the summer before on a trip to Key West, Florida. The work contains echoes of Hindemith's treatment of jazz, understandable because most of it was composed during the summer of 1941 when both musicians were at Tanglewood. David Glazer and Bernstein gave the first performance on April 21, 1942, in Boston.

Gas rationing kept the Boston Symphony out of Tanglewood the following summer. But the student orchestra was there, and this time

Bernstein conducted it not as a pupil but as Koussevitzky's assistant. Koussevitzky subsidized the 1942 summer with his own money and that of a few patrons. His wife had died in January, and he wanted to keep working, not only for his own emotional health but to see to it that Tanglewood would survive. So Koussevitzky produced a season with the help of students and teachers. All the important instructors, with the exception of Hindemith, were back on the campus, and Koussevitzky conducted the student orchestra in six concerts. One of the six was of particular importance, because Koussevitzky conducted the first American concert performance of Shostakovich's Symphony No. 7, the *Leningrad* Symphony, there. (The Russians had infuriated him by giving the broadcast rights to Toscanini, who had conducted it with the NBC Symphony on a network radio broadcast a short time before.)

For Bernstein the most important event of the summer was most probably not that concert. More likely it was his meeting with David Oppenheim, a young clarinetist in the Tanglewood orchestra. Now that Bernstein had found in Koussevitzky a loving musical father who supported him through all of his trials and had his career interests at heart, his search for such a figure came to an end. Instead, Bernstein devoted himself to Oppenheim and dedicated his recently composed Clarinet Sonata to him.

Oppenheim recalls their meeting: Bernstein told him, "I had a dream about you. I had a house and the house had a cellar and you were in the cellar."

Although Bernstein put Oppenheim in the cellar in his dream, he and Oppenheim spent much of their time in a tree, according to several Tanglewood residents that year. At the end of the summer they hitchhiked through New England with nothing but toothbrushes and the clothes on their backs. Oppenheim says it was Bernstein's idea: "We decided that if we needed anything—like another pair of socks—we would buy it en route. We hitchhiked through Vermont and New Hampshire and returned to Sharon, where we stayed with his family for a few days. Later, in New York, Lenny played *Rhapsody in Blue* for my aunt and brought me to the Vanguard to show me to his friends. The Revuers were playing there then. It was that evening I first met Judy Holliday." Oppenheim married her after the war.

By the end of the summer, Bernstein knew his interests lay in New York. "I decided," he says,

that I would not go back to Boston and try and give piano lessons or anything but I would—yet again—seek my fortune in New York. And so I did go to New York again in the fall of 1942. I found a room for eight dollars a week on West Fifty-eighth Street... sort of a basement room, and I looked every-where for a job. I had a little money saved up from various jazz band gigs and things I had done in Boston that wouldn't last very long. I still couldn't find a job anywhere. And then one day I ran into Irving Caesar ... and he said, "What, you haven't got a job?" Mind you. I am now a Harvard graduate, a Curtis grad-uate, a Tanglewood graduate, and Koussevitzky's assistant and I still can't find a bloody little job in New York. He was amazed. He said, "I will talk to my friend Herman Starr, who is the pres-ident of the music publishers at Warner Brothers," a jazz sort of publishing outfit [called Harms], and I did get a job there doing odd jobs around the house, making piano arrangements, four-hand arrangements and eight-hand arrangements of Raymond Scott tunes and Coleman Hawkins improvisations on the tenor sax which nobody could write down and I wrote them down. I got twenty-five dollars a week. That was something.

They later signed me up as a composer, because there was a very nice man there called Frank Campbell Watson who was interested in my music. There wasn't much of it at that time. As a matter of fact my only real completed piece then, outside of the juvenilia I had written at college, was a clarinet sonata I had just completed and he said, "We'll publish that," which was very sweet of him; and so there came to be added to my twen-ty-five-dollar-a-week salary another twenty-five dollars a week as an advance on royalties, and of course nobody had any hope or clue that this advance could ever be paid back because who's interested in a young composer's clarinet sonata that's not going to give many royalties? But still I was now getting fifty dollars a week and I felt I was really rising in New York....[3]

Bernstein and Oppenheim played the sonata over WNYC, the city-owned radio station, To fill out the fifteen-minute segment they were given, Bernstein composed about three and a half more minutes of music on a theme by Adolph Green. The score for that piece has disappeared. Meanwhile, during the time they were playing, twenty or thirty people were looking through the window into the studio. Oppenheim and Bernstein were delighted. Later, Oppenheim recalls, they learned that the crowd had been for Frank Sinatra, who was supposed to be there.

Heady with the new money, Bernstein started to think about living more comfortably than he had been in his one-room basement apartment. One evening Elizabeth Reitel, by then divorced from Adolph Green, arrived at the Village Vanguard with a friend from Chicago. The woman, Edys Merrill, was looking for an apartment. She and Bernstein decided that if they pooled their money, they could do better than on their own. "We both went traipsing around," she remembers, "and found this apartment on the top floor of West Fifty-second Street, on the same block with Leon and Eddy's [a popular nightclub]. It had the two entrances we needed for each of us to remain somewhat independent."

The brownstone was a building owned by Nelson Rockefeller. The front of the apartment, Bernstein's half, faced the street, had one large room, a sofa bed, and the only bath. Merrill had two small back rooms and had to go through Bernstein's room to get to the bathroom. But it cost only a hundred dollars a month, which they shared equally. "There was nobody with money in our group," she says. "We used a cafeteria on Sixth Avenue where we could eat for a dollar thirty-five. Once in a while we went to my aunt's, where we would have a square meal. Lenny had no help from home. He was completely on his own."

Nevertheless, they often spent their evenings at a bar in Sheridan Square in Greenwich Village, called Jack Delaney's. "There was a piano there," Merrill says, "and Lenny would always go to it and play jazz. Once he played so hard he broke a string. I remember we all went out roaring."

During that year Bernstein did not talk about conducting, Merrill recalls. Composition occupied his life and he spent his free time on *Jeremiah*. "Copland had sent in a Steinway grand—we had to hoist it through the window—and Lenny used it to coach singers, rehearse dancers, arrange for Harms, and help the Revuers rehearse their material." Music was a constant presence, apparently too much for Merrill. "I was working in a war plant," she says, "and I was at the factory all through the day and music kept going all through the night. I would walk around the apartment with my hands over my ears screaming, 'I hate music—la de da de da,' and Bernstein wrote a cycle of songs based on what I screamed and dedicated it to me." He called the piece *I Hate Music.*

A good deal of sexual experimentation was going on on the top floor of the house on Fifty-second Street. According to Merrill, Bernstein's important relationships were with men. "He would verge on a relationship with a woman," she says, "but he was unsuccessful with them. Once he tried with me but it went badly. It would not be right to blame either of us. We were both clumsy at the time.

"Most of the men were acquaintances, borderline friends. There was no solid affair with one man. Leonard was seeing a woman analyst then, a refugee from Germany, whom he used to call 'the Frau.' It was an exchange arrangement. She gave him analysis and he gave her English lessons. I remember saying when I picked up her phone calls that if her treatment had the effect his English lessons were having, nothing good was happening." Merrill says there was no open, flagrant homosexuality in evidence, just the sense of it. Bernstein's friends apparently thought it more desirable to be straight. They even attempted to encourage an intimacy between her and Victor Kraft, Copland's friend who went on to become his long-term partner. They did this, she said, in the belief that it would be better for Kraft to have a woman. At least that is her interpretation of the motive.

One of the visitors to the Fifty-second Street apartment in January 1943 was the composer Ned Rorem, who had just begun his studies at Curtis. He was paying Shirley Gabis's mother ten dollars a week for room and board. Rorem says he hated Curtis, learned nothing there, and used to go to New York to get drunk. In 1983 Rorem recalled, "Shirley told me I should look up Lenny. When I knocked at the door of his Fifty-second Street apartment, he was practicing his Clarinet Sonata with David Oppenheim. I spent an alcoholic weekend with him. I was very pretty then and Lenny made a pass at me. We slept together.

When Edys came in she asked, 'Who's that in bed with you—Adolph?' That didn't imply a homosexual relationship between Lenny and Green. They could easily have slept together on the large mattress with nothing going on."

As always there was music as well as sex. "I remember sight-reading the Copland sonata," Rorem says, "and Lenny asking, 'Can't you sight-read any better than that?' He complained that I had ignored the dynamics. I stayed with him a few weekends that spring. One weekend we went to Café Society Downtown. The Revuers were playing there. Judy Holliday ordered double gins. I did the same. I was very impressed. That night Bernstein accompanied them in a chunk of their show he had prepared. I didn't know how to talk to New Yorkers then; I was just nineteen. Lenny let me in the first time not because I was sophisticated but because he was drawn to me. For me Lenny was New Yorky, very glamorous. He had great authority from the beginning. He impressed me a lot."

Though Bernstein had denied that he ever considered changing his name, he did talk about it at that time and many friends recall his going through lists of names that began with *B*. Merrill says, "Jews were not making it then and name changing was common. We used to sit around suggesting names for him. At Harms he used the pseudonym Lenny Amber [the translation of "Bernstein"]. This was 1942, the winter after Koussevitzky suggested the name change. But I really do not believe that Koussevitzky had so much to do with Leonard's concern with the name change then. In any event, I cannot be sure of this, of course, but I do recall that Koussevitzky was not on the scene at all that winter. No letters or phone calls from him."

Bernstein entered *Jeremiah*, his first large-scale serious work, in a competition sponsored by the New England Conservatory of Music. Koussevitzky was the principal judge. The entries were to be submitted anonymously and the deadline was December 31. In late December all of Bernstein's friends were working frantically copying the score. "Leonard and I were going to Sharon so that I could deliver the score to Koussevitzky," Merrill says. "The only attack of asthma I remember seeing him have was when we were rushing to get it done on time.

"In Sharon, Bernstein was very warm to his sister, a pretty girl who went to Mount Holyoke College, and to his brother, who was about nine. But his parents never exchanged a kind word and I was made to feel like an outsider, bent on getting their star-son. The attitude was 'He's the genius; who is this girl from New York?'"

Jeremiah lost the competition and Koussevitzky later let Bernstein know that he should not be disappointed; it was, after all, just a first work. The competition was won by Gardner Read, a conservative composer.

In those years Bernstein's success was invariably in performance. In February 1943, at a Town Hall concert devoted to new music, he spoke about Copland's Piano Sonata before he played it. The audience responded to the performance with great enthusiasm. Lukas Foss was there and recalls he heard a man behind him say, "All this applause is very nice, but where is the money?" It was Sam Bernstein.

By the spring Edys Merrill had become disenchanted with the frenetic life in New York. Along with Liz Reitel, she joined the Woman's Army Corps. With four months left on the lease, she owed two hundred dollars as her share of the rent. "But of course," she says, "I did not have it. Soon I received a letter from a lawyer representing Bernstein that I owed the rest of the rent. A few months later, he sent me a warm note telling me to forget the bill."

Bernstein may have been unable to pay the rent alone. He left almost immediately and moved to a room in the Chelsea Hotel, where Virgil Thomson and Paul Bowles lived. He had met Bowles at Copland's apartment in 1935. In 1939 they developed a strong friendship. "We used to wander along the back roads of Staten Island together," Bowles wrote in a recent letter. "He was inclined to be depressed about his life, but his genius seemed so obvious to me that I dared to prophesy. 'You'll not only be a success; you'll be world famous.' He did not appear to take my words very seriously. 'As what?' he countered. That I could not answer, but my conviction was in no way weakened. The talent was far too great to remain submerged; an explosion was inevitable."

Although the explosion did not take place in the spring of 1943, it was comforting for Bernstein to be among artists who encouraged him. "It had some kind of atmosphere," Bernstein says, "and I felt I was among friends."

On March 16, 1943, Bernstein conducted Bowles's *The Wind*

Returns, a one-act work, on a program at the Museum of Modern Art. Bowles had based the work on a text by Federico García Lorca. Bowles says, "I had written a zarzuela, which was to be performed at the Museum of Modern Art. Lenny agreed to conduct the orchestra. One night I gave him a piano version of the overture to look at. Pianistically it was tricky and difficult. He kept it overnight. The next morning we met at Schirmer's to make a recording of the piece. Not only was he able to play it perfectly throughout, he had memorized it as well. I still believe that no one else could have accomplished this prodigious feat."

Bernstein recalls the summer of 1943 as being particularly hot, and he says that his depression mounted. Not only wasn't the Boston Symphony at Tanglewood that summer, neither was the student orchestra, because the war prohibited many such civilian activities that required auto travel. Koussevitzky was living in Lenox, Massachusetts. For the benefit of the Red Cross, he gave a series of lectures and concerts at the library in Lenox, which were attended by the local residents. He asked Bernstein to come up and provide musical illustrations at the piano. Koussevitzky told him there would also be a recital given by a new singer, and that he wanted Bernstein to accompany her. Bernstein invited Helen Coates, his former teacher, and his sister; the three took the train to Lenox on a Saturday morning near the end of the summer.

I grabbed onto that with some vim because it was something to do and it was a way of getting out of New York for a while. I got permission to leave my job for a week. This was in August 1943, and my twenty-fifth birthday was rapidly approaching on the twenty-fifth of that month. I guess I was at the low point of my life. Mainly because while I was in Lenox doing these illustrations for Koussevitzky's lectures, I was summoned yet again by the draft board in Boston to report for a physical, and again I failed it. So, on top of everything else, I felt I wasn't any good to my country. I wasn't any good to music. I couldn't find anything to do that was substantial. I kept writing music but I just didn't have any place in the musical world. I felt I was no damn good. And so, having been turned down in Boston, I went back to Lenox to complete these illustrations. Koussevitzky had also invited Jennie Tourel up, the mezzo-soprano who was at the beginning of her career then, to sing in the Lenox library. He asked me to accompany her. That's the way I met Jennie Tourel.... [3]

Within a few years of leaving home, Bernstein had found a second Shirley and a second Jennie as well. Burton Bernstein surely had the depth of the original connections in mind when he titled his memoirs *Family Matters*. When Bernstein first heard Tourel sing during the summer of 1943, he raised his head in astonishment and cried out, "You're good!" Her voice had startled him. He never expected that a Jewish Jennie could sing.

Bernstein brought *I Hate Music* with him to the rehearsals with Tourel. Koussevitzky liked the songs even less than he had liked the score to *Jeremiah*. Here the jazz quality was not even camouflaged in a form that could pass as serious art. According to Lukas Foss, the popular aspect of Bernstein's gifts offended Koussevitzky from the earliest days. It threatened the career he had planned for his most prized of protégés: that of the classical European-style *chef d'orchestre*. Although Koussevitzky refused to allow the Bernstein songs to be programmed that evening, Tourel and her accompanist outfoxed him; they presented them as encores.

On August 25, the day after the recital and Bernstein's birthday, Olga Koussevitzky told Bernstein that Artur Rodzinski wanted him to visit him in nearby Stockbridge. Rodzinski had met Bernstein a few years before when he was conducting near Philadelphia. Renée Longy had brought Bernstein backstage and admonished Rodzinski to "remember this name. This boy is a genius, a real phenomenon." She knew Rodzinski because the Polish conductor had started his career in the United States with a post at Curtis, where he taught conducting and conducted the conservatory orchestra. All that Bernstein knew about Rodzinski was that he had been the conductor of the Cleveland Orchestra for many years, and now was the newly appointed music director of the New York Philharmonic for the coming season.

Bernstein took the bus to Stockbridge; he did not own a car. Before Rodzinski went to bed, he told Bernstein to be up at 9 A.M. so they could wash the Rodzinski car together. Bernstein, a late sleeper, appeared at eleven. When he greeted his hosts he did so with tearing eyes. The room he had slept in was one usually occupied by the family cat, and his allergy had been activated.

In 1985 Halina Rodzinski recalled the details of this first visit: "Lenny was shy, innocent, and sweet on that first overnight visit in Stockbridge, and I remember him lying down in the living room in front of the fireplace talking about his family. He was not at all fresh then. My husband had been looking for an assistant conductor for some time, ever since he had been given the post with the New York Philharmonic. He wrote to all the good schools, all the conservatories in the United States. And he hired Thor Johnson, who was at Ann Arbor at the time. But almost immediately Mr. Johnson was drafted and Artur had to look all over again. All the young musicians were in the army and I recall how much effort he put into this search. Then, in the summer of 1943, Koussevitzky told him he had this 'phenomenal student, the most talented of my boys,' I remember him saying. Artur had taken Thor Johnson on the basis of a recommendation and he may have taken Bernstein the same way—without ever hearing him conduct." She must be correct for if her husband had heard Bernstein conduct the student orchestra in the summer of 1942, he surely would have remembered him. And in 1943 Tanglewood was closed.

Bernstein recalls that at their meeting in Stockbridge Rodzinski met him on a motor scooter wearing a great beekeeper's hat. In addition to keeping cows and goats, Rodzinski tended bees on his farm. They sat down in a haystack. Bernstein remembers:

> Rodzinski said, "You may know that I am about to take over the New York Philharmonic. I begin in October or late September. It is a month away and I am going to need an assistant conductor. I have gone through all the conductors I know of in my mind and I finally asked God whom I shall take and God said, 'Take Bernstein.'"
>
> Well, I freaked out, I mean, you know, God! I had had recommendations from Aaron Copland, Roy Harris and—but, I mean, God! I don't know how Rodzinski had managed to find access to this extraordinary recommender but I didn't ask. I just said, "Yes, of course!" I was happy as a bird because what that meant was that beginning September, I would be assistant con-

ductor of the New York Philharmonic. I was offered a room to live in in Carnegie Hall.... I would now make one hundred twenty-five dollars a week instead of twenty-five dollars. I was signed up by Arthur Judson, who was the manager of the Philharmonic and also the manager of everything else musical in this country through his agency, Columbia Artists Management, Incorporated. My whole life had changed suddenly, on my birthday, on that remarkable coincidental birthday, the twenty-fifth birthday on the twenty-fifth of August. I was suddenly going to get a real salary, live in a real place in Carnegie Hall and have a real job.[3]

Ned Rorem reports that he was sitting at an outdoor café in Greenwich Village soon after that when Bernstein passed and casually understated what had happened: "I have a job—it's assistant conductor at the New York Philharmonic." But to Helen Coates he revealed his elation. When the *New York Herald Tribune* published the announcement of his appointment and accompanied it with a photograph, Bernstein clipped and sent it to her with a note in the margin: "Here we go! Love, Lenny."

Bernstein delights in centering this story on his "coincidental birthday" and says that his life is full of coincidences like that, "which I tend to believe in, the way I believe in everything. I mean there is nothing— no cockamamy fad or group or cult or belief or doctrine—that you can name that I don't believe in because I'm a believer, and even though one doctrine may contradict another or render the other invalid, I still believe in them because I believe."[3]

During Bernstein's first year at the New York Philharmonic, Rodzinski, too, was a "believer." He had just joined Frank Buchman's Moral Rearmament movement and, according to his widow, had been transformed from a difficult man with intense mood shifts to a calm and orderly one, who frequently did consult with God.

A stunning array of stars had taken their turns on the podium during the 1942–1943 season of the New York Philharmonic: Toscanini, Walter, Rodzinski, Reiner, Mitropoulos, and the outgoing Barbirolli. When Rodzinski took over in the fall of 1943, there was a collective sigh of relief from the board, the

© WHITESTONE PHOTO/HEINZ H. WEISSENSTEIN

"The next thing I remember is my mother and father—especially my father— coming backstage ... all aglow.... And he suddenly realized it was all possible. And there was a great moment of forgiveness and very deep emotion."

musicians, and the audience. He was to be the orchestra's first music director. This meant he would not only conduct but control the personnel, choose the guest conductors, select the soloists, and plan the repertory for the whole season, coordinating his own programs, with those of his guests.

From 1929 to 1933 Rodzinski had molded the Los Angeles Philharmonic into a much improved ensemble, and from 1933 to 1943 he made the Cleveland Orchestra an instrument Szell was delighted to take over. Just before coming to New York, Rodzinski had been courted by the Chicago Symphony. In addition to possessing a straightforward conducting style with steady tempos and a clear beat, he was adventurous in admirable ways. It was Rodzinski who conducted the American premiere of Shostakovich's *Lady Macbeth of Mtsensk*, and he was one of the first conductors to present opera in concert form.

Rodzinski did not shrink from his new responsibilities. His first move was to fire fourteen musicians including the concertmaster and six other first-desk men. The response was devastating. This was a time of growing sympathy for the union, and public reaction went against him. Forced to reinstate five of the players, Rodzinski still managed to let enough of them go so there would be room for the cellist Leonard Rose and the violist William Lincer as well as a few other first-rate musicians from Cleveland whom he hired for New York.

Rodzinski was a complicated man. On the one hand he could instigate a mass firing. On the other he was courteous to his musicians and never ridiculed them at rehearsals. Moreover he was extremely generous to as formidable and unneedy a colleague as Koussevitzky and repeatedly did large favors for him. Halina Rodzinski, in her memoir, claims they were never returned. She details the many generous acts Rodzinski performed for Koussevitzky but notes that Koussevitzky never invited her husband to conduct the Boston Symphony. Surely one of Rodzinski's most important favors was to give Koussevitzky's protégé Bernstein a great career boost when he was still virtually unknown. The powerful men who ran the Philharmonic, Arthur Judson in particular, were dead set against Bernstein's getting the job, most particularly because of his age and inexperience. But Rodzinski did not want an aging, failed European musician as his assistant conductor and fought the Philharmonic management to put Bernstein in. Bernstein says that he does not remember ever seeing Rodzinski at any student performance of his in Tanglewood.

So the lesson of his first "job" could not have been lost on Bernstein: that this extraordinary coup had not come about through disciplined study, an audition, or a competition. It had come about because the renowned Koussevitzky believed in him and because Rodzinski admired Koussevitzky and did favors for his friends. The dynamics of this remarkable appointment reveal a pattern characteristic of Bernstein throughout his life. Socially he has always traveled in packs; he says he has never dined alone in a restaurant. But professionally he has mostly moved alone, resisting "schools" and organized styles, and, when it mattered, gaining the support of an influential person.

After smoothing out the agitated feelings stirred up by his personnel shake-up including his insistence on Bernstein as his assistant, Rodzinski was ready for his new post. During Bernstein's first weeks as assistant conductor in the fall of 1943, Rodzinski delivered a stunning performance of Mahler's Second (*Resurrection*) Symphony. And because he was grateful to the United States for all that it had given him and believed in the value of American talent, he not only insisted on a native son as his associate but he often programmed American works. Of course these were the years of World War II when things German and Austrian were suspect and American composers were getting a hearing. Still, his contribution was noteworthy. Once, at an anniversary concert of his own, he devoted the entire program to American music and featured a part of Ives's Fourth Symphony, this at a time when Ives was virtually never played. But Halina Rodzinski's rich portrait in *Our Two Lives* of her husband as a deeply troubled, unpredictable man was confirmed by Bernstein's initial impression. Here he is almost forty years later describing the Stockbridge visit.

It turned out that he was a member of the Oxford Movement, the Buchmanite movement known as the Oxford group, which is a confessional kind of group and talks to God three times a day and listens to the still, small voice and is based on the rather beautiful idea of losing the ego, which all great religious ideas are based on, whether they're Christian or Buddhist or whatever or *est*, any ideas that involve mysticism involve the losing of the ego naturally. That is the first thing. He lectured me about this and he began to proselytize. He said, "You will be very interested in this and I hope you will become a member of this group. Once we are working together we will become great friends. Let's go in and have some tea."

And we went into the house and the first thing he showed me was a wall of recordings and he said, "Look at all those recordings I made with the Cleveland Symphony. Do you know what my royalties were this year on those records alone? Twenty-five thousand dollars." And I thought, for a man who has just been lecturing me about how all material things are shadows, how they don't matter, the only thing that matters is the still small voice and that money is stupid and that private possessions are vain—that that was a very odd statement to make a big point about how much royalty he had gotten on his records that year. But that was the first indication I had that Rodzinski was a rather problematic and a self-contradictory man, and, in fact, as it turned out, a rather almost psychotic man. Full of superstitions. He carried a gun in his pocket all the time, and he had to have someone kick him in the backside in the wings before he entered the stage. All these things were ritualistic and compulsive. Very odd man but very likable, very warm and a marvelous conductor. [3]

Once the professional association began, there were good and bad surprises for both. Rodzinski was delighted at Bernstein's ability to read and judge scores. From the mountain of material that came into his office, Bernstein would sift through and select those which deserved Rodzinski's own eye. But, according to Rodzinski's wife, Bernstein's insinuation of himself into the Green Room after performances drove her husband mad. She writes that the twenty-five-year-old assistant would "edge himself into the situation, either by accepting a compliment for a distracted soloist or conductor, or by letting no one misunderstand precisely who he was. This irritated Artur. In fact Artur had [Philharmonic associate manager Bruno] Zirato forbid Lenny to enter the Green Room. Artur's quasi-military upbringing precluded pushy behavior."

Bernstein's appointment as assistant conductor of the New York Philharmonic was a newsworthy event. For one thing an American conductor was almost unheard of. The only American conductor most people knew was Howard Barlow, who led the Sunday afternoon CBS broadcasts but was clearly a token and would never have been considered for a top post. For another, Bernstein was a Jew, and not, like Mahler or Koussevitzky, converted to Christianity. The fact is that despite the horrors of World War II, anti-Semitism continued in the United States. It was only in New York, where Jews have always influenced the cultural life, and at a time when anti-Nazi sentiment was at its height, that Bernstein could have secured the position that he did. Finally Bernstein was twenty-five, and conductors had always been authority figures of an advanced age. When Mitropoulos had made his U.S. debut in 1936 with the Boston Symphony Orchestra, he was forty-one, yet the press persisted in referring to his "extreme youth."

More important than the fact that Bernstein was an unlikely choice as Rodzinski's assistant was the improbability of his ever getting a chance to conduct a public performance. Up to 1943, there had never been an occasion when a scheduled Philharmonic conductor was ill enough to turn over his baton to an assistant conductor. At least no member of the Philharmonic staff can remember such an incident. Bernstein has described his predecessors this way: "All the assistants had just sat there growing increasingly bitter, frustrated, knowing all the scores, being always ready, having their tailcoats hanging in a locker backstage, ready to come on at a moment's notice, never getting the opportunity to do so."

Bernstein's own opportunity came on November 14, six years to the day after he had first met Copland on Copland's birthday. Next to August 25, his own birthday and the date of his appointment as assistant conductor of the New York Philharmonic, November 14 has always held the most magical significance for him.

On November 13, a Saturday evening, Jennie Tourel was making her recital debut in New York in a concert at Town Hall that was to include *I Hate Music*. Because it was her own concert, because she made the rules, this time she was including it as part of the printed program, not relegating it to an encore. Again the composer would accompany her. The occasion was special enough to warrant bringing the Bernstein family down from Sharon. Shirley, a student at Mount Holyoke, was unable to come. But Sam, Jennie, and Burtie checked into the Barbizon Plaza late Saturday afternoon. Burton writes that Sam rushed them through dinner so they could be at the theater one hour before the performance. To the conventional concert-goer, *I Hate Music* seemed out of place here. Both singer and accompanist were established figures. Tourel had made a remarkable American debut under Toscanini at the opening of the New York Philharmonic's season the year before in Berlioz's *Romeo and Juliet*. She had come to the United States with a reputation as one of the greatest Carmens, which she had sung at the Paris Opera. Bernstein was now assistant conductor of the New York Philharmonic, and here were these established people collaborating on a cycle of songs in which the protagonist, a ten-year-old girl, sings:

> *Music is a lot of folk; in a big dark hall*
> *Where they really don't want to be at all;*
> *With a lot of chairs, and a lot of airs,*
> *And a lot of furs and diamonds;*
> *Music is silly: I hate music!*
> *But I like to sing.*

An artist who had already launched a major career, Tourel's agreement to program this song suggests her relationship with its composer transcended a purely professional liaison.

"Even with the exhilaration the evening promised—" Burton Bernstein writes,

Lenny's first hearing as a composer before a sophisticated New York audience—my brother seemed unusually atremble when he met us in the lobby. What he didn't dare disclose was that the Philharmonic's associate manager, Bruno Zirato, had informed him of some terrifying news earlier in the day: Bruno Walter, the guest conductor of the Philharmonic that week, had been taken ill with influenza. He had a fever and his stomach was upset. It was possible, remotely possible, that Maestro Walter would not be in condition to conduct the rather exacting program on Sunday afternoon, which was to be broadcast throughout America by CBS. If such a dire situation did arise, and Rodzinski wasn't able to drive through the snow from his

Stockbridge farm to substitute for Walter, then Lenny would have to step in. [1]

The program consisted of Schumann's *Manfred* Overture, Miklós Rózsa's *Theme, Variation and Finale*, Strauss's *Don Quixote*, and a prelude from Wagner's *Die Meistersinger.*

Tourel's performance that Saturday night went well. Of *I Hate Music,* the composer says that

> people yelled and stamped and cheered and I had to take a bow.... And then Jennie gave a party at her house that night. I was at the piano and drinking and singing blues and we were all carrying on like mad until dawn. I had just gotten to bed when the phone rang splitting my skull and it was Bruno Zirato on the other end saying, "Well, this is it. You have to conduct at three o'clock this afternoon. No chance for a rehearsal. Bruno Walter is ill. He has the flu. He is all wrapped up in blankets at the hotel and he says he will be happy to go over the scores with you for an hour or so ... but there is nothing else he can do. There is no way to get the orchestra together and you will report at a quarter of three backstage at Carnegie Hall and conduct this afternoon." [3]

Bernstein got dressed and went to see Walter, who had conducted the same program on Thursday, Friday, and Saturday. The members of the orchestra knew the music but had played it only under Walter. The old man went through the scores with Bernstein, pointing out tricky details in the Strauss work, such as giving an extra upbeat to the clarinet at one point and helping the tuba to come in on time. But Bernstein was suffering from a hangover and says he didn't absorb much of the advice.

When Bernstein left Walter, he went to the pharmacy at Fifty-seventh Street and Seventh Avenue, where he always took his morning coffee. The pharmacist, who knew him, said that he looked sick. When Bernstein explained what was going on the pharmacist handed him two pills, presumably a barbiturate and an amphetamine to calm him and lift him at the same time, and told Bernstein to put them in his pocket and take them just before he went onstage. Bernstein then went for a walk in Central Park.

His family had not come to the Tourel party after the performance the night before. Instead they had gone straight back to the hotel. The plan for the next day was to lunch in the hotel coffee shop and take a one o'clock train back to Boston. Just before they left the hotel, the telephone rang. It was Leonard telling them to cancel their return trip, to book the hotel for another night, to go to Carnegie Hall and pick up three tickets for the conductor's box because their Lenny was going to conduct the New York Philharmonic that very afternoon. Leonard told his family to wish him luck and to come backstage at intermission.

Here is Bernstein on what followed:

So there I am standing in the wings. All atremble with these two little pills in my pocket, listening to Bruno Zirato who had come out on stage address the audience and tell them the unhappy news that they would not be hearing Bruno Walter that day. Many groans. But instead they would be hearing a young conductor called Leonard Bernstein, the assistant conductor of the Philharmonic, and on I had to come and suddenly I remembered the two pills. And I took them out and looked at them and said, "I'm going to do this on my own. I am not going to take any pills. I don't want any aid from anybody but God," and I just flung them across the entire backstage and strode out and that's the last thing I remember until the end of the concert when I saw the entire audience there, standing and cheering and screaming. But from the time of my entrance until the time of my last exit I remember nothing. There's nothing I can tell you. It was all a dream.

I do remember giving the upbeat for the *Manfred* Overture because it's a very tricky piece to begin and I've heard it several times beginning in a very messy way. It begins on a syncopation in the middle of the bar, and if they misunderstand, then the whole thing is over. This is the first beat I had to give. And I remember giving it and they came in like angels on this syncopation, and that's it. I mean I blank out from then on.

The next thing I remember is my mother and father—especially my father—coming backstage…. And I remember receiving a telegram from Koussevitzky saying, "Listening now. Wonderful. Love, Koussevitzky." He had caught it on the radio. And a telegram from Rodzinski, and my mother and father walking into the dressing room and my father all aglow. It was the first time in his life. And baffled. He couldn't understand what happened because he had been so against my being a musician all those years. "Where will it lead you? To playing in a hotel lobby for the rest of your life and with palm trees and playing Cole Porter songs." You see his tradition was that a musician in the Russian-Jewish ghetto was among the lowest order of being…. And it was very hard for him to adjust to the fact that there was such a thing as a musical world in which one could succeed. I didn't even know as a child … that there were such things as concerts that one could go to. That there was such a thing as a musical life. That there were musicians. That there was a community of musicians, that there were music lovers, and there were people who took it all very seriously. I had no background at all in music from my family and here was my father standing there absolutely dazzled, bewildered, stupefied because he had seen thousands of people … on their feet screaming and cheering for his little Lenny who had been standing there conducting all afternoon. And he suddenly realized it was all possible. And there was a great moment of forgiveness and very deep emotion.

The next thing I remember is the next morning. Picking up *The New York Times* and finding myself on the front page. I couldn't believe it. And this long story about how I had substituted at the last moment for an ailing Bruno Walter and continued on page sixteen with pictures and Lord knows what and Olin Downes who was then senior music critic writing very glowingly about what had happened. Suddenly I was famous and also I was famous all over America because of that radio broadcast. So then it all began. It was just that simple.[3]

The publicity department of the New York Philharmonic had alerted the press that an unknown conductor would be making his debut and the coverage was extensive. *New Yorker* magazine critic Robert Simon wrote, "Some of us had noticed him last year when he conducted a concert at the Museum of Modern Art. For the record, he is the youngest man ever to direct a Philharmonic Symphony subscription concert, one of the comparatively few American-born conductors in the Society's history, and the only maestro who ever led a major orchestra wearing a gray sack suit." The tabloid *Daily News* quipped, "Like a shoe-string catch in center field, make it and you're a hero. Muff it and you're a dope.... Bernstein made it."

Both the *New York Herald Tribune* and *The New York Times* put their stories on page one. In his *Times* review, Downes wrote:

Mr. Bernstein thought for himself and obtained his wishes. He was remarkably free of the score which he followed confidently but without ever burying his nose in it, or, for an instant, losing rapport only maintained by the eye and such elucidative movements as conductors may make to their colleagues of the orchestra. He conducted without a baton, justifying this by his instinctively expressive use of his hands and a bodily plastic which, if not always conservative, was to the point, alive, and expressive of the music.

On the editorial page the *Times* held that

Mr. Bernstein had to have something approaching genius to make full use of his opportunity. The spotlight dwells on him, then it moves to the audience and shows his parents, Mr. and Mrs. Samuel Bernstein of Sharon, Massachusetts, and his little brother Burton, who dropped into New York at just the right moment. It's a good American success story. The warm, friendly triumph of it filled Carnegie Hall and spread over the airwaves.

In 1838 Thomas Carlyle wrote, "No man lives without jostling and being jostled. In all ways he has to elbow himself through the world, giving and receiving offense." Bernstein's overnight success gave many musicians offense and immediately he felt the retribution. Rumors spread like wildfire that Samuel Bernstein had bribed Walter to feign illness so that his son could have the chance to conduct. It is difficult to determine which is more preposterous: Walter's accepting such a bribe or Sam Bernstein's offering it. That such a rumor could have risen and had the staying power it did is attributable partly to jealousy among musicians. Bernstein of course did his own jostling, which contributed to the angry reactions his success provoked in many circles. Rodzinski himself was angry at much of Bernstein's behavior during the ensuing months. This may explain why: The night before Bernstein's headline-making debut, Bruno Zirato, the Philharmonic executive, telephoned Rodzinski in Massachusetts and told him that his guest conductor for the next day, Walter, was sick and that he should come back to New York right away. According to Halina Rodzinski, her husband said, "That is what Bernstein is for. This is his chance. Use him." Zirato replied, "I think you're wrong, but you're the boss." In that version, Rodzinski did it to himself.

Here is Rodzinski in the mid-1950s: "Bernstein made the front page of *The New York Times* and *Herald Tribune* and overnight he became so great you couldn't talk to him. Some time later I missed him at a rehearsal and was told he had gone home with a stomach upset. About an hour afterward I met him in the barber shop, feeling fine. And I gave him hell. And he was terribly embarrassed. So embarrassed he kept saying over and over: 'Doctor'—he always called me doctor—'you really are a great conductor.' It was so corny I could hardly stand it. But he kept calling me doctor and praising me....

"When Bernstein was just getting started, Otto Klemperer came by to hear a rehearsal. While the orchestra was playing, Bernstein sat listening and following the score—I was conducting—but even to Klemperer this upstart would not hand over his copy of the score. So Klemperer had to lean over Bernstein's chair to follow the score Bernstein was holding. Even in those days he was a terribly fresh guy. Ever heard the Jewish word 'chutzpah'? It roughly means a fresh and aggressive guy with lots of guts and it fits Bernstein exactly."

In discussing those early months Bernstein says:

> You can imagine what Rodzinski's position was, being the conductor of the New York Philharmonic in his first year and

having to make good. And suddenly this little assistant of his was all over the front pages and getting all the publicity. And although he knelt three times a day and talked to God and tried to lose his ego, he became increasingly jealous and unhappy. And our relationship, which had begun warmly and was a great friendship—although I did not yield to his proselytizing about joining the Oxford group—began to sour. I would come into the room and he would turn away and suddenly there was no friendship, and I was his assistant and our professional relationship, which depended on our personal relationship, became a troubled one. [3]

Here is how it ended, in Rodzinski's words: "After 1944 Bernstein was in great demand as a guest conductor. He accepted all the invitations instead of taking the steady jobs he needed to get the experience he should have had. I would have hired him again. Lots of other people would have given him good jobs. But he traveled as guest conductor instead...."

Bernstein was never comfortable for long in the role of devoted disciple, of self-abasing or adoring student, or as a conductor's assistant, if he could be the conductor.

In 1956 Comden and Green were asked by a reporter

to describe Bernstein in the early years of their friendship. Among the things Green said was that Bernstein had had no girlfriends then. "Lenny was always very selective; and like all attractive people known to be exceptional, he had a certain shyness." Comden added, "He hung

PHOTOHOUSE PRIOR, TEL AVIV, ALLENBY, K. D. SIELMANN

Brother and sister. Sibling Burton Bernstein writes, "Perhaps it was inevitable that Shirley's future should be inextricably entangled with Lenny's."

around with us a lot. We always traveled in a pack."

Bernstein's affection for and interest in his sister seemed to preclude any romantic involvement at that time. From the moment he inducted Shirley into Rybernia when she was five, through the nights he crept into her room to hold her finger while she slept, to the evenings during their adolescence when they huddled together as their parents fought, to the performances he directed her in at Singer's Inn in Sharon and *The Cradle Will Rock* at Harvard, through the days William Schuman watched them singing at the top of their lungs in a café in Cambridge, to the Tanglewood years when everyone remembers them virtually always hand in hand, Shirley was Leonard's love.

David Oppenheim says, "She was a dazzling woman. When I first saw Lenny in the opera shed at Tanglewood, I saw him with this beautiful girl. She had her head on his shoulder throughout the evening. I was very attracted to her. She was a knock-out. Smart, warm, witty, intelligent, gifted. They were great pair. They knew each other's private languages, Rybernian in particular, and they had a million secrets with each other. There was very close communication. No fighting. No jealousy." In fact, when Bernstein and Edys Merrill left their Fifty-second Street apartment on December 31, 1942, to submit the score for *Jeremiah* to the New England Conservatory of Music competition, Bernstein arranged for Oppenheim and Shirley to have the apartment to themselves. On his return Bernstein expressed disappointment that a romantic liaison had not taken place.

In his memoir Burton Bernstein writes:

> Perhaps it was inevitable that Shirley's future should be inextricably entangled with Lenny's. Since her childhood, she had been under his spell—a kid sister who looked upon him not only as a big brother but as a kind of father, too. The attraction of her imaginative, charming, pedagogic, talented older brother was overpowering. Part of the reason for this closeness to Lenny was her place in the family structure, an unfortunate legacy from the Old Country. She was a girl child, the second born, of whom nothing much was expected or demanded save the *nachas* that comes from her being one day a good homemaker and a bearer of children—after she was suitably educated, of course. [1]

The only periods in Bernstein's pre-debut years when he and his sister were separated for any length of time were the semesters he spent at Curtis. At that time he filled the void with the Philadelphia Shirley, Shirley Gabis, who looked remarkably like the original. Just after Bernstein's debut, when that Shirley visited New York and asked Bernstein to let her use his piano, she met Shirley Bernstein for the first time. Bernstein used to tell her that he wished she had another name because "Shirley" got in the way.

In the fall of 1943, Shirley Bernstein was still in Massachusetts. It was during these months, just preceding Bernstein's big break, that he composed a suite of piano pieces for seven people whom he loved. He included one for his sister among them. Called *Seven Anniversaries* they appeared in this order: I. "For Aaron Copland"; II. "For my sister, Shirley"; III. "In Memoriam: Alfred Eisner"; IV. "For Paul Bowles"; V. "In Memoriam: Natalie Koussevitzky"; VI. "For Serge Koussevitzky"; VII. "For William Schuman." Later when he needed to select three from the seven for a recording, he chose those composed for Copland, Shirley, and Koussevitzky.

It was also during the fall of 1943, after Bernstein had played the piano for the lecture-demonstrations given by Koussevitzky, that he found himself attracted to an older woman. Jennie Tourel had recently arrived in the United States. In the 1940s Boosey & Hawkes, the British music publishers, maintained a concert bureau in New York and assisted Europeans who had come here. Béla Bartók, for example, was among its beneficiaries. Hans Heinsheimer, later director of publications at G. Schirmer, and Friede Rothe, now personal representative for Claudio Arrau, both worked for Boosey & Hawkes then. Among those artists Boosey represented was Sir Thomas Beecham.

One day a colleague called Rothe to ask if she could arrange an audition with Beecham for a soprano who had come here from France. She could not. But when, soon after, she learned that Toscanini was searching for a French singer for a Berlioz *Romeo and Juliet* he was to conduct at Carnegie Hall in commemoration of the New York Philharmonic's hundredth anniversary, Rothe suggested Tourel. For her audition the mezzo sang songs by Debussy. Toscanini engaged her and she was an overnight success. Tourel engaged Rothe as her personal representative, a business liaison that turned into a friendship that lasted until the singer died in 1973.

By the time she and Bernstein met the following summer at the library in Lenox, Tourel was already a star. "Jennie was about forty and a real beauty," Rothe recalls. "She dressed elegantly and was radiant on stage. Lenny was brilliant, hyperactive, talkative, and although he was not then as handsome as he later became, they fell in love immediately. They reacted with such intensity to one another that it was not unusual for those close to Jennie to think that during the months between the Lenox concert and her Town Hall debut they were having a little affair."

Bernstein followed Tourel's lead and hired Rothe as his first publicist. But the liaison was short-lived. "Everything I wrote," Rothe says, "he rewrote and made better. Lenny had an unerring sense of newspaper headlines."

To quote this is not to suggest that Rothe believed Bernstein's success was primarily the result of self-promotion. "Lenny possessed enormous talent," she says, "a genuinely amazing talent. I remember his going over the Ravel *Shéhérazade* with Jennie and he was playing it at sight. He had all the feeling for it. He played it exactly as Jennie had visualized it after going to a great deal of work. Neither of us had ever seen a musician who could do anything like that."

Tourel gave many parties. Comden and Green would invariably join Lenny at them. Throughout Bernstein's career, his night life with show business people, the Revuers and their friends, and his work for Broadway have been cited as the most important sources for any problems he has had with his other, "serious" career. Those who believe this tend to agree with Rothe on the value of Bernstein's very early pop songs. Here she is on the particular cycle Tourel introduced to New York at her first recital there: "I hated them when I heard them at Town Hall. They are not art songs but cute little songs that should be sung at a house party. They did not rise to Jennie's style or stature."

Bernstein's original Jennie, his mother, in her mid-eighties in 1984, said she was "concerned about Leonard's health. He works too hard. He overloads himself. He is demanded wherever he goes. I always say to him: 'It's a good thing you weren't born a gift because you don't know how to say no.'"

Bernstein's overloading himself is not new. His appetite was always gargantuan; when the activity placed him in the limelight, he could never get enough. In the three days after the Philharmonic concert, as many as eight crews of photographers covered him at once. Bernstein told a reporter that no two of the photographs looked alike: "In some I look like a dope fiend." Warner Brothers considered him for the leading role in a movie about Gershwin, but Robert Alda got the part.

Meanwhile two weeks after his Philharmonic debut, in an arrangement he had made before the beginning of the season, Bernstein conducted the orchestra in Ernest Bloch's *Three Jewish Poems*, this time with the benefit of rehearsals. In his review, Downes noted the performance received a warm response. On the same program Rodzinski conducted the Mahler *Resurrection* Symphony in an interpretation Downes called "magnificent." Two weeks later, Downes wrote, "The proverbial luck that seems to have nurtured the aspirations of Leonard Bernstein, assistant conductor of the Philharmonic-Symphony, and the bad luck that seems to haunt other conductors of that august organization, was again in force last night when Howard Barlow, scheduled as guest conductor, was taken ill with influenza, and Mr. Bernstein accommodated by again substituting at short notice." Bernstein's performance of the Brahms *Variations on a Theme by Haydn*, Delius's orchestral nocturne *Paris*, and the Beethoven Violin Concerto with Albert Spalding as soloist was favorably reviewed: "An evening of effectively presented music and an audience uncommonly enthusiastic."

Virgil Thomson's remarks in the *New York Herald Tribune* suggested that he thought more than luck was involved: "For a second time this season, epidemic influenza has given us a concert conducted by Leonard Bernstein. In previous years guest conductors didn't fall ill. Maybe it is the knowledge that Mr. Bernstein will meet all such emergencies more than capably that enables them nowadays to give in."

Thomson's praise for Bernstein in this review was in excess of virtually anything that anyone had written until then: "I suspect that Mr. Bernstein's striking quality as a conductor is largely due to his rhythmic understanding. His enlightenment in this respect is superior to the contemporary great, save only Beecham..." It should be noted that Toscanini, Koussevitzky, Stokowski, Reiner, and Klemperer were still living.

Rodzinski, in his first year as music director of the New York

Philharmonic, was receiving virtually no attention, being completely eclipsed by the assistant of his choice. When Bernstein reminded him that he had agreed to allow Bernstein to take off a week in January to conduct *Jeremiah* in Pittsburgh, Rodzinski became enraged. The story behind Bernstein's invitation to conduct the Pittsburgh is this: It was generally known Reiner was critical of Bernstein's manner, of a lack of responsibility he had sensed at Curtis. But what irritated him even more was that all the publicity surrounding the young man credited Koussevitzky as Bernstein's primary teacher. None credited him. To counteract that, Reiner decided to generate some publicity for himself by having Bernstein conduct the first performance of his first orchestral piece in Pittsburgh. When the concert date approached, Rodzinski began to react oddly.

Here is Bernstein on those events:

> Rodzinski began to develop a cold. He began to go around with his handkerchief and he was sneezing and I mean, if ever there was a psychosomatic cold, this was it. Because he worked himself up to a hundred four degrees of temperature and the day approached that I had to leave for Pittsburgh.... Rodzinski said, "Now look, just when I need you you're going." A real Jewish mother. And I said, "I'm sorry. It's in my contract that I have this week off and it's terribly important to me as a composer and I must go, and I hope your cold is better, and please forgive me," and I went and the Philharmonic had to get somebody finally to substitute for Rodzinski. They got William Steinberg.
>
> When I came back, flushed with success and joy and thrill from my experience in Pittsburgh, I found a depressed bunch of people at the Philharmonic, including Arthur Judson, Bruno Zirato, Rodzinski, and everybody else. William Steinberg had apparently not fared very well with the orchestra or the press— whereas I had fared very well, so I came back all bubbling and they were not glowing at all. And my relation with Rodzinski worsened from that moment on. He tried—and I must say he tried very hard—and he was up against a very tough thing. If I had been in his position I don't know if I could have behaved any better, really, than he did. But he was really pathologically

jealous. Very upset. And he tried to discredit me. Even framed me in a couple of cases. He tried to prove I wasn't doing my job, that I was too heavily involved in other activities, in composing, whatever. That I went to parties, that I was not really a serious person, and of course I had never been such a serious person as I was at twenty-five. I was the most serious person you can imagine.[3]

Because of the enthusiastic reviews printed in the New York papers, Bernstein received dozens of invitations to conduct. But because his contract as Rodzinski's assistant tied him down, he couldn't accept them. The complexity of the relationship between Bernstein and Rodzinski was exceeded only by the competition among the three great conductors—Reiner, Koussevitzky, and Rodzinski—who were vying for the credit of being the young genius's primary influence. The competition served Bernstein well. It was only after Reiner invited him to Pittsburgh to conduct *Jeremiah* that Koussevitzky and finally Rodzinski programmed the work.

It was around that time, when major musical organizations were actively courting Bernstein, that Rodzinski found Bernstein in the barbershop. In 1967 Bernstein told the author John Gruen that one day he fell sick at a morning rehearsal and told the personnel manager that he would be upstairs in his room if needed. In the afternoon he felt better and went out to get a haircut at the Essex House barbershop, where in the chair next to him sat Rodzinski. He glowered at Bernstein, made a caustic remark, and then the two men sat in silence having their hair cut for half an hour.

The next morning at 9:30, according to Bernstein, Rodzinski went to Judson's office and said, "Now I have him! He said he was sick, and there he was in the barber shop. What's going on?"

Bernstein told Judson what had happened and asked what he had done. Judson said, "I don't know, but whatever it is, we can't have this at the Philharmonic. There is an atmosphere of murder. You've got to go backstage and apologize to him, because he's on the warpath."

Bernstein asked, "Apologize for what?"

Judson answered, "I don't know, but whatever it is, just apologize! Make things well again."

Bernstein went backstage to Rodzinski's dressing room—whereupon, according to Bernstein's later recall of the incident, Rodzinski pinned him to the wall. "He was brutally strong. He had this huge, almost humped back, like a bull, solid muscle. And he was calling me a liar, a cheat—I don't know what. I squirmed free somehow, or somebody came into the room and he had to let go, because he was killing me...."

Bernstein ran into Judson's office and was told to apologize to Rodzinski and to stay away from him for a while. He was ordered not to attend any rehearsals.[5]

On February 17, 1944, *The New York Times* printed an announcement that Bernstein would no longer have to go on as assistant conductor, but he would conduct the Philharmonic for two weeks in the new season as a guest. Other guests that season would be Stravinsky, for his first time with the New York orchestra, Pierre Monteux, the French conductor of the San Francisco Symphony, and George Szell, then with the Metropolitan Opera. Not bad company. In addition to being a guest at the Philharmonic, Bernstein was now able to say yes to all the invitations pouring in.

During the week of March 29, Bernstein conducted the New York Philharmonic in an entire program: Mendelssohn's *Italian* Symphony, Stravinsky's *Firebird* Suite, Copland's *El Salón México*, and his own *Jeremiah*. The *Times* sent Noel Straus, then an assistant critic, to review Bernstein's conducting as well as his composition. Straus concluded that "at present, Mr. Bernstein makes his deepest impression as conductor."

Jennie Bernstein has said that her son began to compose at twelve and that he would ask her to listen to different versions of a piece and then decide which she preferred. His next musical adviser, Helen Coates, was even more giving. Scheduling his lessons for the end of the day, she allowed him to go on for hours playing his own pieces and talking endlessly.

Bernstein says he brought much of his early music to Copland and Mitropoulos for their advice. Although he says Mitropoulos often told Bernstein he had talent, there is no evidence that either Copland or Mitropoulos ever encouraged him to pursue composition. Each thought conducting should become his career. For Mitropoulos such a choice would be natural; as a conductor he could be expected to recognize Bernstein's special gifts in his field. But for Copland, it was indicative of his reservations from the start about Bernstein's promise as a composer that he never seemed to speak favorably about Bernstein's scores.

Thus Copland and Mitropoulos appeared to have shared with Piston a certain caution regarding Bernstein's potential as a composer of art music. Not that Bernstein was untalented or that he lacked critical facility in composition. On the contrary, when he was forced to address himself to composition, he brought his very real gifts.

In 1939, Henry Cowell, a composer older than Copland, Schuman, and Blitzstein and more eccentric than they, was running a record company called New Music Records. Cowell knew Diamond's set of *Preludes and Fugues for the Piano* and wanted to record one of them in the fall of 1940. When Diamond asked Bernstein if he would play No. 3 in C-sharp Minor, Bernstein agreed. It was probably Bernstein's first professional recording. But before it was actually made, Bernstein made remarks to Diamond about the work that Diamond found insulting. Diamond was always vulnerable. And Bernstein was often cruel in his assessment of a colleague's score. In reply to a note Diamond sent Bernstein in which he responded bitterly to Bernstein's attack on him, Bernstein wrote on November 4, 1940, from Philadelphia:

> Dear David, I was shocked by your letter. I'm afraid you misunderstood. I intended no criticism of the music per se, but simply referred to the probable reaction of a record audience. I suggested the 3rd fugue, unpianistic and unrelieved as it is, might be an unfortunate choice with which to introduce yourself via recording. If you want it, then certainly I will be glad to do it.
>
> But why the violence? I understand you've been ill and down, and probably out, and kind of out of the world but lord, David ... I thought you knew me better than to intimate that I would make superficial dicta about your music. Believe me, I know what the fugue is worth. I can list for you all the fine points—your achievements in it. But there are "stains"; your second stretto, for instance, is anticlimactic because it is a four-measure stretto, whereas the preceding one was a one-measure stretto. This is especially true of a subject in unrelieved half-notes. Again, you speak of nuances to be mastered thoroughly but you haven't one in the piece except the opening ff: From

my point of view there must be a dynamic growth—involving especially a drop to *piano* in the 17th measure, & a rise to the first climactic stretto, and possibly the same thing again (modified) before the second stretto. Write me what you think of this. And is ♩ = 63 strictly to be maintained throughout?

I shall make a test record as soon as possible and send it to you. Let me know about the above very soon. And please keep well, & somewhat happier—Best, Lenny.

Bernstein was then twenty-two, Diamond twenty-five, and Diamond took virtually all of Bernstein's advice. "In my little prelude and fugue," Diamond says today, "he put the hairpins in it and made it perfect."

The first work that appears in Bernstein's list of works is the Sonata for Clarinet; during the season of 1944–1945, Oppenheim and Bernstein recorded it for Hargail Records. Another early work was *Seven Anniversaries* written to celebrate seven people he loved. Probably the most notable feature of these piano pieces is the omission of Mitropoulos. If one is to believe what Bernstein has said about the enormous influence the Greek conductor had on him, one must question the reason for his not being represented here. Either it is because Bernstein was still suffering from Mitropoulos's unrealized promises to him and a consequent confusion about the state of their relations, or he was moved by Koussevitzky's overweening jealousy. Probably it was a little of both.

Bernstein's first large-scale work, scored for orchestra and soprano, was *Jeremiah*. The composer provided the original program notes: "In the summer of 1939 I made a sketch for a *Lamentation for Soprano and Orchestra*. It lay forgotten for two years. In the spring of 1942 I began a first movement of a symphony. I then realized that this new movement and the scherzo that I planned to follow it made logical concomitants with the *Lamentation*. Thus the Symphony.... The work was finished on December 31, 1942, and is dedicated to my father."

The first two movements are entitled "Prophecy" and "Profanation." The program involves the prophet's admonition against his people, his struggle with the sad content of his message, and his wresting with its divine source. All of it is mirrored in the music, with the prophecy evoked by melancholy unison sighs interrupted by sudden orchestral outbursts and the profanation suggested by an agitated background with which an obviously jarring message is juxtaposed. The third movement takes its text from Lamentations and contains moments when the music and Jeremiah's personality appear genuinely to coalesce.

The work did not receive the same unreserved reviews that Bernstein's conducting debut had elicited. Virgil Thomson remarked, "It is not a masterpiece by any means but it has solid orchestral qualities and a certain charm that should give it a temporary popularity. Bernstein orchestrates like a master but does not compose with either originality or much skill. His pieces lack contrapuntal coherence, melodic distinction, contrapuntal progress, harmonic logic, and concentration of thought." Like Copland's and Mitropoulos's, Thomson's celebration of Bernstein was restricted to conducting.

Despite the fact that *Jeremiah* had lost a national competition, received qualified responses from Koussevitzky and Rodzinski when they first saw the scores, and elicited something less than raves from the major New York papers, the work went on to win the Music Critics Circle Award for 1943–1944. This was the third year of the award. In 1941–1942 it had gone to William Schuman's Symphony No. 3, in 1942–1943 to Paul Creston's Symphony No. 1. Bernstein's work was nominated from a list of more than twenty new compositions and ran off with the majority vote on the first ballot. It was played by the NBC Orchestra under the direction of Dr. Frank Black.

Bernstein's celebrity as a conductor fed his recognition as a composer. The phenomenon of the herd always played a large role in New York's musical life. But there was something else at stake. The work, orchestrated at breakneck speed in less than ten days, revealed a fresh voice with a handwriting that was individual and suggested that here was a new personality in music who might develop into a composer of stature. The important fact about *Jeremiah* is that Bernstein composed it when he had little else to do: during the depressing summer of 1939 when he had no work at all and during the fall of 1942 when nothing more important than a twenty-five-dollar-a-week job orchestrating pop tunes occupied him.

With no conducting or piano playing to divert him at this time,

Bernstein put genuine effort into this early work. Although there is an inconsistency of style between the first two movements and the last one, separated, as they were, by a period of several years—with the light-weight second movement cutting into the sustained mystery of the surrounding ones—Bernstein's *Jeremiah* showed a schooled musician who could write exciting music and sad, soaring melodies for mezzo-soprano. In 1983 when Bernstein rehearsed *Jeremiah* with the Boston Symphony at Tanglewood, he called it "my poor little symphony." That was appropriate. The musicians had just finished rehearsing the Funeral March from the Beethoven Third Symphony. In 1944, however, *Jeremiah* was not just a poor little symphony but, as the New York Music Critics Circle judged, better than any other work premiered in New York that year.

The only twentieth-century composers who became rich did so by composing for the ballet. In his early career Stravinsky wrote for Diaghilev, in his late years for Balanchine. It was the income he received from the repeated performances of these works—as well as from the fees for conducting—that

FRANK DRIGGS

1943

Bernstein, Jerome Robbins, and Sol Hurok. "…Lenny played a few bars…. Bernstein recalls that Robbins 'went wild. "That's it! That's it!" he screamed. And we were off.'"

allowed him to die a wealthy man.

Nadia Boulanger required her students to write for the dance. Under her tutelage, without commission or choreography, Copland started his first ballet. Based on the German Dracula film *Nosferatu*, it was called *Grogh*. But it never found its way onto the stage. Copland worked on it in 1923 and 1924, his last two years in Paris, and the first year he was back in the United States. Later he used parts of it for his *Dance* Symphony, a concert piece.

Copland's first score in collaboration with a choreographer was *Hear Ye! Hear Ye!* Composed for Ruth Page in 1934, it was quickly dropped from the repertory. Again Copland salvaged parts for the second of his *Four Piano Blues*.

Copland wrote his best music for dance in the mid-1930s. That was after he abandoned the austere intellectual style he had been using in favor of one accessible to a larger audience. The repudiation of art for art's sake in Blitzstein's *The Cradle Will Rock* had been consistent with the Marxist view of art as a servant of the revolution. This approach was adopted by Blitzstein, Copland, the WPA painters, and John Steinbeck among many other artists of the period. One of the leading exponents of this American version of socialist realism was the Group Theater under the direction of Harold Clurman, Copland's first cousin and his roommate in Paris. Copland has often said that the time when he lived with Clurman was when he decided to change his style of composition.

In 1938, after Copland and Bernstein had met at a dance recital in New York, Copland accepted a commission from Ballet Caravan for *Billy the Kid*. Cowboy songs and stretched-out familiar folk melodies gave the work a bright Western flavoring that made its premiere in Chicago a success.

When in the fall of 1942 Copland began work on *Rodeo* for Agnes De Mille, he again used cowboy songs. *Rodeo* was given its first performance by the Ballet Russe de Monte Carlo in New York. With a scenario that dealt with the love of a "tomboyish girl" for "the handsomest cowboy," it approximated Copland's own sex life. Bernstein was living on West Fifty-second Street in Manhattan at this time, playing for dancers, coaching singers, peddling his music until he landed a job at Harms, where he transcribed jazz improvisations and even wrote a few songs. One of them, "Riobamba," was sung by Frank Sinatra at the opening of a nightclub by that name in the spring of 1943.

After *Rodeo*, Martha Graham commissioned a piece by Copland. He responded with what he described as a musical portrait of the choreographer. *Ballet for Martha* was its working title; when it was finished Graham called it *Appalachian Spring* after a poem by Hart Crane.

In *Appalachian Spring*, Copland did something he had not done until then. He composed his own folk songs, borrowing only the traditional tune. He was not the first composer to do this for an extended piece. Virgil Thomson had composed his own hymns and ballads, and in 1935 Gershwin simulated blues and folk songs for his *Porgy and Bess*. In an article published in *The New York Times*, Gershwin wrote, "I wanted the music to be all of one piece."

During Bernstein's Harvard and Curtis days as well as his early years in New York, he spent considerable time reading Copland's ballet scores and watching them being performed. He loved the dance and must have envied Copland's direct participation in it. In October 1943, after Bernstein started working as Rodzinski's assistant, a dancer named Jerome Robbins came to his studio one night around midnight and asked him if he would write a ballet score.

How Robbins came to him is an important question, because the collaboration between Robbins and Bernstein led to such creations as *On the Town*, *West Side Story*, and *The Dybbuk*. The alliances set up in New York in the early 1940s are as critical to an understanding of some of the most important American art as the alliances set up in Paris in the postwar years among Boulez, Stockhausen, and John Cage are to the understanding of European music.

At least two composers recommended Bernstein to Robbins. Morton Gould was one. Gould had first met Bernstein during the 1942–1943 season, the first year Bernstein lived in New York. "It was at Lindy's," Gould remembers. Lindy's was a restaurant at Broadway and Fifty-first Street that was frequented by garment industry and show business people. "Bernstein was with Marc Blitzstein, and Marc introduced him saying that he was from Boston. At that time I had not heard of him.

"It was clear Marc thought highly of him. I remember later, at Marc's death, that Bernstein said publicly that Blitzstein had seduced his soul. Perhaps they were lovers. In any event all I knew then was that

Lenny seemed to be aware of himself. I was a little surprised. I thought, maybe he knows something that I don't know. He had the pose of an accomplished person."

After that first encounter, Gould heard that Bernstein was looking for work. "I was in radio then. I had a weekly show with a full orchestra, *The Cresta Blanca Hour*, and I was a hot name. Offers kept coming in, I remember Decca wanted me to do something and I recommended Lenny. I also remember Lenny coming to my radio show and my introducing him to the live audience as 'the Frank Sinatra of conductors.'"

Early in 1943, when the Ballet Theater hired Robbins as a dancer with the company, Robbins approached Gould with a proposition. "He had been told," Gould says, "that he could choreograph a work on spec. He said he had an idea about three sailors and asked if I would compose the music. I told him I couldn't do that. I was paying alimony and had children to support. I remember asking him who was going to pay for the copying of parts and the orchestration. I gave him a list of three names—Alex North, Henry Brant, and Lenny—who I told him were worthy of consideration."

Vincent Persichetti was a second route to Bernstein. Now on the faculty of Juilliard and a composer in the tradition of Copland, Persichetti never used jazz in his scores, but in 1942 he had written a piece, *Dance Overture*, that had won a prize given by the Juilliard School. Persichetti was a student at Curtis, a year ahead of Bernstein. Persichetti recalls that Bernstein was known to everyone there because he talked so much and because he played jazz piano. Persichetti studied the piano with Olga Samarov, Stokowski's former wife, and Robbins went to Samarov and asked her about the young composer who had written *Dance Overture*. "Robbins came down to Philadelphia," Persichetti recalls, "and spent four hours with me. He described his idea for *Fancy Free*. I thought it needed jazz. I like jazz but I don't get involved with it as a composer. So I suggested Lenny."

Robbins decided to pursue Bernstein but did not know where to find him. One day he was seated on a bench in Central Park with Oliver Smith, the set designer for *Fancy Free* and the man who, with Lucia Chase, was a co-director of Ballet Theater. Smith asked him who was going to compose the score. When Robbins said it would be Bernstein but he didn't know where he was living, Smith steered him to the

Carnegie Hall studio. This was still before Bernstein's November debut. The two men got along from the start. In many ways, Robbins exerted a powerful influence on Bernstein in moving him away from lighthearted, commercial endeavors into a headier realm.

Paul Bowles, the composer, novelist, and poet for whom Bernstein had just written one of his *Seven Anniversaries,* wrote in a letter in 1984, describing the change he saw in Bernstein at that time, "Jerry and Lenny saw a great deal of one another and I can only surmise that Jerry persuaded Lenny that I had been a pernicious influence with my cynical and frivolous attitude towards existence.... Jerry was in analysis and inclined to be what seemed to me over-serious about everything, not in a merry state of mind...."

In 1943 Robbins and Bernstein set to work on their first ballet. The night Robbins came to Bernstein's studio, Lenny played a few bars of what he says he had been "fooling around with." Bernstein recalls that Robbins "went wild. 'That's it! That's it!' he screamed. And we were off."

They were off in that frenetic way that has characterized Bernstein's life ever since and that makes his mother worry about his health. It was during the time between Curtis and Tanglewood or Tanglewood and something else that Bernstein would either go to Key West, a popular town for homosexuals, or sleep around the clock and write to Shirley Gabis about how depressed he was. But in this glorious fall of 1943, there was no time for depression. Within a few months of saying yes to Robbins, Bernstein conducted the New York Philharmonic four times, premiered *Jeremiah* in Pittsburgh, Boston, and New York, and composed *Fancy Free,* drawing at one point on his pop song "Riobamba." No wonder Rodzinski was almost literally driven out of his mind. Morton Gould remembers visiting Rodzinski in the Green Room after a Philharmonic performance and being reduced to conversing with him in a Carnegie Hall stairwell. "What can I do?" Gould quotes Rodzinski as saying. "Bernstein takes over the whole place."

The mechanics of putting *Fancy Free* together posed some problems under these circumstances. Bernstein was conducting mostly in New York but also in Pittsburgh and Boston. Robbins was on tour with the Ballet Theater. Oliver Smith was in Mexico. The three kept in touch by telephone and telegram. Whenever Bernstein finished a section, he and Copland would make a four-hand piano recording and he would send it to Robbins, who would wire back comments. Changes would then be made. Throughout their collaboration, Bernstein generally acquiesced to Robbins; he says he cannot deal with this kind of confrontation.

Probably because of Bernstein's spectacular conducting debut, Sol Hurok bought the ballet. (Bernstein told friends at the time that he did not believe the work would have been mounted if all of the principals still had been unknown.) The first performance was makeshift. Shirley Bernstein had done the vocal for a jukebox song in her deep voice and it was supposed to be heard as the curtain went up. But about a half hour before the first ballet began, Comden and Green, sitting out front, realized there was no phonograph in the house on which to play the piece, "Big Stuff." According to Comden, there was "sudden hysteria," and she and Green jumped into a taxi, sped to her apartment, and picked up a record player.

The ballet was a success. Recently Bernstein described it this way: "[It was] a brief, wonderful look at twenty-five minutes in the life of three sailors who had twenty-four hours' shore leave in New York and had some balletic adventures in a bar-indulging in a certain amount of competition culminating in a fight, and then wound up pals again. Beautiful ballet."[7]

The details in the scenario had been designated by Robbins, who was a principal dancer as well as choreographer. All the program said was that it was about three sailors on shore leave. The time was "the Present, a hot summer night"; the place "New York City, a side street." Among the street's attractions were a bar, three girls, and three sailors who treated two of the girls to beer, entertained them with solo dances, fought over them, lost them, and wound up in pursuit of the third.

Hardly your prototypical love story about a man and a woman. But the piece captivated audiences, and within a year of its first presentation, *Fancy Free* was danced more than 160 times. Bernstein deserves a good deal of the credit. His music is theater music at its best. Never strained, sentimental, or phony, it is hard-edged in its urban sexuality. Probably more significant than anything else in Bernstein's own development was a total absence of anything related to cowboys or the West. Bernstein went beyond Copland here, and if there are moments in *Fancy Free* or anything else that remind the listener of Copland or Tchaikovsky or Brahms, the sound is still unmistakably Bernstein. The music-theater voice is entirely his own. Aggression is at least one of the ingredients, and in this case the tone was not limited to the score. *The New Yorker* magazine critic Robert Simon wrote, "Bernstein conducted *Fancy Free* with an almost pugnacious direction."

There were two dozen performances of *Fancy Free* at the Metropolitan Opera House that spring. The following season the Ballet Theater took it on tour. It was considered the finest ballet on an American theme. Choreographed and composed by Americans, it became the signature piece for the Ballet Theater.

Bernstein recalls the experience as being "terribly exciting." He says Hurok came to see him and said it had to go everywhere on tour—San Francisco and the Hollywood Bowl—and that Bernstein would have to conduct it himself. Hurok took Bernstein to lunch at the Russian Tea Room and told him that although he had a number of concert performances lined up, Hurok could do better for him. He asked Bernstein how much he needed a year to live. Considering the rent at the Carnegie studio, the fact that he had no dependents, and the prices charged at the Russian Tea Room where he then wanted to eat the rest of his life, Bernstein said fifteen thousand dollars. Hurok told him he would guarantee that, "come hell or high water," and in return for Hurok's getting him engagements, he would give Hurok everything in excess of fifteen thousand dollars that he earned. Of course Bernstein was obliged to conduct every engagement Hurok booked for him. That was the quid pro quo of the deal. Bernstein says that although he never had a head for business, something told him this was some form of slavery, and he turned it down. "He never really forgave me for that or for not saying, 'How about making it a hundred thousand dollars?'"

In a profile in *The New Yorker,* author Robert Rice wrote, "Almost from the beginning, Bernstein's annual income was around $75,000, incomprehensible for a serious musician."

At the time of the Philharmonic debut, initially
Sam Bernstein had taken credit for Leonard's success. A headline on
the feature page of the Sunday *Boston Post* read: FATHER IN TEARS
AT BOY CONDUCTOR'S TRIUMPH. BOSTON MERCHANT
CALLS SON'S ACCOMPLISHMENT, "MY CONTRIBUTION

1944

The On the Town *cast: Green, Comden, unidentified cast member, Battles, Osato.*
"Green says they fought the idea of the three sailors because they were afraid they
would come up with a Grade B movie. What they had not counted on was the power of
the music to transform a Grade B movie into something much more."

TO AN AMERICA THAT HAS DONE EVERYTHING FOR ME." The
article went on to say that Sam had invested twelve thousand dollars
in his son's musical education but that it had all been well worth it.

For his part, Leonard told reporters that his father had done everything possible to prevent him from pursuing a musical career and that
he had not invested anything at all.

The older Bernstein was subscribing to a clipping service and reading what his son was saying. He developed ulcers and became deeply
depressed. Finally he fell victim to shingles. His physician recommended that he consult a psychiatrist. After the initial visit Sam said he would
never go again, that he could get the same advice from his rabbis.

But for Leonard psychoanalysis became a lifelong addiction.
Several of his friends and colleagues including Jerome Robbins were
trying Freudian psychotherapy, then still new to the United States.
Bernstein's situation was complex. Predominantly homosexual, he was
drawn both to men and to women. Then, too, as much as he fought
Sam Bernstein over his career, he could never have escaped intact from
his father's rage if he had exhibited this additional aspect of his personality. Finally, Bernstein wanted a big career; he worried that a commitment to professional success would not allow him the luxury of following his sexual bent whenever and wherever he felt it.

Bernstein went in and out of analysis, probably not entirely because
of his sexual conflicts. It is likely he spent at least as much time talking
about his career uncertainty: What should he be, a composer, a conductor, a pianist? Bernstein says he has gone to at least a dozen psychi-
atrists during his life. Although this may be exaggerated (his sister suggests that it is), he has entered and left treatment many times, remaining most devoted to two New York psychoanalysts: Dr. Milton H.
Horowitz and Dr. Willard Gaylin.

In the spring of 1944 Koussevitzky contacted mayor Fiorello La
Guardia and asked him to arrange for Bernstein to conduct some of the
summer concerts at Lewisohn Stadium in Manhattan. It was to be the
stadium's twenty-eighth season. The seats were inexpensive, the crowds
enormous. Koussevitzky probably took this action to try to keep his
wandering protégé on the conducting track. He surely saw *Fancy Free*
as a threatening experience.

On July 14, the New York Philharmonic played the Mendelssohn Violin Concerto at the stadium with Bernstein conducting and Nathan Milstein as soloist before ten thousand five hundred people. The *Times* wrote that Bernstein gave the soloist "able support" and that his interpretation of William Schuman's *American Festival* Overture was "filled with exuberance and vitality." Bernstein also conducted the Sibelius First Symphony on the same program, probably because of the relationship he had seen as early as his Harvard days between Sibelius and Schuman. In this work he was reported to have "made manifest his inherent gifts as an orchestra leader, his authority over the players."

A few evenings later Bernstein conducted Tchaikovsky's *Romeo and Juliet* and, with Lukas Foss conducting, played the solo in the Ravel Piano Concerto in G. This time the *Times* critic noticed some blunders but said the problem may have been lack of sufficient rehearsal time.

If Koussevitzky had intended that these assignments would wean Bernstein away from his pop music and show business life, he did not succeed. Almost as soon as Bernstein finished the stadium concerts, he was again at work with Comden and Green and his new friends Robbins and Smith, as well as Paul Feigay, his Carnegie studio roommate, transforming *Fancy Free* into a Broadway musical. It was Smith's idea. He and Feigay were the producers of the show. Smith says that Robbins and Bernstein at first had not jumped at his proposal. "They wanted to do something more serious," he says. "I tried to persuade them as hard as I could, and at a certain point they said, 'OK, let's go.' I was introduced to Betty and Adolph, I think by Lenny, and of course I was immediately enchanted by them. They were enthusiastic about the idea, and, as I remember, we went at it very rapidly."[7]

Within months, *On the Town*, as they called it, was ready. At the beginning they raised twenty-five thousand dollars. Then for a long time they couldn't raise the rest of the money needed to mount the show.

In the summer of 1944 Bernstein needed an operation for a deviated septum in his nose and Green had been told to have his tonsils removed. They decided to have their surgery at the same time in the same hospital and to share a room. That way they could work on *On the Town*. Bernstein was uncomfortable about wasting time.

It was quite a scene in that hospital room—rather like a Marx Brothers movie. Radios blared. Arguments accelerated over card games.

Pieces of *On the Town* were sung full voice. But they did a lot of work. Initially there was resistance to the three-sailor idea. According to Comden:

> We thought it was too light. We also resisted the title, for the same reason ... Anyway we finally settled on the sailors and the title and then made a list of locales with Oliver—if we were going to show a day in New York we could cover all these locales, no matter what the story was going to be.[7]

Green says they fought the idea of the three sailors because they were afraid they would come up with a Grade B movie. What they had not counted on was the power of the music to transform a Grade B movie into something much more.

Bernstein insists that *On the Town* was not an expansion of the *Fancy Free* score. "There was not a note of *Fancy Free* music in *On the Town* ... We started from Square One with a totally new series of conceptions ... different plot ideas, different scenarios which we had great fun bouncing off each other's brains and souls." Bernstein also makes a distinction between the plots of *Fancy Free* and *On the Town*: "*On the Town* was not about three sailors competing. It was about three sailors with 24 hours' shore leave in New York, period."[7] Their ship is berthed at the Brooklyn Navy Yard. The sailors are just back from sea duty and have never been to New York before. So they head over to Manhattan. On the subway one of the sailors falls in love with Miss Turnstiles, the girl in a poster that says that she studies dancing at Carnegie Hall and painting at the museums. His friends spend the day helping him find her, and of course their efforts take them all over New York. As it turns out, the girl is a belly dancer at Coney Island and has told the subway people a lot of glamorous lies.

Bernstein was in on the book discussions from the start but was often away doing something else. Smith brought the show to the Theater Guild, whose head, Lawrence Langner, fell asleep during the audition. Elia Kazan, then a budding director, turned it down. Then they brought it to George Abbott, the hottest director on Broadway and the man responsible for a hit show called *On Your Toes*. Smith says Abbott was a great enthusiast of ballet and had seen *Fancy Free*.

Abbott said, "I like the smell of this—let's do it tomorrow."

In a conversation in 1985, Abbott said that Bernstein was "always very sure of himself but always cooperative. He was doing everything for the good of the show. He was *not* an egotistical maniac. I was the father figure there and the only problem I can recall with Bernstein was that he would seem to over commit himself. When we were trying out in Boston, he would have to rush back to New York one day. The next day he would have to make a speech for a cause. Twice he left for a distant city to conduct orchestras. Since, at that time, he did his work perfectly—wrote a new song and ballet music—none of us objected to this."

Abbott agreed to direct the show and he quickly established his control. Comden recalls:

> We'd written an almost final version as a flashback. The show opened in a night court where all the characters were gathered, and the judge rapped his gavel and said, "Now tell your stories one at a time," and then you told your story and did *On the Town*, and then you came back to night court where everybody was sitting around and the judge was making his final decisions. We thought it was great. It gave the show form, shape, and importance. Then one day Mr. Abbott told us he loved the score, the book, everything. We were so excited. Then he said, "There's just one thing. Cut that prologue, that flashback. You don't need that."

Comden says she and Green left the room in a rage. "We talked about it and decided to tell Mr. Abbott why we needed this flashback as the whole backbone of the show." Abbott replied, "OK. I'll tell you what. You can have either me or the prologue." From that point there was no ambiguity about control. There were changes and deletions. Abbott showed them that many of their ideas—like having three songs in a row with no intervening dialogue—were not feasible for a Broadway show. Abbott also made radical changes in a Robbins ballet in the second act, cutting it right down the middle and putting a scene between the halves.

As for the core of the book itself, a fifteen-minute sequence in which the boy pursues the girl and finds her in a theater at intermission was annihilated.

Bernstein says about eleven numbers were cut—some before Abbott was brought in—but he adds that

> what I was very much afraid of was cutting a lot of the so-called symphonic music—which was quite long and complicated and would entail a lot of extra rehearsal time and a slightly larger and more expensive orchestra. I was scared it might go the way of that intermission sequence, with the easy snipping of Mr. Abbott. He used to make sort of friendly fun of some of my music by calling it "that Prokofiev stuff," and I was afraid all "that Prokofiev stuff" would go, but it didn't—not a bar of it. This man George Abbott is such an extraordinary creature, such an absolutely practical man of the theater, that I was amazed to find how deeply esthetic his instincts were.[7]

Abbott's reputation was such that as soon as he agreed to direct the show the money was oversubscribed. MGM made a preproduction deal with him; it was reportedly the first time film rights to a musical were sold before the stage production got off the ground. But later, when Abbott told MGM he wanted to direct the movie, the company turned him down. It also cut several fine Bernstein songs—among them "Lonely Town," "I Get Carried Away," "Do-do-re-do," and "I Can Cook Too." But the studio left in all "that Prokofiev stuff." In addition Roger Edens, an associate producer of the film, composed several new songs that were inserted into the film, upsetting Bernstein. But MGM's contribution of more than $350,000 and Gene Kelly and Frank Sinatra in starring roles made any complaints foredoomed to failure.

When *On the Town* opened at the Adelphi Theater on West Forty-fourth Street on December 28, 1944, other shows it was competing with were *Oklahoma!*, *Bloomer Girl*, *Mexican Hayride*, and *Follow the Girls*. Sono Osato, who had recently made a big success with *One Touch of Venus*, had been persuaded by Bernstein to play the lead role. She was joined by Nancy Walker and Betty Comden. Originally Kirk Douglas was slated to portray Gabey, the sailor in search of Miss Turnstiles, but because Douglas could not sing he was replaced by John Battles. The opening dockside set and song were an urban counterpart to the opening farm scene and song that had contributed much to the success of *Oklahoma!* a year before.

Bernstein acknowledges his debt to Rodgers and Hammerstein, as do many others involved in the countless shows that were influenced by that watershed musical. Virtually all the participants in *On the Town* except George Abbott were operating on Broadway for the first time. Until then Comden and Green had appeared as the Revuers in nightclubs and had once done a show at Radio City Music Hall. Robbins was also new to Broadway as a choreographer. In 1940 he had joined the Ballet Theater as a dancer and in 1941 appeared there in Agnes De Mille's *Three Virgins and a Devil.* Although Robbins had appeared on Broadway as a chorus dancer, he had never before choreographed for the theater. But it was principally Bernstein's contribution to the show that made it a landmark. In *The New York Times,* Howard Barnes wrote, "When the work chases after three gobs on the loose in New York, it has all the attributes of a Class B picture." Barnes said it was not Abbott's fault. "The fact is that the Betty Comden-Adolph Green book is a feeble frame for sustained entertainment."

No matter. The music transformed the feeble frame into a bona fide Broadway hit, and the public and other critics responded. Olin Downes, dealing with the music alone in his remarks wrote, "*On the Town* brought a new style, technique, and tempo to New York." But Bernstein's skill brought only anxiety to Koussevitzky who, at the Boston tryout, spent hours after the performance berating his conducting student for wasting time on this show when he should have been working on far more serious, that is, European-oriented pursuits.

In a Dramatists Guild symposium held in 1981, Bernstein said:

> [*On the Town*] is funny, light-hearted, satirical—but not terribly satirical. It was a very serious show from a structural point of view and from the point of view of everybody's contribution and the integration of esthetic elements. The subject matter was light, but the show was serious. I think I can speak for all of us when I say that what we meant about being afraid when Oliver first came to us was that it might get too lightweight. We were very much influenced by our masters, our

teachers—people like Koussevitzky, Lucia Chase, and others who were trying to goad us into doing more serious things; serious in the sense of being non-Broadway, because ... shows on Broadway were then in a very low estate. What we accomplished was a happy and moving show about wartime, in the lightest possible vein but with a most serious esthetic means.

Bernstein might have added that the one experience that probably provided him with all the musical tools he needed to create this kind of music was arranging sheet music for Harms. He was doing that until only a little more than a year before *On the Town* opened.

During the winter of 1944, just after Sam Bernstein bought a house in Brookline, a high-income suburb of Boston, Shirley left home to live with her brother in New York. She had graduated from Mount Holyoke College, and she missed him. In 1968 she spoke of her college years: "The romances came, and all that. But they never

1947

Bernstein conducting the New York City Symphony at the Masonic Temple on West Fifty-fifth Street. "In 1985, on the subject of the City Symphony concerts, Bernstein said that while he was conducting 'all this exciting stuff' on Fifty-fifth Street ... Rodzinski was plodding along with routine programs just two blocks north at Carnegie Hall ... Even forty years later ... what comes to Bernstein's mind is how he upstaged Rodzinski, suggesting that the battle with his father never lay far beneath the surface."

compared with my relationship with Lenny. And that was a kind of a curse, because none of the boys, no matter how bright or how darling or how whatever, had his mental capacities or ways of looking at things."[5]

In a letter to her younger brother, written in the winter of 1944, Shirley described a party at the home of Leonard Lyons, a newspaper columnist:

> Lenny and Sylvia Lyons gave a great party the other night—all the usual people plus, mind you, Ethel Barrymore, Bernard Baruch, Joe DiMaggio, Charles Boyer, Ezio Pinza, Moss Hart, John Steinbeck, Garson Kanin, Al Hirschfeld, Abe Burrows, Frank Loesser, John Ringling North—and people like that there; how about that?

It was during Shirley's first months in the big city that she entered show business with her recording for *Fancy Free* at the Met. She said Billie Holiday was her model; later Holiday recorded the piece with Bernstein. When *On the Town* opened, Shirley was in the chorus.

Hollywood continued to attract Leonard. In 1945, he took a screen test to play Tchaikovsky in a projected Hal Wallis movie. Irene Diamond, who had worked for Warner Brothers but was then a story editor for Wallis, says, "The script had not been started when Lenny took the test. I remember the studio; it was very far west, near the Hudson River, on Forty-eighth Street. Many musicians were interested in Hollywood then. Horowitz wondered why we didn't do a movie about Liszt, whom he found much more interesting than Tchaikovsky. At any rate we abandoned the Tchaikovsky idea. Paramount, then distributing Wallis's films, was not crazy about it and Lenny proved to be much too modern to play Tchaikovsky. Years later Lenny wanted to see the test but we couldn't put our hands on it."

Bernstein never became a movie star. According to Diamond, he did go out on a few dates with Lana Turner, the blond "sweater girl" of the day, but Diamond adds that "nothing much happened." Still there was no doubt that Bernstein's fame transcended the field of music. In 1944, the U.S. Chamber of Commerce named him, along with Nelson Rockefeller and author John Hersey, one of the outstanding young men of the year. Bernstein became a frequent guest on *Information Please*, a popular radio quiz show hosted by Clifton Fadiman, the literary figure, and displayed the knowledgeability and wit he had shown long before.

Conducting remained a constant in his life. In the summer of 1944, in addition to his Lewisohn Stadium concerts, he appeared at the Ravinia Festival near Chicago. He opened the Ballet Theater season with *Fancy Free* while Sir Thomas Beecham conducted the rest of the program. The dance critic Edward Denby celebrated Bernstein as a great conductor for the dance in a review that appeared in the *New York Herald Tribune*:

> His downbeat, delivered against an upward thrust in his torso, has an instantaneous rebound, like that of tennis balls. He can give the illusion of an increase in speed by increasing his buoyancy and adding a dynamic crescendo, so he doesn't have to quicken the tempo.... Such a beat gives a lift to the dancers and it gives them confidence; they feel he won't hurry them breathlessly in a lively spot, nor die out on them in a nostalgic cadence....

That autumn Bernstein conducted the Detroit Symphony in a series of broadcast concerts. Through the 1944–1945 season, he served as guest conductor in Boston, Cincinnati, Pittsburgh, St. Louis, Montreal, Minneapolis, and Vancouver. It should be noted that Koussevitzky, who was stingy about letting others conduct his orchestra, offered it to Bernstein that year. In New York, Bernstein appeared not only as guest conductor but as piano soloist in the Ravel Concerto in G. RCA Victor signed him to a recording contract.

In an interview that appeared in the New York daily *PM* on the eve of the opening of *On the Town*, Bernstein said that the show "represented a six-month period out of my life. I'm primarily a conductor. It's not easy to grow as a conductor when you're diverting your energies in so many other directions." At that particular moment Bernstein sounded as though he was trying to placate Koussevitzky, who could be counted on to read any statement Bernstein gave to the press. To the end, Koussevitzky never understood Bernstein's deep roots in popular music and the theater. The life Koussevitzky held out for Bernstein was that of the classic conductor and the concert hall, nothing more. In the *PM* interview, Bernstein described the way one activity could interfere with the other: "I was guest conductor of the Boston Symphony for a week in November. It requires everything for you to do the job right. And all through the week I was getting calls from New York—the show needed two more measures for this song, or another verse for that."

During the week Bernstein was guest conductor in Boston, Koussevitzky must have felt the kind of anger and frustration experienced by Walter Piston at Harvard, who complained that "Bernstein was always putting on a show or something," and Vengerova and Reiner at Curtis, and Rodzinski, of course, in New York. Koussevitzky was doing everything in his power to ensure that Bernstein would inherit his own post, among the most prestigious in music in the United States. And this impossible boy, instead of doing everything he could to persuade the trustees he was a "serious artist," was putting together a musical comedy based on what Koussevitzky called "jezz," which was part of what the trustees considered to be the tawdry night life of New York.

Koussevitzky would have a hard time trying to transform Bernstein into a figure palatable to the trustees. First, Bernstein was not a wealthy European but a middle-class American. Second, of course, he was a Jew. Third, he was not married. Fourth, he held no terror at all for the musicians in the orchestra, who had known him from his Tanglewood days when he was only a novice.

Probably more destructive than any of these factors, as far as the Boston Symphony's trustees were concerned, was Bernstein's tie to show business. Known to the world not as Maestro but as Lenny, he spent his evenings not with the intellectual and cultural figures in American and international society, but with Comden and Green, who had done "Mabel Mabel" to Tchaikovsky's Fourth with the whole symphony orchestra at Radio City Music Hall. Morton Gould says a trustee of the Boston Symphony told him she hoped *On the Town* would fail because then Bernstein might give up Broadway and become eligible for the Boston Symphony post. *On the Town* did not fail. It ran for 483 performances. But Bernstein did not go near Broadway again until after Koussevitzky died, which was almost ten years later. When Comden and Green wrote their next show, *Billion Dollar Baby*, Bernstein was unavailable. Abbott directed, Robbins choreographed, but the score was composed by Morton Gould.

In March 1945, the *Times* announced that a festival would take place in Paris that June, under the joint sponsorship of the U.S. Office of War Information and the French government. Copland was to be the director, Bernstein the chief conductor. There would be several concerts devoted to American composers as well as to those Europeans who had found refuge in the United States during the war. The stated purpose was "to demonstrate to Europeans who had undergone five years of Nazi occupation the cultural progress achieved in this country under democratic government." On the surface, the festival appeared to he unexceptionable. In terms of musical politics, however, it was highly charged. Arnold Schoenberg, a refugee from Hitler who had pioneered the twelve-tone system of composition, had been living and working in California since 1933. Yet he was not on the list. The programming took its direction entirely from the style of Stravinsky and therefore from Copland and those who followed them.

What Copland and Bernstein did not understand was that although the United States had won the military war, an aesthetic war was to follow in which America might not be the victor. In France in particular, a method of composition was developing that would soon rule out Stravinsky and Copland and all the Koussevitzky-sponsored composers. In April the music festival was canceled. Transport difficulties and the generally unsettled conditions of Europe were given as the reasons. The fact is that if the festival had taken place, there would have been an intense reaction from young composers in France and elsewhere. They were in revolt against the Russian and other more traditional composers who had dominated France since the days of the Russian émigré impresario Diaghilev. In its place, they were promoting a new music language, German in origin, initiated by Schoenberg in 1923. The more traditional style of Stravinsky, which still seemed to be progressive to the musically naïve Bernstein, was already considered reactionary by the new generation of European composers.

Schoenberg's revolution of 1923 was not only difficult for many listeners to accept, or at least enjoy, but impossible for many composers to adopt. Musicians—especially those outside Austria and Germany—

resented the imposition of a new set of rules, far more stringent than any they had subscribed to until then. Those opposed to twelve-tone music included such diverse composers as Stravinsky, Hindemith, Bartók, Milhaud, and the Americans around Copland, all of whom found themselves thrust together under the amorphous umbrella called neoclassicism.

Each of the two major schools of the first half of the twentieth century was presided over by a godlike figure: Schoenberg over twelve-tone and Stravinsky over neoclassicism. Each created a kind of idolatry. Neither questioned the correctness of his way. Schoenberg and Stravinsky, who lived ten miles apart in Los Angeles after they fled Europe, never met except once at the funeral of a mutual friend.

In Europe twelve-tone music went underground during the 1930s and early 1940s when Hitler set out to destroy modern art as decadent and a disservice to the People, in much the way that Stalin and the Communists were doing it. But René Leibowitz, a composer and conductor, proved to be a conduit between Arnold Schoenberg and the post-World War II composers who adopted the twelve-tone method. Just before Schoenberg left Germany to settle in the United States, Leibowitz, then nineteen, heard a performance of Schoenberg's *Pierrot Lunaire*. The work impressed him profoundly, and he determined to find the composer. Gathering together his savings, he first looked in Vienna, then in Berlin, where he found the composer teaching at the Prussian Academy. Schoenberg allowed Leibowitz to attend his class for six weeks.

In 1933 Hitler dismissed Schoenberg, a Jew, from his teaching post. By then Leibowitz had returned to France and was studying conducting with Pierre Monteux and playing violin in a Paris nightclub to make enough money to buy all the Schoenberg scores he could find. It was through the study of these scores that Leibowitz discovered the twelve-tone technique; Schoenberg never defined or discussed the method in class. To confirm his notion that a new system of composition governed these post-1923 Schoenberg works, Leibowitz contacted Schoenberg's brother-in-law, Rudolph Kolisch, the violinist who had given the first performances of many Schoenberg works. Kolisch told Leibowitz that Schoenberg believed the twelve-tone technique would assure the supremacy of German music for the next hundred years.

When World War II broke out, Leibowitz went into hiding in Vichy, then in Paris until the liberation in 1944. At the same time that Copland and Bernstein were planning to bring Stravinsky-oriented concerts to Paris, Leibowitz began to conduct and record the first postwar performances of Schoenberg in Europe. Despite the fact that he had an expatriate passport and therefore had difficulty gaining access to the French radio, Leibowitz managed to conduct, record, and broadcast performances of the Schoenberg school. These performances became major events among the European avant-garde. René Leibowitz was being celebrated as the Father of the New, while Nadia Boulanger, Stravinsky's idolator, Koussevitzky's colleague, and Copland's mentor, was holding the reins of the dying neoclassicism.

While *On the Town* was rollicking along Broadway, Leibowitz was teaching the twelve-tone method to Pierre Boulez and other Conservatoire students in his Paris apartment. Then these parallel forces began to collide. At the Théâtre de Champs-Élysées, during a concert devoted to Stravinsky, two pieces he had composed in the United States were booed and hissed. Leibowitz had organized this demonstration, but Boulez and his classmates did the work. They were proclaiming that Boulanger and neo-classicism were dead, the musical life of the past would not return, the future would go the Austro-German way.

Bernstein knew very little of this deadly serious, joyless world. The cancellation of the Paris project disappointed him, but by the summer he had another opportunity to conduct the same kind of music, though not in Europe. On August 25, 1945, his twenty-seventh birthday, he was appointed conductor of the City Symphony of the New York City Center of Music and Drama. Bernstein succeeded Leopold Stokowski, the very same conductor who had snubbed him in Philadelphia.

The City Center of Music and Drama was housed in what can best be described as an Islamoid building on West Fifty-fifth Street. Originally a Shrine auditorium, the Mecca Temple, it had reverted to the city in 1943 for nonpayment of taxes. Public officials, seeking ways to produce some income, renamed it the Cosmopolitan Opera House. Stokowski conducted several NBC concerts there, and soon afterward a permanent orchestra, the City Symphony, was established. In the winter before Bernstein took over, the building was renamed again, this time the City Center of Music and Drama.

Bernstein announced that the season would begin on October 8 with a ten-week series of Monday and Tuesday evening concerts, that the men would receive union scale and that he, like Stokowski, would serve for nothing. "I might talk about plans for 15 years," he said, "but it is too early to talk specifically about plans for the season just ahead. America is now definitely the cultural center of the world and New York is the cultural center of America, and hence the world. There should be a fountainhead in the city for music and art, and it seems to me that the City Center fills the need. No change in the personnel of the orchestra is now in view, although, in consideration of the end of the war, it is impossible to say what might happen in the next month. Undoubtedly many changes will occur in time."

Time ran an article in its October 22, 1945, issue in the gee-whiz style it reserved for its culture heroes:

> The 27-year-old wunderkind of the musical world, Leonard Bernstein, opened his fall season last week. His Broadway musical, *On the Town*, still packed them in. His ballet, *Fancy Free*, was the most popular attraction at Manhattan's Metropolitan Opera House. Nervous, earnest, Bernstein has still not decided whether he wants to be a composer or a conductor, a jazzman or a classicist. Last week he led the municipally owned New York City Symphony for the first time, after only one week of rehearsals. He had replaced more than half of the musicians inherited from Leopold Stokowski. Now there was only one slightly bald head in the whole orchestra. There were twelve ex-servicemen. The orchestra thumped its way through Brahms's Second Symphony which Brahms wrote at 44, but critics liked best young conductor Bernstein's version of Shostakovich's First Symphony which he wrote at 19.

Downes did not agree that they thumped and gave Bernstein a review that echoed the one for the young conductor's debut:

> Leonard Bernstein, with an orchestra materially improved over that of last season, conducted a concert of exceptional bril-

liance last night in the City Center of Music and Drama. His program was principally of modern music, in the instances of Aaron Copland's *Outdoor Overture* and Shostakovich's First Symphony, though he showed a significant development of his musicianship and interpretive powers when he closed with Brahms's Second. In the sum of it he gave plain proof of another conductor of distinguished gifts coming rapidly into his own. The audience rejoiced in his temperament and sensibility, in his youth and instinctive command of the orchestra. There might be an overstatement here and an understatement there; the sum of it was the accomplishment of singular arid unquestionable gifts, and what is more important, capacity for growth and accumulating mastery of his medium.

Bernstein's special contribution with the City Symphony was not, however, a good interpretation of Brahms, it was in presenting twentieth-century works that while not unknown were not yet in the repertory. In combing the century for worthy revivals, Bernstein invariably came up with gems.*

On at least one occasion Bernstein departed from so-called neoclassical works to present parts of a piece by Alban Berg, a disciple of Schoenberg. With Rose Bampton as soloist, he conducted excerpts from Berg's opera *Wozzeck.* Howard Taubman wrote in the *Times* that the performance had been "incandescent ... unforgettable ... Bernstein shaped [the work] with striking logic and sensitivity. There was a wealth

---

* *In his three years in the post, he conducted such Stravinsky works as* Oedipus Rex, Symphony of Psalms, *the* Firebird Suite, Petrouchka, Ragtime for Piano, *the* Violin Concerto, Pastorale for Violin, Woodwind Quintet, *and the* "Royal March" *from* L'Histoire du Soldat. *Bernstein called on his friends to perform, as he did, for nothing.*

Other twentieth-century works included Hindemith's Concerto for Strings and Brass, Randall Thompson's Symphony No. 2, Walter Piston's Concerto for Orchestra and Concerto for Violin and Piano, Carlos Chávez's Sinfonia India, Blitzstein's Airborne Symphony in its world premiere with Orson Welles as narrator and The Cradle Will Rock with Bernstein at the piano, Rachmaninoff's Piano Concerto No. 2, Harris's Third Symphony, Barber's Essay No. 2, Milhaud's Création du Monde and Concerto for Two Pianos, and Bartók's Portrait No. 1 in D, transformed for the first time, according to Bartók's own suggestion, into a violin concerto, with Joseph Szigeti as soloist. Bernstein also conducted Bartók's Music for Strings, Percussion, and Celesta, the piece he had conducted in place of a work by Brahms at a Boston Symphony rehearsal four years before. Also on Bernstein's list of twentieth-century works were Vaughan Williams's Fantasia on a Theme by Thomas Tallis, David Diamond's Symphony No. 2, and Ives's Lincoln the Great Commoner for chorus and orchestra. The Robert Shaw Chorale donated performances, as did Tospsy Spivakovsky, David Oppenheim, and Jennie Tourel during the season.

of contrast in the orchestral tone: the pacing was right and the tenderness and pathos of the music came through with blazing intensity."

In 1985, on the subject of the City Symphony concerts, Bernstein said that while he was conducting "all this exciting stuff" on Fifty-fifth Street that was causing such a stir among the public and in the press, Rodzinski was plodding along with routine programs just two blocks north at Carnegie Hall. With prices that ranged from 90 cents to $1.80, Bernstein had apparently mobilized an audience that the standard repertory could not attract, young intellectuals committed to twentieth-century music. Even forty years later, however, what comes to Bernstein's mind is how he upstaged Rodzinski, suggesting that the battle with his father never lay far beneath the surface.

In fact, almost as soon as he was named director of the City Symphony, he publicly attacked its sponsor, Mayor Fiorello La Guardia. In November, 1945, at a meeting run by the National Council of American-Soviet Friendship, Bernstein departed from his prepared text to say that New York had no such thing as its own orchestra despite popular opinion to the contrary. "When I travel around the country," he said, "people always come up to me and ask me what they can do to give their cities a civic orchestra like New York's. And I look at all the people in amazement and wonder what they are talking about. 'Can't you realize that it is a complete fraud?' I always tell them. I hasten to assure you, in front of all these people, that it is a fraud. We haven't had a penny from the city." Bernstein said the mayor had been interested in the project and had given it a kind of passive support, but had not intervened in complex legal matters where his intervention might have helped the orchestra. Bernstein noted that the symphony had to pay the city rent for the hall, that the musicians made five hundred dollars for the season, and that box office, radio sponsorship, and private donations were what kept the orchestra alive. He ended by saying that what he wanted to do most was to tell the men that they could count on making a reasonable living next year.

But as Bernstein was always able to dish it out, so he started getting it back. In 1946 Virgil Thomson attacked him in the *New York Herald Tribune*:

Leonard Bernstein would be a delightful conductor if he

could ever forget ... that he is being considered by Warner Brothers to be a potential film star.... With all the musical advantages he has, he seems to have turned, in the last two years, even more firmly away from objective music making, and to have embraced a career of sheer vainglory. With every season his personal performance becomes more ostentatious, his musical one less convincing. There was a time when he used to forget occasionally and let the music speak. Nowadays he keeps it always like the towering Italian bandmasters of forty years ago, a vehicle for the waving about of hair, for the twisting of shoulders and torso, for the miming of facial expression of uncontrolled emotional states. If all this did not involve musical obfuscation, if it were merely the prima donna airs of a great artist, nobody would mind. But his conducting today, for all the skill and talent that lies behind it, reveals little except the consistent distortion of musical works, ancient and modern, into cartoons to illustrate the blithe career of a sort of musical Dick Tracy.

When this appeared Bernstein told friends and even one reporter (though not for publication) that Thomson's vendetta was a personal one stemming from two sources: The first, Bernstein said, was his refusal to take Thomson as a lover, and the second was his failure to program Thomson's own works. Bernstein said, though not to Thomson, that he had never liked the music and could see nothing in its "plagal cadences."

Still, almost forty years later the violinist Matthew Raimondi, who had played with the City Symphony in 1947, said, "What Bernstein did was to visualize for the audience what he was feeling about the music. None of *us* really watched him at all." Raimondi's recollections gain support from even as loyal a critic as Downes, who in November 1947 wrote that "we do not see each gyration of Leonard Bernstein on the platform as essential to the most efficient conducting," although he added, "It must be admitted that he conducts very successfully."

In addition to being the most readable and provocative critic in the 1940s, Thomson was also a sharp observer. In this instance he hit on something important when he noted Bernstein's ambitions as a movie star. Surely Bernstein was handsome enough to qualify, and he had experienced in his three years of public life enough applause and adulation to know how much he needed both. Where could he get more of what he was then getting? In Hollywood!

Bernstein began spending time there in 1944. In 1946, he made a verbal agreement with producers Lester Cowan and Mary Pickford to work on a movie. Based on an English short story, *The Beckoning Fair One* was to be about a composer and pianist who went through an extrasensory experience. In 1985, Cowan said, "I was to pay Lenny twenty-five thousand dollars and build the picture around him in every respect. Louella Parsons [a gossip columnist] ran a banner headline announcing his participation. But Lenny was about to go off on a concert tour and came up with the suggestion that he write the musical themes and have my wife, Ann Ronell, fix them up and make them work for the film. That wasn't my idea. I wanted him all the way. But he felt that Hollywood would have put a blemish on his career."

Ronell, composer of such songs as "Willow Weep for Me," says that Helen Coates kept calling Bernstein during his month-long visit with the Cowans at their ranch near Hollywood. "She insisted he couldn't do both, that he would have to choose between the movie and the upcoming tour. So he turned the movie down."

Bernstein was still trying to build a career that would make him acceptable as Koussevitzky's successor in Boston. To compete for that post, he also had to remain in the public eye as an administrator and organizer of first-rate concerts, so he stayed with the City Symphony.

In 1946, a year after the aborted Paris festival project, Bernstein went to Europe to conduct two concerts of American music at the First International Music Festival in Prague. The program included Barber's Essay No. 2, Schuman's *American Festival* Overture, Harris's Symphony No. 3, Copland's *El Salón México*, Bernstein's *Jeremiah*, and Gershwin's *Rhapsody in Blue*, which brought down the house. Other concerts in the festival were devoted to English, French, and Russian music. Nothing German or Austrian. The conflict between schools of composition as much as the recently ended fighting was the reason for those exclusions. After the concerts Bernstein delighted Rafael Kubelik, the conductor of the Czech Philharmonic, and a group of listeners by playing his renditions of "Honky Tonk Train" and "Empty Bed Blues."

In June 1946, Bernstein conducted the London Philharmonic. British reserve and American ebullience have always conflicted. In this instance Bernstein suffered. According to the *London Daily Express*, "Bernstein's conducting looked as if he was playing a part choreographed by Jerome Robbins. He swayed, stabbed, crouched and leaped in the air, both feet off the ground several times, like a pocket-sized Tarzan." The *Daily Telegraph* wrote, "Bernstein conveys his relish of the sounds Brahms and Mozart make. There is a less convincing assurance from the performances that he allows and respects them for masters, that he can be enriched or taught or wounded as well as stimulated...." When Bernstein returned to New York, he told reporters that the London Philharmonic was "a terrible orchestra."

In London Bernstein also conducted *Fancy Free* at Covent Garden. On his return he was guest conductor in Rochester, Cincinnati, San Francisco, Vancouver, Boston, and Detroit, as well as with the NBC Symphony.

By 1947 speculation about who would be Koussevitzky's successor was growing. He invited his protégé to conduct the orchestra in a full concert at Carnegie Hall, the first time he had allowed any outsider to do that. Bernstein chose a demanding program: Schubert's C Major Symphony and Stravinsky's *Le Sacre du Printemps*, a program he repeated that summer in Tanglewood. This time Downes outdid himself: "Mr. Bernstein understood the music.... He felt its whole structure and germination, felt it in his bones, and so released it that it seemed almost to rend the orchestra itself with elemental power. He is a born conductor, a musician of his period, and one of its voices in art."

But the Boston audience with its Puritan history was probably uncomfortable not only with Bernstein's gestures but also with music as visceral as *Le Sacre du Printemps*. Just about the same time, Charles Munch arrived in Boston and conducted programs exclusively French, describing a new Honegger work as "horizontal music, rather stern and unsentimental, and as such an expression of our time." He was talking the language of the Boston sensibility. On February 3, 1947, in an article on Munch, *Time* magazine reported an important fact: "In Boston, where he made a big hit, Beacon Hill rustled with rumors that he would succeed 72-year-old Serge Koussevitzky as the Boston's permanent conductor."

Koussevitzky sensed the danger was real. According to Halina Rodzinski, he issued an ultimatum: "If you don't want Bernstein, I shall retire right now." He thought that the Boston Symphony would never permit him to resign. The Boston Symphony trustees stunned Koussevitzky and accepted his resignation on the spot. In the spring of 1949 Munch became the conductor of the Boston Symphony. *Time* wrote:

> The choice of Koussevitzky's successor was something of a surprise, but not a shock. Koussevitzky's 29-year-old protégé, Leonard Bernstein, had long had the inside track with his sponsor, but not with the symphony's trustees. The post went to 56-year-old Alsatian Charles Munch, who first came to the United States in December, 1946, and has since conducted in Boston, New York, Chicago, and Los Angeles.
>
> Bostonians will find some things about Charles Munch very Koussevitzky. As the elegant conductor of the Paris Conservatory Orchestra—"the oldest and best orchestra in France," says Munch, "le beau Charles" was the idol of lady concert-goers. Like Koussevitzky himself (whose second wife was rich), Charles Munch is independently wealthy. His wife, the daughter of a Swiss condensed-milk millionaire, inherited a fortune said to be close to $1,000,000.

Bernstein resigned as director of the City Symphony on March 7, 1948. The available funds had diminished, and the American Federation of Musicians, which had contributed ten thousand dollars to the orchestra in 1947, wouldn't do it the following year. At a press conference announcing his resignation, Bernstein spelled out all he found wrong at the City Center, provoking an angry reply from Newbold Morris, chairman of the board. After the public statements, Bernstein moved to the side and chatted with some of the press. Miles Kastendieck, music critic for the *New York Journal-American*, recalls being thunderstruck when Bernstein, surely the most "successful" of all the serious musicians in the United States, confided he was worried about his future. He told Kastendieck he didn't see how he could make a living through music.

In 1946, at Tanglewood, the first summer the festival opened after the war, Koussevitzky said to Bernstein, "I think Copland is pederast. I think David Diamond is pederast. I think you, too, may be pederast."

Koussevitzky's attitude toward homosexuality was not dissimilar

Helen Coates. "She not only took care of his professional arrangements and correspondence with his friends when he was too busy, she also said no to those proposals she believed would be harmful to him. (This role became a legend....)"

to Sam Bernstein's. Such behavior was shameful, reprehensible. In his lectures to the conducting students, Koussevitzky emphasized the importance of feeling "clean" before the conductor mounts the podium. Feeling clean meant, at the very least, feeling heterosexual.

But he was fighting a losing battle, for even those artists he brought to Tanglewood from abroad turned out to be homosexuals, too. The highlight of the 1946 season was the first American production of *Peter Grimes*. In 1942 Koussevitzky had commissioned Benjamin Britten to compose an opera. It had its world premiere in London in 1945. For the American premiere, Britten brought an entourage to help prepare the production. The tone of the British group did nothing to dispel the effete American ambience, and when Bernstein conducted the rehearsal from the pit bare-chested, Koussevitzky must have felt helpless. Nevertheless he loved "*Peter und Grimes*," which is what he always called the Britten opera, and believed it to be second only to *Carmen*.

To say that most of the artists then at Tanglewood were homosexual is not to imply the same was true of the people filling the Bernstein house. When Bernstein arrived that summer he was not viewed as Koussevitzky's assistant anymore. Now he was a towering personality in music, with ballet, Broadway theater, and London performances behind him. So much had happened in the intervening years that he no longer had to ask Copland if he could have a place in Copland's house. Instead Bernstein rented a house on the Stockbridge Bowl, the only body of water in the area. Helen Coates, his former teacher, had by then replaced Shirley as his secretary and lived in the house that summer. Visitors included Shirley and Burton Bernstein; Adolph Green and his fiancée, Allyn Ann McClerie; Betty Comden and her husband, Steven Kyle; David Oppenheim; William Kapell, the pianist; and David Diamond.

Diamond found the usual chaotic mix of people at Bernstein's place. He had some of his own music with him that he wanted Bernstein to see, but remembers one could never get him alone. "There would have to be waterskiing first with Burtie, then a ride into Stockbridge with Shirley." But the most intriguing figures in the ménage that summer were those who were new to Tanglewood and Bernstein. One was Arthur Weinstein, who later became an interior designer. Good-looking, cultivated, he was anxious to serve Bernstein in whatever small domestic ways he could. Another was Felicia Montealegre, the daughter of Roy Cohn, a California Jew with business interests in Chile (not the attorney by the same name who was an associate of Joseph McCarthy), and Clemencia Montealegre, a Latin American Catholic who had educated her three daughters in a convent in Chile. Felicia had taken a few lessons with concert pianist Claudio Arrau.

Leonard and Felicia had met in New York the previous winter. Arrau was to be soloist with the City Symphony in the Brahms Concerto in D Minor. Bernstein had heard him perform the work under Koussevitzky years before with the Boston Symphony. Because Arrau's press representative, Friede Rothe, was also the representative of Jennie Tourel, Bernstein entreated Rothe to see if Arrau would play for nothing. Arrau said yes and it was on this occasion that he served as a means for Felicia Montealegre to meet Bernstein. Before she ever met Bernstein, Felicia told friends that she was determined to marry him. Of course she was not alone in this; Bernstein had captivated women in audiences from the start of his career.

Arrangements were made for a small dinner after the concert at the Arrau house in Queens. Felicia waited there with the pianist's wife, Ruth, for Arrau to return with Bernstein and Friede Rothe. Rothe says that the two "fell in love at first sight." Apparently Felicia told people that this was what happened.

A number of Bernstein's associates describe their initial encounters with him as being "love at first sight." When one hears it for the fifth or sixth time one tends to become skeptical. Ned Rorem's observations on Bernstein's personality might help explain why otherwise intelligent people feel no embarrassment at using these particular words to describe their first meetings with him: "I've known a lot of famous people in my life but no superstars. Lenny is the only one. I felt whenever I was with him that I was the most important person in his life. He never looks over his shoulder while he is talking to you at who else more important is in the room. He takes a person into a corner at a party to talk. I know that if I say hello he won't be too busy to talk to me. That was true of Noel Coward, Jean Cocteau, Nadia Boulanger. It is a fame that surpasses fame, not the hardness that comes to some. You can't fake it, can't buy it, that humanity, that charm."

Bernstein's infatuation with Felicia Montealegre appears to have been as real as hers was for him. During the next few months he occasionally brought friends to her apartment on Washington Place in Greenwich Village to introduce them to her. Apparently he did not call before he came, and no one seems to have ever come to the door. Either she wanted to try to impose some discipline on her undisciplined lover, or she simply was never home. In any event his friends were all told that they would "adore her" when they met her.

They finally did meet her in the summer of 1946. What she found in the house on Stockbridge Bowl was a parade of good-looking men and Shirley Bernstein and Helen Coates, two women so crucial to Bernstein that she would have to compete with them the rest of her life. His sister, Shirley, was his first love. Helen Coates, then in her mid-forties, was so devoted to Bernstein she did not tell him she could not type, and paid someone out of her own salary to come in on Saturdays for the important letters. Coates had solidified her position with Bernstein by telling him that, during the war, she had turned down a soldier who offered to divorce his wife to marry her, because she knew Bernstein needed her. He did. She not only took care of his professional arrangements and corresponded with his friends when he was too busy, she also said no to those proposals she believed would be harmful to him. (This role became a legend. More than twenty years later Stephen Sondheim gave Bernstein a fiftieth-birthday present, a game he had made himself. One part was a maze the goal of which was Bernstein at the center, with Helen Coates the chief obstacle. As soon as the players started this part of the game, a recording of Coates's high-pitched voice came on.)

Despite the formidable competition—Coates, Shirley Bernstein, and Arthur Weinstein—Felicia stuck it out through the summer and even went so far as to visit Bernstein's parents in the fall. Although her father was a Jew, her manner was so strikingly un-Jewish that the meeting, according to Bernstein's brother, was not successful.

In January 1947, Bernstein and Felicia Montealegre became officially engaged. Leonard Lyons, the gossip columnist, claimed:

> This is how Leonard Bernstein's engagement to Felicia Montealegre was announced. Lester Cowan, producer of "The Beckoning Fair One," in which Bernstein will co-star, conduct and compose the musical score, gave a hoe-down for them at

his ranch. Sinatra sang, Gene Kelly danced, and John Garfield donned boxing gloves.... Then came a song written by Ann Ronell, author of Willow Weep for Me, Big Bad Wolf, etc. The tune was a blending of Haydn's *Surprise* Symphony, Mendelssohn's Wedding March, and Bernstein's *Fancy Free, On the Town,* and *Jeremiah.* The lyrics ended with the announcement: "This party has been staged because they got engaged. Len and Felicia are now officially two."

It may have happened that way.

Soon after, Felicia gave up music and returned to acting. Before she had met Bernstein, in 1944 and 1945, she had attended Herbert Berghof's acting class in Manhattan. The move from music was probably good for the survival of their relationship. Bernstein, while hugely talented, was fiercely competitive; his brother, Burton, angered him by beating him at tennis. Through the years he challenged and beat practically anyone in musical trivia games identifying musical themes or lyrics. In later years Samuel Barber refused to visit Bernstein in Martha's Vineyard because the playing of such games was too fatiguing for him; Bernstein always had to win.

In December 1946, Bernstein received a certificate of meritorious achievement at the Academy of Arts and Letters. Others honored were James F. Byrnes, secretary of state; John Hersey, popular novelist; Dr. Harlow Shapley, astronomer; Mary Margaret McBride, radio commentator; and Helen Hayes, actress.

The following spring, Bernstein, accompanied by his father and sister, went to Palestine to conduct a tenth-anniversary concert of an orchestra founded in 1936 by Jews who had fled Hitler's Germany. Bernstein's first appearance with the orchestra was in Edison Hall, a movie house in Jerusalem. Hundreds of people stood in the aisles and hundreds more were turned away. The program consisted of the two works Bernstein had heard Mitropoulos conduct: Robert Schumann's Symphony No. 2 and Ravel's Piano Concerto in G, as well as Mozart's *Linz* Symphony. Bernstein's *Jeremiah* had been programmed, but the parts did not arrive in time, so for the first of the Palestine performances, the Mozart was played instead. The day after the performance, Bernstein told reporters, "The Palestine Orchestra is potentially one of the greatest in the world. It should make a trip to the United States next fall, but first it needs two solid months of real hard work under a single conductor." He added, "I hope I can be the guy to pull that off." To Clifton Daniel of *The New York Times* he was even more specific. By then Koussevitzky knew he could not persuade the Boston trustees to take Bernstein as his successor. In fact he was trying to promote a shared season, half with Bernstein and half with Eleazar de Carvalho, a conductor who had also studied at Tanglewood and was older and more reserved than Bernstein. If that was acceptable, Bernstein still would have time for Palestine, where he was well received. Writing in Tel Aviv, Peter Gradenwitz noted that "not since the days of Toscanini ... has a conductor been recalled so many times and been given a similar ovation."

To Clifton Daniel, Bernstein emphasized that it was essential that the musicians, made up of Jewish refugees from Europe, should have a permanent conductor and a hall large enough for its audience and acoustically fit for its rehearsals. He suggested that a tour of the United States might be the occasion for a campaign to raise the funds for such a concert hall. The tour, he told Daniel, "would be one of the most important things that could happen, not only musically but politically."

After the concerts in Jerusalem, Bernstein went back to Tel Aviv and then on to Haifa, finishing his series in the big Jewish settlement of Ain Harod. By then he had laid a groundwork that made Americans connect him to the Palestine orchestra. Lyons published a letter from Bernstein in his newspaper column:

> I gave a downbeat at this morning's rehearsal. It coincided with a perfectly timed explosion outside the hall. We picked ourselves up and calmly resumed our labors. We've had four incidents in two days: a kidnapping at this hotel, a train demolished, a police station blown up, a military truck bombed. But the care sitters don't put down their newspapers, the children continue to jump rope. The Arab goatherd in the square adjusts another milking bag, and I give the next downbeat. The orchestra's fine. Shalom.

After nine concerts in Tel Aviv, Bernstein made a tour of Europe.

He conducted the Czech Philharmonic in Prague, the Radio Symphonique Orchestre in Paris, the Brussels Philharmonic, and the Hague Orchestra in Scheveningen. From Paris he sent a card to Diamond: "Palestine was a fabulous dream. Paris is agonizingly beautiful. The weather is tropical, and the langoustines at the Doyen are fabulous. Love from Munch [the conductor] and Claude Alphand [a chanteuse] and Peggy [Copland's friend] and Shirley [Bernstein] and Jennie [Tourel] & Friede [Rothe] and me."

The fact that Felicia was not there augured trouble. The previous winter, when Bernstein was thinking about starring in the Lester Cowan film, he and Felicia had announced their engagement on the Cowan ranch near Hollywood. A few months later, in the spring of 1947, Felicia called Ann Ronell and told her that she was frightened: Bernstein had invited all his friends to Tanglewood for the summer but had not invited her. Ronell suggested she go anyway.

It was useless. Nothing could have helped Felicia hold Leonard during the summer of 1947 except perhaps news that the Boston Symphony was reversing its move toward Munch and giving the post to him. But that was unlikely and Bernstein, as well as Mitropoulos, Reiner, and all the others who had coveted that assignment, had to lick their wounds and reassess their career plans. By the fall, Bernstein was back to living the life of a homosexual, which certainly worked against the career he wanted. David Diamond recalls, "In those days, a homosexual was called a fruitcake or a pansy. I remember one day when I was in the Russian Tea Room with a boy and we were very loving, kissing each other with abandon. It got around that I was behaving that way and many people thought that this was the reason I had trouble with my career. Mitropoulos, who was very honest about his own homosexuality, and who was very demonstrative, full of caresses, used to say to me, 'People envy you your honesty and sincerity.' "

Diamond tells a story about Bernstein, who he says used to walk away "with all of my boyfriends." Once in the early 1940s, Bernstein entered Diamond's room when he was in bed with his lover. Bernstein climbed into the bed. Diamond left it and lost his lover. This was a pattern that was to be repeated many times in Bernstein's life. Any men he wanted he pursued, no matter to whom they were tied—to strangers, family members, or close friends. "It was in and out as usual with Lenny," Diamond says. "Lenny is a short-timer regarding sexual relationships."

In the late 1940s, Rorem met Bernstein in New York for the first time in a while. "One evening," he says, "when I was very drunk, I ran into Lenny on West Eighth Street in Greenwich Village. He was living on West Eleventh at the time. We went back to his place. The next morning, when Helen Coates came in, she found us together in Lenny's bed." This is unlikely to have fazed Coates. Men who were far more anonymous than Rorem report that when they emerged from Bernstein's bed in the morning, with Bernstein still asleep, Coates asked for their names and numbers in the event the maestro wanted to call on them again.

After Bernstein broke off the engagement in 1947, Felicia went out with men generally connected to the theater. One, Morton Gottlieb, was then the general manager of New Stages, a Greenwich Village theatrical group. In 1986 Gottlieb recalled, "We were creating the ground rules for Off-Broadway, the two hundred-ninety-nine-seat house and everything that went with it. Felicia was glorious. She was stylish, intelligent, concerned, and always available if you needed help."

Felicia became interested in working in film, and went to Hollywood again, a year after her engagement to Bernstein had been announced there. But this time he was not with her. Felicia called the Cowans from the airport and asked if she could stay again at their ranch while she looked for work. They refused. Ronell says that in the intervening year she had lost her servants so she could not accommodate Felicia.

In 1949 Felicia Montealegre won the Motion Picture Daily Critics Award as the best new television actress of the year. She had made appearances in such programs as *Studio One*, the *Kraft Theater*, and the *Philco Playhouse*. Still, between 1947 and 1951, this young and gifted woman had to have learned that Bernstein had brought her a style of life that would not be available to her without him.

In August 1947, Bernstein wrote to Diamond:

> I've made a few decision.... I'm cancelling my whole
> European trip, with the possible exception of Palestine, to

which I feel such an obligation. This means composing, analysis, solitude, maybe getting to know myself again (or for the first time). I know you'll approve. I feel better for it already.

Bernstein's break with Felicia and his pulling away from projects to which he had, to some degree, committed himself meant an effort to define himself not only as a musician, but in sexual terms. A 1970 *roman à clef* called *Philharmonic* by Herbert Russcol and Margalit Banai which, Bernstein acknowledged in the summer of 1983, was based on his life, tells of how a handsome young conductor named Danny Lourand was pulled between a blond, "delicately boned, crisp woman" who "always looked sexy and preoccupied with high affairs at the same time," and a jazz musician named Peter.

But his hunger for Peter had frightened him. He was bewitched by Peter's dark masculinity. It was as though Peter had aroused a beast within him that had been sleeping and now the beast was in view. That was when he decided to see Dr. Rudolph, driven not so much by want of Peter as by his haunting fear that later he would be at the mercy of other Peters and that in the end he would be inescapably alone, condemned to chance encounters in hidden avenues.

This Peter was based, in the main, on a jazz pianist named John Mehegan. Mehegan had written the incidental music to Tennessee Williams's *Streetcar Named Desire*, had been educated at Juilliard, later taught at Juilliard and Yale, and was, at the time he first met Bernstein, appearing nightly at Marie's Crisis, a club on Grove Street in Greenwich Village. Every night they were free Bernstein and Blitzstein went to the club to hear Mehegan. In *Philharmonic*, the character who represents Felicia drops in one night unannounced,

and discovered that it was not only jazz that attracted him. She saw Danny and Peter at the bar in deep conversation. Peter's arm was around Danny's in a manner that instantly alerted and shocked her. She could always spot a homosexual, she always sensed their special sensitivity and nuances of feminine feeling, and she knew instinctively that this striking ... man seated so familiarly with Danny was a homosexual.... Homosexuality repelled her. She just couldn't come to terms with it, couldn't be tolerant, let alone sophisticated. In her mind she knew that she was being square, middle-class and culture bound—traits that she scorned in others and above all in herself—but she just couldn't accept ... the fact that men sometimes liked to make love to each other.

Gay Mehegan, John's third and last wife, and a woman a generation younger than her husband, shared Felicia's reactions to homosexuality. Coming from a proper upper-middle-class background, with a conservative Republican father, she says that the Greenwich Village life was "new to me. John's sexual kinks were very odd to me.

"But John was a remarkably attractive man. Brilliant, funny, cynical, he conveyed a masterful presence. He entered a room like a hurricane, sweeping into it in his trench coat with the collar turned up—and everywhere people's heads would turn. He was extremely left politically, fiercely independent, flaunting, with a mocking sense of humor. He spent seventeen years on the Juilliard faculty and never agreed to attend a party. Leonard was fascinated by him and in 1946 wrote one of his *Anniversaries* for him. Around the same time John cut an album of piano improvisations on Leonard's songs."

The conflict taking place in Bernstein's life in the middle 1940s found reflection in his next work. On November 4, 1946, the Ballet Theater presented *Facsimile*, a new work by Robbins, Bernstein, and Smith. Bernstein's role was not limited to composing the music. *Time* magazine described the first performance:

It was the most eagerly awaited premiere of the Manhattan ballet season. The three young collaborators, Robbins, Bernstein, and Smith, had teamed together twice before. Their good-natured, casual *Fancy Free* was still, after two and a half years, one of Ballet Theater's best attractions. Then they joined hands in *On the Town*, and it became a Broadway hit. Last week Ballet Theater put on the trio's latest, *Facsimile*.

The scene was described as "a lonely place," the cast as "three insecure people" and "some integrated people." It involved a lonely girl in a bathing suit (shapely Nora Kaye) and two young men who come along and make love to her, quarrel over her, and then leave her. The set was a sparse Daliesque landscape.

To a frantic score by Leonard Bernstein, the three insecure people (the integrated ones never appeared) rolled on the floor, kissed indiscriminately, tussled. Then the two men tossed Nora Kaye back and forth like a shuttlecock until she fell sobbing on the floor (on opening night she went down so hard that many seat holders thought she had sprained her ankle). At this point, ballerina Kaye cried out "Stop!" One unkind critic felt she had said everything that needed saying.

Although there were those who thought the choreographic movements in *Facsimile* were an improvement over the motions of *Fancy Free*, they were in the minority. The general reaction to the sadistic treatment of the woman was so intense that by April 1947 the company presented a revised version that was not only less offensive but even provided a few laughs. Here a trivial resourceless woman trifles with two trivial resourceless men. John Martin, drama critic of the *Times*, thought "it was less sardonic than satirical." Bernstein's music, in any event, was tough, witty, and colorful. But critics were beginning to complain that his scores were derivative. That may have been a function of his remarkable memory. Stravinsky once said of himself that it was because he had such a bad memory that he had to be original.

Bernstein's concerns with humanity that went back to his Harvard years of meetings and marches apparently continued unabated. In November 1947, his first article appeared in *The New York Times*, "The Negro in Music." Bernstein said many things that needed to be said. He wrote, "There is not a single Negro musician employed in any of the major symphony orchestras, and that goes right down the list. There are no Negroes employed in the orchestras of the ballet or opera companies...." He attributed the situation not to malevolence on the part of directors but to the absence of training opportunities for black musicians. In the summer of that year, probably when he was working on the article, Bernstein accompanied Marian Anderson in a recital of Handel arias and black spirituals before twenty thousand people in Lewisohn Stadium.

Just before the fall season of the City Symphony, Bernstein's last one with the orchestra, he began a work based on W. H. Auden's long poem *The Age of Anxiety.* That fall a game of musical chairs was being played out in New York among some of the greatest conductors of the world. At seventy, Bruno Walter accepted a one-year appointment as musical adviser of the New York Philharmonic, a job he had turned down four years before because, he had said then, he was too old. The management of the New York orchestra was using the 1947–1948 season to shop for a permanent conductor. The year's guest conductors were the favorites in the race: Dimitri Mitropoulos of the Minneapolis Symphony, George Szell of the Cleveland Orchestra, Charles Munch of Paris, and the Hollywood Bowl's Leopold Stokowski. All but Stokowski were clients of New York Philharmonic manager Arthur Judson. At one time even Stokowski had been a client. Bruno Walter, a pre-Hitler conductor at the Vienna State Opera, was at his greatest conducting Mozart, Beethoven, Brahms, Mahler, and Bruckner. His weakness was that he did little else. The big question was who would replace Walter after his one-year tenure.

Although Bernstein was concentrating at the City Center on American compositions and on the European neoclassicists, the biggest event of this season was his conducting of the Mahler *Resurrection* Symphony. This was a work that Bernstein had had trouble conducting in 1943 when Rodzinski had handed him his baton at a rehearsal. Now Bernstein was conquering the piece. It was the first Mahler he had ever conducted, and he was pleased with the results. "Given the fact that the Mahler I conducted last Monday night," he told reporters, "was the first thing by that composer I ever did, it was darned good. But there's no use giving me credit or lambasting me on that ground alone. After all, practically anything I do is the first time for me. I've only been around three years." In that sense the City Symphony had been enormously useful for him. "I have done more there in repertoire than in any other place in the world. What I have learned astonishes me."

Bernstein conducted the *Symphony for Classical Orchestra* by Harold

Shapero, his Harvard schoolmate, with the Boston Symphony in the spring of 1948 and gave concerts with the Hague Orchestra. Then came a concert at Lewisohn Stadium, followed by Tanglewood. He took a house in Richmond, Massachusetts, where he managed to work on his score for the Auden poem. At the end of the summer, Bernstein decided to drive his new Buick convertible to some isolated spot out west to continue work on his new piece. He also decided to take his brother along. The British poet Stephen Spender had been visiting Tanglewood at the time and suggested that they join him at the ranch that belonged to Frieda Lawrence, the widow of D. H. Lawrence, in Taos, New Mexico. The isolation of the place was intolerable to Bernstein and within the week he fled with his brother to Sheridan, Wyoming, where they had been invited by a Tanglewood student to spend time on his family's cattle ranch. Burton reports that they "plunged into the strenuous Wyoming life, working, in effect, as hired ranch hands from dawn to dusk and then drinking beer in town at night with the local cowboys." The conditions on the ranch were not conducive to composition.

In the fall of 1948 Bernstein conducted the Philadelphia Orchestra for the first time. He chose to introduce himself to that city with a work the musicians had never played before: Bartók's *Music for Strings, Percussion, and Celesta*. Irving Kolodin in the *Saturday Review* wrote, "Only a conductor as young and uninhibited as Bernstein would confront an audience for the first time with a work of this complexity. For that matter, only one with his authority and domination of such a score could have carried it through to so convincing a climax. One who recalls the imagery accomplished with his eager if unskilled [City] symphony found even more remarkable Bernstein's address with these masters of the craft."

He conducted many of the same American works as in 1946— Harris's Third Symphony, Gershwin's *Rhapsody in Blue*, his own *Jeremiah*—and additionally Barber's *Capricorn* Concerto, in a 1948 European tour that included Munich, Milan, Budapest, Vienna, Paris, and Scheveningen. The plan he had written about to Diamond of cutting down his touring did not materialize. The most important visit of the year, however, seems to have been the one to Israel that he started only a few months after the end of the War of Independence. In mid-September, Bernstein left the United States to become the musical director and conductor of the seventy-eight-man Israel Philharmonic from October 2 to December 1.

The official concerts—seven in eight days—took place in Jerusalem, Tel Aviv, and Haifa. But when Bernstein called for volunteers who wished to go farther, thirty-five musicians joined him, piled into two dusty buses, crossed the Negev desert to Beersheba, the battle-scarred Old Testament town. There they gave the first symphony concert in its history. Israel had been ordered to evacuate Beersheba by the United Nations the day before but had refused. Bernstein conducted a concert of Mozart, Beethoven, and Gershwin. While he was playing *Rhapsody in Blue* his chair, balanced tenuously on a pile of flat rocks, began to slip. Bernstein stood up and continued to play while the first violinist adjusted the seat. Bernstein had played the piano standing up at parties during his high school days. He had played the piano standing up in 1940 when, between rehearsals for a student performance of *The Peace,* he rehearsed Beethoven concertos for a performance of his own. But this was the first time that his playing the piano standing up was reported in the press.

For the last concert in Tel Aviv, Bernstein played the Mahler *Resurrection* Symphony, the work he had played for the first time with the City Symphony the year before. After concerts in Rome, he returned to the United States. There he told reporters he had arranged to go to Israel for a still longer engagement the following year. Bernstein said he was thinking of establishing a permanent connection with the orchestra, dividing his time between Israel and the United States.

Bernstein and the Israeli orchestra had worked at a formidable pace. They had played more than forty concerts in sixty days, touring every part of the country under the most difficult conditions, often playing to soldiers within the sounds of gunfire.

Azaria Rapoport, now coordinator of Israel projects for B'nai Zion, was an Israeli soldier assigned to accompany Bernstein on the tour. "The traveling from Tel Aviv," he recalls, "was still dangerous and there was an alternate route we used which was called the Burma Road. Everyone had great admiration for Bernstein not only because of the warmth of his music but because of his nerve. His tour to Beersheba was particularly courageous. The day after the liberation they cleared out the rubble in the center of town and he conducted Mahler's *Resurrection* Symphony with Jennie Tourel singing. In Beersheba Bernstein conducted and played a Mozart concerto. In Tel Aviv I remember him conducting and playing both Mozart and Ravel.

"When Bernstein came to Israel," Rapoport goes on, "he felt a big excitement there. He wanted to identify both with the fighting and with the state. He saw in me and a few friends a symbol of Israel and became infatuated with the historic occasion. He came again and again. He was involved with every dugout, every battle. He visited every place that had been taken. He traveled all across Israel between the concerts into places the orchestra could not go."

In Israel, according to Rapoport, Bernstein worked on the part of *The Age of Anxiety* entitled "The Dirge." "It reflected the mood of the country in mourning," Rapoport says. "Being so close to the end of the war, with six thousand dead and twenty thousand wounded, everybody lost someone. The coincidence was obvious. Bernstein would read paragraphs from Auden's poem with excitement, and then he would read chapters from the Bible with an inner glow. He was also interested in World War II and how it was won. Bernstein loved the Song of Songs and wrote about it in Hebrew. There was his link with his Jewish heritage and he seemed to need to identify with it. How many boys from a Boston suburb know the Song of Songs and Jeremiah, and can speak Hebrew? He spoke of his father with warmth. He also spoke about Mahler and the need to appreciate him. I remember that Mahler's conversion to Christianity presented a problem for him. He spoke of it more than he spoke of Koussevitzky's but that was because Mahler was dead. I believe that what occupied his thought then was Koussevitzky's conversion and he could not come to terms with it."

Bernstein was then reassessing his ties. As early as August 1947, he had written to Diamond, "I had a home-going this week, which turned out to be a splendid and relaxing visit! What a wonderful family I have! Once I can break the old chains, I can really feel very warm about them."

As for his feelings about Koussevitzky, Olga Koussevitzky's niece, who lived with the Koussevitzkys from 1947 to 1949, staying with them at Seranak, a large and beautiful old house on the Tanglewood grounds, says, "In the beginning there was a great bond between Bernstein and Koussevitzky. Then it lessened. Bernstein was critical of him at times. He almost made fun of him. I never understood this because Koussevitzky was a wonderful human being. He did more for contemporary music than anyone, including Stokowski."

Other friends report Bernstein's mocking of Koussevitzky. Koussevitzky did do more for contemporary music than any other conductor, particularly contemporary American music. Still, if one wanted to mock someone, there were aspects of Koussevitzky that made him vulnerable. For one thing his vocabulary in English was severely limited. For another he never learned to read a score. For a third he always had difficulty counting; old recordings testify to that. Still Koussevitzky was a powerful force in the music world. By 1940, the year he took Bernstein under his wing, he was a conductor who possessed the big line and the big gesture. With color and drama in everything he did, his performances were memorable. In the last decade of his life, Koussevitzky was considered one of the great conductors of his time.

By 1949, Bernstein no longer could look to him for the Boston Symphony post. That was when he began to question Koussevitzky's ways, most particularly his defection from Judaism. It was at precisely this time that Bernstein dedicated *The Age of Anxiety*, his second symphony, to the older conductor.

Bernstein's dedications invariably came after the period of his dependence on or intense intoxication with the dedicatee had ended. In 1939, when he saw his father in only the darkest hues, he dedicated *Jeremiah* to him. In the early years, of 1947, when Jennie Tourel had been replaced by Felicia as the primary female in his life, he dedicated *La Bonne Cuisine* to her. In 1949, when Bernstein was looking to Israel to provide the security of an orchestra post, and Koussevitzky played no role at all in that, he gave the old man his Symphony No. 2. Bernstein appears to have used a dedication as a kind of consolation prize. It was a gift to compensate for the withdrawal of his love. With it he must have felt he had paid whatever debt he owed.

Sam Bernstein, the son and grandson of rabbis, was
a talmudic scholar. As soon as his firstborn could comprehend, he
taught the boy everything he knew. When Leonard began to rebel
and to resist his father on matters of style, language, and métier,
he resisted him on religious grounds as well. Throughout his life

© WHITESTONE PHOTO / HEINZ H. WEISSENSTEIN

"Bernstein's choice of Felicia Montealegre over all of the Jewish women he had known
reflected the same ambivalence about his heritage."

Bernstein's connections to Judaism remained as fragmented as his connections to virtually everything else.

Bernstein's behavior toward God was like his behavior toward his father and other father figures. Initially awed by Sam Bernstein, Koussevitzky, and Rodzinski, he wrestled with them and brought them under his control. Bernstein's God is on Bernstein's side. Bernstein's belief in the magical significance of coincidence—his appointment with the New York Philharmonic coming on his twenty-fifth birthday, which fell on the twenty-fifth day of the month; his meeting with Aaron Copland falling on Copland's birthday, which turned out to be the very same day of the same month, some years later, that Bernstein filled in for Bruno Walter—reassured him that he was touched by God.

To believe that one is loved by God and endowed with gifts only He can endow does not carry with it the implication that such a person will be docile before Him. In fact the Hasidic belief in personal confrontation with God is the one Bernstein seems to have adopted since his adolescence. When he had just turned into his teens, he assumed a stance of combatant with the Lord. Those were the days he was charging his friend Sid Ramin a dollar a lesson plus a few candy bars. Once, when a lesson fell on Passover, which imposed particular dietary restrictions, Ramin handed Bernstein the dollar. But he held back the candy bars, because he didn't know precisely what he should do about them. Bernstein was quick to show the contempt he held for such ritual. Ripping off the wrappers, he gobbled them down.

A similar incident happened at Harvard, where Mitropoulos offered Bernstein the oyster from his own fork. According to Bernstein's own description, he "slurped" it down with gusto, reveling in an act that was at least anti-Jewish, at most anti-God. Even after his debut the pattern continued. In 1945, when Moyshe Kuzevizky, the great cantor who had been interned in concentration camps in Poland, was singing at a Brooklyn synagogue for the High Holy Days, Bernstein went with Jennie Tourel and Friede Rothe. Rothe says, "It was a glorious Kol Nidre, a cry out of the deep. Everyone was overcome. Yet immediately afterwards Lenny bolted out of the synagogue into an Italian restaurant. Not only was there no question of fasting; he ate a large meal, and he ate it right away."

Bernstein's choice of Felicia Montealegre over all of the Jewish women he had known reflected the same ambivalence about his heritage. Although Felicia's father was a Jew—her great-grandfather had been a renowned rabbi who founded San Francisco's Temple Emanu-El—she presented herself as a Roman Catholic and always distanced herself whenever Yiddish was used, insisting she could not pick up a word. Despite such a claim, she told Bernstein she had been drawn to him because he reminded her of her own father.

However anti-Jewish some of Bernstein's behavior might have been, his deep connection to his own father is reflected not only in the fact that he didn't change his name, but also in the music he composed. In *Jeremiah*, the listener hears prayer cadences, and biblical chants. At the time he composed it Bernstein said, "The symphony does not make use to any great extent of actual Hebrew thematic material. The first theme of the scherzo is paraphrased from a traditional Hebrew chant, and the opening phrase of the vocal part in Lamentation is based on a liturgical cadence still sung today in commemoration of the destruction of Jerusalem by Babylon. Other resemblances to Hebrew liturgical music are a matter of emotional quality rather than the notes themselves."

Bernstein finished *Jeremiah* on December 30, 1942, eight months before he became assistant to Rodzinski. Almost five years passed before he began his next concert piece, *The Age of Anxiety*. Bernstein completed this, his second symphony, a work for large orchestra, on February 9, 1949, and orchestrated it in six weeks. At the bottom of the last page, which he completed on March 20, he wrote, "NYC— the first day of spring."

In April 1949, only weeks after Bernstein completed the score, Koussevitzky gave the work its world premier in Boston with the composer at the piano. Like *Jeremiah*, it was certified fight away. The Boston Symphony gave Bernstein a one-thousand-dollar Merit Award, and Koussevitzky, delighted his protégé was now devoting his composing energies to "serious" music, even reconciled himself to Bernstein's language: "It is very interesting music," he confided to friends, "and you know, the third movement, it is a jezz."

For that performance, and for those that followed, Bernstein wrote program notes describing the work. Perhaps the most striking revelation comes in discussing Part II: The "Dirge," which Azaria Rapoport believed to have been composed in reaction to the loss of the Jews, reflects, according to Bernstein, a mourning for "the loss of the 'colossal Dad,' the great leader who can always give the right orders, find the right solution, shoulder the mass responsibility, and satisfy the universal needs for a father-symbol." Koussevitzky, who a decade before had fulfilled that role so thoroughly, clearly no longer did. Here is a part of those program notes:

> Auden's fascinating and hair-raising "eclogue" had already begun to affect me lyrically when I first read it in the summer of 1947. From that moment the composition of a symphony based on *The Age of Anxiety* acquired an almost compulsive quality; and I have been writing it steadily since then, in Taos, in Philadelphia, in Richmond, Mass., in Tel Aviv, in planes, in hotel lobbies, and finally (the week preceding the première) in Boston. The orchestration was made during a month-long tour with the Pittsburgh Symphony.
>
> I imagine that the composition of a symphony with a piano solo emerges from the extremely personal identification of myself with the poem. In this sense the pianist provides an almost autobiographical protagonist, set against an orchestral mirror in which he sees himself, analytically, in the modern ambience. The work is therefore no "concerto" in the virtuosic sense, although I regard Auden's poem as one of the most shattering examples of pure virtuosity in the history of British poetry.
>
> The essential line of the poem (and of the music) is the record of our difficult and problematical search for faith. In the end, two of the characters enunciate the recognition of this faith—even a passive submission to it—at the same time revealing an inability to relate to it personally in their daily lives, except through blind acceptance.
>
> No one could be more astonished than I at the extent to which the programmaticism of this work has been carried. I have never planned a "meaningful" work, at least not in the sense of a piece whose meaning relied on details of programmatic implication I was merely writing a symphony inspired by

a poem and following the general form of that poem. Yet, when each section was finished, I discovered, upon rereading, detail after detail of programmatic relation to the poem—details that had "written themselves" wholly unplanned and unconscious. Since I trust the unconscious implicitly, finding it a source of wisdom and the dictator of the condign in artistic matters, I am content to leave these details in the score.

For example, I recently discovered, upon rereading the "Masque" movement that it actually strikes four o'clock! Now there is no mention of four o'clock in the poem; there is only the feeling that it is very late at night, that everyone is tired, that the jokes are petering out, and that everyone is valiantly trying to keep them going. So we find the music petering out, while the celesta strikes four as naively as day and the percussion instruments cheerfully make a new stab at energetic gaiety. I was thrilled to find this in the score, since I had not really "written" it. It had simply been put there by some inner sense of theatricality.

If the charge of "theatricality" in a symphonic work is a valid one, I am willing to plead guilty. I have a deep suspicion that every work I write, for whatever medium, is really theater music in some way and nothing has convinced me more than these new discoveries of the unconscious hand that has been at work all along in *The Age of Anxiety*.

I have divided Auden's six sections into two large parts, each containing three sections played without pause. A brief outline follows:

Part One:

(a) The *Prologue* finds four lonely characters, a girl and three men, in a Third Avenue bar, all of them insecure and trying, through drink, to detach themselves from their conflicts, or, at best, to resolve them. They are drawn together by this common urge and begin a kind of symposium on the state of man. Musically the *Prologue* is a very short section consisting of a lonely improvisation by two clarinets, echotone, and followed by a long descending scale which acts as a bridge into the realm of the unconscious, where most of the poem takes place.

(b) The Seven Ages. The life of man is reviewed from the four personal points....

And so he goes for several more paragraphs explaining a long piece of music based on a long poem. If it is necessary to read all of this to comprehend the music, it is reasonable to ask about the function of the music and of the Auden poem, and whether in fact Bernstein is trying to inundate the poem if not the poet with his exegesis, as though Auden himself had become yet another father figure to be annihilated with a torrent of words.

During the summer of 1949, Bernstein conducted the Boston Symphony Orchestra in *The Age of Anxiety* at Tanglewood with Lukas Foss at the piano. Rodzinski, by then out of the New York Philharmonic, no longer stood in Bernstein's way. He was at Tanglewood at the time.

Years later Rodzinski told this story: "Bernstein was then teaching conducting at the Berkshire Festival—think of it, teaching conducting after such a short time. He was lecturing on his *Age of Anxiety*, and he asked me to come to the lecture. 'Doctor,' he said, 'would you please come to my lecture?' So I went. It was wonderful, intriguing, a great success. He delivered his lecture beautifully. Then he went to the piano to play the score and as he stood before the piano, before he started to play, he caught sight of me sitting in the class and he said very gaily, 'Arturo, would you turn the pages of the score for me?' He didn't call me 'Doctor' then. I said I forgot my reading glasses.... Later he said to me, 'Of course the last movement is strictly Warner Brothers.' He said that himself. He can never make up his mind whether he belongs to Broadway, Hollywood, or Carnegie Hall."

In 1972, Bernstein addressed the issue of the last movement in an interview with Phillip Ramey, a composer and later an annotator for the New York Philharmonic program notes.

RAMEY: Olin Downes once denigrated the ending of *Age of Anxiety* as being a "sort of tinsel-bourgeois evocation of some distant plush paradise" while Virgil Thomson saw it as a "finale out of Strauss's *Death and Transfiguration*." Was your

1965 revision of the finale a response to such criticism?"

BERNSTEIN: No. But let me explain for it's rather complicated. In the original version of the Finale, the piano—who is the protagonist, remember—is silent and that was part of the theatrical concept. At the time, I had some notion about contemplating faith on a movie screen—a Bette Davis version of faith if you will, faith as seen on the silver screen. So, my original idea for the whole big end was to produce a kind of mockery of faith, a phony faith. The piano was to be detached from all this and, consequently, was to be silent and only play one chord of affirmation at the end.

RAMEY: In other words, that one chord was to be the only real thing in the finale.

BERNSTEIN: Right.

RAMEY: But if this was all part of the original theatrical concept, why did you eventually come to feel that you must involve the piano?

BERNSTEIN: Because a strange thing happened when I looked over the score years later. I had thought I was making a big Hollywood version of faith in the finale but I realized then that I meant every note. So the silence of the piano didn't work, and I rewrote the ending, even giving the piano a cadenza near the coda. I suppose the original didn't work because I had once been trying to convince myself that I was talking about faith—once removed—and it just wasn't true. Also, there seemed to be something very odd about the solo piano sitting there during the whole finale—and pianists complained.

What had been "fake" to Bernstein when he created it turned out to be "real" to him later on. A little less than a year after the premiere of the work in Boston, Bernstein conducted it with the New York Philharmonic and Lukas Foss at the piano, with the last movement scored as it had been at Tanglewood. Olin Downes, in his review, did more than characterize the last movement as one that was laden with "tinsel," he also said it was "wholly exterior in its style, ingeniously constructed, effectively orchestrated, and a triumph of superficiality." After remarking that "as emotional commentary … it is counterpoint, not emotion," Downes went on to soften his judgment. "Is not the glitter of this score, its restlessness, its unease, its obvious artificiality, precisely the sincere expression by a young musician of today, of today's 'anxiety'?"

Not only does Bernstein's "fake" become "real," Downes's "superficiality" is transformed into "sincerity." Clearly the post-World War II years were confusing ones for art.

But if Bernstein was not continually anxious over the Berlin Wall, the atom bomb, the state of blacks in music, he surely might have been made anxious by the continual carping of critics over the complaint that he was spreading himself "too thin." In 1949, in response to this pressure, Bernstein made a statement to the *Times*:

> It is impossible for me to make an exclusive choice among the various activities of conducting, symphonic composition, writing for the theater, or playing the piano. What seems right for me at any given moment is what I must do, at the expense of pigeon-holing or otherwise limiting my service to music. I will not compose a note while my heart is engaged in a conducting session; nor will I give up so much as a popular song while it is there to be expressed, in order to conduct Beethoven's Ninth. There is a particular order in this which is admittedly difficult to plan; but the order must be adhered to strictly. For the ends are music itself, not the conventions of the music publishing business, and the means are my own personal problem....

Maria von Leuchtenberg de Beauharnais, Olga Koussevitzky's niece, belonging to a European noble family, was Koussevitzky's first choice as a wife for his protégé. Koussevitzky called Maria by the diminutive "Mashenka" and Bernstein by the diminutive "Lenyushka." Despite Koussevitzky's hopes, no liaison developed and, in 1949, Maria married Joseph DePasquale, then the Boston Symphony's first violist. During the years after his broken engagement, Bernstein's connections were homosexual. Although, for the most part, he kept his behavior under wraps in the United

States, in Europe Bernstein behaved as he wished.

Jonathan Sternberg, an auditor of Koussevitzky's conducting class at Tanglewood, remembers a sunny day in Paris in the late 1940s when Bernstein and his sister arrived at Gare Saint-Lazare. As usual, when Bernstein was present, there was considerable commotion. One of the details Sternberg noticed during the melee was that Bernstein wore an "enormous chronograph watch on his left hand. Because I often fumbled over my own watch when I conducted, I asked Bernstein if when he conducted, he took his watch off. I've never forgotten the answer. He said, 'When I conduct I take everything off.'" Sternberg recalls Bernstein showing him a little black book filled with names of cafés frequented by homosexuals, which he had gathered from concierges in Paris. Some weeks later, the two shared a box at the Vienna Volksoper for a performance of *The Gypsy Baron.* "The baritone was holding a live pig in his arms," Sternberg says, "and the pig peed, making a great arc into the orchestra. Lenny loved it. He shouted an enthusiastic response. Naturally everyone in the house turned to look at him."

Bernstein's uninhibited ways surely played a significant role in keeping him from securing the posts he wanted. During the 1940s, he was in the running for the Rochester Symphony. When the job went to someone else, the rumors were that he had been turned down because of anti-Semitism on the board. But David Diamond, a native of Rochester, says that although he would not deny this was a possible reason, he believes Bernstein's homosexuality was the more important factor. Diamond's assessment appears to be correct, for Erich Leinsdorf, a descendant of a highly cultivated Jewish family, was named conductor of the orchestra in 1947.

The difficulty homosexuality could cause during this period is well illustrated with a bizarre story connected to the Boston Symphony post. Mitropoulos, among others, was under consideration as Koussevitzky's successor. Mitropoulos said to several of his close friends that Bernstein had actually told him that Bernstein had informed on Mitropoulos's homosexuality because he wanted the post so much for himself. One cannot know if Bernstein did what Mitropoulos claimed, but if it is true, Bernstein made whatever remarks he reportedly made during the period when he was first engaged to Felicia.

Over the years Mitropoulos suffered the effects of turning his back on Bernstein as an assistant in Minneapolis in 1939 and 1940, and as a composer throughout his career. Despite his championing works of other American composers—Morton Gould, Samuel Barber, Gunther Schuller, and David Diamond among them—he never conducted Bernstein. Diamond tried to help his friend by sending Mitropoulos the score to *Jeremiah*. Faith Reed, Mitropoulos's secretary, says that Mitropoulos turned it down with a covering letter that questioned why "Bernstein had to write such Jewish music. What he meant," Reed explained in 1985, "was that *he* didn't write *Greek* music."

Toward the end of his life Mitropoulos characterized Bernstein as a man ungrateful for the kindnesses he had extended to him. But, in reality, the only kindnesses Mitropoulos had extended were the checks he sent to Bernstein for a trip to Minneapolis during a Christmas holiday from Harvard and to supplement the forty dollars a month Sam Bernstein sent during the two years Leonard was at Curtis. Perhaps the suggestion that Bernstein study conducting was a kindness, too, however it was intended.

In 1949, along with Leopold Stokowski, Mitropoulos was named principal co-conductor of the New York Philharmonic. There were two guests that season. One was Victor de Sabata, the leading conductor at La Scala and a recent guest with the Pittsburgh Symphony. The other was Bernstein. That year he had even rescinded his decision not to conduct in Austria or Germany. After his tour in Israel and his concert with the St. Cecilia Orchestra in Rome in 1946, he had gone into Germany and received a tremendous ovation when he conducted the Bavarian State Orchestra in front of a German and American audience. He also made some kind of history when he directed an orchestra of displaced persons at two former concentration camps near Munich.

During the late 1940s Bernstein received his greatest renown as a guest conductor. No longer "permitted" by Koussevitzky to compose for Broadway, being obliged to inhibit his theatrical flair and to confine his jazz in art works, conducting had become Bernstein's primary career activity. Conducting was the only musical activity through which he could earn the income he wanted. All the *Jeremiah*s in the world could never produce the equivalent of the $100,000 he had earned from *On the Town*. But guest conducting engagements could add up to a livable sum. In 1949, after totaling up the ballots from seven hundred critics and editors, the magazine *Musical America* gave Bernstein an award as "the best guest conductor." Other awards that year: Toscanini for the sixth time in a row as "the best regular symphony conductor," Fritz Reiner for "conducting the Met's broadcast of *Salome*," and Arthur Fiedler of the Boston Pops as "the best program conductor." The prize must have carried with it a hollow ring for Bernstein. Everyone thought him a dazzling "guest," but nobody wanted to live with him.

Even the Israel Philharmonic (formerly the Palestine Symphony Orchestra), for which Bernstein had held such high hopes, turned into a disappointment for him. In 1949, the year after his pronouncements about how the orchestra needed a consistent directorship and a new space in which to perform, concerts were still taking place under a variety of leaders and in movie houses in Haifa and Jerusalem and an eleven-hundred-seat hall in Tel Aviv.

The history of the orchestra, not surprisingly, mirrors the history of the nation; the primary concern for both was independence. Starting, in 1936, as a cooperative for the musicians, the ensemble had increased its performances from ninety a year to almost two hundred in the 1949–1950 season without a permanent conductor. Developing steadily against the background of Arab disturbances, World War II, and the Israeli War of Independence, with musicians traveling in armored cars under fire, the group seemed unlikely ever to surrender its autonomy and give an outsider the authority to hire and fire its members.

Bernstein's efforts to maneuver the orchestra into choosing him as permanent director led to an ambitious tour of the United States under the auspices of the American Fund for Israel Institutions at the end of 1950. But even here Bernstein was thwarted for he shared the podium not only with the Christian convert Koussevitzky, but with Eleazar de Carvalho. Although the conductors made a point of including a few Israeli works, the bulk of the programs came from the standard repertory. There were complaints from the press: "Hearing Koussevitzky or Bernstein is a pleasure," Virgil Thomson wrote, "even when the pieces played have little to offer that is fresh to the ear. But bringing a whole orchestra from Tel Aviv to America just to offer these excellent artists in their familiar repertory is surely like bringing perfume to Paris. Has Israel no confidence in its own conductors? Or its own music?

Bernstein fared no better in his quest for a music directorship with the Israel Philharmonic than he had with the Boston and Rochester orchestras. In each instance Bernstein's expectations failed to materialize.

It was during this frustrating time that Bernstein wrote *The Age of Anxiety*. He believed his Symphony No. 2 called for a more prestigious publisher than Harms. It had published Jerome Kern, George Gershwin, Richard Rodgers, Cole Porter, Harold Arlen, and Vernon Duke, as well as Bernstein's *I Hate Music*, Clarinet Sonata, *Seven Anniversaries*, *Jeremiah*, and *On the Town*, a mixed bag of works. But with the firm's concentration on show music, it projected an image that Bernstein then wanted to leave behind. In 1948 he made a deal with the venerable house of G. Schirmer for a three-year contract with a guarantee of two thousand dollars a year against royalties. Hans Heinsheimer, an executive with Schirmer at the time, recalls, "It was a little more than usual but by then Bernstein was a well-known conductor and composer." Gus Schirmer, running the family business, took to Bernstein immediately and became a kind of confidant to him.

In 1950 Bernstein started to record with Columbia Records. By then Decca had issued a disc of Bernstein conducting the Ballet Theater Orchestra in *Fancy Free* with Billie Holiday singing "Big Stuff." Victor had issued the rest: Bernstein conducting *Facsimile* with the RCA Victor Orchestra; Bernstein playing the piano in Copland's Piano Sonata, a major work that had been commissioned by Clifford Odets in 1939 and took up five sides of a six-side seventy-eight-r.p.m. album (on the last side Bernstein played three miniatures from his *Seven Anniversaries*).

Though Bernstein was clearly trying to upgrade his image, in the spring of 1950, he agreed to write both the words and the music for a Broadway production of *Peter Pan*. The subject must have seduced him. Here was a play celebrating a boy who refuses to grow up, who would rather battle the formidable Captain Hook than go to school or take a job. With Jean Arthur and Boris Karloff playing the leading roles, and Bernstein's energetic, unsentimental score, the play avoided being sticky and proved a considerable success. The three children in the James Barrie classic actually had real-life counterparts in Lenny, Shirley, and Burtie. Only weeks after the opening, the three took off for a summer in Europe, though Lenny left the others from time to time to conduct major orchestras. During this tour, Bernstein moved into a place where brave men would have feared to tread. In Scheveningen, with the Hague Orchestra, he conducted the Mahler *Resurrection* Symphony, the work first introduced to the world in that same city in 1904 by the great Willem Mengelberg. It is hard to believe that the man who created such a personal triumph with the *Resurrection* Symphony that year in Holland is the man described here by his brother:

> From the moment we fastened our seat belts on the airliner to Paris, the three of us regressed to our old, puerile, Rybernian form. The private jokes and allusions, the uncontrollable giggles and mad laughter, the infantile sense of sheer pleasure in one another's existence poured out nonstop, no matter how many eyebrows were raised in bemusement. It was difficult for the Europeans we encountered to fathom a brash young American maestro who didn't use a baton and moved athletically on the podium; it was impossible for them to comprehend one who blended in quite happily with his dribbling siblings. Were we being vulgar Americans, loud Jews? we didn't care. Throughout the tour, it was as if there were only three people on earth and we were the fortunate trio.
>
> The self-perpetuating fun carried us mindlessly through France, England, Scotland, Holland, West Germany, and Ireland. In Paris, where we stayed longest, Lenny was the *"chef d'orchestre distingué"* to everyone, and it was endlessly amusing to Shirley and me that the *chef*—our very own Lennuhtt—would mumble asides in Rybernian even as he was being lionized by some terribly grand *comtesse*. We could hardly wait to leave elegant receptions and special excursions to cultural landmarks so we could rush back to our hotel for some unmuffled jokes, and, of all things, a long game of Canasta. Canasta—loud, riotous, hysterical Canasta—was the obsession of the tour. We played it not only in hotel rooms but in any enclosed space, secluded or otherwise: planes, trains, green rooms at intermission, waiting rooms, lobbies, and, on one memorable occasion, a taxi speeding across Ireland—the melds and packs balanced on laps and tucked into upholstery crevices, behind

the rate card and the lap-robe holder, while the driver snatched astonished glances in his rearview mirror. Perhaps the zenith of our exclusive insanity (and rudeness) was our stay as guests in a Donegal castle—there, among British nobility, artists, and a deferential staff of deerstalkers, gillies, maids, chars, and an aged butler named Whiteside, we carried on as though we were in our own Sharon living room....[1]

The host of this particular visit told American friends that Bernstein astonished other guests by leaving the dining table first, even when dukes and duchesses were present. And that the servant assigned to bring breakfast to the rooms would invariably find Bernstein with his sister and brother, all under the same blanket.

Burton ends this reminiscence:

When they saw me off on the plane at Shannon, it was a grievous parting. While we hadn't advanced the cause of American civilization much, we did have a spectacularly good time, a kind of last fling with our Rybernian childhood, our arrested development. We knew that sooner or later we three—especially *chef d'orchestre distingué*, thirty-two-year-old Lenny—would have to grow up, and that things would never be quite the same again.[1]

Bernstein's guilt about his homosexuality expressed itself not only in declarations to heterosexual male friends about an occasional attraction to a woman, it also revealed itself in remarks on his regret that he was the way that he was. There were many such examples. During the early 1940s, the Revuers days, Judy Holliday

HERSCHEL LEVIT

An obviously disconcerted Felicia, with Shirley, during the summer of 1947, when Bernstein was about to break their engagement. (Later, in 1951, a photograph of him smiling politely with his arm around the waist of his beaming bride accompanied a note he wrote for his book Findings, *describing himself as having become a "very well behaviorized chimpanzee.")*

was a lesbian. She later married and probably remained heterosexual the rest of her life. But at the time of her entrance into show business, she and her lover, a policewoman, shared an apartment that contained a pool table and was generally crowded with their lesbian friends. Once, when the policewoman entered the living room, she found Bernstein at the piano with tears running down his face. When she asked what had happened, he answered that everyone in the room was homosexual and that was reason enough for him to cry.

In the late 1940s, Bernstein embarked on a friendship with a young furniture designer named Harvey Probber. A story told by Probber illuminates Bernstein's ambivalent attitude toward heterosexuality while living in a homosexual world. Bernstein walked into Probber's showroom one day and, says Probber, "fell in love with the furniture and me." Probber went to Bernstein's Park Avenue apartment to advise him on how to decorate it and the two men became close friends.

In 1949 they took a train to Key West. This was after Bernstein had completed *The Age of Anxiety* and had lost any chance of succeeding Koussevitzky with the Boston Symphony. Bernstein was working on *Peter Pan*. Probber says that on the train to Florida, "he was trying to compose the Wendy song, 'Peter, Peter,' while lying down in the berth above mine. He explained to me how he generally composed, how he got the music in his eyes and ears and then set it down on paper. But it wasn't working for him then. When I suggested he use a song he had written for Comden—which had never been published or recorded— substituting 'Peter, Peter' for 'Betty, Betty,' Lenny shouted 'Done' with delight. Comden never forgave me for that, for taking her song away from her."

In Key West the two men went to bars. Probber says that Bernstein liked the seedy areas, enjoyed slumming with "the low life." At a bar they sat at a table and were joined by a man and a woman. "I went for the woman," Probber says, "who turned out to be very cool. Then I found she was a lesbian. Lenny went for the boy. He asked me to wait in the car and then disappeared for an hour and a half. When he came back he described exactly what had gone on. He told me how the boy had licked his toes and how much he had loved all of that. But he also spoke of his own self-loathing, of the contempt he felt for himself for being the way he was."

Probber says that on the train home, Bernstein told him it had been a wonderful trip and that "he was so glad I wasn't gay. He said he couldn't have stood it if I were. He rumpled my hair in my eyes as he said this, the only sign of physical affection he made during the whole trip."

When they got home, Bernstein suggested they share an apartment. They looked at ten- and twelve-room apartments on East End Avenue and a penthouse on Central Park West. "I was uneasy," Probber says. "First there was the guilt by association. Everyone knew Lenny was gay. Then I found myself becoming increasingly engulfed by him. I became more and more concerned with *his* career, *his* friends, *his* parties. I was afraid of being swallowed up by him and knew I would have to get out—or die."

In describing his own background, Probber says it was similar to Bernstein's, "but I was younger, uneducated, shy, discreet, with little interest in classical music. I was neither promiscuous nor homosexual, and even then I had the feeling that Lenny hoped these last traits would rub off on him."

Probber sang with a dance band. "I was a baritone," he says, "with a sweet, untrained voice, something like Dick Haymes. Lenny told me that if we had met a few years before, he would have used me as Gabey in *On the Town*."

Once Bernstein arranged for a date between Probber and his sister. Probber remembers her as being "talkative and very impressed with her famous brother." Probber had been dating a girl from Mount Holyoke, Shirley's college, and once or twice she brought along a friend for Leonard. "Nothing much happened," Probber says. But he recalls one Sunday afternoon driving back from Leighton's, a restaurant in Westchester, when the girls asked him to sing something. "I did it reluctantly," he says. "It brought Lenny to a dead silence. He couldn't bear it." Bernstein was never able to tolerate attention being drawn away from him.

Even so, Bernstein brought this non-classical musician and heterosexual man into the fabric of his life. On the stage of the music shed at Tanglewood, he introduced Probber to Koussevitzky. He had Probber sit in the waiting room of his psychoanalyst in Lenox while Bernstein underwent his hour of treatment. He would bring him along to a restaurant for a dinner with such friends as Copland and Blitzstein.

Bernstein even brought Probber with him on his only visit to Toscanini. "We went to Riverdale," Probber says, "and there was this formal meeting in Toscanini's cathedral-style house. He was tiny, pale, aloof, Sicilian looking, like a mini-don. He didn't smile. There was no warmth." No wonder. Toscanini's idiosyncratic temperament was confronted with something he could not have enjoyed. Bernstein says he told Toscanini that the tempo he had taken in a recording differed from one he had used in a radio performance of the same work. Bernstein says that Toscanini later wrote to him to tell him that he indeed was right.

Probber says he was always disconcerted by Bernstein's absolute lack of discretion. "The day we met," he says, "Lenny told me about a party when he went into the bedroom of the host's apartment and telephoned Farley Granger in Hollywood. He was making love to him on the phone and someone, in jest, had turned on the loudspeaker and connected it to the living room. Lenny found this out only after he came out of the bedroom, and told me how embarrassed he was. Lenny always referred to Farley with a diminutive. He was the kind of man Lenny preferred: tall, dark, slender, beautiful. That was the pattern."

Not only was Bernstein's behavior outrageous, his capacity for self-assessment appears to have been nonexistent. Bernstein's inability to evaluate his chance to carve out a career as music director of the New York City or Boston or Israel symphony was matched by his miscalculation in Rochester. He had begun to serve as guest conductor in Rochester in 1945 and went back in 1946 and again in the early months of 1947. That year when he conducted four performances— January 16, February 27, March 13, and March 27—he went so far as to try to influence the board members by giving them a "new" orchestral work of his own. He changed some music in the last of the four parts of his score to *Facsimile*, which he had introduced as a ballet at the Broadway Theatre in New York only a few months before. Then he presented Rochester with a "choreographic essay" and a program note quoting Santiago Ramón y Cajal that read, "Small inward treasure does he possess who, to feel alive, needs every hour the tumult of the streets, the emotion of the theater, and the small talk of society." Certainly he was telling this audience precisely what was troubling him. And he went further, noting that the title referred to the superficial nature of those relations that could, at best, be only substitutes, "facsimiles" of the real thing.

If Bernstein thought the people of this company town dominated by staid Eastman Kodak would respond with sympathy to his confession to feelings of alienation or his implications of his homosexuality, he was wrong. There was no place in Rochester where one could proclaim the age of anxiety or confess to a problem of sexual identity. If his personal and sexual problems were not enough to disqualify him there, his political liaisons certainly were. This was immediately after World War II. Not only hadn't Bernstein served in the armed forces or the Red Cross, or even done much entertaining of troops, all through the 1940s he was allowing his name to be used in connection with particular events and meetings associated with a variety of leftist groups. During the period 1945–1947 alone they included:

1 Sponsor and co-chairman: American Youth Congress
2 Dinner sponsor: American Slav Congress
3 Board member: National Committee to Oust (Senator) Bilbo, Civil Rights Congress
4 Sponsor: Action Committee to Free Spain
5 National Committee member: American Birobidjan (Soviet Jewish Region) Committee
6 Sponsor: Spanish Refugee Appeal of Joint Anti-Fascist Refugee Committee
7 Sponsor: National Conference of Civil Rights Congress
8 Board member: American Committee for Democratic Greece
9 National Committee of America-Soviet Friendship (Bernstein signed a statement by this organization that appeared in the Communist *Daily Worker.*)

To list these organizations is not to suggest that, as a private citizen, he did not have the right to follow his conscience or his political impulses and do as he pleased. It is rather to emphasize that to do so and then expect to become the music director of a major symphony orchestra reveals an important aspect of Bernstein's personality: He wants it all. He thinks he should be able to do whatever he wishes without paying a price. But grownups know this is not possible. So the portrait of Bernstein in the late 1940s is one of a handsome, vulgar, flamboyant musician, politically left and homosexual, with the career that Koussevitzky had promised him still eluding him.

Bernstein's recognition of his own homosexual nature and his awareness of how it interfered with his career underlie a long poem he wrote in 1948. While his early symphonies have pretentions to intellectual seriousness and social commentary that make one feel uncomfortable, Bernstein's poetry manages to avoid all of that. Here is an excerpt from the 1948 poem:

> *Oh, that was a different time, Before!*
> *Then someone taught me to be clean,*
> *and someone to be still and wait.*
> *And everyone became a friend*
> *who knew a way. But less with more*
> *became a paradox too lean*
> *to bear with. Always in the end*
> *the barrier rose, barbed wire and all,*
> *between the seeing and the seen,*
> *the hearing and the call, between*
> *sensation and experience.*
> *The hurt renewed, the hurt renewed*
> *itself from day to day. And now*
> *I find myself upon this hill,*
> *seeking the first connection still.*
> *I suddenly recall a burning night*
> *of sour sleeplessness. There was a train,*
> *and in it I was flinging back the earth,*
> *extending stiffly in my upper berth.*
> *I can remember raising up the shade*
> *to find a million stars upon a plain,*
> *then closing it again in sudden fright,*
> *and snapping on the light. The stars*
> *had been too bright. They were not mine.*
>
> *I find there is a sharper sting*
> *than that of failing in one's art,*
> *or being lonely in the spring.*

The pain is this: to make the fight
with Time, to tell the days apart,
advance, seek answers, muddle through,
make love, feel growth—and find that you
have finished where you made your start.

On February 15, 1951, *The New York Times* ran the following news item:

> Leonard Bernstein, who begins a fortnight' as the Philharmonic-Symphony's guest conductor tonight at Carnegie Hall, has decided to take a long sabbatical leave from concert appearances at the end of his current conducting schedule after April 15. He will remain away from the podium for at least a year and a half. During this time, he said, he will "take stock, gather inner sustenance," and continue his activities as a composer. He has already refused to appear next season with several American orchestras and also for appearances abroad with Salzburg and La Scala in Milan.... During the next two months he will conduct the Israel Philharmonic in twelve more concerts of its American tour and in five concerts in the Scandinavian countries. He will then fly to Mexico City for two concerts and spend the first few months of his long vacation in the Mexican capital.

When his tour with the Israel Philharmonic ended in April, Bernstein left Mexico City, the last stop, and went on to Cuernavaca. There he rented a house and spent the next few weeks getting it staffed and ready so he could proceed with his next creative effort. The piece would deal with the life of an unhappy suburban couple whose despair stemmed from not being in love. Irony would be achieved through a trio interrupting the couple's scenes with jazzy songs extolling the joys of suburban life. Publicly celebrated, but privately often depressed, Bernstein, as early as 1951, wanted to convey the message that life in reality is far from the picture presented by the mass media. The work was *Trouble in Tahiti*. Bernstein called it an opera, probably to satisfy Koussevitzky's demands on him, but that would not stop him from using popular song in the work. In fact, before he had completed it he said, "It's a lightweight piece. The whole thing is popular-song inspired and the roots are in musical comedy, or, even better, the American musical theater."

Just as he was about to begin composing, on June 1, Olga Koussevitzky called to say that Serge was too ill to handle Tanglewood by himself. Bernstein flew home almost immediately. On June 4, the last night of Koussevitzky's life, the two men talked for hours in the hospital room. By noon on June 5, Koussevitzky went into a coma, and he died later that day. Olga; Victor Sakharoff, his valet; and the hematologist who had attended him were at his deathbed.

Koussevitzky was buried in a Christian cemetery belonging to a Congregational church. Nearly a thousand people attended the funeral. Pallbearers included the composers Piston and Schuman, and Bernstein.

The Berkshire Music Center at Tanglewood began its ninth season on July 2 with vows to continue Koussevitzky's ideals. At the time of his death, Koussevitzky was no longer music director of the center or of its festival concerts. Charles Munch had taken over both these positions, though he had retained Koussevitzky to conduct some of the concerts and to direct the music school.

Little revision of plans for the season was required beyond substitutions for Koussevitzky by people already attached to the center. Koussevitzky's conducting dates were assumed by Munch, Bernstein, Carvalho, and Goldovsky. His conducting class was taken over by Bernstein. The general direction of the school was carried on by the heads of the departments: Copland for composition, Bernstein for conducting, Goldovsky for opera, Hugh Ross for choral conducting, and William Kroll for chamber music. "So smoothly does the whole thing run," Thomson wrote in the *Herald Tribune*, "that a visitor to Tanglewood nowadays would scarcely be aware, save for the lack of his physical presence, that the founder and animator of the project is no longer there to guide it."

Probably true of the casual visitor. Not true of Bernstein. Here the effect appears to have been so profound as virtually to change his life. Of all of Bernstein's father figures, Koussevitzky had not only been the most loving and giving, he was also the only one who, like Sam, was Russian and heterosexual. At his death Bernstein stepped into his shoes.

On August 10, the last weekend of the season, with Adele Addison as soprano, David Lloyd as tenor, and E. Power Biggs on the organ, Bernstein conducted a monumental performance of Beethoven's *Missa Solemnis* with the Boston Symphony and 140 students from the center, in honor of Koussevitzky.

During the 1949–1950 theater season, Felicia had met Richard Hart, an actor. They were both in the cast of *The Happy Time*, a Broadway play. Felicia was the understudy to Leora Dana, and Hart played the male lead. In recalling those days, Morton Gottlieb, Felicia's former suitor, said of Hart: "He was very dashing and seemed to live a life of excess. Hart was an exceptionally interesting actor and probably would have been even better if he had not been such a heavy drinker."

On January 21, 1951, at the age of thirty-five, Hart died in his sleep. The obituary in *The New York Times* attributed his death to a heart attack. According to David Diamond, Hart had always appeared to be suicidal. Whatever the actual cause of death, the fact of it made Felicia distraught. Still, her friends report that throughout the period of the broken engagement with Bernstein, she was never out of love with him.

A few months after Hart's death, Gottlieb invited Felicia to the opening of *The Small Hours*, a play by George S. Kaufman and his wife, Leueen MacGrath. Michael Wager, a good friend of Bernstein's, played one of the roles. Along with Gottlieb and Felicia, Bernstein was in the opening night audience. He had his sister with him.

"After the show," Gottlieb says, "the four of us went to Bleeck's, a restaurant on West Forty-first Street near the old *Herald Tribune*. It was then that the whole thing between Lenny and Felicia got reactivated. Soon after—I think it was actually the next day—Felicia was leaving for Europe. I went down to the boat to see her off. Lenny was there to see her off, too."

Felicia stayed abroad for three months. When she returned, she went directly to Tanglewood. Over lunch she and Bernstein talked about marriage. Just two days after the Koussevitzky memorial concert, at a buffet supper in Lenox, Olga Koussevitzky announced the engagement of Felicia Montealegre to Leonard Bernstein.

Before the marriage, Felicia converted to Judaism. On September 9, 1951, thirty-three family members and friends attended the religious ceremony performed at Mishkan Tefilah, the synagogue of Bernstein's childhood, with H. H. Rubenovitz, the rabbi of Bernstein's childhood, and Rabbi Israel Kazis officiating. The marriage and reception were held at Bernstein's parents' Brookline home. Leonard Bernstein was married in Koussevitzky's white suit and wore Koussevitzky's shoes. In his book *Findings*, a photograph of him smiling politely with his arm around the waist of his beaming bride accompanies a poem he stopped writing when, he notes in introductory words to the poem, he realized he had become a "very well behaviorized chimpanzee." It was like a caption.

The marriage may have made Bernstein's future career possible. Besides what it did to help him "ingest" Koussevitzky, it also was a signal to the community of patrons and managers of his willingness to compromise. He was delivering a positive message: You know me; if I am willing to get married, I am willing to behave in every way. Bernstein certainly came to regard Felicia with some of the tenderness and attachment he felt for the women in his family. But how much passion, how much calculation lay behind the decision to marry is open to question.

Felicia had her own emotional needs. First, she responded to Bernstein as tens of thousands of other women would have if they had had the chance. Here was a handsome, brilliant, virile-seeming man, a "Renaissance man" with talent bordering on genius who was courted far and wide and, at thirty-two, possessed international renown. In this period before women's liberation, what better road to fulfillment was there for an ambitious woman with limited talent? Second, Felicia did virtually what her mother had done. She married a Jew whom she found vulgar and then proceeded to try to tone him down. "Stop being so vulgar, Lenny" was a common reprimand heard in public. Finally, Felicia appears to have needed a man with an overwhelming weakness. Richard Hart, at the least, was an alcoholic. Many believed him to have been bisexual. After Hart's death, Felicia consulted a variety of sources as to what she should do if given the chance to marry Bernstein. Friends report she would use a Ouija board, and in answer to her question a disembodied Spanish lady's voice would say, "*Sí*." Real-life women like Jennie Tourel and Ruth Arrau advised her that when there was love, anything was possible. In the novel *Philharmonic*, after proposing to the young conductor, the Felicia character makes discretion a condition of the marriage; it concerns "the other man."

"I'd like to add a rider to my proposal."

"You want me to promise not to see him again?"

"No. There's no point in your making promises when you don't know whether you'll be able to keep them. But I do want you to promise me one thing…. That you'll keep your private affairs—very private. I don't want you to wreck your career with that sort of thing."

"That sort of thing?" he echoed sardonically. "… Dearest, you are behind the times. Swinging from both sides of the bed doesn't hurt anyone in the arts these days. In fact, half the successful artists are members of the Homintern."

"I don't care. I hate all that. It makes me feel dirty." Her impassioned voice startled both of them. She hadn't meant to declare her feelings so strongly…. Sensing his withdrawal, "Please don't misunderstand me. I'm not all that bigoted. I'd vote for liberal reforms in the laws concerning homosexuality. But I can't help my private feelings about the subject, even if they're irrational. There's a big difference between public acceptance and private tolerance. I can't be hypocritical and tell you I don't mind. I do mind. I'm old fashioned. I think that homosexuals are different from the rest of us. I wish there were no homosexuals on this earth."

In response the young conductor replied, "That's quite a speech…. In the same breath you declare that you loathe—all that—and yet you still want to marry me. Make up your mind. Which is it?"[6]

The porcelain blond lady in the novel articulates what Felicia's close friends say she indeed felt:

"I was trying to be honest with you and myself. Yes, I loathe all that. And yes, I want you more than I've ever wanted any man. You see, my desire to be your wife makes everything else unimportant. And the marriage will work because my love for you is strong enough to overcome whatever feelings I may have about your sexual inclinations.... Please marry me, darling."[6]

It appears Bernstein tried to remain faithful to his wife. But even in the first year of marriage he invited Mehegan to participate in a jazz festival at Brandeis. The action was, in part, probably due to his longing to see Mehegan again, but it was also in response to an album Mehegan had made of improvisations based on Bernstein's songs. According to Mehegan's widow, Gay, her husband told her Bernstein had said, "John, what have you done to my tunes? What is this plethora of notes?" Bernstein's unhappiness came from Mehegan's notes burying his own music.

Bernstein's presence at Brandeis was entirely because of Koussevitzky. In its original plan, Brandeis included a school of music, which was enthusiastically supported by Koussevitzky who offered to be a consultant. At Koussevitzky's death, Bernstein was the logical choice to succeed him. He became visiting professor and director of the annual Brandeis festival as well as serving as a consultant. The first festival ran from June 12 to June 15, 1952; the major events were the world premiere of *Trouble in Tahiti*, the world premiere of Marc Blitzstein's adept translation of the Brecht-Weill *Threepenny Opera*, and the jazz symposium with an unexceptionable group of jazz intellectuals, Barry Ulanov, Leonard Feather, and George Simon. Bernstein articulated his purpose to the press: "Jazz has become highly intellectualized. It's lost its beat. Maybe with the experts we've invited, we'll get the answers...." One of the pianists was Lennie Tristano. Another was John Mehegan, whom *The New Yorker* had characterized as the "trigonometrist of jazz." Bernstein was bringing Mehegan back into his life when his new wife was pregnant with their first child. That must have caused her considerable anguish. It probably was not pleasant for Mehegan either.

But no outsider could have guessed at such tensions. Bernstein rented Leonard Burkat's house in Brookline, and then, surrounded by the usual contingent of friends and family, set about finishing an opera about a desperately unhappy couple who lived in Brookline.

The misery in Bernstein's libretto may have been his own, but he charted it through his parents' lives. The book for the opera places Sam and his wife in a neat, modern, little white house similar to the many houses Bernstein had lived in during the 1920s and 1930s when his father was moving up the economic ladder. In the opera the couple is so profoundly unhappy that their conversations invariably degenerate into fights. Neither Sam's visits to his gym nor his wife's to her psychiatrist provide them with enough emotional nourishment to allow them to attend their son's school show. Junior, his name taken from Junior Mister in Blitzstein's *The Cradle Will Rock*, represents Bernstein but the child never appears on stage. The preoccupied and battling parents take up all the space literally and metaphorically.

To underline the meaning, Bernstein names the protagonist Sam. But probably to avoid upsetting his mother, who has always been sensitive to revelations about herself made by either of her sons, Bernstein selects another name for her: Dinah, the name of his paternal grandmother, who lived with the Bernsteins for a short, harrowing time. Because Junior is a young child in this scenario, Bernstein's sister and brother, in reality five and fourteen years younger, make no appearance.

A work of art is always a mixture of imagination and truth, with the balance in one direction or the other. Burton Bernstein's memoirs, written thirty years after *Trouble in Tahiti*, suggest the balance lies strongly in the direction of the truth. After describing the wedding of Sam and Jennie, Leonard's younger brother writes:

> Before long sharp differences emerged between them—differences in personality and in their goals…. Sam was the driven, diligent Horatio Alger hero, willing to slave and sacrifice in order to better his lot. Also he was intellectual, albeit a parochial one, the descendant of noted rabbinical scholars; his avocational pursuits were solely concerned with the mind—Talmudic study, philosophical discussions, the science of business….
>
> On paper, at least, Jennie was more "educated" than Sam. She had, after all, gone to night school and studied a variety of academic subjects, while Sam's formal education had never progressed beyond a few years at a shtetl yeshiva…. Her chief interests seemed to be food, the small available pleasures of life in Mattapan, movies and their celluloid celebrities, romantic novels, the local Hearst newspaper, and gossip with her coevals.

None of these ... held the slightest interest for her husband.

Increasingly he grew contemptuous of what he saw as her dullness, her passive acceptance of the superficial, the second-rate.... Jennie, while incapable of being contemptuous, made light of Sam's consuming ambition, his penny-pinching, his Talmudic studies.... She was trapped in confining wifehood with a man who no longer made her laugh. [1]

Burton Bernstein believes that "in no way did Sam worship the golden calf"—far from it, in fact; he took the biblical strictures against greed very seriously—but money itself emerged as a symbolic excuse for expressing his dissatisfactions with his marriage, his in-laws, his children's alien way of life, his own dilemmas. It is no coincidence, the author writes, "that in Lenny's short opera, *Trouble in Tahiti*, the husband and wife (named Sam and Dinah) bicker over money as a starting point for deeper quarrels.... And Dinah's suspicions about an affair that her husband allegedly had with his secretary, Miss Brown, spring from a biographical incident. The malevolent wife of one of my father's employees once telephoned Jennie to hint that Sam was sleeping with a woman who worked in his office...." [1]

The characteristic that generated the title of the opera is also grounded in reality. So passionate was Jenny about movies that she named her only daughter after the actress Anne Shirley. In the opera Dinah also finds relief in escapist films. Despite the fact that she had spent the afternoon watching a movie called *Trouble in Tahiti*, which she ridicules in an aria that is the high point of the opera, a *tour de force* for a gifted soprano, she chooses to sit through it again rather than face a few hours alone with Sam.

The opera opens with a vocal trio, "dance-band ensemble style," huddled around a microphone dressed in evening clothes. It comments on the action as though it were a Greek chorus. The tone is one of irony.

> *Skid a lit day: skid a lit day:*
> *Lovely day!*
> *Lovely life:*
> *Happily married: sweet little son:*
> *Family picture second to none:*

> *It's a wonderful life!*
> *Up-to-date kitchen: washing machine:*
> *Colorful bathrooms, and* Life *Magazine,*
> *And a little white house in Brookline!**

The trio celebrates Sam's business acumen:

> *Oh, Sam, you're a genius, you marvelous man!*
> *Oh, Sam, you're a genius, you marvel of a man!*
> *When it comes to the dollar,*
> *No one touches marvelous Sam!**

Sam's need to triumph over everyone, to win every competition, is captured in a scene in which he showers in the locker room of his gym. In an aria he expresses his view of the world:

> *There are men who will study the books 'til*
> > *Judgment Day,*
> *And examine the techniques of winners galore;*
> *There are men who will practice the rules religiously:*
> *Ev'ry day they'll improve just a tiny bit more:*
> *And they'll put all their soul behind it;*
> *And their ego, power, drive and will and desire*
> > *behind it,*
> *And they'll throw themselves in:*
> *But they never will win, they never will win,*
> *They never, never, never, never will win!**

Winding up this self-congratulatory song he sings:

> *There are men*
> *That whatever they touch will turn to gold,*
> *And their ev'ry decision will always be right.*
> *There are men*
> *Who can handle the work of seven men,*
> *And will manage to sleep seven hours a night.*
> *You can throw all your weight against them.*
> *All your fire, snow and hail and darkest disaster*
> > *against them:*
> *They'll respond with a grin,*
> *For they always will win,*
> *They always, always, always, always will win.**

While there may be a little of Felicia in Dinah, there is surely a great deal of Leonard in this Sam. The composition of the opera itself represents a public victory of Leonard over his father, reminiscent of the public airing of his complaints against Sam back in 1943, when he told the press every time he could of his father's stinginess. *Trouble in Tahiti* goes even further; it impales Sam in a kind of caricature to which generations will have access. In doing that, Leonard comes out an even bigger winner.

If the libretto was a tool in Bernstein's battle with Sam, the score was a tool in his contest with Mehegan. In place of what he viewed as Mehegan's diluting the essence of jazz with his "plethora of notes," Bernstein, in his opera, distilled its heavy syncopation and bouncy counterpoint into arias, duets, and trios.

Reviews of *Trouble in Tahiti* were mixed. Some reviewers were put off by the combination of art and popular music forms. But others were more than sanguine about the results. Howard Taubman said, "Mr. Bernstein writes with delicious and irresistible vitality." Irving Kolodin described the score as "crisp and flavorsome, even witty.... The strains designed to give credibility to the personal drama of the people involved are often inventive and, if not precisely moving, possessed of a kind of wistful poetry." The presence of pop music sounds as the underlying idiom appears to have prevented the critics from acknowledging the beauty of the main theme and the long stretch of genuinely operatic music with which *Trouble in Tahiti* ends.

This first Brandeis festival included a performance of Stravinsky's *Les Noces*, Irving Fine's *Notturno*, Copland's Clarinet Concerto with David Oppenheim as soloist, William Schuman's *Symphony for Strings* and a new work by Ben Weber. There were, in addition, Britten's *Serenade*, and Pierre Schaeffer's *musique concrète*, which accompanied Merce Cunningham dancing. Hardly a regressive program. Then came a seminar where Bernstein said the concert hall was probably a thing of the past. (This came fifteen years before Boulez said pretty much the same thing when he proposed that all the opera houses should be bombed.)

Because of the Jewish connection, Brandeis and Bernstein appeared to be suited to one another. An experiment in Jewish sponsorship of nonsectarian education, the university was founded in 1949 by leaders of the greater Boston Jewish community. Its name honored Louis Dembitz Brandeis, who had been a lawyer in Boston before he was appointed a justice of the U.S. Supreme Court. For its first president, Brandeis selected Abram L. Sachar, former director of the Hillel Foundation, and the university took over the buildings and campus of Middlesex University, a defunct medical school in Waltham.

Heading the university's school of creative arts, Bernstein occupied the Frederick and Sylvia Mann Chair in Music, but Irving Fine played a far more active role in the day-to-day life of the music department. Frederick Mann, a Philadelphia paper manufacturer, had studied piano with Rafael Joseffy at the old Juilliard School before going to the Wharton business school at the University of Pennsylvania. Throughout the rest of his life he directed his philanthropic gifts to Jewish institutions of music. Bernstein's first project for Brandeis was the 1952 festival. Echoing his priorities while an undergraduate at Harvard, theater triumphed over academic pursuits with both *Trouble in Tahiti* and Blitzstein's version of the Brecht-Weill *Threepenny Opera*.

Bernstein was not destined for success in the American university system. While a student at Curtis, he had applied to Princeton for a teaching post. Interviewed by Roy Dickinson Welch, then chairman of the music section of the department of art and archaeology, he was turned down. People at Princeton at the time attribute the rejection to Bernstein's obvious "Jewishness." But Dickinson Welch may have intuited what Piston had experienced: that Bernstein would always be putting on a show or something, and that would not have suited Princeton, whose music department has always favored academic interests above performance. Even at Brandeis, where Bernstein could do virtually what he wanted, and did, he was unable to live up to his commitment. He taught in the 1952–1953 academic year and again in 1953–1954, but the pressure from his other projects prevented him from teaching the next year. He said that he would be back the following academic year, but he couldn't make it.

In those years, Bernstein was working nonstop, producing his best, most important, most memorable work. As the head of a growing family, his energies seemed to have coalesced and were working for him in the best of all possible ways. His first child, a girl named Jamie, was born in 1952. The second, a son with the burdensome name of

Alexander Serge Leonard, arrived in 1955. In 1956, Bernstein told a reporter, "I value control and self-control. Sure I was perhaps a big orgiastic at one time. But marriage and children change everything."

BERNSTEIN 15

The review of a Bernstein performance by
Virgil Thomson in 1947 accused Bernstein of having Warner Brothers
always on his mind. Ten years later Rodzinski echoed the complaint
when he said, "Bernstein wants one thing: to be talked about. Look at
the way he dresses, with flashy neckties and turtleneck sweaters and

LESTER COWAN PRODUCTIONS

1946
Canoga Park, Los Angeles: Ann Ronell, Bernstein, Felicia, and Lester Cowan.
Of film-struck Lenny, Artur Rodzinski later wrote, "I think Bernstein
would correspond with me only if my name were Darryl Zanuck or Spyros Skouras
or one of those people who could do him some good."

all those bright colors. Still, he's a good looking boy with wonderful eyes and a great smile and I still have a soft spot in my heart for him, even though it has been years since I have seen him and we never correspond. I think Bernstein would correspond with me only if my name were Darryl Zanuck or Spyros Skouras or one of those people who could do him some good."

Bernstein did take one screen test and looked toward Hollywood from time to time. Movies were, after all, the fastest route to unlimited fame. But he never persisted in these efforts and always came back to music. In their remarks Thomson and Rodzinski were probably reacting more to Bernstein's theatrical behavior than to any genuine concern that he was seeking another career.

Charges of excessive theatricality in his conducting have pursued Bernstein from the start. In the 1950s in defending himself, he told a *New York Times* writer a story that suited his purpose but is unverifiable. After a rough going-over by one of the critics, he conducted a concert in a restrained way, relying primarily on his fingers. He was conducting the Beethoven Fourth: "Everything came out correctly but it was dead. After the concert the orchestra came around to see me. They thought I was sick. And I got bad reviews for a dull performance. Since then I conduct the way I feel." In the late 1960s a CBS interviewer confronted him on the issue again. This time, irritated, he replied, "It is the conductor's responsibility to bring the composer's intention alive. It is a matter of identifying with the composer. You get ideas, and then invent at the moment, and the spontaneity of the music is what is hoped for. It does not happen very often."

Bernstein was theatrical before he understood the meaning of the word. He was theatrical in Boston Latin when he spoke up in Marson's class, when he produced Gilbert and Sullivan and *Carmen* at Singer's Inn at Sharon, when he performed Molière in drag, and later when he played the piano in *The Cradle Will Rock* on a bare stage at Harvard. His mentors, Mitropoulos and Koussevitzky, were both theatrical. "Whatever Koussevitzky conducted," Bernstein has said, "it was a gala occasion. He was such a great theater man."

The question here is not whether Bernstein's theatricality comes to him naturally. It is whether at twenty-five, he could have engendered the excitement he did if he had not been histrionic. To ask this is not to suggest that Bernstein used excessive gestures to hide the technical defi-ciencies he had at that time. Rather is it to emphasize that his person-ality and temperament served his genuine talent by propelling him to fame and notoriety. Such instant recognition could hardly have been achieved through sheer artistic virtuosity on the podium.

Clearly the theater was his proper vehicle. That would help explain why throughout his life, Bernstein never made friends any closer than Adolph Green and Betty Comden, whom he had known before his Philharmonic debut.

But Bernstein's mentor was Koussevitzky, not Irving Berlin or Frank Loesser, and on opening night of the Boston tryout of *On the Town,* his first Broadway show, Koussevitzky, who had been in the audi-ence, came backstage and laid it on the line: no more Broadway if Bernstein wanted to remain a contender for the Boston conducting post. He reportedly spent three full hours giving Bernstein hell for low-ering himself and his image by squandering his talents.

Although the Broadway musical was moving toward new peaks, it did so without Bernstein, and that is too bad. For it was Bernstein's idio-syncratic voice—with its brash, frantic, funny, symphonic, jazzy, oper-atic sound—that had made *On the Town* a singular musical. In the years that followed, Comden and Green wrote a number of musicals, four of them in collaboration with Jule Styne, but none with the panache of their first effort. Styne in 1947 composed *High Button Shoes* with Robbins as choreographer. The high point of that piece was a ballet by Robbins in the style of silent movie director Mack Sennett. But it was a far cry from his work in *On the Town.* Here two con men, played by comedians Phil Silvers and Joey Faye, are chased by villagers, bathers, Keystone Kops, and a bear. No longer was dance used as a vehicle to further the plot. No longer was there the magic of the dream ballet of *On the Town.* Robbins did not make another significant mark on Broadway until 1951, when he created the dance "The Small House of Uncle Thomas" for Rodgers and Hammerstein's *The King and I.*

But Bernstein turned his back on Broadway. His identification with Koussevitzky was so profound that the older man's European values colored his own attitude toward "high" and "low" art. Concentrating almost exclusively in those years on Koussevitzky's values, Bernstein went on to become one of the greatest conductors—some would say indeed the greatest—of the late twentieth century.

Through the 1940s and early 1950s, Bernstein did not tell his theater colleagues that he was unavailable to them. It just turned out that way. Here is his own reconstruction, published in the fall of 1957, of a log he kept on a particular project that did not materialize until then:

New York, Jan. 6, 1949. Jerry R. called today with a noble idea: a modern version of *Romeo and Juliet* set in slums at the coincidence of Easter-Passover celebrations. Feelings run high between Jews and Catholics. Former: Capulets; latter: Montagues. Juliet is Jewish. Friar Laurence is a neighborhood druggist. Street brawls, double death—it all fits. But it's all much less important than the bigger idea of making a musical that tells a tragic story in musical-comedy terms, using only musical-comedy techniques, never falling into the "operatic" trap. Can it succeed? It hasn't yet in our country. I'm excited. If it can work—it's the first. Jerry suggests Arthur Laurents for the book. I don't know him, but I do know *Home of the Brave*, at which I cried like a baby. He sounds just right.

New York, Jan. 10, 1949. Met Arthur L. at Jerry's tonight. Long talk about opera versus whatever this should be. Fascinating. We're going to have a stab at it.

Columbus, Ohio, April 15, 1949. Just received draft of first four scenes. Much good stuff. But this is no way to work. Me on this long conducting tour, Arthur between New York and Hollywood. Maybe we'd better wait until I can find a continuous hunk of time to devote to the project. Obviously this show can't depend on stars, being about kids; and so it will have to live or die by the success of its collaborations; and this remote-control collaboration isn't right. Maybe they can find the right composer who isn't always skipping off to conduct somewhere. It's not fair to them or to the work.[2]

By this time the Boston Symphony post was gone. Munch had taken over. But Koussevitzky was still very much alive, and he and Bernstein spent summers at Tanglewood, probably with the understanding that at least in regard to the conducting division, Bernstein would take over when Koussevitzky bowed out. Also Bernstein had been altogether seduced by Israel; in 1948 he had conducted forty concerts there in sixty days. The following year he committed himself to a tour with the Israeli orchestra, and plans were being made for the orchestra to travel in the United States with Bernstein and Koussevitzky its co-conductors. In other words, when Bernstein turned down what was to become *West Side Story*, suggesting his colleagues find someone else, "the right composer who isn't always skipping off to conduct," Koussevitzky was still a large presence in his life.

In June 1951, Koussevitzky died. That set in motion an immensely complicated circuit of threads in Bernstein's mind that moved him to make the decision to marry. It also freed him to write for Broadway. Not immediately, of course. In the most immediate sense, Koussevitzky's death led to a post as professor of music at Brandeis. At Brandeis he was not only in a position to get experience conducting, he led the orchestra in his own *Trouble in Tahiti* and Blitzstein's translation of *The Threepenny Opera* the following June. And he honed his lecturing talents in front of demanding listeners. According to Irving Fine, who addressed this issue in the late 1950s, "When he talked on the modern symphony or on the opera—and incidentally, he would go through it, singing practically all the roles—the hall would be jammed with students enrolled in the course, other students, faculty members, everyone who could possibly squeeze in. It was always a brilliant performance."

When Bernstein finished his duties at school, he and his wife went to Cuernavaca, where he planned to complete *Trouble in Tahiti*. Because Munch fell ill, Bernstein returned to Boston to fill in for him. In March 1952, he led the Boston Symphony in Alban Berg's *Der Wein*, a work composed between *Wozzeck* and *Lulu* and one of considerable complexity. Bernstein's performance was its first in sixteen years; critics credited him with a significant revival at a time when Berg was not frequently heard.

In June there was the Brandeis-festival—the only opera he had conducted previously had been Britten's *Peter Grimes* six years before—and in August, at the end of the Tanglewood season, Bernstein conducted the Boston Symphony in Sibelius's Symphony No. 2, Chávez's *Sinfonia India*, and Brahms's Symphony No. 2. In addition to the Boston Symphony, during that year that was supposed to be a total sabbatical from conducting, he led the Robin Hood Dell and Ballet Theater orchestras. On September 8, 1952, his first child, Jamie Anne Maria, was born. In a letter three years later he described her as looking "like a princess, namely Felicia, and is unutterably blond and delicate and fey." (Her second name, Anne, was the same as his sister Shirley's.)

In November 1952, NBC produced *Trouble in Tahiti* on television. The cast was not the same as at Brandeis. Bernstein had not liked the way the original Dinah had used her hands and on television such a detail could be an insurmountable problem. In 1983 he said, "My dream of the first set of the television premiere was to have Saul Steinberg design it. But he wasn't in the right union. I gave the indication that when the girl sings 'Ratty Poo' the boy goes to the blackboard and draws a little white house, a sun and a moon, and a little tree. Then they return and sing 'Ratty Poo'.... Then when you move into the so-called foreground it is hell on wheels. It is murder...."

This first work completed after his marriage was not dedicated to Felicia. The only published piece he ever dedicated to Felicia during her lifetime was one of the *Four Anniversaries*, completed in 1948, after Bernstein had broken their engagement. *Trouble in Tahiti* was dedicated instead to Marc Blitzstein, who had helped him with problems in the libretto. By the time of the television premiere, Bernstein and Felicia had been married more than a year. In thinking back to that production, he says he was most concerned that Sam and Dinah not come off as caricatures. It is possible that by then the similarities between his marriage and that of his parents had darker resonances than when he had written the piece. Those similarities certainly occurred to others. Rorem recalls one night in 1952 in the Bernstein apartment: "Felicia and Lenny sang a duet from *Trouble in Tahiti* for me. Everyone was wondering, 'What do you think about Lenny writing this opera about a disintegrating marriage while he is on his honeymoon?'"

At the end of 1952, George Abbott called Comden and Green and said he had a book and Rosalind Russell and that he needed a score. "Can you get one together in five weeks?" he asked. They said they didn't know. He told them to call Bernstein and find out: "Is he yes or no?" Bernstein was yes. Later Green remarked that working on such short notice had certain marvelous advantages: "Everyone is afraid to criticize for fear of o'ertipping the creative bark." The book Abbott had was an adaptation by Joseph Fields and Jerome Chodorov of their play *My Sister Eileen*, which had enjoyed a success on Broadway and which in turn had been based on Ruth McKenny's autobiographical stories for *The New Yorker*. The titles considered during the course of the creation were *My Beautiful Sister, A Likely Story*, and *The Sherwood Girls*. But the final decision was to use two words from the movie version of a song Bernstein had written ten years before: "New York, New York, it's a *wonderful town*." (On the stage the lyric had been "helluva town.")

When Bernstein invited Sono Osato to play the lead in *On the Town*, he had described the musical as "a show I'm working on with friends." It had started with an idea of Robbins's, developed with music by Bernstein, finished its conception with Comden and Green, after which Abbott had pulled it into shape. Nothing could be further from the way that *Wonderful Town* was born. Because it is more typical of the ways of Broadway, it is worth describing in some detail.

Several producers had expressed interest in doing a musical version of *My Sister Eileen*, the hit show that had also been a successful movie starring Rosalind Russell. In 1948 Max Gordon, knowing from the Revuers' material what a splendid backdrop New York can make for a musical treatment, approached Herbert and Dorothy Fields to do the book and the lyrics. He asked Burton Lane to write the music and George S. Kaufman to direct. Two years later Leland Hayward announced plans for the same work with Joseph, Herbert, and Dorothy Fields writing the book and Irving Berlin or Cole Porter doing the score. Still a third plan emerged with Ella Logan in the starring role. Because Columbia Pictures had screen rights to the work and Harry Cohn's negotiators kept presenting problems, each of these projects was aborted.

In June 1952 Robert Fryer, who had produced *A Tree Grows in Brooklyn* in 1951, took a crack at the property. With a book co-authored by Ruth McKenny and George Abbott, he decided to move ahead on *My Sister Eileen* and deal with Cohn when he had things in place. In addition to signing up Joseph Fields for the book, he asked Jerome Chodorov to collaborate with him. The plan was for Frank Loesser or Irving Berlin to do the score. Fryer was planning to try to get Rosalind Russell to repeat her screen role.

Russell was reluctant. She had never sung or danced. When she was invited to hear some of the music and lyrics, she found Abbott and Fryer in a state of despair. Something had happened between conception and execution, and the music they had was by Leroy Anderson and the lyrics by Arnold Horwitt, who, in 1948, had been a collaborator on the lyrics for Beatrice Lillie's *Inside U.S.A.*

On November 12, unconfirmed reports in the press had Bernstein doing the music and Comden and Green the lyrics. By then Abbott had called Comden, and wheels had been set in motion. Five days later Anderson and Horwitt stepped aside with the obligatory comment about a viewpoint conflicting with management's. Each was bought out of the deal for twenty-five hundred dollars.

The final lineup was this: producer, Robert Fryer; director, George Abbott; book, Joseph Fields and Jerome Chodorov; lyrics, Betty Comden and Adolph Green; choreographer, Donald Saddler, who had just come to New York from Hollywood. Obviously Abbott did not seek out Robbins for this venture and Bernstein was in no position to dole out jobs to his friends. He was an employee hired to do the work, and he did it brilliantly and fast.

Changes were made from both the show and the film. The book for the musical moved out into the streets of Greenwich Village, settled for a time in a Village garden, included a new jail scene and a nightclub sequence for the finale.

On January 19, 1953, *Wonderful Town* opened in New Haven to rave reviews. There were the usual crises in New Haven during the tryout. Rosalind Russell came down with a fever the second day and the show had to be canceled. By the third day a chorus girl substituted for her in the part. A ballet for the opening scene was dropped, several new scenes were written, and a new song was added for Russell, who surprised herself and everybody else by being able to carry out her musical numbers through a joyous enthusiasm and comic talent that made a real singing voice unnecessary.

A week after the New Haven opening, the show went into the Shubert Theatre in Boston. The production set a house record in its first week of previews. And Koussevitzky wasn't around to cast a pall on the occasion. Robbins was called in to help with the dances; a chorus boy had dropped Russell in "Conga," an uproarious burlesque, and they didn't want that to happen again. Still on the road, the show moved on for a final two-week pre-Broadway run at the Forrest Theater in Philadelphia. It ran an extra week because of unexpected demand for seats.

The Broadway opening came on February 25 at the Winter Garden. It received eight favorable reviews. All of them agreed that Bernstein's score was the outstanding aspect of an altogether first-rate work. Bernstein showed how he could combine the vernacular with sophisticated techniques, and use jagged, offbeat meters and distinctive Bernstein dissonances to give a hard edge to a popular sound.

Whatever reservations Olin Downes had had about Bernstein's *Age of Anxiety* were nowhere present here. He wrote that *Wonderful Town,*

> utterly American in conception and execution from head to toe, is current and characteristic of our people, and not paralleled by any other musical theater, for better or worse, of the contemporaneous world…. The electricity shoots back and forth over the footlights in a show which projects such spirit, and is maintained with such ingenuity and taste, that it is not for an instant vulgar or banal or less than the triumph of invention….
>
> This is an opera of which dance is warp and woof, an opera made of dance, prattle and song and speed. Its unflagging pulse is characteristic of its restless time and nervous environment….When the American opera created by a composer of the stature of the Wagners and Verdis of yore does materialize, it will owe more to the robust spirit and the raciness of accent of our popular theater than to the efforts of our prideful emulators in the upper esthetic brackets, of the tonal art of Bartók, Hindemith and Stravinsky.

This came not from the *Times's* theater critic but from the music critic.

In fact Brooks Atkinson, the paper's theater critic, echoed Downes's acclaim. Audiences agreed that Bernstein's score, an effervescent tone poem in praise of New York, contained some beautiful melodies. "A Quiet Girl" and "It's Love" were two memorable ones. And with "Christopher Street," the ebullient opening number, and "Wrong Note

Rag," the rollicking finish, the show was unmistakably Bernstein. Not that he still didn't show other influences. But here early Copland and Stravinsky sounds were replaced by older styles. "Why Oh Why Oh Why Oh, Did I Ever Leave Ohio?" came from the third movement of the Brahms Piano Concerto No. 2. But with Bernstein's handling of the melody, it was entirely consistent with the sound of the whole. In "On the Town," almost a decade earlier, Bernstein had used a melody from the last movement of the Brahms Piano Concerto No. 1 for "New York, New York."

Everyone profited from the show which ran over five hundred performances. Tony Awards went to Fryer as producer of the year, Saddler as choreographer, Russell as best actress in a musical, Abbott for the best musical of the year, and Bernstein for the score. Russell's last performance on Broadway had been in Rodgers and Hart's *Garrick Gaieties* in 1930. After that she made forty movies in Hollywood. In her return to Broadway, working for 10 percent of the gross and 10 percent of the profits, she took home almost eight thousand dollars a week in 1953.

On April 8, something happened that portended big trouble. Fryer canceled the performance that night because a left-wing publication called the *National Guardian* had bought a block of three hundred tickets and planned to mark them up and sell them to raise funds. Ed Sullivan, a newspaper columnist and TV show host, wrote in his *Daily News* column that the tickets were going for twelve dollars to finance this "leftist sheet." In closing the show that night Fryer said, "Our object is to prevent an organization from reselling tickets to our production at a profit that it then will use to disseminate ideas thoroughly hostile to the interests of America."

By that time the anti-Communist heat was on. Hollywood, the labor unions, Broadway—all of them were scared to death.

16

The success of the Bolshevik revolution in 1917

brought new power to the radical movement in the United States. Two years later the American Communist party splintered off the socialist movement to form a direct link to that revolution, and its policies were dictated increasingly by the political needs of the Soviet

"... No one factor crystallized his [left-wing commitment] more than the emotional tie he made with Marc Blitzstein...."

Union. Initially the Bolsheviks were seen by many people, especially the children of those Russian Jews who had fled the pogroms of the czars beginning in the 1880s, as the liberators of Russia from czarist tyranny. The immigrants themselves had generally uncomplicated feelings of gratitude for what they had found in the United States. After all, the waves of Jewish immigration from Russia and Russian Poland to America had begun with the virulent pogroms that followed the assassination of Czar Alexander II in 1881 and largely ended by the start of World War I in 1914, well before V. I. Lenin, Leon Trotsky, and their associates made the first successful Marxist revolution. However, many of their children, often better educated and socially privileged, became either supporters of left-wing causes or actual Communists. Many were moved by guilt: They could not reconcile the big money they were earning, especially those who succeeded in the theater and particularly in Hollywood, with the poverty and despair of the 1930s Depression.

The record of Bernstein's support of pro-Soviet causes is voluminous and contrasts strikingly with his relations with those active in support of the United States. To say this is not to suggest that Bernstein implemented his left-wing commitment with any action, such as fighting the fascists in Spain. Rather is it to emphasize that in a long and richly textured life, he always allied himself with the left.

Although these alliances began in his Harvard days, no one factor crystallized this commitment more than the emotional tie he made with Marc Blitzstein the day Blitzstein watched him playing piano on a bare stage in Cambridge directing a performance of *The Cradle Will Rock*. In his music-theater works Bernstein followed Blitzstein's example, greatly echoing the score of Blitzstein's *Freedom Morning*, an orchestral work of 1943, for his *On the Town* of 1944. In his handling of his sexual life, Bernstein also built on Blitzstein's model, even marrying, as Blitzstein did, although Bernstein's homosexual drive seems always to have been the predominant one. In the political arena, Bernstein also followed Blitzstein's model, only here he never went far enough; Bernstein says Blitzstein was always prodding him to do more for the movement.

Blitzstein was a well-to-do Philadelphia Jew from a family with a cultivated background. Unlike Bernstein, he was aware as a young man of the richness of the musical tradition Western Europe was passing on to the United States. During the 1920s, Blitzstein was on the periphery of big developments in modernism in art, witnessing the early works of the neoclassical and twelve-tone movements. In the 1920s he was in France with Boulanger and in Germany with Schoenberg. But in the early 1930s he put modernism behind him and shifted to the principles held by Hanns Eisler and Bertolt Brecht, the German artists who had committed themselves to a fight against "art for art's sake" in favor of art in the service of the revolution. During this period, Blitzstein wrote a number of articles that were published in radical journals such as *New Masses* and *Masses and Mainstream.* In essays that appeared in the summer of 1936 he attacked Stravinsky's *Apollon Musagète* for "its suave, dry, elegant maneuvers, its French court nymphs and gods," and he characterized Ravel's *Boléro* (adored by Bernstein a few years before) as "a piece whose vulgarity and cheapness are consummate.... This choice opium package was not smuggled in; we got it at the hands of Toscanini and the Philharmonic."

Blitzstein devoted an entire essay to celebrating Eisler, concentrating his remarks on the evening of December 7, 1935, at Town Hall where Eisler was joined by Aaron Copland and Henry Cowell. Before paraphrasing Eisler's statements, Blitzstein described the composer this way:

> Eisler is more than a composer. Rather he is the new kind of composer, whose job carries him to the meeting-hall, the street, the mill, the prison, the school-room and the dock.... He is a leader as Gorky is a leader; he has experienced deeply the life and problems of the working class, his thought propels him to music and to action. Sometimes the action is the organizing of a music *front;*... sometimes it is the music itself, or the teaching of socialism, through the clear, light, wiry structure of the *Lehrstück*, which he created with Brecht....

Brecht, who was to Blitzstein what Blitzstein became to Bernstein, a model par excellence, is here described by Blitzstein:

> Brecht, the German poet ... saw ... that you couldn't just give the new public what it wanted; for what it wanted had been conditioned by generations of capitalist exploitation and

treachery. He saw the need for education through poetry, through music. Note that as he had become more and more revolutionary in content, Brecht turned more and more to Eisler for musical collaboration.... I have written of Eisler and his contribution to the movement in music which belongs not only to the musical revolution but to the world revolution as well. This is the stage at which composers at last feel themselves joined to the proletarian movement, to the struggle of laboring classes everywhere for liberation, self-realization.

Within a year of the publication of this article, *The Cradle Will Rock* started on the journey that began with a federal subsidy and an advance sale of eighteen thousand seats in a Washington, D.C. theater, and ended in Blitzstein sitting alone at a piano on a bare stage in a New York theater, a scene that was repeated by Bernstein the following year at Harvard. If Bernstein, wearing Koussevitzky's suit and shoes, "became" Koussevitzky at his own wedding, then Bernstein directing Blitzstein's work from a piano on a bare stage became Blitzstein for the night. The presence of Boston critics assured that for the first time Bernstein's fame transcended school activities.

Blitzstein responded to that performance not with anger that a younger man was threatening his world, but with affection and admiration that bordered on awe. He told all of his friends that Bernstein was "me when I was that age." And so the love was not only great but mutual. Blitzstein's pressuring of Bernstein in any direction moved Bernstein to respond.

Blitzstein pressured Bernstein to give his name and work to the leftist movement. But Copland, Bernstein's father figure in art music, was also a model in a political sense. In May 1934, Copland entered a contest to set to music a poem by Alfred Hayes that had been printed on the cover of the May Day issue of *New Masses*. Copland's competitors included Lan Adomian, Wallingford Riegger, and Elie Siegmeister under a pseudonym. The competition was sponsored by the Composers' Collective, an organization that met every week to support the labor movement. Charles Seeger, chairman of the committee that judged this competition, later wrote that the Composers' Collective was "Communist controlled," and that "we criticized everybody's contribution and they criticized themselves, true Communist style. (As far as I know there was only one real Communist there, Marc Blitzstein, as Henry Cowell was out by this time.)" The poem on which the words were based is presented here:

> Into the streets May First!
> Into the roaring Square!
> Shake the midtown towers!
> Shatter the downtown air!
> Come with a storm of banners,
> Come with an earthquake tread,
> Bells, hurl out of your belfries,
> Red flag, leap out your red!
> Out of the shops and factories,
> Up with the sickle and hammer,
> Comrades, these are our tools,
> A song and a banner!
> Roll song, from the sea of our hearts,
> Banner, lead and be free;
> Song and banner together,
> Down with the bourgeoisie!
> Sweep the big city, march forward,
> The day is a barricade;
> We hurl the bright bomb of the sun,
> The moon like a hand grenade.
> Pour forth like a second flood!
> Thunder the alps of the air!
> Subways are roaring our millions—
> Comrades, into the Square!

In announcing the winner, Ashley Pettis, the paper's regular writer on music, wrote that "one of the most significant developments within the revolutionary movement has been the growth of music and music-making of a nature which helps to inspire masses of workers," and that the judges had unanimously selected Copland's setting for its "balance of good music and accessibility." The plan was for the work to be sung by a group of combined choruses of eight hundred voices at the auditorium of the College of the City of New York at Twenty-third Street and Lexington Avenue. In fact only the *Daily Worker* Chorus had the time to rehearse. It sang under the direction of one of Copland's competitors, Adomian. Pettis, in his review, claimed that the performance, though "trivial and detached," had nevertheless been effective and "a tribute to Copland's craftsmanship."

Blitzstein followed *Cradle* with *No for an Answer,* his own response to the question of America's involvement in the war. To raise money for an orchestral version, Blitzstein accompanied singers at the piano on three Sunday evening performances in January 1941. Carol Channing, in one of her earliest professional roles, played the lead. But in June 1941, Germany invaded the Soviet Union, which moved most American Communists to support the war. Blitzstein's own answer now was yes. He entered the army and composed the *Airborne* Symphony, which Bernstein conducted at the City Center with the City Symphony the first chance he had.

The aftermath of World War II was a time of great confusion and difficulty for American Communists and fellow travelers. The Soviet purges of worldwide party leadership in the 1920s and 1930s had resulted in the expulsion and resignation of many U.S. party members and the creation of such splinter groups as the Trotskyite parties. Stalin's doctrine of "socialism in one country" had pretty much ended the idea of a world revolution powered from the USSR. The assassination of Leon Trotsky by a Stalinist agent in Mexico in 1940 had eliminated the Communist leader most likely to provide an ideological base outside the Soviet Union. Stalin's projection of himself during World War II as the Little Father struggling to save Mother Russia revealed a nationalism that was inconsistent with Marxist ideology. Those who remained loyal to Soviet communism included both well-intentioned people and die-hard conspirators working for a link to power or money or some residual mystic force that for most others had become "the God that failed."

In 1947 Hanns Eisler, a Communist sympathizer whose brother Gerhard was the principal Soviet espionage agent in the United States, became a target of the House Un-American Activities Committee. The House committee had a long history of investigating subversives, generally on the left but during the war on the right as well. At one committee hearing, Robert E. Stripling, chief investigator for the committee, asked the German composer about an article he had written, "The Destruction of Art," which had appeared in a Soviet journal. Stripling read several paragraphs in which composers Copland and Cowell were noted in a sympathetic context. Eisler claimed that it was fascism, not democracy, he had indicted in his piece. But to no avail. As an alien, Eisler was ordered to leave the country. A number of artists organized a fund-raising event at Town Hall to help him get home. Among them were the playwright Clifford Odets and the composers David Diamond and Leonard Bernstein.

That same year Brecht, then a refugee in the United States, was called before the committee. His *Threepenny Opera*, with a score by Kurt Weill, had been an overwhelming success in Europe, playing more than five years in Berlin. When it was mounted on Broadway in 1933 it was largely overlooked and died almost immediately. With a libretto that illuminated the heinous injustices Brecht saw in the capitalist system, the work attracted Blitzstein, who translated the libretto for American audiences. He did not alter the Weill score. The Blitzstein adaptation was scheduled for its premiere in the spring of 1952 at the New York City Opera, but conservative groups intervened and the first performance took place at the first Brandeis festival, the one that premiered Bernstein's *Trouble in Tahiti*. The connection between Bernstein and Blitzstein was revealed in several ways in this piece. Bernstein had recently married Felicia; therefore it followed he would dedicate it to Blitzstein, in the tradition of consolation gifts. But there was an even more hidden tribute: For part of the passage the trio sings, Bernstein used the syllables "A-bar-ba-nel," the name of the actress who was the mother of Blitzstein's late wife and a woman to whom Blitzstein had remained deeply attached. In addition, Bernstein named the figure who represented himself "Junior," after the son of the capitalist in *Cradle*, and, a few months later, made Blitzstein godfather to his first child.

When Brecht was called before the House committee and asked if he had ever been a member of the Communist party, he said no six times, and then said never. He explained it had been necessary for him to stay close to the party because he wanted the Communists to produce his plays. If he was speaking the truth, Brecht was at least a fellow traveler. Within hours of his testimony, Brecht fled the United States.

In 1947, when ten Hollywood writers were called before the

committee, they refused to name anyone they knew to be associated with Communist causes and ideas. Instead of pleading the Fifth Amendment of the Constitution, which would have marked them but not incriminated them, they chose to invoke the First Amendment and question the authority of the committee itself. Cited for contempt, they refused to purge their contempt and several were eventually sent to prison. Immediately a group of Hollywood producers gathered in New York's Waldorf-Astoria Hotel to determine what to do. They decided to go along with the committee and issued the following statement: "No Communist or other subversive will be employed in Hollywood."

In 1948 Whittaker Chambers, a former Communist courier, testified that Alger Hiss had been a member of a Soviet spy ring in Washington in the 1930s. Hiss denied what Chambers said. He was tried twice for perjury. The first trial ended with a jury deadlocked eight to four for conviction. The second time, in 1950, Hiss was convicted and sentenced to prison. The Communists and their associates rallied round Hiss and have supported his cause ever since.

By choosing to deny any involvement in Communist activities throughout, Hiss missed a unique opportunity to clarify some historic issues confronting the nation at that time. A high official in the State Department, one of the architects of the UN, and then the director of the Carnegie Endowment for International Peace, Hiss stood an excellent chance of being believed and understood if he had told the world why a person well endowed and educated could have become entwined in communism amid the poverty and misery of the 1930s and why such a person would have left its thrall later. At the least, some of the fear and ignorance of the postwar days and some of the virulence of the aggressive headline hunters might have been dissipated by such a courageous act. At best, it might have rendered Senator Joseph R. McCarthy, who emerged in early 1950 as the preeminent Communist hunter, ineffectual without endangering the security of the nation. But Hiss did not do that.

Many others involved in and around Communist activities of the period—and many who were not—were brought up before congressional committees, put on proscription lists, and harassed in other ways. There were thousands of them in entertainment, the arts, the academic world. Any list of entertainers and writers who supported

Communist causes and interests was likely to include detective novelist Dashiell Hammett and his companion, playwright Lillian Hellman, as well as people whose lives had touched Bernstein's own, such as Judy Holliday, Orson Welles, and Howard da Silva. (Welles had been the producer of *Cradle*, and da Silva had played a leading role.) It was a bad time, particularly for people with only tenuous involvements, who wouldn't dream of stealing and passing government secrets but who thought little before writing a check that might end up financing some Communist effort.

In May 1953, a month after *Wonderful Town* had closed for a night because it had been discovered that tickets were being sold for a fellow-traveling paper's benefit, Jerome Robbins was called by the committee. Frank S. Tavenner, counsel to the committee, asked Robbins how "dialectical materialism" had influenced *Fancy Free*. By the time he was called, Robbins had left the Communist party. When Tavenner asked him why, he said it was because of the arguments that had taken place at the meetings. Then he named several people he had known as party members: They included writer Jerome Chodorov, co-author of the book to *Wonderful Town*, and Edna Ocko, who had got Bernstein and Adolph Green an apartment in the summer of 1939. Robbins told the committee that Ocko had been in the middle of an argument when he walked out on his last meeting. In 1985, when Ocko was asked to recall the nature of that argument, she said she thought it had to do with the meaning of existentialism.

Robbin's naming of Ocko is probably a good example of the random brutality of the time. In the late 1930s, when Robbins was known as Rabinowitz, his family name, Ocko was a dance critic under various pseudonyms for *New Masses*, *Cue*, and *Masses and Mainstream*. She wrote a glowing review of his dance in a cabaret with Anita Alvarez to Billie Holiday's recording of "Strange Fruit." Robbins even sent a letter thanking her for the boost to his career. Still, in 1953, Robbins cited Ocko to the committee. That is probably as much as anything a function of the indifference of ambitious people to everybody and everything but their own careers.

A lot of this sort of personal violence took place during the period. Many people, probably including Robbins, named people they knew would be mentioned by others as well to avoid bringing new names before the committee. But the games the interrogators played usually required that the list of names contain at least one that was brand-new to the committee. At least nobody has accused Robbins of naming anybody who was not a party member just to save his own skin. Some others certainly did.

Many witnesses were convinced of their own wrongdoing and wanted to redeem themselves. Most often it is not possible to know what moved people to act as they did. Elia Kazan, the director, named playwright Arthur Miller, who responded to the experience with *The Crucible*, a play set in the late seventeenth century in which children accuse people of being witches. It has been suggested that these children pointing at witches in their midst were analogous to Robbins and Kazan pointing their fingers at Communists.

Kazan tried to justify his behavior, first by taking out an advertisement in the *Times* in which he wrote that love of country had moved him to do what he had done. Second, he made *On the Waterfront*, a film that could be construed as a metaphor for the crisis in his life, as Miller tried to do with *The Crucible*, but with an important difference. In the movie the protagonist, played with eloquence by Marlon Brando in an early film role, "rats" on his brother and his brother's mob associates, because it is the morally correct thing to do. When Sam Spiegel, producer of the film, first asked Bernstein to write a score, the composer turned him down. But in February 1954, Bernstein saw a work print of the movie and changed his mind. He took a leave of absence from Brandeis and moved out to Hollywood. It is his only movie score.

Bernstein had worked on Broadway and was accustomed to yielding to other needs than music in a show. But movies—at least this one—presented him with serious technical demands. In a May 30 article in *The New York Times* and placed at "Upper Dubbing, California," he described the problems of composing the movie score:

> I had become so involved in each detail of the score that it seemed to me perhaps the most important part of the picture. I had to keep reminding myself that it really is the least important part: that a spoken line covered by music is a lost line; and by that much a loss to the picture; while a bar of music completely obliterated by speech is only a bar of music lost, and not

necessarily a loss to the picture. Over and over again I repeat-ed this little maxim to myself like a good Coué disciple, as I found myself pleading for a beloved g-flat.

Sometimes there would be a general decision to cut an entire piece of music out of the picture because it seemed to "generalize" the emotional quality of a scene, whereas the director wished the scene to be "particularized." Sometimes the music would be turned off completely for seconds to allow a line to stand forth stark and bare—and then be turned on again. Sometimes the music, which had been planned as a composi-tion with a beginning, middle, and end, would be silenced seven bars before the end.

And so the composer sits by, protesting as he can, but ulti-mately accepting, be it with a heavy heart, the inevitable loss of a good part of the score. Everyone tries to comfort him. "You can always use it in a suite." Cold comfort. It is good for the picture, he repeats numbly to himself: it is good for the picture....

Despite the excisions made at "Upper Dubbing," which was in fact a large dubbing room on the third floor of the sound building at the Columbia studios, where sound and image were synchronized, what came through was music that aptly illustrated the murder and mayhem of the waterfront. There were, of course, echoes of others: The begin-ning and end recall Copland's *Billy the Kid*; the rhythms are particular-ly Stravinskyan. But the vivid emotional shifts, the striking alternations of pace and color, the episodes of violence where driving rhythms gen-erate terror are pure Bernstein, sound like only him, and could have been composed by no one else.

At the second Brandeis festival in June 1953,
Bernstein conducted the American premiere of Francis Poulenc's *Les
Mamelles de Tirésias [The Breasts of Tiresias].* It is not surprising that
the opera was receiving its first performance in the United States.
The score was characteristic Poulenc: skillful and elegant. But the

1953

With Maria Callas in Milan. "Bernstein asked Callas to sing sections from Tristan *in
Italian.... He did not try to hide his reaction." He let the other guests at the party
know "how appalled he was at 'the difficulty she was having getting things out
vocally.'" Bernstein's wish to present Callas in the most unflattering of ways was in
evidence almost thirty years later when he selected this photograph as the only one of
her to appear in his own book* Findings.

libretto by Guillaume Apollinaire was idiosyncratic and would have had little appeal for a conductor with a routine interior life. Bernstein, always hungry to experience everything, must have felt envy at his wife's having gone through childbirth. In this work, a housewife sick of being a woman turns into a man, and a man turns into a woman, making a number of babies in the bargain. Sometimes Poulenc's style is lovely and light as in an operetta. At other times he is portentously heavy, clearly satirizing grand opera in the context of this absurd situation. Sung in an English translation, the piece was led by an ebullient Bernstein.

During the summer of 1953, Bernstein conducted and taught at Tanglewood. In the fall he toured, first in Rio de Janeiro, where he received fourteen curtain calls at his first appearance, and then in Israel and Italy. He had toured Italy before; in 1950, he conducted some orchestra concerts at La Scala. But it was not until the 1953 tour that the stage was set for Bernstein to conduct his first grand opera. The piece was *Medea* by Luigi Cherubini; Bernstein had never heard of it. Except for *Peter Grimes, Trouble in Tahiti, The Threepenny Opera*, and *Les Mamelles de Tirésias*—all twentieth-century works—Bernstein had never conducted opera.

In *My Wife, Maria Callas*, published in 1982, Giovanni Battista Meneghini tells how the engagement came about. In the fall of 1953 Antonio Ghiringhelli, the director of La Scala, told Callas she would sing the second opera of the season and that it would be *Mitridate*, by Alessandro Scarlatti. The previous two seasons she had sung the first opera. This time that coup was to be reserved for Renata Tebaldi, who would open with Catalani's *La Wally;* it was the centenary of Catalani's birth. But because Callas had had a large success with *Medea* in Florence the season before, and because Ghiringhelli wanted to inject some life into the new season, he suggested at the last minute that they substitute *Medea* for *Mitridate*. Callas agreed but noted that the problem lay in finding a suitable conductor at that late date. Vittorio Gui, who had conducted in Florence, was unavailable. Victor de Sabata, who would have been a fine choice, was also busy at the time. Callas told Ghiringhelli that a few evenings before, on a radio broadcast, she had heard a performance that had thrilled her. She said she did not know who had been conducting but suggested that the La Scala director find him and invite him to conduct her *Medea*.

"Ghiringhelli pursued the lead immediately," Meneghini writes,

and was informed that the concert had been conducted by Leonard Bernstein, a young American who was almost unknown in Italy. Because he was unknown, Ghiringhelli did not want to engage him. But Maria was insistent. Ghiringhelli then sounded out the conductor by telephone. Bernstein told him he was unfamiliar with the opera and therefore not interested in the assignment. "Let me talk to him," Maria said. I don't know what they discussed, because they were speaking in English, but I could tell at one point they were talking about Rossini's Armida. By the end of the phone call, Bernstein had accepted.

Three days after La Scala opened on December 10, Callas sang *Medea* with Bernstein in the pit; it was the first time an American had conducted in the famous Milan house. *Time* reported that Bernstein had never conducted grand opera in his life, had had five days to learn the score, and that the score itself, dating from 1797, had been so filled with dust that it activated an old allergy. But the speed with which he conquered new works, which had filled his fellow students at Curtis with disbelief, was still in evidence. *Time* said:

Once the curtain went up he was the old assured Lenny, he bounced athletically, contorted his features in the dramatic passages, let his face relax to an expression of drugged bliss in the lyric ones. He sang to himself and punctuated the more striking moments with hoarse growls.

The results wore fine. Out of a stiff and rather unremarkable score, with few melodic arias and a mediocre book, conductor Bernstein produced a lively and dramatic show. At the end, white-tied Milanese cheered up a half dozen curtain calls for leading soprano Maria Callas and Bernstein.

A few months later Luchino Visconti, the Italian director, wrote to Callas suggesting he direct her in a *La Sonnambula* with Bernstein in the pit. Although Bernstein had shifted several scenes and numbers in *Medea* and even cut an important aria, Callas agreed. With few exceptions Bernstein could have his way with women, no matter how he treated them.

After the opening of *La Sonnambula*, the Ricordis, the Italian music-publishing family, hosted a party. Bernstein asked Callas to sing sections from *Tristan* in Italian and she began to read through selected passages with him. He did not try to hide his reaction. According to others present, he let them know how appalled he was at "the difficulty she was having getting things out vocally." The peculiar, and mean, note of this incident is that when Bernstein came back to New York, he raved to Tourel about how great and glorious a singer Callas was. Friede Rothe says that Tourel was consumed with jealousy.

Bernstein has never been kind to women, and Callas surely sensed his disapproval at the Ricordis' on that evening. Still she went along with whatever he wished. This included participation in the parlor games that are so obsessive a part of Bernstein's life. Later, seated on the piano stool, with Visconti at the other end of the room. Callas looked at the director, then the conductor, and asked, "Why must it be that all the attractive men are homosexuals?" Nobody replied. Then she demanded of Bernstein, "I want to know the truth and all the truth: Are you homosexual?" There was no answer.

Bernstein told a *Time* interviewer that with a leave of absence from his usual summer chores at Tanglewood, he planned to write a "really big opera" in Europe. The only trouble was, he said, "when you're conducting you itch to compose, and when you're composing you itch to conduct."

The itch to compose in the summer of 1954 did not produce a "really big opera," but *Serenade*, a half-hour work for solo violin, strings, and percussion, a piece many critics hold is his best "serious" work. According to Bernstein, the piece was inspired by a rereading of Plato's *Symposium*. Bernstein may say that music expresses only itself, echoing a statement made by Stravinsky over fifty years ago. But when he composes it is almost always with a program in mind. Other composers may do this, too, without being aware of it. But with Bernstein the translation of literary images into musical notes appears to be a conscious process, despite some of his statements to the contrary.

Commissioned by the Koussevitzky Foundation, *Serenade* is dedicated to the memory of Serge and Natalie Koussevitzky. It was after he wrote the music that Bernstein added the program. Although he says that it is not to be taken literally, he claims that, like Plato's dialogue, "the music ... is a series of related statements in praise of love."

Here then are five movements celebrating Eros in the context of Greek life and thought. During the early years of his marriage, Bernstein appears to have been devoted to his wife and daughter, often praising their beauty in letters to friends. Although the lively sexual life that had characterized his behavior in the 1940s was at least inhibited in the 1950s, the program to *Serenade* confirms that it was never far from his mind. Starting with a fugue based on a lyric theme, the opening movement calls to mind Piston's early criticism of the melodic fragment that Bernstein had presented to him when he asked for a motive that could be used for a fugue. Here again the theme, precisely because of its lyric quality, fights bona fide fugal treatment. The most beautiful movement in the piece is the fourth, an adagio, and a section of such power and concentration that it can sustain the work as a whole. The finale is Bernstein at his most capricious. Here, according to the notes, Alcibiades and his drunken revelers interrupt Socrates' discussion with Diotima. "If there is a hint of jazz in the celebration," Bernstein writes, "I hope it will not be taken as anachronistic party music, but rather the natural expression of a contemporary American composer imbued with the spirit of that timeless dinner party."

Despite the verbal pretension in the accompanying notes, Bernstein's music in *Serenade* is among the most charming, honest, engaging scores he produced for the concert hall. Because he composed it during the summer of 1954 when he was in Europe with his wife and daughter when he had little to distract him in the way of conducting or performing assignments, he worked on it with sustained attention. The concentration shows. The world premiere took place at the Venice Festival that September with Isaac Stern as soloist. Unlike other composers, Bernstein never had to wait long to hear his own work. As a conductor, he could program it for performance almost as soon as he produced the last bar.

Some critics complained about the jazz infusing the last movement. Writing in the *Times* in 1956, after Bernstein conducted the work in its American premiere, Howard Taubman noted, "Mr. Bernstein writes jazz with a flair, but does it really belong in the context of this piece?"

And then: "Leonard Bernstein has written a Serenade that is attractive in places and ought to be better in sum. Just as this work ... has begun to persuade us that it is going to be all music, it fritters away the opportunity. Then fine passages appear and are again dissipated in easy excitement. Too bad."

Bernstein, from the start, has ignored the critics. Except for his early success with *Jeremiah*—and he himself has acknowledged that it was tied to his successful debut as a conductor—he has not received many kind words about his concert pieces. Yet he has never stopped writing them. His overwhelming ambition has been to compose a great work of "art." In fact, at the Trattoria restaurant in New York, just after the American premiere of *Serenade*, Bernstein told some friends including Stern and Diamond, "Look at Mahler. He had to wait for the summers to compose." About the same time Bernstein wrote a letter to Mitropoulos saying he was going to give up conducting in order to concentrate on composition. Faith Reed says Mitropoulos did not reply, that Bernstein's letter "did not call for a reply."

One area that has always elicited praise from reviewers, although it initially enraged Reiner, is Bernstein's work on television. His career on television started with his several appearances on a show financed by the Ford Foundation called *Omnibus*. The first was broadcast on November 14, 1954. Later there were *The Young People's Concerts* on CBS. Here is Bernstein, in recent years, describing how it all came to be:

It was kind of prophetic that my debut as a conductor should have been involved with the electronic medium, the medium of radio, because that was to play—in other manifestations—such a great part in the rest of my life. For a while I was quite accustomed to radio broadcast and I conducted the NBC Symphony at NBC and the broadcasts at Carnegie, a series of broadcasts in Detroit, San Francisco, and various places around and I came to know about timing and about the various hazards and advantages of electronic media. But it really wasn't until 1954 when I got involved with television that I realized the tremendous power of the medium, the power it could have in terms of music, and I got involved with it in a rather odd way.

Again it was coincidental. One of the producers of *On the Town*, which had been done in 1944, was Paul Feigay. Now, in 1954, he was working with Robert Saudek in producing what was then known as *Omnibus*. Alistair Cooke, as narrator, was holding the whole thing together. It was a kind of magazine show with segments. And they had been planning one segment on Beethoven's Fifth Symphony, concentrating on the sketch books that he had written for that symphony. They had somebody or other do this segment and they weren't happy with it. And one day Paul Feigay called me and asked if I would be willing to do it instead. And I said I'd have a shot at it.

And I got involved with the sketch books of Beethoven and developed a short but rather complex program about the first movement only of Beethoven's Fifth; the first movement is a short movement. I tried to analyze the struggle and battlefield on which the thing was written, the millions of changes, the millions of ideas, the crossings out, the additions, and that show became what is now, I guess, a rather famous show. It's been repeated over and over again. But what I realized about it was not only what I thought and felt about these matters—about Beethoven and the creative process—but that I could share it with millions of people face to face, eye to eye, nose to nose, and that I could also use visual aids, which was a whole new wrinkle. For example, we had the first page of the Beethoven Fifth, the whole score, painted in white on a black floor and we had musicians standing—each one on the designated line. Then I dismissed the ones that Beethoven had dismissed in his own mind. Because he begins the Fifth Symphony only with strings and clarinet, out went the flutes, oboes, horns, trumpets, leaving only the people who were relevant standing there. This made such an impression on people because it had this visual connotation of what I was saying, which they were also receiving in an auditory way, and it was unforgettable. I realized suddenly that my own teaching instinct, which I had inherited from my father ... and all my teachers ... who taught me how to teach, this old quasi-rabbinical instinct I had for teaching and explaining and verbalizing, found a real paradise in the whole electronic world of television and I was able to do one show after another. That one was so successful that they invited me immediately to do another one and do an hour long and then ninety minutes long and one show succeeded another with increasing success....[3]

Other *Omnibus* shows dealt with what makes jazz jazz, why an orchestra needs a conductor, what makes Bach Bach, why modern music sounds so strange, what this distinctive form called musical comedy is, and what makes an opera grand.

The manner in which Bernstein crystallized his own ideas on Beethoven and the creative process so that he could present them to a nationwide audience was the model for the rest of the shows. He was formulating these notions for himself as he went along, and that gave the programs the urgency that they had. In 1956 Bernstein won an Emmy, television's equivalent to Hollywood's Oscars; this was the year comedian Sid Caesar, television journalist Edward R. Murrow, and playwright Rod Serling also received Emmy Awards in their fields. The *Omnibus* shows provided the model on which *The Young People's Concerts* were based.

In his recollections of these projects Bernstein said that "between CBS and the Philharmonic we got these on television and I think I am prouder of these fifty-odd shows than of almost anything else I have done in the way of teaching."

Although Bernstein mentioned only the New York Philharmonic, he conducted the first *Omnibus* program with the Symphony of the Air. It was telecast on November 14, probably because Bernstein felt that would ensure its success, November 14 being the date on which he had met Copland in 1937 and made his debut in 1943. It marked the beginning of an affair with the old NBC orchestra that lasted a little more than a year.

The Symphony of the Air was essentially a new name for the NBC Symphony, which had been created in 1937 for Arturo Toscanini. In 1926 Toscanini had taken over the New York Philharmonic. Ten years later, on April 29, 1936, he conducted it for the last time. The legendary conductor had been dismissed partly

November 1954
With Alistair Cooke, host of Omnibus, *and Jerome Toobin, manager of the Symphony of the Air. In* Agitato, *a memoir, Toobin writes that Bernstein* "was a logical candidate for the music director's post. He was young, famous, versatile, well-connected, experienced.... Bernstein had no regular post then and was definitely interested in the Symphony of the Air...."

because of his legendary temper but also because he had demanded a salary of $100,000 at the time when the musicians in the orchestra were earning only $2,700. Members of the board recall that Toscanini also objected strenuously to the power of orchestra manager Arthur Judson and to the fact that Judson, who also was permitted to serve as booking manager for the conductors and soloists who appeared with the Philharmonic, received a percentage of Toscanini's salary. But the quality of his conducting was never an issue.

In 1937 Samuel Chotzinoff, an executive of the National Broadcasting Company, the broadcasting subsidiary of the Radio Corporation of America, went to Italy to persuade Toscanini to return to the United States to become the music director of a new orchestra to be sponsored by NBC. Toscanini agreed and performed with such distinction that he created a second orchestra in New York that was as good as and perhaps better than the Philharmonic. Moreover, the sale of recordings of the NBC Symphony made millions for RCA.

On April 4, 1954, after seventeen years, Toscanini conducted his last concert with the NBC orchestra. At eighty-seven, he was simply too old to continue. Jerome Toobin, who later became the manager of the Symphony of the Air, says that the resignation was not Toscanini's idea but that of David Sarnoff, chairman of RCA. In *Agitato*, Toobin writes:

> Within a matter of hours of the Toscanini "retirement," and the announcement that the Toscanini orchestra, as it was popularly and accurately called, was to be disbanded, the members of the orchestra were given six weeks' notice, and that was to be that. There was, naturally, a great deal of agitation both within and without the orchestra's ranks and in less than a week, there were reports that the orchestra intended to stay alive, independent of Sarnoff and his organization, and the structure of the reconstituted group was to be that of a cooperative, ruled by a committee of member musicians.

It was an uphill fight. Not only did NBC obstruct the efforts of the musicians to remain together, the Toscanini family showed no interest in the orchestra's survival. The motto of the musicians became: "the orchestra that refused to die." Although reports held that they were a proud, conductorless ensemble, the musicians knew that if they could find the right man for the post, their chances to keep the orchestra alive would increase. Bernstein was a conductor on the move. When conversations led to his invitation to them to appear with him on the first of the *Omnibus* shows, the musicians were delighted. Not only did it mean unprecedented fees, there was also the psychological gratification that this was to happen on CBS, the rival to NBC. The program was a tremendous success. Recently, Howard Taubman of the *Times* recalled his reaction to the telecast: "I thought the reproduction of the staff and the illustrations were absolutely marvelous for communication with people. There is great music that is not just for the elite. I am willing to concede that some great works—like the late Beethoven quartets—are accessible only to those with training. But there is much great art that holds that the reverse is true. And there was Lenny proving the reverse."

Virtually all of the critics—both television and music critics—delivered encomiums on the show, to the advantage not only of Bernstein but of CBS and the Symphony of the Air. Two months later, in January 1955, Bernstein and the orchestra played together again, this time at a concert in Carnegie Hall. The program consisted of Copland's *Appalachian Spring*, Hindemith's Clarinet Concerto, and Prokofiev's Symphony No. 5. Taubman's enthusiasm for Bernstein remained intact: "It is still a magnificent orchestra and Mr. Bernstein reminded us that he can be a brilliant conductor.... He conducted as if it were a pleasure and privilege to lead these men who have kept an orchestra in being by their self will. And the men continued to play as if the chance to make music were the most precious gift that could be granted to them."

On January 23, 1955, Bernstein left for Italy, where he conducted *La Sonnambula* and *La Bohème* at La Scala. Then he led the Israel Philharmonic in its first tour of Europe, a tour that brought these Jewish musicians into cities in Germany for the first time since the Holocaust. Bernstein was out of the United States touring for five months.

While he was moving around Europe during that spring, the Symphony of the Air was on a tour of its own to Japan, the Philippines, Taiwan, Korea, Thailand, Okinawa, Ceylon, and Malaya with conductors Thor Johnson and Walter Hendl, both of whom had been fellow students of Bernstein's at Tanglewood in the early 1940s. The concerts were a success. When the orchestra returned to the United States, plans were made for another tour the following spring to Turkey, Egypt, Israel, India, and elsewhere.

Bernstein arranged to conduct a series of six concerts with the orchestra for the 1955–1956 season. Because he was the first conductor after Toscanini to lead a series of concerts with this orchestra, it was assumed by many that he would take over its direction. Toobin writes, "Bernstein ... was a logical candidate for the music director's post. He was young, famous, versatile, well-connected, experienced.... Bernstein had no regular post then and was definitely interested in the Symphony of the Air...."

For the first of the concerts of the 1955–1956 season, Bernstein conducted the orchestra and the Schola Cantorum in Copland's *Canticle of Freedom*. It was a concert for the benefit of the National Conference of Christians and Jews and was designed to call attention to the continuing fight against prejudice. Taubman wrote, "The Symphony of the Air is still a first-rate orchestra. All it needs to make it shine in something like the glory it had when it was the NBC Symphony and its maestro was Arturo Toscanini, is an accomplished conductor. It had one at Carnegie Hall last night in Leonard Bernstein, and the performance had crispness, precision, and richness of style. Mr. Bernstein was directing the first of six concerts the Symphony of the Air calls its own series. Since this is an independent ensemble and its members must eat, it hires itself out to sundry program arrangers. On some of these occasions this season the orchestra seemed to have slipped downhill. With Mr. Bernstein in control last night, all was well again."

But the courtship that was taking place between the conductor and the musicians was suddenly interrupted. On March 19, 1956, a congressional subcommittee headed by Representative John Rooney, a Brooklyn Democrat, held that Bernstein, identified at the hearings only as "No. 5," and several members of the orchestra, were security risks. The trip to the Middle East was canceled.

In *Agitato*, Toobin describes a meeting that took place in Bernstein's nine-room apartment across the street from Carnegie Hall. Along with Toobin and Helen Coates, Bernstein's lawyer, Abe Friedman, who also represented Blitzstein, was present. Toobin recalls Friedman as calm and sagacious, always totally in control, whereas Bernstein appeared anxious and overwrought, obsessively stroking his throat in a characteristic gesture of anguish. Apparently he was concerned not just about his future with this symphony orchestra but most particularly about *West Side Story*, a project he was then working on with Robbins. At the time Robbins was probably a pariah to some; it generally took the theater community some time to forgive those who had informed to the committees. But Bernstein's sympathy for Robbins remained intact.

For reasons that have never come to light, the crisis ended. Toobin writes, "This was practically the last time I saw Bernstein ... and certainly the last time we discussed the political affair. The series with the orchestra ended shortly thereafter, and there was no inclination on the part of Bernstein or the orchestra to renew the association.... I never found out how he avoided any public discomfiture over the Rooney affair."*

Bernstein's luck was remarkable. Six weeks after his anguished meeting with his lawyer, an article in the *Times* literally turned his life around. In 1985 Taubman talked about it: "Olin Downes died in August 1955. I took over the number one spot in September. I began to go to all of the main events of the Philharmonic. Now that I was going every Thursday night, I found what was happening deplorable. Mitropoulos was struggling; the orchestra was shot; the entire enterprise was in grave trouble. This was reflected month after month. What was needed was shock therapy.

"Sulzberger, the father of the present publisher, held daily lunches at the *Times*. When important musicians were there I was invited. There were serious conversations on the sad state of the New York Philharmonic. Each time Sulzberger asked me what I thought, and each time I would say I had not yet decided what to do. Sulzberger, of course, had friends on the board of the orchestra, and he asked me to let him see what I was doing before I did it. I nodded.

"In April 1956, I sat down and wrote that piece. It took me a few days to do it right. What I was doing then—what I proposed to do—

---

* *The FBI files in all probability have additional information on this episode. Although Bernstein was generally cooperative in responding to questions for this book, his office specifically refused the author permission to consult these records. (The Freedom of Information Act provides basic access to such material. In the event, however, that the subject of a report is still living, his permission must be obtained before the relevant data are made available to a third party.)*

was to take over the entire music page. Lester Markel was the Sunday editor. He was a law unto himself. When I proposed the idea to him he refused to let me take over the entire page. But when I sent the piece to him, the whole eight columns, Markel refused to send it to Sulzberger. 'I am the editor,' he said and published it.

"The response was enormous. There were many knowledgeable people—like Leopold Mannes—who wrote in support of what I said. It was a bomb. The blast was not only on Mitropoulos; it dealt with Arthur Judson and the whole organization. The piece was a watershed for the history of the New York Philharmonic. David Keiser, the president, told me it tore them to bits."

Entitled "The Philharmonic—What's Wrong with It and Why," the essay dealt systematically with each of the orchestra's problems. The ensemble, Taubman claimed, was demoralized and had become second class. Mitropoulos, he wrote, was "overmatched by the requirements of the post." Taubman claimed Mitropoulos was weak in critical areas of the repertory and inadequate as a drillmaster. The choice of guests was a narrow one, he noted, and the programming haphazard, lacking in an overall design.

Then he went on to attack precisely what Rodzinski had attacked fifteen years before: a setup in which the manager of the orchestra, Arthur Judson, was permitted to maintain a commercial enterprise, Columbia Artists Management, which managed the careers of conductors and soloists. The logical result of such a conflict of interest would be for Judson to hire his own clients for the Philharmonic at the expense of other artists and the general good of the orchestra.

Taubman was specific in his recommendations. Appoint a new musical director. Select the programs first, then choose the guest artists who would best implement them. Most important: Reach the largest possible audience. (By this time Bernstein had appeared in three *Omnibus* telecasts.)

Paul Henry Lang, a professor of musicology at Columbia who had succeeded Virgil Thomson at the *New York Herald Tribune*, echoed Taubman's complaints in three Sunday pieces that appeared in June. Nor were they alone in finding a moribund tone to the orchestra. During the previous five years, the three most regularly employed guest conductors had been Bruno Walter, George Szell, and Guido Cantelli, the favorite of Toscanini. All were conservative in their programs. Although Mitropoulos may have favored Mahler and some of the moderns, management tried to make up for that by hiring these conductors year after year.

Trustees and boards of directors of American musical organizations are generally a docile lot, and no one in the music business in the United States has more power than the chief critic of *The New York Times*. In its annual report of 1955–1956, the Philharmonic Society stated that it had "received considerable notice in the press containing valuable recommendations for which the Society as a public institution is always grateful. Many of the items brought up by the press were, at that time, and are, under active consideration by the Society's directors. Rather than answer the articles directly, it is hoped that the ultimate results of the Society's actions will speak for themselves." This was distributed on September 10, 1956. Almost immediately Judson's "retirement" was announced. Clearly things were going to change.

But who could have anticipated the dramatic turn of events that was signaled on October 16, two days before the opening concert of the season? On that day Mitropoulos, obviously a weak and by then beaten man, allowed this release to be given to the press: "At the request of its musical director, Dimitri Mitropoulos, the New York Philharmonic has engaged Leonard Bernstein to share the direction of the orchestra beginning with the 1957–1958 season...." In a letter to David Keiser, Mitropoulos gave as his reasons for requesting the administrative change the large number of invitations he had received to conduct in Europe and a bid to increase his activities with the Metropolitan Opera House. "After thinking the matter over very carefully," he added, "I would like to suggest that my colleague, Leonard Bernstein, be invited to work with me and I am sure that together we will be able to prepare a very sound and stimulating season...."

What an unenviable position Mitropoulos found himself in: First of all, he was being assaulted by the specter of Bernstein, whom he had managed to keep away from the New York Philharmonic since 1950, when he first took over the sole directorship of the orchestra. Moreover, the new guests could not have pleased him. None was a specialist in Mahler, Schoenberg, or Berg, the Austro-German moderns he loved. Nor was any in a class with the great interpreters of the classics who had shared the podium with him during recent years. Instead they included André Kostelanetz, Franco Autori, Paul Paray, Max Rudolf, and Igor Stravinsky, who would conduct programs of his own works. But the most tragic note involved Guido Cantelli, Toscanini's protégé. As Toobin reports in *Agitato*, in 1955 Cantelli begged the management to relieve him of his obligation to conduct in 1956, because of the bad treatment he had received from members of the orchestra. But management refused the request. Cantelli died in a plane crash en route to fulfill his obligation in New York. Bernstein took over Cantelli's concert on December 12, 1956, and led the program Cantelli had planned: Hindemith's *Mathis der Maler*, Cherubini's *Anacreon* Overture, and Tchaikovsky's *Symphonie Pathétique*. In his review of the Hindemith, Taubman praised the "well-defined" polyphonic strains, the "well-marked" rhythms, and the sense of "spaciousness" the performance conveyed. To make certain that no one would mistake this program for Bernstein's own, Taubman added, "Since Mr. Bernstein is slated for a weightier share in the Philharmonic fortunes next season, his concerts ... will be worthy of special scrutiny. It is only fair to be patient until he takes on programs of his own choice."

So here he was in the spring of 1957, one year after the Rooney hearings, planning to take over a post transcending, in both money and power, anything he might have dreamed of with the Symphony of the Air. Although at that moment he was co-conductor of the New York Philharmonic, one did not need Felicia's Ouija board to know which of those co-conductors would emerge on top.

As Taubman said correctly in 1985, "There is no doubt that I had a tremendous impact on Lenny's career when I wrote that blast. It gave the Philharmonic courage to give the post to an American—and a young man."

Not only to an American and a young man. But to a Jew. And not a converted Jew with a name like Mahler or Koussevitzky but a Jew with the name Bernstein. Whatever Bernstein was at the time—composer, conductor, pianist, television educator—he was also a Jew and one who worked with other Jews, played with other Jews, never shied away from his identity as a Jew. He had, in fact, been honored in 1955 by the American Jewish Congress for his "contribution toward the enrichment of the musical arts in the country and the Jewish community."

In the early summer of 1955, Bernstein led the

Lewisohn Stadium orchestra and Louis Armstrong's ensemble in W. C. Handy's "St. Louis Blues." The aged Handy was in the audience. Although the venerable Handy song could hardly be called a piece of contemporary jazz, it was certainly a seminal work. On the

1957

Bernstein and Louis Armstrong, Lewisohn Stadium. "Despite his deep ties to jazz, Bernstein has never been considered a jazzman by jazzmen. And if he considered himself a jazzman, he would be playing jazz for the public much more than he does; Bernstein does not hide his gifts."

same program, Bernstein also led Dave Brubeck and the orchestra in Billy Strayhorn's "Take the A Train."

Jazz was on his mind. He was preparing his second *Omnibus* performance, an exploration of America's indigenous musical language. In the show, he presented a jazz piece he had written some years before. In the earliest years of Bernstein's career, Woody Herman had commissioned him to write something for his band. By the time Bernstein delivered it, that Herman band had gone out of business. Bernstein sent Herman the piece anyway but never heard from him.

Prelude, Fugue and Riffs lay around until 1953, when Bernstein had to write a score for *Wonderful Town* in less than five weeks. Bernstein hates to waste anything; pieces of compositions once discarded invariably turn up in other works. On this occasion he used the piece for a ballet number but the choreography didn't work and it was cut from the show in New Haven. Still, *Prelude* was not yet a total loss. Benny Goodman had heard about it, put a band together at his own expense to hear it, and planned to record it. One thing or another intervened.

When the 1955 *Omnibus* came up, Bernstein resurrected the piece. He dedicated it to Goodman, who played a clarinet solo on the show. The program, narrated by Alistair Cooke, the English journalist, was so successful that Bernstein suggested Columbia Records issue a recording. For the disk Bernstein wanted what he called more authentic examples. He used some old Bessie Smith records to illustrate blues and called on Miles Davis for his version of "Sweet Sue."

When it comes to jazz, Bernstein's interest in authenticity reflects a major problem. The term itself came into use around 1915 and has since been applied to many evolving styles. But one factor remains constant. Throughout its history, which began in New Orleans at the end of the nineteenth century, its vocabulary has been tonal, diatonic—in other words, the vocabulary of Western music up to Schoenberg. It is not surprising, then, that Bernstein should feel far greater ties to it than to the so-called classical scores by his contemporaries who have been influenced by the twelve-tone method.

Despite his deep ties to jazz, Bernstein has never been considered a jazzman by jazzmen. And if he considered himself a jazzman, he would be playing jazz for the public much more than he does; Bernstein does not hide his gifts.

What Bernstein is able to do is something few of his colleagues can do. Like Gershwin he can brush by jazz, lifting it out of its original context and transforming it into something new. Through his skilled handling of the sophisticated techniques he learned through his study of classical music, Bernstein uses jazz as a base and brings its beauty and vitality into the concert and opera world.

Bernstein spent the summer of 1955 at Tanglewood. Among his concerts was one devoted entirely to Mozart. He accompanied Jennie Tourel in arias from *Idomeneo*, conducted the overture to *Don Giovanni*, and played the piano solos in the G Major Concerto. Although Bernstein's Mozart did not then compare to his Mahler or twentieth-century Americans, he was a sensitive accompanist and his performing as both pianist and conductor was an effort that only Mitropoulos had matched at that time. For the last week, Bernstein led the premiere of his *On the Waterfront* Suite and Copland's *A Lincoln Portrait* with Claude Rains as narrator; he also appeared as soloist and conductor in *Rhapsody in Blue*.

Bernstein also conducted Beethoven's *Missa Solemnis* with the same soloists he had had at the Koussevitzky memorial concert in 1951. When, on July 7, 1955, Bernstein's son was born, he named him Alexander Serge Leonard. Throughout the 1950s Koussevitzky's ghost seemed to become more, not less oppressive.

In the fall of 1955, right after his second *Omnibus*, a reporter asked Bernstein to explain his continuing interest in jazz. "It's part of my musical thinking," he said. "It's the stuff I've soaked up ever since I heard music."

Another battle—between "low" and "high" art—began paralleling the one between composing and conducting. In 1956, when Bernstein knew he was heading for a preeminent post as a "classical" conductor, he was working on *Candide*, on the surface a comic operetta but in reality a sophisticated parody of opera, the genre best suited to parody, and the one most likely to be used to ridicule everything that is thought to be "high" about art.

The parodying of opera may have been Bernstein's private reason for composing the score. But there was a more public motive. He and Lillian Hellman, whom he had met through Blitzstein in 1949, decided to do the work as, he says, "a political comment in the aftermath of Joe McCarthy." It was the McCarthy hearings that prompted the bitter treatment of the political process in the Hellman-Bernstein *Candide*.

As early as September 1950, Hellman suggested the idea to Bernstein. But she could not pursue it at that time because she was working on another play. Her desire to react to the political harassment of the day through her work, as Kazan, Miller, and others had done, was surely not surprising. In its earliest days the investigations of communism had intruded on her life. Hellman had gone to the Soviet Union in the late 1930s and never said a word against Stalin's purges. In the 1940s she had been involved in Communist activities here. But it was in 1951 that the hearings took a turn that devastated her. Dashiell Hammett, her lover, refused to answer the questions of a congressional committee and challenged its authority. As a result a radio serial based on his best-known character, the private detective Sam Spade, was removed from the air, and Hammett went to prison.

In 1952 the committee subpoenaed Hellman. She later wrote that all she had wanted to do then was emerge with her decency and self-respect intact. She sent a now-famous letter to the committee saying she would testify about her own politics but not about others'. She was allowed to remain silent and unpunished, though she was blacklisted for a time in Hollywood.

The play Hellman was working on, an adaptation of *The Lark* by Jean Anouilh, related to her version of the anti-Communist probes and her view of herself at the center. *L'Alouette*, produced in France in 1953, is a work about Saint Joan, the virgin from Orleans who, at the behest of the voices she hears, takes command of the French army, defeats the invading English, and then is martyred at the stake because she won't stop talking about her "voices," presumably the metaphor for Hellman's refusal to yield to her own inquisitors.

Invited to compose incidental music for *The Lark*, Bernstein produced ten minutes of music for a cappella voices to simulate a medieval sound. Even this minimal contribution was mentioned by drama critics. *Times* reviewer Brooks Atkinson wrote, "Leonard Bernstein's musical recreation of Joan's medieval voices gives the play a new dimension." *The Lark*, with Julie Harris as Joan, was not only praised by the critics, it ran for 229 performances in late 1955 and 1956.

Hellman had planned *Candide* to take the same form as *The Lark*: a play with incidental music. But when Bernstein reread the Voltaire novel, he became so enthusiastic about it that he persuaded Hellman to alter it from a play with music into a bona fide musical, or as he called it on the title page, "a comic operetta." She was reluctant, but finally acquiesced.

James Agee was selected as the first lyricist. Soon he was replaced by Dorothy Parker, who was replaced by John Latouche, who was replaced by the poet Richard Wilbur. While Hellman did not get along at all with his predecessors, she liked Wilbur enough to dedicate *Toys in the Attic*, her next play, to him. With the exception of "I'm So Easily Assimilated," with words by Leonard and Felicia Bernstein, and "Eldorado," with words by Hellman, the lyrics of this first *Candide* were by Wilbur, with minor contributions by Parker and Latouche. Hershy Kay, who had transformed Bernstein's piano score for *On the Town* into a brilliant orchestral arrangement, was chosen to do the same for *Candide* (although Bernstein orchestrated the overture).

Candide opened on December 1, 1956. Directed by Tyrone Guthrie, it had a book by Hellman, a score by Bernstein, and lyrics credited to Richard Wilbur, John Latouche, and Dorothy Parker. Oliver Smith designed the scenery, Irene Sharaff the costumes, and Samuel Krachmalnick conducted. This original production ran fewer than eighty performances. The problem was that the various elements did not jell in the way that would have made the piece work, maybe because there were just too many large talents and large egos involved. Tinkering continued throughout the production process with nobody ever feeling satisfied with his own or anybody else's contribution. Betty Comden remembers that Bernstein—unnerved by what was going on at rehearsals—would come back to his friends and complain, "But I've never had a flop before."

Harold Prince, who directed a 1973 revival, says that when he was first approached he rejected the notion. Then, when he found time in his schedule, he decided to try. First, though, he read Voltaire's original. "I had never read *Candide*," he writes. "I was surprised by how light and impulsive and irreverent and unimportant it is....Voltaire wrote it quickly and denied having written it, putting it down as a schoolboy's prank. And that's the spirit of it. The … years that separated Voltaire's writing and the Guthrie version served only to make a classic of it and spoil all the fun." The years and Hellman's intention to use the work as an attack on the anti-Communist investigating committees.

When it opened Bernstein wrote a "Colloquy" in the form of a dialogue between his ego and his id, which was published in the Sunday *Times*. His major point was that Voltaire's satire may be international in scope but that "the matters with which it is concerned are as valid for us in America, with its puritanical snobbery, phony moralism, inquisitory attacks on the individual, brave-new-world optimism, essential superiority—aren't all these the charges that are levelled against American society by our best thinkers?"

With that article Bernstein made a gesture in Hellman's direction, spelling out the moral of the piece, because he must have known that his lilting, delightful score was at cross-purposes with her dark message. He also made these points: that because the author, composer, and lyricists were Americans, this was an American work; that because the period it covered never touched modern times, it was the only Broadway score in which he did not use his kind of jazz sounds; that, as his music played hopscotch with periods, jumping around in style, so did the scenery of Oliver Smith and the costumes of Irene Sharaff. Brendan Gill in *The New Yorker* held that *Candide* was a musical adapted from an eighteenth-century novel in a twentieth-century *commedia dell'arte* style, with its tongue in cheek all the while. The problem was that Hellman's tongue was never in her cheek. She was dead serious. In its December 10, 1956, review, *Time* commented:

> Lillian Hellman's libretto ... bears her own strong impress, which is foreign to Voltaire's. When Voltaire is ironic and bland, she is explicit and vigorous. When he makes lightning, rapier thrusts, she provides body blows. Where he is diabolical, playwright Hellman is humanitarian.
>
> Whatever its own weight and thrust, the libretto distorts Voltaire's formula without really forging one of its own, and seems too serious for the verve and mocking lyricism of Leonard Bernstein's score which, without being strictly 18th century, maintains, with its gay pastiche of past styles and forms, a period quality. Instead of show tunes, the score goes in

for something akin to Sullivan's spoofing in *The Gondoliers*, offering the wonderful "paste" coloratura of a "Glitter and Be Gay," duets and quartet finales and schottisches and waltzes that can be danced.

In his effort to satirize opera, Bernstein drew a good deal from what he learned from Francis Poulenc while conducting *Les Mamelles de Tirésias*. Poulenc's work taught him how to ridicule the pomposity of the genre. It is hard to believe that he didn't know his music was drowning Hellman's words. But even if he hadn't figured it out himself, his wife persistently pointed it out. In rehearsals, Felicia supported Hellman in pushing for the words to be heard through the score. Hellman, never self-abasing, made well known her unhappiness with the result. She went on record describing *Candide* as her most unpleasant experience in the theater.

Despite the conflicting motives of this complex project, the score turned out to be its star. The overture is the most frequently played concert piece that Bernstein ever composed. For sheer musical virtuosity, the entire score transcends any other Broadway music. Tyrone Guthrie, its original director and a major figure in world theater, described the story of the work in some detail in *A Life in the Theater*:

> From the start the great risk was that the whole thing would seem wildly pretentious. And that is just what it did seem. Only Bernstein's mercurial, allusive score emerged with credit. For my part I do not at all regret the skirmish. It was an artistic and financial disaster from which I learned almost nothing about anything. But it was fun to be closely associated with a group so brilliantly and variously talented.
>
> Bernstein's facility and virtuosity are so dazzling that you are almost blinded, and fail to see the patient workmanship, the grinding application to duty which produces the gloss. This may not be an original or creative genius, but, if I ever have seen it, the stuff of genius is here.
>
> Hellman fought this battle with one hand tied behind her back. We had all agreed that when necessity demanded we would choose singers to do justice to the score, rather than

actors who could handle the text but for whom the score must be reduced. Consequently, line after line, situation after situation, fell flat on its face because—no blame to them—singers were asked to do something for which they had no gift ... nor experience nor understanding. Miss Hellman stooped fatally to conquer. None of her good qualities ... as a writer showed to advantage. This was no medium for hard-hitting argument, shrewd humorous characterization, the slow revelation of true values and the exposure of false ones.

I wonder whether it was an unconscious reaction to the diamond quality of Bernstein's brilliance? She and I, and an eminent squad of technical collaborators—Oliver Smith for the scenery, Irene Sharaff who designed the clothes made by Karinska—all seemed to lose whatever share of lightness and gaiety and dash we might possibly have been able to contribute. My direction skipped along with the effortless grace of a freight train heavy-laden on a steep gradient. As a result even the score was thrown out of key. Rossini and Cole Porter seemed to have been rearranging *Götterdämmerung*.

Bernstein and his friends picked up *West Side Story* while he was still at work on *Candide*. The experience with the Voltaire project was not lost on him. In his new Broadway show he self-consciously abandoned the more sophisticated musical techniques that he had used in *Candide* and went quite obviously in the direction of Broadway. In their initial discussion of the "*Romeo and Juliet*" project in 1949, Arthur Laurents had said, "Whatever we do it can't be opera." Not even a *parody* of opera, was the lesson that Bernstein learned in the fall of 1956.

Less than two months before the opening of *Candide*, Bernstein had appeared in his fourth *Omnibus* show and devoted his presentation to musical comedy. He started by telling the audience that a new musical comedy by Rodgers and Hammerstein or Frank Loesser was anticipated with the same excitement and partisan feeling as a new Puccini opera used to be in Milan or the latest Brahms symphony in Vienna. "Yet no one," he said, "seems to be able to define what this phenomenon is." Bernstein held that the more a Broadway show moved away from pure diversion, the more it tried to engage the interest and the emotion of the audience, the closer it slid toward opera. He said that the more a show used music to further its plot, again the more it moved toward opera.

In turning to a discussion of opera, Bernstein described *recitative* as a tool the composer used to set up the situation for the song that followed. Taking a random sentence, he showed how the *recitative* would sound in the hands of Mozart, Verdi, and Wagner if they were trying to convey that "chicken is up three cents a pound." And then he demonstrated how those same composers would create a lament on the high cost of living. What Bernstein was doing here was probably not far removed from the satire he was creating at the same time for his musical *Candide*.

Taubman, so enthusiastic about Bernstein in the role of classical conductor, did not respond favorably to this. After criticizing Bernstein's use of "some feeble illustrations and annoying examples of condescension," he concentrated on Bernstein's irreverent approach to a form he didn't want treated irreverently:

> Whether he was aware of it or not, his performance amounted to a ribbing of opera. Of course this is not a crime. Even the most ardent, single-minded devotee of opera will concede that it has more than its share of silliness. But what ensued was a homily on the virtues of musical comedy, and it seemed to some of us that opera was being denigrated to build up musical comedy.

Taubman clearly did not subscribe to the notion that the two forms were anything less than antithetical modes of artistic expression, or that enlarging the purposes of one could lead to something comparable to the other. He wrote:

> There is no argument that shows like "Guys and Dolls," "Pajama Game," and "My Fair Lady" represent a joyous American accomplishment. Nor could one dispute the contention that they have drawn inspiration from opera, operetta, revue, vaudeville, and all the other styles of musical theater and have created an original blend.

One's quarrel with Bernstein and "Omnibus" is that they did not probe deeply enough in their analysis of opera, operetta, and musical comedy.... They should have made clear that the glory of great opera is its use of music to achieve penetrating characterization and emotion. It is precisely because many theatergoers do not wish to be troubled by too much depth and seriousness that operetta and musical comedy are gay and superficial in musical content. In such works as "South Pacific," "Fanny," and "My Fair Lady," there are moments when the content is serious and touching. But the musical language employed to convey these emotions lacks the diversity and the musical sophistication of the most enduring musical theater.

Taubman's Sunday essay put a definite limit on how much musical comedy can grow:

The American musical comedy can be a fresh, delightful amalgam of the arts of the musical theater. Let us rejoice in it. But let us not magnify it beyond its desserts. There may be a Mozart along some day, as Mr. Bernstein hopes, to lift it into the realm of lasting art. But chances are that a Mozart would gravitate elsewhere.

One of Bernstein's least apparent characteristics is that despite his seemingly aggressive ways he is, at heart, a passive man. Not only does he receive ideas and sometimes musical passages from others and submit to the personalities of those composers he conducts, he also allows himself to be bullied in matters like this one instead of charging ahead, secure in the knowledge of his awesome talent. At the outset of his program, Bernstein said no one could precisely define what musical comedy was. Then when Taubman went ahead and defined it, Bernstein was affected by what he said.

Thus the fall of 1956 found Bernstein receiving conflicting messages. On the one hand, with the commercial failure of *Candide*, he knew *West Side Story* would have to be more Broadway. On the other hand Taubman, his longtime supporter as a conductor, was echoing Koussevitzky's prejudices of fifteen years before. Moving into the respectable position of the leader of the New York Philharmonic, it was natural for him to identify with the establishment and accept the notion certified by the arbiters of taste that the only high-class form of music theater, the only one that could be considered to be art, was opera, the very genre he had just subjected to such scathing parody.

On April 16, 1985, the Dramatists Guild sponsored a round table discussion on *West Side Story* at Manhattan's St. Peter's Church. The four principals were there: Arthur Laurents, book; Jerome Robbins, choreographer-director; Leonard Bernstein, composer; Stephen Sondheim, lyricist. The house was filled and

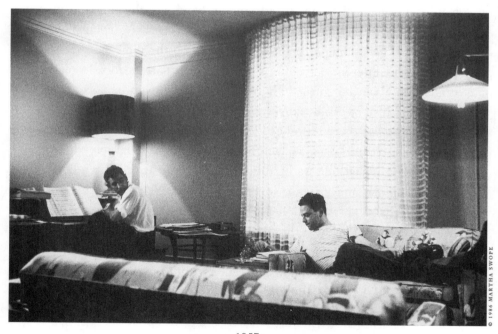

1957

Bernstein and Stephen Sondheim putting finishing touches on West Side Story *in the Jefferson Hotel, Washington, D.C. Brooks Atkinson, drama critic of* The New York Times, *in his book* Broadway: *"Enthusiasm travels fast and infects theatergoers everywhere; and it was not long before* West Side Story *was recognized as an achievement of the first order...." Then comes this comment: "The next year Leonard Bernstein capitulated to respectability by accepting the post of conductor of a famous symphony orchestra." Atkinson was not noted for his use of irony. So it is safe to assume that by not even mentioning the name of the orchestra, Atkinson was denigrating Bernstein's choice.*

playwright Terrence McNally chaired the discussion.

Five minutes into the discussion, Laurents said that Hal Prince, one of the two producers of the show, had written about it in his memoir and had gotten just about everything wrong. On that point all the participants agreed: that they disagreed with Prince's memoir. From then on it was difficult to find a single incident that even two of them recalled in the same way. Bernstein punctuated the lively counterpoint with such remarks as "These are our truths …" and "Steve, you have the meanest memory.…"

More than once Bernstein agreed with Laurents' characterization of the meeting as a *Rashomon-West Side Story*, which the others generally endorsed. *Rashomon* is a Japanese film in which a bandit murders a man and rapes his wife. Or he doesn't. The wife may have seduced the bandit and persuaded him to kill her husband. Or the husband may have chosen to die and orchestrated his death in this particular way. The film is generally perceived as one in which the same story is told through the different perceptions of each of the participants. In reality it is a film about lying, for only one of the stories can be correct. Or parts of each story can be correct.

In *Rashomon* there is no need for the writer to intrude and clear up the ambiguity with objective fact. But in history and biography there is such a need. What follows here is a coherent narrative, with a beginning, a middle, and an end, something impossible to have obtained from the chaotic presentation at the church. It is a narrative that has been pieced together with those quotations from each of the principals that seem most plausible in each instance. The quotations come from the St. Peter's discussion, published reports, and conversations with the principals. To have followed Mallarmé's method and given multiple possibilities for each of the details would have been to devote more space to these nuances than they deserve. One fact transcends all the others: that, in the mid-1950s, four remarkable artists came together and made a work that is a landmark in the cultural history of the United States. *West Side Story* is somewhat reminiscent of a collaboration almost fifty years before when Nijinsky created the choreography, Nicholas Roerich the scenario, and Stravinsky the music for *Le Sacre du Printemps*, with each of the three also becoming involved in the work of the others.

"I met Bernstein briefly in 1943," Laurents says. "I was in the army. They weren't. I was in and that was the time all of their careers took off. I knew Jerry. We were good friends. I was stationed in Astoria and there was an ex-Ballet Theater person in my unit. I went to *Fancy Free* by happenstance. The audience went wild over the ballet. The song at the outset was a shocker. Never had there been such a thing in the Metropolitan Opera House.

"There was a war. What they were doing in art didn't seem that important, and I didn't think about it. *Fancy Free* was a terrific, jazzy ballet but dancing sailors were not the primary interest of many when a war of the nature of World War II was going on."

In 1949 Robbins was in New York working at the Actors Studio. He had recently choreographed *The Guests*, a Marc Blitzstein ballet which has been described as "an exploration of the Romeo and Juliet theme." "One day," Robbins says, "a young actor approached me and told me he had been assigned to do Romeo. He asked for my help. I wondered if I could make a story about Romeo and Juliet today. I called Bernstein and arranged for us to meet with Arthur Laurents."

Robbins called Bernstein on January 6, 1949, and Bernstein noted in his log that day that Robbins had come up with an idea for a "*Romeo and Juliet* set in the slums at the coincidence of Easter-Passover celebrations." The project excited him and he agreed to the meeting with Laurents.

Recalling the meeting Laurents says that Robbins made the suggestion of "a contemporary version of *Romeo and Juliet*—one Jew and one Catholic—and I said it was *Abie's Irish Rose* to music and wouldn't have any part of it." (*Abie's Irish Rose* was a Broadway comedy in the 1920s.) At this meeting Laurents also made clear that under no circumstance would he serve as librettist for a big Bernstein opera. In other words he articulated his passionate unwillingness to play the secondary role of a Boito to a Verdi, even if it could lead to an *Otello*. If they were to move ahead, as far as Laurents was concerned, the collaboration would have to be more balanced than that.

Three months later Laurents sent Bernstein a draft of four scenes. Bernstein wrote in his log that there was much that was good here but noted his concern about "this remote-control collaboration."

Koussevitzky died. Bernstein started to teach at Brandeis and composed *Trouble in Tahiti, Wonderful Town,* and *Serenade.* He began *Candide.* He continued to conduct, touring South America, Italy, and Israel, started his *Omnibus* telecasts, and began his series with the Symphony of the Air. He also had impregnated his wife with their second child. Meanwhile Robbins was working on Broadway and Laurents was in Hollywood. Bernstein and Laurents were discussing another collaboration, a musical adaptation of James M. Cain's *Serenade,* which they asked Robbins to join. He wasn't interested; he wanted to stay with "the *Romeo* show."

Laurents and Bernstein ran into each other quite by accident on August 25, 1955, at the pool at the Beverly Hills Hotel. Bernstein was conducting at the Hollywood Bowl, Laurents writing the screenplay for *Summertime,* a movie based on his play *The Time of the Cuckoo.* There had been a story in the *Los Angeles Times* about gang warfare in a Mexican neighborhood, and they brought up the *Romeo* project again. Laurents says that Bernstein asked why they couldn't put it in Los Angeles and have the Mexicans and Anglos as the two groups. "I suggested the blacks and Puerto Ricans in New York," Laurents says, "because this was the time of the appearance there of teenage gangs, and the problem of juvenile delinquency was very much in the news. It started to work."

Bernstein's log, September 6, 1955: "Jerry loves our gang idea. A second solemn pact has been sworn. Here we go, God bless us!"

Bernstein recently said, "At the time I had madly agreed to take on the lyrics as well as the music. In 1955 I was also working on *Candide.* The music for *West Side Story* turned out to be extraordinarily balletic, and there was tremendously more music—symphonic and balletic music—than anything I had anticipated. I realized then I couldn't do all the lyrics and do them well."

Here then are the musical chairs as they were arranged early in November of 1955: Robbins, then with the New York City Ballet, was ready to go. Laurents, still connected to *Serenade,* which Bernstein had left by then, was also writing *A Clearing in the Woods* for Broadway. But he was ready to go. Bernstein as usual was occupied on several fronts, but he also was ready. A call was put in to Comden and Green to get them to write the lyrics, but they were committed to a movie in Hollywood. So Robbins, Bernstein, and Laurents needed a lyricist.

When *Fancy Free* opened at the Met in 1944, Stephen Sondheim could hardly have been aware of it. Only fourteen, he was living on a farm in Doylestown, Pennsylvania. His mother had brought him there three years before when her marriage to a well-to-do dress manufacturer had fallen apart. At ten, Stephen went to a military school where he says he reveled in its confining order and rules. The most nourishing contact of the time was, nevertheless, with neighbors; the Oscar Hammerstein II family lived only three miles away. Stephen's mother was friendly with the Hammersteins and Stephen became friendly with one of their sons.

During the first years of the friendship, Hammerstein was at work on a Broadway musical. He was writing the lyrics; Richard Rodgers was composing the score. It was *Oklahoma!*, a show that broke new ground in that, for the first time, every song served to tell a part of the story. Dialogue would turn into song, action into dance. The heroine's dreams of anxiety were realized by choreographer Agnes De Mille with chorus girls dressed up like whores. This was the first Broadway show to be called "a musical play," rather than a "musical comedy." Producers thought it not commercial enough; for one thing there were no undressed girls.

Bernstein saw *Oklahoma!* and credits it with influencing him. In one touch alone one can see the influence. The conventional opening for a show about a farm would be a colorful barn dance. Instead *Oklahoma!* opened with one woman alone on stage churning butter. *On the Town* opened a year later. In earlier times, it might have led off with a dozen sailors dancing on the deck of their ship; instead it opened with a lone sailor singing on a stark dockside set. While Hammerstein was working on his musical, he kept encouraging Sondheim, according to Sondheim's own recollections, to cultivate an interest in Broadway. Hammerstein proved to be to Sondheim what Koussevitzky had been to Bernstein. Each of these substitute fathers set the tone that determined his gifted son's life.

At fifteen Stephen and two classmates wrote a musical about campus life. Called *By George*, it was about the Quaker-run George School, which Sondheim was then attending in Bucks County, Pennsylvania. "I really thought it was terrific," Sondheim is quoted as saying in a biography by Craig Zadan. "And when I finished it, I not only wanted Oscar to see it but I wanted him to be the first to read it, because I knew he and Dick Rodgers would want to produce it immediately and I'd be the first fifteen-year-old ever to have a musical done on Broadway."

Hammerstein devastated the boy by telling him the work was terrible. But he also gave him the greatest compliment possible by devoting half a day to a lesson on how to write for Broadway. Sondheim says that Hammerstein "proceeded from the very first stage direction to go through every song, every scene, every line of dialogue.... in that afternoon I learned more about song-writing and the musical theater than most people learn in a lifetime. I was getting the distillation of thirty years of experience." And he was getting it from one of the foremost lyricists of the time and a man for whom writing for Broadway represented no kind of aesthetic compromise.

In 1947 Sondheim went to Williams College. He considered a major in English and a major in mathematics but finally decided to concentrate on music. On graduating he received the Hutchinson Prize, which provided him with a two-year fellowship he used to study with Milton Babbitt, professor of music at Princeton and the leading advocate of serialism in the United States. Despite Babbitt's recondite approach to his own "serious" composition, he had always loved American popular music. Sondheim says they spent the first half of each lesson analyzing Kern, Berlin, da Sylva, Brown, and Henderson, and then they would turn to Mozart. He never addressed Schoenberg, his own most formidable influence, because, Sondheim explains, "Milton said he went into atonality when he had exhausted all the tonal resources, but since I had not, I should stay with tonality."

Through the Hammersteins, Sondheim met many people in the world of entertainment. One evening at a dinner party, Hammerstein introduced him to George Oppenheimer, who had just produced a pilot for a new television series based on Thorne Smith's *Topper* stories. The pilot had been accepted, and Oppenheimer needed a writer to help him turn out scripts. Hammerstein recommended Sondheim, who accepted the job.

After Sondheim returned from Los Angeles, he served as an usher at the wedding of a friend. One of the other ushers was Lemuel Ayers, producer of *Kiss Me, Kate*, based on Shakespeare's *The Taming of the Shrew*, transformed into a musical with a score by Cole Porter. Ayers had still another property, one called *Saturday Night*. Ayers listened to some of Sondheim's work and hired him to write the score and lyrics. Jack Cassidy and Alice Ghostley were cast in leading roles; half the money had been raised; then suddenly Ayers died. With the cancellation of that show, Sondheim was left without a project.

Oppenheimer, Sondheim's former employer on the *Topper* show, was a good friend of Martin Gabel, the producer of Cain's *Serenade*. By this time Bernstein had left *Serenade*, and Gabel was looking for a composer and lyricist. Gabel listened to Sondheim's score for *Saturday Night* with Laurents present. Laurents recalls that "I thought Sondheim's lyrics were brilliant, but not the music." Whatever Laurents thought, Warner Brothers bought *Serenade* and made it into a movie starring Mario Lanza.

Several months later Sondheim attended an opening night party. "I didn't know anyone there," he says, "and then I spotted Laurents. I went over to make small talk and asked him what he was doing and he said he was just about to begin a musical on *Romeo and Juliet* with Bernstein and Robbins. I asked, just idly, 'Who's doing the lyrics?' And Arthur literally smote his head, which is, I think, the only time I saw anyone literally smite his head. There seemed a real indentation there. And he said, 'I never thought of you, and I liked your lyrics to *Saturday Night* very much.' "

Laurents remembers smiting his head, and the words he recalls saying were " 'My God, you're the lyricist.' I thought he would jump for joy. Instead he said he'd have to think about it. He wanted to do the music, too. I invited him to meet with Bernstein and play some of the material to *Saturday Night*."

Sondheim says, "Although I had limited interest in doing the lyrics, the project sounded terrific. And there was the glamour of meeting Bernstein. We met at his studio on the second floor of the Osborne and I played *Saturday Night* for him. He said, 'Don't you have more poetic lyrics to show me?' I don't use poetic in that way—to mean florid. Since this was a colloquial show taking place in Brooklyn, 'poetic' lyrics would have been inappropriate. Certainly there was an intellectual tension from the start.

"A week later," Sondheim says, "Lenny called and asked if I would do the lyrics with him. I talked to Hammerstein who knew how much I wanted to compose the score, but he advised me to take the opportunity to do the lyrics because it would be good for me to work with professionals of that caliber. One week later I started to work."

The contract held that Bernstein would compose the score and that there would be a double credit for the lyrics. Because music and lyrics together were to receive four percent of the royalties, Bernstein would get three percent for doing the music and half of the lyrics and Sondheim one percent for his half of the lyrics. That was November 1955. The first piece Bernstein played for Sondheim was the song "Maria."

At St. Peter's Church, Sondheim said Bernstein had written the name "Maria" as "a lyric line." Bernstein answered that he had completed the song as a tune "but not as a lyric, not as a satisfactory lyric." When Robbins explained, "The whole experience was a wonderful sort of mutual exchange: what we gave each other, took from each other, yielded to each other...," Bernstein finished the thought with "stole from each other."

Stealing is what many great artists do. Picasso and Stravinsky repeatedly claimed they took anything they wanted from anyone. Faulkner remarked, "If a writer has to rob his mother, he will not hesitate. The 'Ode to a Grecian Urn' is worth any number of old ladies." Bernstein appears to have done a little more of this than makes him comfortable. In 1983 he told a radio interviewer, "I am beginning to think that I have only begun to compose my own music. At the beginning there was more than a little of Copland, Stravinsky and Debussy that got into it…. The better a conductor you become, the harder it is to be a composer."

No doubt "known" music crowding into a conductor's head may impede the emergence of fresh musical ideas. But Bernstein is particularly hard on himself here. Generally he needs to use found material to get off and running; then the piece becomes idiosyncratically his own. As *On the Town* borrowed from Blitzstein's *Freedom Morning*, and then took on a tone quite removed from Blitzstein, so "Maria" came from *Regina*, the opera Blitzstein had composed a few years earlier, but then went its own more aggressive way. The passage that Bernstein picked up was one between the prologue and first act; he inverted one interval but left the harmonies and rhythms virtually intact.

Sometimes Bernstein takes from himself. "One Hand, One Heart," sung in *West Side Story*'s bridal shop scene, was taken from *Candide*. Bernstein and Sondheim paid *Candide* back with a song, originally from the same scene, about an imagined visit that Tony and Maria make to her mother's house for tea.

Bernstein and Sondheim were in constant contact while they were working on the show. They would write in separate rooms in Bernstein's apartment and then, after an hour or so, get together to see what each had done. In addition to "Maria," Sondheim recalls that at the start, Bernstein gave him "Boy, boy, crazy boy,/Get cool boy!" He says he accepted it but discarded another Bernstein piece. According to his memory, which may or may not be the "meanest" one, Bernstein would fight him "on every word. I would say: 'I just met a girl named Maria,' and Lenny would interrupt with 'I just *saw* a girl…' It was that way from beginning to end. It is true Lenny put in a lot of time on the lyrics but when I sat down to write, it was *I* who wrote them."

Whatever tension there had been was kept under wraps. "I freaked out when Steve came in," Bernstein says. "From that day to this we've been loving colleagues and friends." Sondheim's assessment is more measured but does not contradict Bernstein's: "We argued but it was never ugly. It was even fun. We got our hostilities out on the anagram table. Lenny never won."

Bernstein may have lost at anagrams and in the use of a word or a phrase. But in the big competition, that is in *West Side Story* itself, he won overwhelmingly because it was he who composed the score. It was not for nothing that Laurents attacked the idea of producing a libretto for a Bernstein opera, or that Sondheim was resistant to writing lyrics for the show. Music is a powerful art. *Le Sacre du Printemps* is Stravinsky's masterpiece, not immediately associated with Roerich, Nijinsky, or even Diaghilev.

Laurents appears to be nourished by constraints. If they are not there, he imposes them on himself. The constraint he chose for *West Side Story* was Shakespeare's play. Laurents chose to parallel it blow by blow, scene by scene, while Bernstein, Robbins and Sondheim went their more freewheeling twentieth-century ways. Following the model so skillfully that nobody was the wiser, he achieved his goal. The book is one of the shortest in the history of Broadway but it contains hidden gems.

Shakespeare's plot centers on two star-crossed lovers surrounded by a sea of violence; so does Laurents's tale. Juliet has a confidante in her nurse, so Maria has one in Anita, her friend. Juliet has a suitor, Paris; Maria has Chino. Shakespeare's lovers meet at a ball, Laurents's at a high-school gym dance. The hatred in Shakespeare is concentrated in the Montagues and Capulets, two feuding families. The hatred in *West Side Story* is invested in the Jets and the Sharks, two teenage gangs.

Laurents transforms the balcony into a fire escape, Friar Laurence into Doc, the apothecary into the local drugstore. The crisis in both is precipitated by the same series of events: In Shakespeare, Tybalt kills Mercutio, Romeo's friend, so Romeo kills Tybalt. In *West Side Story*, Bernardo kills Riff, Tony's friend, precipitating Tony's killing of Bernardo.

Laurents says his colleagues could not understand his insistence on remaining faithful to Shakespeare, but there is one big plot difference: Juliet dies and Maria lives. Most Broadway veterans believed that if after Bernardo and Riff died, both hero and heroine were to die, the show would be unable to attract any of Broadway's traditional audience.

As the show approaches its climax, Maria picks up the gun that has been lying beside her lover's body. Seemingly unable to sing, apparently reduced to whispered speech, she murmurs what she has to say. The fact is this was an accident, not a planned conceit. The idea was for Maria to sing a "mad aria" at this point. But Bernstein was not satisfied with any of his four or five attempts.

Robbins has always been the choreographer best suited to Bernstein. As music generally contains literal meaning for Bernstein, so dance "meant something" to Robbins. Whenever Robbins was faced with choreographing a dance for this work, he would always ask, "What's it about?" None of Balanchine's abstract classicism here. Originally the heavily instrumental prologue had lyrics; then the lyrics were thrown out and the music was made to convey precisely what it did through Robbins's masterful use of movement. In fact, when *West Side Story* opened, it was the choreography that provoked the most praise. Bernstein did not win a Tony for *West Side Story*. The *West Side Story* awards came when the movie was made in 1961. Meredith Willson's *Music Man* won the award in 1957 for the best musical on Broadway.

For four months after Sondheim entered the *West Side Story* project, he, Bernstein, Robbins, and Laurents worked on it. Then *Candide* came alive again. As Stravinsky put aside *Le Sacre du Printemps* to work on *Petrouchka*, so Bernstein put *West Side Story* aside for almost a year. Robbins went off to direct *The Bells Are Ringing* for Broadway, Laurents supervised the production of his play *A Clearing in the Woods*, and Sondheim returned to television, this time working on a project that suited his talents far more than *Topper* had. With Professor Bergen Evans, he wrote a show devoted to language called *The Last Word*.

On March 17, Bernstein wrote in his log:

> *Candide* is on again; we plunge in next month. So again *Romeo* is postponed for a year. Maybe it's all for the best; by the time it emerges it ought to be deeply seasoned, cured, hung, aged in the wood. It's such a problematical work anyway that it should benefit by as much sitting time as it can get. Chief problem: to tread the fine line between opera and Broadway, between realism and poetry, ballet and "just dancing," abstract and representational. Avoid being "messagy." The line is there, but it's very fine, and sometimes takes a lot of peering around to discern it.

Less than a year later *Candide* had opened and closed. However disappointed he was, Bernstein appears never to have placed the blame on any single figure. For February 1, 1957, his log reads: "*Candide* is on and gone; the Philharmonic has been conducted; back to *Romeo*. From here on nothing shall disturb the project; whatever happens to interfere I shall cancel summarily. It's going too well now to let it drop again."

This time Bernstein must have meant what he said, for virtually everything that could interfere did. First there was the question of who would produce it. Roger Stevens said yes, but everyone else turned it down, and Stevens did not want to do it alone. Hal Prince, a friend of Sondheim's since 1949, turned it down initially. George Abbott, then directing *New Girl in Town*, which was being produced by Prince and Robert Griffith, turned it down. Richard Rodgers, who had known Sondheim from his preadolescent days and whose daughter Mary was Sondheim's good friend, and Oscar Hammerstein turned it down.

Leland Hayward turned it down. Many said it was an angry, ugly show; there was so much violence in it, with two dead bodies on stage at the end of the first act. The group had a backers' audition. "We all got up," Bernstein says, "and did our damndest. It was in an apartment on the East River. There was no air-conditioning. The windows were open and there were a lot of tugboats. Later we put the tugboat sound into the score."

Cheryl Crawford finally said yes. Generally an honorable, reliable producer, she appears to have been thrown by this group, because she behaved in an eccentric way. She reportedly told each collaborator angry things that his colleagues had said about him. She also wanted the show to explain why the poor in New York, who had once been Jewish, were now Puerto Rican and black. At one meeting she expressed dismay that, with all the special locution, no one in the show ever said, "That's how the cookie crumbles." The fact is Laurents avoided the slang of the day, knowing how quickly it would become stale.

Six weeks before rehearsals were to begin, the four collaborators met in Crawford's office. She was angry. She said she wanted the show's book to explain why these kids were the way that they were. When someone said the piece was a poetic fantasy, not a sociological document, she replied, "You have to rewrite the whole thing or I won't do it." According to Bernstein, "We all went to jelly." Without saying a word to each other they rose simultaneously, as though a conductor had cued them and walked out. First they went to the Algonquin Hotel but were not admitted because Laurents wasn't wearing a tie. Then they walked to the Iroquois Hotel, where Laurents used a public telephone and called Stevens collect in London. Stevens told him, "Whatever happens, keep working."

Still they knew that Stevens could not produce the show alone. Bernstein says he was even considering giving it to the City Center for a two-week run. Prince was in Boston with *New Girl in Town* and called Sondheim to tell him about the difficulties he was having with his show. Then he asked how Sondheim was. "We don't have a producer" was Sondheim's reply. Prince told Sondheim that he and Griffith would come to New York that Sunday, would listen, and, if they chose to produce the musical, would return that same afternoon to Boston because their own show needed their concentrated attention. Under no circumstance was anyone in the *Romeo* project to expect them until after *New Girl* opened.

It worked out precisely that way. Prince and Griffith listened to a run-through, agreed to take over, and returned to their own troubled show. The day after that show opened, they began raising money for *Romeo*. In seven days they had pulled together $300,000. Rehearsals began within weeks of the original date. Laurents notes that once Lillian Hellman phoned him at midnight. He says he knew her only slightly. She said that he was in for terrible trouble because Bernstein was a monster and had created the *Candide* disaster. Crawford and Hellman, both strong women, had found themselves unable to work with him.

Hellman was not alone in her dismal prognosis. Bernstein recalls he and Sondheim played the score for Columbia Records and were turned down: "We both slaved. We sang sextet, played four hands. It didn't work. 'Too many words in the lyrics…. Too many tritones in the music.'"

Even after the money was raised the proceedings were delayed because Robbins wanted Oliver Smith to redesign the sets. Then there were problems with the casting because this was to be a show about slum kids, so stars couldn't play them. But they needed people who could move, dance, look young, and sing. The critical consideration was that although they needed performers who could sing, they shouldn't be singing with anything resembling "trained" voices. On that issue Sondheim was adamant. He says Babbitt introduced him to opera and tried to activate his interest in it, "but I have never responded to opera or to the forcing of voices that opera demands."

Larry Kert tells how he was cast as Tony: "In 1956 I was in *Mr. Wonderful* starring Sammy Davis, Jr., and Chita Rivera. I was in the chorus doing a number behind Chita. She had just gotten the part of Anita and told me there was an open call the next day for the chorus. That summer I had been the male lead in a show *Fat Tuesday* playing at a resort in the Catskills. It was about gang warfare and I did a number, "No More Mambo," about never going out at night because God knows what's going to happen to you. Cheryl Crawford and the four big guys were there. They said, 'Thank you very much,' and I went back to *Mr. Wonderful.*

"In the spring of 1957 Sam Zolotoff had a story in the *Times* that Crawford had pulled out of the show saying it would be an artistic success but a commercial failure. The show went into rehearsal in June. By then *Mr. Wonderful* had closed. My sister Anita Ellis, then singing in Bermuda, told me they wanted to see me again for the role of Bernardo, the Puerto Rican leader. [Anita Ellis and Arthur Laurents were close friends.] Again I auditioned. Again they said, 'Thank you very much.' I was clearly terrible, and they needed a dancer for Bernardo.

"A little later I was working on a TV show called *Washington Square*. Robbins had five people auditioning for Riff, and I was called again. I did 'Cool' for them, but again there was too much dancing involved. Until then I was strictly a chorus boy and had no ambitions for a star role. I was happy in the chorus line. I didn't dance well enough for Riff.

"Burt Shevelove called. Shevelove was directing an industrial show for *Esquire*. Sondheim showed up. He used to go to everything. After the show Sondheim said, 'My, you sing high. How come you never auditioned for Tony?' I told him every newspaper had said Bernstein was looking for a six-foot blond Polish tenor, and that I was five-eleven, dark, and Jewish. He asked me to try for Tony. At the audition I sang 'Maria' in the original key. I cracked on the high note. Still they saw something they liked and had me do it again one note lower. At the time Anna Maria Alberghetti and Frank Purretta, a top tenor and a glorious singer, had been their choices for the two roles. As I was leaving, Ruth Mitchell, the stage manager, introduced me to Carol Lawrence in the lobby. Just then the big four passed us there; they asked us to walk on stage together. They asked us to sing 'Tonight.'" That song had been a recent addition. Originally the balcony scene had included "Somewhere," written about the time of *On the Town*, followed by "One Hand, One Heart." When Hammerstein saw a run-through he said that what the balcony scene needed was a song that really soared. "Somewhere" was transferred to the end of the show, "One Hand, One Heart" was put into the bridal shop, and Bernstein and Sondheim sat down together and created "Tonight."

Carol Lawrence asked if she and Kert could go home and memorize the song. "That was a risk," Kert explains. "People tend to be more lenient when performers have the music in their hands. But Carol decided to go for broke, and we worked on 'Tonight' for three or four days. At that time, it was a twelve-minute scene; there was so much glorious music in it. But, for theatrical reasons, much of the music was cut and it emerged a seven-minute scene. That was probably the correct decision, because the dialogue was redundant, but what a lot of gorgeous music was lost.

"When I was doing the audition, I looked around for Carol on stage and couldn't find her. Without any plan to do it, she had gone up a back fire escape she had seen there, just to project the feeling of a balcony. When I had to sing 'I'm coming up,' I shimmied up the pole, also on instinct. It lent a sense of urgency to the moment and showed some physical prowess on my part.

"When we had finished, Bernstein walked up to the front of the house. 'I don't know what's going to happen,' he said. 'We have more people we promised to hear. But that is the most mesmerizing audition I have ever seen.'

"That night I went home and was alone. My roommate was out for the evening. At seven fifty-eight Arthur Laurents called and said, 'We've been sitting around and they all said I should break the news to you.' Break the news sounded ominous. But he went on, 'How does it feel to have a lead on Broadway?' The next morning Zolotoff ran this item in his column: 'Leonard Bernstein has found his Romeo and Juliet in Larry Kent and Carol Lawrence.' The first time my name was in the paper, it was misspelled."

Kert says Bernstein was consistently supportive, that he never ever whispered a complaint. When Kert asked for help, Bernstein sent him to a retired voice teacher living in an uptown hotel: "It was she and my instincts that got me through the role" Kert says Robbins was hard on everyone. "He seemed to control the whole enterprise. He would say, 'That's a B-flat, not a G-major chord.' Or 'That skirt is an inch too short.' I got a lot of trouble from Jerry. He does his homework, and I had never done anything like this before. He had me crying much of the time."

Robbins had more than Kert crying. He followed the Actors Studio version of Stanislavsky's "Method" of intense identification between actor and character. In his *Contradictions: Notes on Twenty-Six Years*, Harold Prince, in discussing this show, writes, "The whole relationship between dancer and choreographer contains powerful elements of sadomasochism." During rehearsals, Robbins had the cast in jackets with JETS and SHARKS printed on them. On a bulletin board backstage, he posted news of the gang battles from the papers. He forbade his actors to use their real names and insisted that they call each other by their stage names even off the stage. Kert says that Robbins generated so much antagonism between the groups that the two male leads, generally best friends, never lunched together during the entire rehearsal period. No one suffered more than Lee Becker, who played the cruelly named character "Anybody's." She found the cruel treatment she received in the script mirrored in reality. She always ate her lunch alone.

This is not to suggest anyone fought Robbins on applying the Method. It was only about the cruel treatment that they complained. Inevitably the collaborator's efforts overlapped. Each took something from the other, and Laurents took a lot from Shakespeare. Bernstein—who is lately given to using hyperbolic language routinely—says that they "raped" Laurents's book, often using it as a starting point for a lyric line. This in itself is not unusual. But to take a book line such as "A boy like that, who'd kill your brother," and think of it as a line in a song struck the romantic in Bernstein as altogether remarkable. What is particularly interesting about this example is not only the idiosyncratic Sondheim lyric, but the idiosyncratic Sondheim-like music it brought forth: tight, circular, based on a small cell. Sondheim says it is the only lyric in the show that he gave to Bernstein "dry." That means they did not develop the song simultaneously, influencing each other as they went along. Instead Sondheim handed Bernstein the complete lyrics before any music was composed.

After eight weeks of rehearsal, and just before the opening in Washington, the collaborators decided that the character of Tony had not been defined in musical terms early enough in the show. Until then, his first song had been "Maria." Bernstein and Sondheim went to work one afternoon and by midnight they had composed "Something's Coming," Tony's song at the end of the second scene. The music is charged with an energy that seems more Sondheim than Bernstein. When they had completed the song, Bernstein called Felicia in to hear it. Sondheim recalls that she came into the living room in her nightgown and gave her approval, something it was clear that Bernstein wanted.

Although there were fewer changes during the tryout for *West Side Story* than for virtually any other Broadway show, one interesting incident took place in Washington. For the second-act ballet, Robbins wanted a sound almost rhythmless, as though from a string quartet. When the orchestra got into the pit for the important technical rehearsal (where cues, places, and sets were checked) the musicians played the piece the way Bernstein had written it. "Jerry got into the front row," Sondheim says, "leaned over Max Goberman who was conducting, and instructed him to circle each of the notes [Robbins] wanted deleted, those that gave him the rhythm he didn't want. I expected there to he a big fight, something I could call home about. Lenny got up and disappeared into the back of the theater. A few minutes later I looked for him but couldn't find him anymore. I could not believe he would have left the theater during a 'tech' rehearsal. I went into the street and walked until I reached the first bar. I went in and there was Lenny, with three scotches lined up."

Titles began with *East Side Story*, moved to *Gangway!* By the time the show got to Washington, it was called *West Side Story*. Its first performance was a success. Bernstein says that at intermission, Supreme Court Justice Felix Frankfurter met him in the lobby and said, "The history of America is now changed." Richard Coe, a critic for *The Washington Post*, called *West Side Story* a "work of art." But he did not mention Sondheim's name and that upset the lyricist. "I ended up writing all the lyrics," he says, "and received no mention in Washington. I was really unhappy. Bernstein knew it and came to me and generously offered to take his name off the lyric credit and even give me the concomitant royalty fee. Instead of dividing it three percent and one percent, he offered to divide it evenly. I said no. All that interested me was the credit. I would do the same today."

G. Schirmer, Bernstein's publisher at the time, reports that Flora Roberts, Sondheim's agent, asked that they "pull the cover off the printed music in order to change it to the single credit for lyrics. We had to reprint the first signature [batch of pages] for the inside titles as well. Some scores had been completed and bound. A smallish amount. What was really involved was the title page, the cover, and the rerun of the first signature."

After Washington the show went to Philadelphia, where new posters reflected Sondheim's new status. On September 12, Bernstein sent a letter to Diamond, the first he had written since the closing of *Candide*, and characterized the previous months as "one monochromatic labor on this show which is now thankfully open, and provisionally a smash hit. The three weeks in Washington were phenomenal sellouts, raving press and public. Now similar in Philly. It really does my heart good—because this show is my baby, my tragic musical-comedy, whatever that is; and if it goes in New York as it has on the road, we will have proved something very big indeed, and maybe changed the face of the American musical theater."

In Philadelphia Bernstein took a streetcar ride with Sid Ramin, his boyhood friend who was also one of the orchestrators on the show: "Lenny went to the back of the streetcar, spread out over several seats, and lay down. Then he said, 'I've been offered the opportunity to become music director of the New York Philharmonic.' All I could think of was, *this* is the music director of the New York Philharmonic? Lying down in a Philadelphia streetcar?" Bernstein accepted the offer.

Brooks Atkinson, drama critic of *The New York Times* from 1925 to 1960, mentioned Bernstein's decision in his book *Broadway*:

> If Leonard Bernstein had not deprived himself of a spectacular career by becoming conductor of the New York Philharmonic, the musical stage would be richer.... *West Side Story* was Mr. Bernstein's finest work. By the standards of Broadway, it looked unpropitious. Instead of glamor, it offered the poverty-stricken life of Puerto Rican street gangs, and it did not conclude with romance and the cliché of living happily ever after. It concluded with the violent death of the chief male character. Although it was deliberately patterned after *Romeo and Juliet*, it dispensed with the wit, poetry, gentility, and ceremoniousness of the Shakespeare drama. In the beginning, some theatergoers were repelled by the ignobility of the *West Side Story* scene and complained that Broadway had betrayed them.

But enthusiasm travels fast and infects theatergoers everywhere; and it was not long before *West Side Story* was recognized as an achievement of the first order. Mr. Bernstein's third
city score (the fourth if the ballet *Fancy Free* is counted) was sui
generis, a harsh ballad of the city, taut, nervous and flaring, the
melodies choked apprehensively, the rhythms wild, swift and
deadly. Since Jerome Robbins, the director, had been trained in
ballet, the staging had a breathtaking pace, and the ballets were
explosive. Carol Lawrence and Larry Kert played the leading
parts with passion and wonder. Everything was superbly blend-
ed in this exotic work—the blunt text by Arthur Laurents, the
lyrics by Stephen Sondheim, the pitiless city sets by Oliver
Smith, in addition to Mr. Bernstein's score. *West Side Story* dispensed with the familiar charms of musical theater and relied
solely on talent and artistic conviction. It had 732 performances
on Broadway.

Then comes this comment: "The next year, Leonard Bernstein
capitulated to respectability by accepting the post of conductor of a
famous symphony orchestra." Atkinson was not noted for his use of
irony. So it is safe to assume that by not even mentioning the name of
the orchestra, Atkinson was denigrating Bernstein's choice.

Respectability was not the only issue. Bernstein must have felt elated at being named sole music director of the New York Philharmonic, knowing that two of his "fathers" had done nothing to help him get it. With his appointment, he proved beyond his wildest boyhood dreams that he was the man his father said he was not. Even

© WHITESTONE PHOTO/HEINZ H. WEISSENSTEIN

1958
South America: "In seven weeks the Philharmonic played thirty-nine concerts in twelve countries ... Bernstein was the only one ... who appeared to enjoy himself.... Felicia left the tour and returned home early because her husband's flamboyant flirtations with men in Chile, her native country, humiliated her."

at the moment of the announcement, Sam shifted attention away from his gifted son to himself: "I tried to give him *ruach Elohim*," he repeatedly told the press, "the Godly spirit. With it a man does not become dizzy when he reaches high places. Without it he is nothing and the food in his mouth is like straw."

Regarding Mitropoulos, Bernstein's triumph must have had even darker resonance. Here was a man who had invited a Harvard junior to Minneapolis, who had promised the young musician a job with the Minneapolis Symphony, who had not delivered on that promise, who had promised it to him the next year and had not delivered again. Here was a man who had watched as Bernstein then rose through the intervention of Koussevitzky, the director of the Boston Symphony and the man who had prevented Mitropoulos, reportedly because of his own jealousy, from returning to Boston as guest conductor in 1938, after his striking success in 1937. Mitropoulos's deep disappointment at this manifestly unfair turn of events could only have strengthened his already apparent reluctance to help Bernstein.

Events that followed increased the chasm between the two men, an estrangement apparently never articulated. In the 1944–1945 season, when Bernstein appeared as guest conductor in Minneapolis, at a post-concert party, he spoke so insultingly about Mitropoulos, who was away for the week, that he was publicly rebuked for his remarks by the concertmaster's wife. A few years later Bernstein told Mitropoulos of his own role in preventing the conductor from succeeding Koussevitzky at the Boston Symphony.

In addition to the personal struggle characterizing relations between Mitropoulos and Bernstein, there was an aesthetic battle. It revolved around the conflict between the tonal and twelve-tone composers. Gunther Schuller, the composer and conductor, who has had success in both fields, knows the situation firsthand. During the 1955–1956 season, Mitropoulos had conducted two Schuller works and commissioned a third, which he presented in the spring of 1960. Schuller says that while there may have been some truth to the claim that Mitropoulos had failed to maintain orchestral discipline, that claim masks another one that management is reluctant to acknowledge. Mitropoulos was determined to conduct those twelve-tone works whose intricacies he heard with more accuracy than virtually any other living conductor, as he had in Minneapolis. Schuller speaks of several "unforgettable" Mitropoulos performances of the Schoenberg *Variations* and the Webern Symphony Opus 21. He says that the tape of a performance of the Webern transcends any recording of that work. The fact is that Mitropoulos was presenting in New York, or at least trying to present, that very repertory that Leibowitz was introducing to Europe just after World War II. According to Schuller, "This was the music that everyone in the Stravinsky-Copland axis had been suppressing. There is no doubt that Mitropoulos was hurt at being displaced, but what hurt him more than anything else was the fact that the post was being taken by someone in the other camp. It seems foolish now, and it seemed foolish to me then, but in the nineteen-forties and even the nineteen-fifties, when a composer came into the profession he was expected to take a stand between the Stravinsky-Copland and the Schoenberg schools. There was always a touch of the standoff in Lenny's relationship to me because he believed I was born on the wrong side of the musical tracks. Lenny has always had me off in that corner and he still thinks of me in the 'enemy' camp."

However much Mitropoulos despaired about the situation, he never made public statements about it. Mitropoulos had grown up in a monastery that rose out of the sea on a high cliff. A two-thousand-year-old retreat, it was under the supervision of his Greek uncle. According to Mitropoulos's friends—and he had many who loved him in New York—he was a long-suffering person; most of them use the word "masochist." Schuller says that Carlos Moseley, important then in the management of the New York Philharmonic and naturally wanting subscriptions to rise, wanted "Dimitri out and Lenny in. Dimitri saw himself as a kind of sacrificial lamb. The point is that all the real pressures on him came from his commitment to new music and that was unshakable. He stuck to his guns. And he did not know how to cope with his situation. He did not have that aggressive, hard-nose, self-centered attitude that most conductors have."

Bernstein's contract held that his appointment as music director was to begin in the 1958–1959 season and continue for three years. The news was announced in November 1957, just after Bernstein had returned from Israel and six weeks into the year of his co-conductorship with Mitropoulos. The scene of the news event was the art gallery of the Century Club in midtown Manhattan, a club whose members have an interest in the arts and humanities and in related businesses. The music press attended.

Mitropoulos took advantage of the presence of the music critics to say, "It is all right to write what you believe. But sometimes you should also think that when you write something disagreeable it doesn't only hurt the conductor; it also hurts the Philharmonic. The Philharmonic needs more support and less criticism. If too many critical things are said, the public loses faith."

Then, in what can be interpreted only as a note of condescension both to the United States and to Bernstein, he added that the appointment was "a sign that America is so grown-up" that it could offer such an important post to an American-born and American-trained musician. Bernstein replied by referring to Mitropoulos's "heartbreaking situation in New York" and saying that the Greek conductor was the first to have advised him to make conducting his own career.

The truth. Just not *all* the truth. Bernstein has confided to very few anything of the relationship between Mitropoulos and himself. But finally he told it to the entire world in 1982 when he published a book, *Findings*, which includes a story he had written for a Harvard composition class in 1938. "The Occult," a *roman à clef*, was so transparent a transferal of real-life events that the student protagonist plays the very same piece for the visiting Greek conductor that Bernstein played for Mitropoulos when they met at the Greek Society the previous year.

It is a fact that Bernstein, in public, spoke only well of Mitropoulos. Since 1943, when he attacked his father in the press for having done nothing to help him succeed, he has never complained about anyone's treatment of him. Something more circuitous takes place. He generally showers just such a man with a host of compliments which inevitably reduce the man. Sondheim notes that after the symposium on *West Side Story*, Bernstein stretched out his arms to gather his three colleagues underneath them in a manner that projected the unmistakable message that he was the father of them all. Sondheim extricated himself from the embrace. In all of the Blitzstein memorial tributes, Bernstein invariably characterizes him as the "survivor" of a "long chain of beautiful work-failures." On the surface it suggests belief in and sympathy for the man. But what it also does is point out to those in the house that Blitzstein never did succeed as a composer. The appearance Bernstein gives is one of infinite goodness: Schuller had described him as "a sweetheart." But underneath the apparent sweetness Bernstein's competitive spirit is working around the clock, and while acting like a beneficent god, dispensing blessings to everyone around, he does manage to command stage-center, to get whatever attention is available.

In addition to the psychic gratification the post of musical director brought, there were the real benefits: Bernstein's salary was reported to exceed that of anybody who had held the post before. It would provide the financial security he had heard Sam rail about all of his life. It also meant being thrust into a position where he could make all manner of things happen. Even without institutional power, Bernstein's record had been exceptional. It began with the performances of *Carmen* and Gilbert and Sullivan when he was in his teens. It continued with *The Cradle Will Rock* at Harvard, to which he attracted such powerful sponsors as the philosopher David Prall, the poet Archibald MacLeish, and the historian Arthur Schlesinger, Jr. It culminated in the rescue of *West Side Story* by Roger Stevens, who offered unconditional support after Cheryl Crawford walked out and before Prince and Griffith came in. Finally the appointment in New York made it possible for him to do what he loved to do most: "Make music for my fellow human beings."

He would do exactly that through concerts, touring, and recordings week after week and telecasts that won one Emmy Award after another. Then there were the less quantifiable rewards, the applause, adulation, adoration that would transcend anything he had ever experienced, even in his days on Broadway. In fact, immediately after the opening of *West Side Story*, Bernstein greeted the opening night party waving the one review that had been qualified. He told everyone that Walter Kerr was "such an inverted snob, such an intellectual, that he cannot stand a musical unless it had a chorus line." Kerr is Roman Catholic and heterosexual. He may have been prejudiced about this show. But the fact that his review was the only one Bernstein singled out on this otherwise magnificent night is proof enough that even as tough a professional as he is not above responding to criticism. In 1980, at a New York party, an unidentified young woman told Bernstein she thought he had been overrated. According to Ned Rorem, Bernstein spent the better part of the evening on the back stairs trying to persuade her that she was wrong.

The day after *West Side Story* opened on Broadway, Bernstein flew to Israel to conduct the Israel Philharmonic in the opening concert at the Fredric Mann Auditorium in Tel Aviv. The house fulfilled those requirements Bernstein had specified during his 1947 trip. The audience included Prime Minister Ben Gurion and several hundred Americans who had arrived on chartered planes as guests of Mann, the Philadelphia businessman, amateur pianist, and music lover who had contributed $250,000 toward the building of the house. The America-Israel Cultural Foundation and the municipality of Tel Aviv made up the remainder of the cost of more than $2 million. In a land of open shirts and no neckties this was a black tie event. Bernstein conducted Ernest Bloch's *Schelomo* with Gregor Piatigorsky, the cello soloist, the Mendelssohn Violin Concerto with Isaac Stern, Beethoven's Concerto No. 5 with Artur Rubinstein, and a new work, *Festival Prelude*, by Noam Sheriff, a twenty-two-year-old Israeli composer. The artists donated their services and scalpers got ninety dollars a ticket.

Ricky Leacock, who had participated in helping move Bernstein's early performance of Copland's *Second Hurricane* to Sanders Theater in 1941, was assigned to film the Israel trip for *Omnibus*. "It was hard keeping up with Lenny," Leacock says. "We missed some wonderful things: Lenny losing his temper at construction workers, Lenny borrowing a vest from Rubinstein, then watching it tear apart on him. But we got wonderful things. One night at the Hotel Sharon when Teddy Kollek, the mayor of Jerusalem, was there, everyone asked Bernstein to tell them about *West Side Story*. He and Felicia sat down at the piano in the room and picked their way through the score." Bernstein alone would never have had to "pick his way" through the score. Here he was clearly slowed down by his wife, who, in the earlier years of their marriage, was always willing to come forth and play.

Leacock says, "I remember Lenny took me to a Yemenite service and then, the next day on the beach, explained what every aspect of the service meant. After the explanations, there were the word games and anagrams. I also recall a holiday when women were not allowed on the Wailing Wall. Lenny and I climbed up to it and Felicia stayed back singing the 'Alleluia' from Handel's *Messiah*. She was great fun. They seemed to be close and happy. Lenny said he was not screwing around.

I remember Paul Feigay saying that Lenny was trying to go straight but that, in the end, he would never make it."

It was during a performance on this trip that Bernstein suffered a pain in his back. He continued to conduct from a chair but later a doctor told him that he had torn a dorsal muscle. The doctor prescribed bed rest. Bernstein ignored him and went to a moonlight beach party given by Isaac Stern. His back pained him severely and this time the doctor insisted on absolute bed rest. Unable to bear missing anything, Bernstein was enraged that he would have to bypass a lunch to which he had been invited by Ben Gurion and a gala dinner at Rehovat. He spent the entire day playing piano in his room and when he returned to the podium he did so with a baton. This was November 1957. It was then he discovered the baton to be the energy-saving instrument that most conductors know it to be. So seventeen years after upsetting Reiner and Koussevitzky by refusing to use a stick, Bernstein took to it.

In addition to separating himself from Mitropoulos in the matter of repertory, he would now separate himself from him in this most visible of ways: replacing his hands with the baton. When Brooks Atkinson used the word "respectable" to describe the nature of Bernstein's choice to leave Broadway for the concert hall, he was not altogether off the track. Beside this change to the more conventional conducting technique, there were other shifts that echoed Bernstein's self-conscious broadening of his *a*'s when he entered Harvard. A memo went out with the message that his name was spelled not "Lennie" but "Lenny," and that the pronunciation of his last name was not Bern-*steen* but Bern-*styne*. In a 1957 article published in *The New York Times Magazine*, his name was said to rhyme with "Rhine," and in person he asked those who mispronounced it, "Would you say Gertrude *Steen*?" In 1985, Nicolas Slonimsky dealt with this particular alteration of Bernstein's behavior in the seventh edition of *Baker's Biographical Dictionary of Music*. He wrote that "intimates used to refer to him as Bern*steen*, and he himself said he preferred the 'democratic Yiddish' Bern*steen* to the 'aristocratic Germanic' Bern*styne*." Slonimsky concludes the entry with the fact that the pronunciation Bernstein preferred in the later years of his life was Bern*styne*.

So by the time Bernstein assumed his prestigious post in the fall of

1958, he was a man infinitely different from the rising artist of the 1940s. Formerly a homosexual, or at least a bisexual with a powerful sex drive, he was now a family man. Formerly a leftist with a plethora of uncelebrated, loving Jewish friends, he was now a Germanic aristocrat with a circle that tended to exclude them. Formerly a composer whose head had filled with the opening bars of *Fancy Free* at the Russian Tea Room—he says he wrote the notes down on a paper napkin without missing a word of the conversation—he was now, as his brother would say, the *chef* of an orchestra *distingué*. Members of the press reported that Felicia was responsible for getting Bernstein to "commit himself for a long time in one place." That could be true. Many of Bernstein's friends say it is and add that it was also Felicia who cut them out so devastatingly from the couple's rapidly expanding and escalating social circle. The fact remains Bernstein chose Felicia, married her, and made children with her, and as a quid pro quo it was not all bad. He loved her in the particular way that he could, and, according to their oldest child, Jamie, her own "earliest childhood memories are basically golden." For a book, *The Men in Our Lives*, Jamie told Elizabeth Fishel, an old school friend:

> I remember no stress. My parents never fought. They were beautiful. They were full of fun. Our friends were full of fun. There was a lot of laughter and carrying on and silliness. Summers were fabulous. There was a period when we would go to Martha's Vineyard every summer. I remember those summers as endless sailing and beaches and sun. And my father was great with us—talking to us and teaching us things. He was the eternal teacher and we were the eternal students.

That period was golden in many ways. In the spring of 1958, a few months after Bernstein's appointment had been made public but still before the conductor took over, Taubman celebrated the new regime: "Bravo for the New York Philharmonic! What looked like a somnambulistic organization two years ago had been transformed into an institution with ideas and imagination. The plans for next season reveal a progressive purpose and a creative point of view." The Philharmonic had announced that Bernstein would conduct a survey of American

music for eighteen of the thirty weeks of the season. Each of his concerts would present at least one American work. Guest conductors
would be free to choose their own programs but these would have to
have a binding theme. There would be a Thursday evening "Preview"
concert to which the critics would not be invited and at which conductors would be free to talk to the audience. Bernstein would not delegate
The Young People's Concerts to guest or assistant conductors but would
continue to do them himself. Jamie's remark about her father as the
eternal teacher is borne out by what he said at the time: "If my children
have done nothing else, they taught me how to translate music to other
children and to make it fun."

Although Bernstein consciously upgraded his roots, he never forgot
what they were. During his first months as co-conductor, he presented
works by Copland, Shapero, Foss, and Diamond, all friends he had
made before he was twenty and all American Jews. He did this while
managing to conduct such demanding European works as Brahms's
Concerto in B Flat with Artur Rubinstein, a Bartók Violin Concerto
with Isaac Stern, Stravinsky's *Le Sacre du Printemps*, and Webern's Opus
6 *Pieces for Orchestra*. He also conducted Honegger's oratorio *Saint Joan
of Arc at the Stake* with Adele Addison, Leontyne Price, Frances Bible,
and David Lloyd as soloists. For the narrator he chose his wife.

In many ways, Bernstein always has been a generous man. While it
is also true that when he could he did favors for those close to him,
where music was involved, invariably they paid a price. When Bernstein
made his first recording, Diamond's prelude and fugue, he was not long
out of Harvard and a few years younger than Diamond. Yet he provoked Diamond by telling him what was "wrong" with the piece.
Schuller says that once, for a televised *Young People's Concert*, he composed a "sort of *Peter and the Wolf* for jazz. It was performed with me
conducting and Lenny narrating, if you can imagine such a thing.
Lenny insisted on a number of changes. He argued. I was younger. I felt
the pressure of his personality. I had no recourse for there was also the
pressure of time. It's a phenomenon you encounter all the time with
Lenny. Lenny, as a composer, has a fundamental respect for the creative
process but when he expresses himself, he leaves no room for argument
or discussion. Lenny's ego is such that he feels the need to revise and
recompose other composer's music in his own terms."

A similar incident happened once when Blitzstein was ill and Bernstein paid him a visit. Instead of sitting by his bedside and talking, Bernstein went straight to the piano and started to play around with a score that Blitzstein had left there, calling out to his friend how he should fix it up. People who were there at the time say that Blitzstein was almost totally spent when Bernstein left, but he had enough left to ask the others present, "How dare he?"

As for Felicia's narration of the Honegger work, Bernstein wrote of her lovely performance to Diamond, who was in Italy at the time. Yet during the open rehearsal at Carnegie Hall, with many people in the audience, when Montealegre intoned these words in the script with great seriousness: "What is that dog howling in the night?" Bernstein called out from the podium, "That's no dog. That's my wife." A joke, of course, but one that hurts.

During Bernstein's first season with the New York Philharmonic, he complemented his emphasis on American music in his concert programs with an exploration of American music on television. In "What is American Music?" he opened with a part of Gershwin's *An American in Paris*. Then he asked the children why that piece would be recognized anywhere in the civilized world as American music. The answer came back in one word, "Jazz."

Bernstein touched briefly on other American musical traits such as youthfulness, optimism, sentimentality, and a sense of the wide-open spaces, notions that were not as common then as they have come to be today, and he illustrated them with selections from Copland, Thomas, Harris, Schuman, and Randall Thompson. Then he turned the podium over to Copland, who conducted a movement from his Symphony No. 3, which he was conducting in its entirety with the Philharmonic that week. About ten million people watched a normal-appearing man dressed in a business suit mount the podium and conduct a work he had himself composed. It was a powerful lesson, another gesture from Bernstein in the direction of demystifying music, of removing the snobbism and stuffiness from the domain of "high art."

Bernstein did not concentrate exclusively on American music in those early days. Soon after this program he dwelt on the principal of development in symphonic form. Moving rapidly from the last movement of Mozart's *Jupiter* Symphony to "Three Blind Mice" and "The

Colonel Bogie March," the familiar British tune used as theme music in the movie *The Bridge on the River Kwai,* and then to parts of two Beethoven symphonies, he revealed how symphonies are built. Even as a pianist he went beyond the United States: for the first time in years he learned a new work, Shostakovich's Concerto No. 2 for Piano and Orchestra. Written for the composer's nineteen-year-old son, it did not present insuperable difficulties for Bernstein, who no longer practiced at all.

From the beginning of his tenure with the New York Philharmonic, Bernstein performed not only twentieth-century music, but music that was not necessarily associated with the Stravinsky-Copland school. This has not been generally recognized by those musicians tied to the Austro-German camp but Schuller acknowledges that it is so. "Lenny learned all of this new music himself. He understood that he had to have a broad range of commitment as a conductor in this post. But once, when he apologized for doing Stockhausen to the audience in advance, that was not good."

So, while it cannot be claimed that Bernstein made a huge effort to encompass the twelve-tone composers, he did extend himself in a wide variety of ways and with composers not necessarily attached to Stravinsky and Copland. Here is a letter written on February 5, 1958. Bernstein tells Diamond about the life that he had taken on and that would continue at the same frenzied pace for at least three more years:

> The conducting, recording, TV, etc. etc. has finally ground to a halt, like an old locomotive, and is replaced by an endless new series of meetings, interviews, conferences, et al. about next year's soloists, programs, details for the South American tour we are making with the orchestra in May & June (8 weeks—all over!) and all of the rest of the administrative detail that goes with being *the* conductor. But so far it's been a joy, far surpassing any expectations. The orchestra had played marvelously, newly, joyously: the men are happy and proud; there is better morale: more money for them (TV, etc.); full houses week after week, in spite of a tremendous amount of contemporary music (Webern & Strav. on one program, for example; Haieff & Macero together on another; you, of course;

Shosty: Shapero, Foss, Bartok—all in a month)…. (We're doing the *Young People's Concerts* on TV now, they're a smash, but oh so difficult & tiring!) And *Omnibus* coming up, 2 more *Young People's* shows, new programs to prepare for April….

The pressure to concentrate more on twelve-tone composition haunted him throughout his Philharmonic tenure—pressure from composers and musical academics; resistance from audiences, orchestra management, and soloists. By the time he had become music director, even Stravinsky had shifted gears and was using his own idiosyncratic variant of the Schoenberg grammar.

Whatever tension Bernstein might have felt in the late 1950s between the advanced composers and the public at large, it was more than compensated for by the honors that began to proliferate. In 1957 Northwestern University gave him, along with George F. Kennan, U.S. ambassador to the Soviet Union, and Joseph Wood Krutch, essayist and former professor at Columbia University, an honorary degree. In 1958 Eleanor Roosevelt honored him with a silver-banded shofar, the ram's horn used in Jewish rites, for his contribution to Jewish culture. Hebrew Union College conferred upon him a doctorate of humane letters and the Ditson Fund presented him with a check for his contribution to American music. Americans, long neglected in music, and Jews, the subjects of such intense recent cruelty, were having their moments because of the choices Bernstein was making then. His playing out the role of the beneficent father may have been irritating under certain individual circumstances, but on a large scale, it did good and humane things.

Bernstein's newfound respectability—a respectability he had not enjoyed as guest conductor, sometime composer of concert music, or creator of Broadway musicals—moved him into circles that included heads of state. Rebellion continued to be the keynote. As he had attacked Mayor La Guardia, so he went on to confront presidents and premiers.

The first opportunity he had to do this was in the spring of 1958 when he and Vice President Nixon were touring South America. While Nixon received boos and was subject to fierce attacks, Bernstein liked to point out that all was perfect when he arrived. And indeed it was. The fact that Felicia—born in Costa Rica and a citizen of Chile—was also on the tour, and that Mitropoulos, then far more famous than Bernstein in Latin America, was also on the tour, did not interfere with the excitement generated wherever the orchestra went. In seven weeks the Philharmonic played thirty-nine concerts in twelve countries, precipitating universal demonstrations of praise during a particularly tense time of inter-American relations.

Bernstein had told friends when he was starting out on the tour that he had some doubts. He was worried because an unfamiliar conductor always has more power with the men in the orchestra than a familiar one. He said he was "the boy next door" whom the men had known almost all of his life. But apparently there was no need for worry. The men appeared to take to him right away. Programs on the tour were a mix of the traditional—Haydn, Beethoven, and Brahms—with the more contemporary—Ravel, Gershwin, Harris, Copland, and Carlos Chávez, who took bows after concerts in his hometown of Mexico City. With city after city hoisting BIENVENIDA FILARMŎNICA banners, tickets were in such short supply that they went for an average of thirty dollars apiece, a great deal of money for that time and place. In Rio a critic wrote, "We never heard such beauty before." In Santiago: "The orchestral interpretations are simply marvelous, with a perfection to which Chile has never been exposed."

There were the inevitable mishaps. In Panama the men's trunks arrived rain soaked. In Guayaquil, Ecuador, the streets were foul because of a six-week garbage strike. Once, when the orchestra played at an altitude of eight thousand feet, Bernstein had to breathe oxygen after each of the works. Still the rewards transcended the problems. Generally it was a day or two after crowds would break up the Nixon tour that the orchestra would receive a thunderous ovation after playing "The Star-Spangled Banner."

This tour was Mitropoulos's last official duty with the New York Philharmonic. After this anything he would do would be at the sufferance of Bernstein—like Koussevitzky when Munch had come in. Among the pieces Mitropoulos conducted were the overture to Weber's *Der Freischütz*, Beethoven's Second Symphony, the overture to Verdi's *La Forza del Destino*, and Strauss's *Don Juan*.

It was not a joyous trip for Mitropoulos. First of all he was not well. He had begun to suffer from a heart condition and was afflicted with gallbladder troubles. He was not conducting the pieces he deeply loved. Finally he did not get the treatment he—or anyone else—would have wanted to receive. Bernstein upstages anyone, even when his relations are less complex than those with Mitropoulos.

Often Bernstein did not fulfill his responsibilities on the tour, running off with Felicia to see and do things, leaving Mitropoulos to fill in for him. On this particular tour, which covered Panama, Venezuela, Colombia, Ecuador, Peru, Bolivia, Paraguay, Chile, Argentina, Uruguay, Brazil, and Mexico, one that played before two hundred thousand people, exclusive of television and radio, Mitropoulos invariably found himself in a position that even as masochistic a man as he did not enjoy. In fact, Bernstein was the only one of the three—the two conductors and Felicia—who appeared to enjoy himself. The men in the orchestra say that Felicia always wore a long face and that when the plane was crossing mountains, she could be heard praying out loud in Spanish. Felicia left the tour and returned home early because her husband's flamboyant flirtations with men in Chile, her native country, humiliated her.

Bernstein, resilient as ever, bounced happily along throughout the siege. On his return to New York, there was a celebration at city hall where Bernstein took the baton away from the conductor of the Sanitation Department Band to lead the group in a rendition of Sousa's "Stars and Stripes Forever." Then he made a short speech describing the musicians as having played on the tour "like angels, if not Gods," and went on to say that these 120 people "who had to gallop all over the Andes, crossing rivers and jungles, proved to be delightful, gracious traveling companions."

With virtually no time to catch their breath, Bernstein and the orchestra opened the stadium concerts on June 2, 1958. This was Lewisohn Stadium's fortieth year. Some twelve thousand people were there. Bernstein pushed the men as he pushed himself. But the excitement, the money, the blare of good publicity were, for most of them, worth the price of this increasingly frenzied musical merry-go-round.

The 1958–1959 season must have been particularly joyous for Bernstein. His income had increased. He was raising a family, and generating heat wherever he went. Just about all those in music tried to ingratiate themselves with him. "Communication," he told the press, "is a way of making love to people, of reaching out to them. It's a most mysterious and deeply felt experience. Love and art are two ways of communicating. That is why art is so close to love."

Bernstein uses art and sex interchangeably. In the 1980s, when he addressed a master class in conducting at Tanglewood, he was trying to help a student conduct Tchaikovsky's *Romeo and Juliet*. At one point he said, "This is exactly how you should feel in the morning when you've been in bed with someone you love." When the student, trying again, interrupted a rising crescendo with a gesture that was definitely counterproductive, Bernstein looked to the heavens and sighed with despair: "You just ruined a whole gorgeous coitus."

After the Lewisohn Stadium concerts, Bernstein went to Europe, where he conducted the Lamoureux and French National orchestras in performances for UNESCO. At a press conference in New York he said, "I will never conduct any other orchestra in the world as long as I am conductor of the New York Philharmonic. I have the fullest possible satisfaction from conducting this most beautiful and flexible of orchestras." Because Bernstein often acts as though music and sex were the same, it follows that as long as he was being apparently monogamous with Felicia, he also would be faithful to his New York orchestra.

In the 1958–1959 season, Mitropoulos was not on the scene at all, and the fare was heavily American. The works Bernstein conducted during the first part of the season were by George Whitefield Chadwick, Edward MacDowell, and Carl Ruggles, all men born in the 1860s and 1870s. In the second part, the music was of the 1930s; in the third, there were pieces composed between the Depression and World War II; in the fourth, postwar compositions.

Bernstein's first opening night did not fall into any of these categories. Still it celebrated the United States with William Schuman's *American Festival* Overture, which Bernstein had conducted in his early days at Tanglewood, Ives's Second Symphony, which Bernstein had presented in its world premiere with the New York Philharmonic, Beethoven's Seventh Symphony, for the traditionalists in the hall, and, as a last-minute addition, Berlioz's *Roman Carnival* Overture. Taubman reviewed the first event like a man who felt everything was in its right and proper place: "The New York Philharmonic began its 107th season last night with a shining, morning face. There was a new music director, Leonard Bernstein, new men in the orchestra, a new program policy, and indeed a new approach to opening night.... Boxes were filled with ambassadors and ministers of the twelve Latin American countries he had visited—and many of our own dignitaries." Taubman was not the only critic to greet the new regime with warm words. In the *Christian Science Monitor,* Miles Kastendieck commented that Bernstein's remarkable performances of the Ives and the Beethoven suggest that the orchestra "has turned a corner and embarked on an exciting new chapter in its long career."

That issue of "turning a corner" is ambiguous.
The difference between Mitropoulos at the end of his Philharmonic
career and Bernstein at the beginning of his is not clear-cut. Gunther
Schuller, whose father played in the New York orchestra for forty-two
years, started to go to concerts when he was four years old. "The

FRANK DRIGGS

*Dimitri Mitropoulos towards the end of his life, after he turned over the New York
Philharmonic to Leonard Bernstein. "[Gunther] Schuller says that Toscanini,
'a tyrant,' was followed by Barbirolli, 'a perfect gentleman,' who was followed by
Rodzinski, 'a tyrant,' who was followed by Mitropoulos, a 'saint.'"*

rebounding effect," Schuller says, "is an important consideration" when trying to understand the musicians' behavior. Schuller says that Toscanini, "a tyrant," was followed by Barbirolli, "a perfect gentleman," who was followed by Rodzinski, a "tyrant," who was followed by Mitropoulos, a "saint." "The men could be bastards," Schuller says. "Sometimes, despite themselves, they would allow Dimitri to mesmerize them in music they really hated. This happened with the Webern Symphony Opus Twenty-one. Even without an 'I'm the boss' attitude, he could get them to play their hearts out for him. They did this in the Mahler Symphony Number Nine and the Strauss *Alpine* Symphony. Also in some Rachmaninoff. Dimitri is unfairly remembered as the proponent of a lack of discipline.

"I believe," Schuller goes on, "that the real reason he had the trouble he did was Rodzinski's painful way of running the orchestra. The musicians were out to get the next man—and the next man was a vulnerable one. He did not fight back. That was not in Dimitri's nature. Lenny was brought in as Sir Galahad. But his ultimate need to be buddy-buddy with everyone, to be loved by all, meant that he would not be able to restore the discipline that had been lost. The men were almost as bad with Lenny as they had been with Mitropoulos. The Toscanini and Rodzinski eras left a more powerful legacy than most people are willing to admit."

In November 1958, Rodzinski died. A sick and disappointed man in the last years of his life, he must have experienced mixed feelings when the man who had been his brash assistant many years earlier ascended the podium he had had to abdicate. During the last week of November, Bernstein dedicated the concerts to the memory of Rodzinski. He said a few words before the concerts about his assistantship in 1943 and added that Rodzinski had been a great conductor. In her memoir, *Our Two Lives*, Halina Rodzinski describes the painful relationship between her husband and Bernstein. But she was so pleased by the dedication of the concerts that she concluded the book's prologue with mention of this tribute by Bernstein.

For the most part everything seemed to go smoothly at the start of Bernstein's tenure. An article in the *New York Herald Tribune* quoted a number of musicians who expressed delight at the appointment. William Lincer, the head of the viola section and a musician who had been brought from the Cleveland Orchestra by Rodzinski fifteen years before, said, "For the first time in our history we've got a solid bridge between the young people around the country and the Philharmonic." What Lincer said turned out to be true. Dozens of American musicians in their fifties today attribute the choice of their careers to Bernstein's having been given that post in 1958. A respectable path in music suddenly opened to them.

With his celebrity came the opportunity for Bernstein to capitalize on a great deal of the work he had already done. The seven shows for *Omnibus* were gathered together in a book, *The Joy of Music*. When it was published, Virgil Thomson wrote, "This is no set of do-it-yourself recipes for writing successful Broadway musicals or for making the New York Philharmonic eat out of your hand. It is about as realistic a book of music appreciation as this hardened assessor has yet encountered."

In 1959, *On the Town* reappeared on Broadway with Harold Lang as Gabey and Pat Carroll as Hildy, and garnered even more praise than it had the first time around. The same year, *West Side Story* and *Candide* were produced for the first time in London. The reactions were similar to those the shows had evoked in New York; *West Side Story* was received with raves, while *Candide* got indifferent reviews at best.

In 1958 Bernstein hired Jack Gottlieb as his first assistant in charge of details and mechanics. Gottlieb had been a student at Brandeis in the early 1950s. He had been in a class where Bernstein, Blitzstein, and Hellman had presented their embryonic ideas for *Candide*, and Bernstein had asked the students to come up with their own ideas. Gottlieb remained Bernstein's assistant throughout the Philharmonic period, and is still employed by him.

From Brandeis, Gottlieb went on to the University of Illinois, where he wrote a dissertation on Bernstein's music and received an advanced degree. Today he says that he cannot imagine his life without Bernstein, that he is so tied to the way Bernstein makes music that he would have connected with him under any circumstances. Indeed he seems to have been the perfect man for the job. As to why Bernstein sought him out, Gottlieb speculated in 1985, "In those *Candide* seminars, I did some things that interested him. I also paid him back fifty dollars and Helen Coates told me that that had impressed him. Half of my salary was paid by the Philharmonic and half by Bernstein. The job included chores from gofer to copying to liaison work. It was not defined."

The conductor Maurice Peress remembers being introduced to Gottlieb in Bernstein's apartment when Gottlieb was carrying in clothes from the dry cleaner. But there was more than messengering to the job of being Bernstein's assistant. Serving as a first reader of scores—in much the way Bernstein had served Rodzinski, though never, of course, conducting anything—Gottlieb went through the mounds of material that were submitted for review. He also did research. If Bernstein wanted to program Soviet music, it was up to Gottlieb to find him a representative score. Sometimes Bernstein needed an extra example for a preview concert or a television show. If Bernstein wanted a piece of ragtime to illustrate a particular characteristic, Gottlieb was commissioned to unearth it.

Gottlieb would make up the cue sheets for the musicians so that nothing would go amiss on the air. He was also responsible for Bernstein's thirteen suitcases and for keeping the conductor's watches and electric shavers in working order.

What he has described as "the more personal tasks" were still in the hands of Helen Coates. She has always handled Bernstein's voluminous fan mail, cross-indexing all the letters, and she had filed every clipping from every country. These, now on microfilm, plus the awards and medals, plus copies of every score and record, are now housed in Bernstein's old studio apartment at the Osborne across the street from Carnegie Hall. It is known as Bernstein's "little museum." Until 1986, Coates tended to it. Her devotion to Bernstein is absolute, and Bernstein rewards her for that loyalty. In the 1950s he provided her with a small apartment in the Osborne where he and his family occupied a nine-room apartment.

The road from his father's Russia to his own post as music director of the New York Philharmonic was one he had reason to think about in the fall of 1959. It was then that he and conductors Seymour Lipkin and Thomas Schippers took the orchestra on a tour of Eastern as well as Western Europe.

The trip began propitiously. They were greeted by excited crowds everywhere. This was the first full-scale U.S. symphony orchestra ever to visit Turkey. In Istanbul, the open-air theater seating five thousand

people overflowed on two nights. People crashed through wooden bar-
riers and stampeded police lines to fill every aisle and every step. In
Salzburg, Bernstein conducted the Shostakovich Fifth, a performance
he repeated many times on the tour as well as on his return to Carnegie
Hall in the fall. He also conducted Barber's Second Essay for Orchestra,
his own *Age of Anxiety*, and many works of the Americans with whom
he had come to be identified. Every seat was sold out for every concert.
Standing ovations were the rule. In Moscow he received many gifts
ranging from official bouquets to spontaneous posies and a photograph
of Arthur Nikisch, Koussevitzky's teacher. On receiving this last present
he, said, "Nikisch is my musical grandfather."

The Moscow experience started innocuously enough, Bernstein
conducting Piston's Concerto for Orchestra and Beethoven's Triple
Concerto with himself as the pianist. He introduced these works with
short speeches he delivered in Russian, which he had studied before the
trip. None of this caused any difficulty.

The trouble came with the concert in which he presented two
Stravinsky works: *Le Sacre du Printemps* and the Concerto for Piano and
Wind Instruments, as well as Ives's *The Unanswered Question*. Before the
Stravinsky he remarked that *Le Sacre du Printemps* had not been heard
in Moscow in thirty years and that the concerto had never been performed there. In addition to explaining how Ives composed, he played
The Unanswered Question a second time. The galley was filled with students, the boxes with official figures headed by Nikolai A. Milhailov,
minister of culture.

Soviet critic Alexander Medvedev attacked Bernstein in *Sovietskaya
Kultura*, calling him "cocky" for his preperformance talks. He also complained about Bernstein's championing of "the late tragic period" of
Stravinsky: "Some kind of show is being played under the title
'Bernstein raises the Iron Curtain in music.'" Medvedev added that the
repeat of the Ives piece, in light of the fact that the audience had
responded to it with nothing more than a ripple of light applause, had
been totally unwarranted.

That exacerbated the confrontation. Even before the concert
Bernstein had been angry. His long and rambling program for *The Age
of Anxiety* had not been printed by the Soviets and he felt its omission
made it impossible for the audience to understand his work. When, on

top of that, he was attacked for repeating *The Unanswered Question*, he claimed repetition of the work had been demanded by the audience, that their rhythmic clapping meant "again."

Behind the public scenes a private drama was taking place. At first Bernstein tried to persuade his father to join him in Russia to see his own brother, Simyon, and nephew. Simyon was a mining engineer who lived in Novosibirsk, Siberia. At first Sam said yes, then he changed his mind. In Moscow Simyon, who, with his son, had made the long trip to Moscow to be united with his family, greeted his nephew Leonard. Bernstein put in a call to his father at his home in Brookline and put Sam's brother on the line. The brief conversation moved Sam to change his mind and he flew to his homeland. Bernstein, in telling the story, says that he was shocked by his uncle's appearance: He had not expected all those stainless steel teeth. But the great disappointment was for the brothers themselves. Each found a stranger.

Almost immediately, Bernstein rushed off to a rehearsal, leaving the men floundering, apparently unable to converse at all. After attending one of his son's concerts in Leningrad and a few other events, Sam Bernstein returned to Brookline, expressing his delight at being home.

When his son Leonard came back to New York, banners lined Fifty-seventh Street: WELCOME HOME, INTERNATIONAL HEROES. *Time* magazine wrote that the tour was one that would "likely go down in history as the most successful of all time." But success did not inhibit Bernstein in his remarks. When he addressed the National Press Club in Washington he said, "The main trouble with Soviet music is their lack of musical experimentation and their preference for rehashing motifs from earliest times."

In 1984 Nicolas Slonimsky said, "Copland says that when Lenny confronts a microphone he loses all control. After his trip to Russia, Lenny told the National Press Club that Russian music was warmed over Glinka and Rimsky-Korsakov. Kabalevsky wrote to me to check it out. To keep the peace I denied it, saying Lenny had always been a good friend of the Soviet Union. I decompressed the situation.

"But Shostakovich, Kabalevsky, and Khachaturian published a letter in *Pravda* denouncing Bernstein. They said they had treated him so well. They gave him every comfort. How could he reciprocate in this way? Would you believe what he said before he conducted *Le Sacre du Printemps*? He said that before the Russian Revolution there had been another revolution: *Le Sacre du Printemps*. He said this in Russia, in Moscow. He compared *Le Sacre du Printemps* to the Russian Revolution!"

Even without a microphone in his hand, Bernstein rarely censors what he says. He says what he wants to say. Often his remarks fall in a destructive way, wounding the person at the other end for no apparent purpose. But sometimes they do have felicitous if not premeditated consequences.

In her memoir, *And Music at the Close*, Lillian Libman writes:

> Bernstein's playing of Stravinsky's *The Rite of Spring* and the Piano Concerto during his Russian tour and his accompanying remarks about how unjustly these pieces were still unfamiliar to these audiences, probably paved the way for Stravinsky's visit there in 1962. There is no doubt that Stravinsky was deeply touched by Bernstein's efforts in behalf of his music, for he spoke of them with appreciation to me and to others.

If Bernstein did nothing more in his life than pave the way for Stravinsky's return to his homeland, he would have assured himself a small place in history for having performed a most valued gesture for one of the greatest artists of the twentieth century. In a diary kept on that Russian trip, Robert Craft, Stravinsky's longtime amanuensis, wrote, "I am certain that to be recognized and acclaimed as a Russian in Russia, and to be performed there, has meant more to him than anything in the years I have known him."

23

In the 1959–1960 season, Bernstein's second as music director of the New York Philharmonic, Mitropoulos partici-pated with him in an ambitious Mahler festival. In January 1960, Mitropoulos conducted the Mahler Symphonies Nos. 1, 5, and 9, and the first movement of No. 10. Stefan Bauer-Mengelberg, a relative of

Jennie Tourel; Alma Mahler, the composer's widow; his daughter, looking at a Mahler photograph and a page of a score during the 1959–1960 season, when "Mitropoulos participated with [Bernstein] in an ambitious Mahler festival."

Willem Mengelberg, the legendary Dutch conductor, was an assistant conductor with the orchestra at the time. The Friday afternoon performance, the one about which Bauer-Mengelberg speaks here, was the performance then open to the critics for review; Thursday evenings were still closed to them. Bauer-Mengelberg recalls, "Bernstein was not supposed to be there but he dropped in unannounced. Mitropoulos was conducting Mahler Number Five. Bernstein was planning to do whatever he had to do and then leave. But he stopped to listen to a part of the concert and then found he could not pull himself away. People around him were tugging at his sleeve, wanting him to do this thing or that. But he kept shaking his head and saying, 'It's so incredible. I cannot leave.'" Others who attended that particular concert remember that Bernstein's presence in the box and the commotion he caused when he was there drew their attention away from Mitropoulos and the Mahler.

Bernstein followed the Mitropoulos performances with his own interpretations of the Symphonies Nos. 2 and 4, the *Four Songs*, and the *Five Songs on the Death of Children*, Bruno Walter completed the festival in April with *Das Lied von der Erde*. This was not the first time the New York Philharmonic had performed Mahler. The composer himself had conducted some of his own works there early in the century. Bruno Walter's performance of the *Resurrection* Symphony has been singled out by Carlos Moseley, chairman emeritus of the New York Philharmonic, as one of the memorable events in a lifetime of music. Rodzinski conducted that same symphony when Bernstein started as assistant.

After Mitropoulos succeeded Rodzinski, the Greek conductor led more performances of Mahler than he is generally credited with. He would have overseen many more, but management imposed a quota of one Mahler work a year. It assumed that audiences would tolerate no more than that. Here is the schedule of Mahler performances during Mitropoulos's tenure at the Philharmonic: In the 1951–1952 season, he himself conducted Symphony No. 1. The next season, Walter conducted *Das Lied von der Erde*; in the 1953–1954 season, Walter led Symphony No. 1. The next season, Mitropoulos conducted Symphony No. 6; the following year, Mitropoulos presented Symphony No. 3. In 1956–1957, Walter conducted Symphony No. 2. Finally, in the year of his co-conductorship with Bernstein, the year that was to have been his last as director in New York, Mitropoulos conducted Mahler's Symphony No. 10 in what may well have been a prescient sense of identification with Mahler who like Mitropoulos, was both a composer and conductor and an anguished spirit as well. Mahler died before completing the work, and Mitropoulos may have sensed his own death was near.

As Bernstein assimilated so many of Mitropoulos's attitudes and gestures, so he echoed Mitropoulos's identification with Mahler and then built on it. In January 1960, he said he understood "Mahler's problem. It's like being two different men locked up in the same body." Although audiences had heard Bernstein do Mahler, they were not prepared for the extraordinary performances he delivered at that time. These were rich and lyrical ones, with correct balances, appropriate tempos, and glowing tone. Virtually all the critics acknowledged that whatever excesses had characterized some of Bernstein's earlier performances, they were not present now. Bernstein's continuing involvement with Mahler was built on the standards he set in this festival and culminated in the recording of the nine symphonies in the late 1960s.

More than twenty years after Bernstein's Mahler concerts, Donal Henahan, chief music critic of *The New York Times*, reviewed Bernstein's performance of the Mahler No. 2, the *Resurrection* Symphony: "His identification with the score and the composer seems complete and unfeigned. No conductor whom I have heard is quite so convincing in this music."

After being forced out of his orchestra post, Mitropoulos took on a grueling schedule at the Metropolitan Opera. Some observers call it suicidal. Between the fall of 1958 and the fall of 1960, he conducted Barber's *Vanessa*, three performances of *Eugene Onegin*, five *Boris Godunovs*, six *Simon Boccanegras*, nine *Cavalleria Rusticanas* and *Pagliaccis*, eleven *Madame Butterflys* and seventeen *Toscas*. He had been scheduled to conduct the Mahler No. 3 during Easter week of the 1960–1961 Philharmonic season. But in November 1960, rehearsing it for a performance at La Scala, he collapsed and died.

Mitropoulos's 1956 interpretation of the Mahler No. 3 had been a memorable one. A gigantic work, lasting more than an hour and a half, it teems with music that ranges from grotesque dancelike tunes to military marches. Containing a mixture of sophistication and banality that is characteristic of the composer, it seems to present this combination in the most exaggerated of ways. Featuring a contralto soloist, the work includes women's and boys' chorus. In April 1961, when Mitropoulos was to have conducted the work in New York, Bernstein substituted for him. First he bowed his head in silence. Then he conducted the Mahler No. 3. Critics who up to then had not taken him to task for his histrionic behavior did so the following day. In the *New York Post*, Harriet Johnson wrote that "his distortions exuded exhibitionism. During the intermission, the prevailing talk was concerned with the conductor's podium manner and, with one exception, those I questioned were vehement in their disapproval."

In this last tribute to Mitropoulos, Bernstein succeeded in ripping the attention away from him as he had done so many times during Mitropoulos's life.

In repeated accounts of the story of how he and Mitropoulos first met, Bernstein says he forgot the invitation to the Greek Society, at which the conductor was supposed to appear, and that it was due to a wrong turn in the road that he remembered he was to be there. In his family memoirs, Burton Bernstein recounts the story this way. But in 1983, in what seemed to be startlingly accurate recall, his mother told the story differently. She said it was because Leonard had anticipated the meeting with so much anxiety that he persuaded her to come along with him. Bernstein probably went to meet Mitropoulos with a host of complicated feelings, ranging from the guilt he must have felt at what he hoped would come of it, to the "paralysis" he writes that he felt on first seeing the Greek conductor in his Harvard story "The Occult."

In this composition the conductor is named Eros Mavro. The meaning of "Eros" is self-evident. "Mavro" may be a rearrangement of the letters of "Avrom," an earlier Hebrew name for Abraham, the father of the Jews. In the story, the student's name is Carl, the name of Beethoven's nephew, and the person who Bernstein has said he believes was the "sole object" of Beethoven's love. If it is true that Mitropoulos fell in love with Bernstein when they met in 1937, which Bernstein now says happened, it is also true that Bernstein fell in love with Mitropoulos. In *The Old Man and the Sea*, Hemingway writes that the old man taught the boy how to fish and the boy loved him for it. So, in

1937, Mitropoulos taught a boy how to bring music to life, and the boy surely loved him for it.

When Mitropoulos died in Italy, the cross he had always worn found its way into the hands of Trudy Goth, a longtime friend, whose mother owned a villa in Florence. According to Oliver Daniel, Mitropoulos's biographer, Bernstein implored Goth to give the cross to him. Like many other people in Bernstein's life, she could not turn him down. Bernstein wears the cross all the time.

In public, Bernstein has admired, sometimes even worshipped Mitropoulos. He wears his mentor's cross around his neck as though to keep the connection fresh and visible. But in reality, Mitropoulos's brutal treatment of his professed protégé must have confused, ultimately enraged Bernstein. If Mitropoulos twice promised Bernstein employment as his assistant, if Bernstein twice structured his life for long periods of time expecting a call that never came, if Mitropoulos did not remain in Minneapolis to give his imprimatur when Bernstein conducted the Minneapolis Symphony but went to New York to guest-conduct the NBC Symphony, if Bernstein, in Mitropoulos's absence, subjected him to ridicule at a post-concert party, then the purity of Bernstein's public affection for his predecessor at the New York Philharmonic is at least open to question.

That is not to suggest that Bernstein's picture of the relationship is entirely false. When two volatile, talented, intense, vain, sensual homosexuals intermittently over the years sense the shadow of the other, each man in his own way may well be both aggressor *and* victim. Bernstein and Mitropoulos had for each other a deep respect and a strong emotional attraction. Each also displayed a callousness that ignored the other's pain.

By the fall of 1961, at least two of Bernstein's conducting fathers were dead, having gone through experiences with him that range from the irritating to the grotesque. Even Reiner, a formidable teacher, had suffered. Lunching one day at the Plaza Hotel, he spotted Bernstein at a nearby table, walked over, and said, "You are a shit." Not one of Reiner's table companions ever did find out what provoked this attack. Some think he was referring to the speed with which Bernstein took over a European tour originally scheduled for Reiner and the Chicago Symphony Orchestra.

Bernstein attacked and seemed bent on consuming and destroying the conductors he saw as fathers. But there has also been a loving side to him, the side known best by friends and contemporaries such as Comden, Green, Oppenheim, Ramin, and Foss and those who sang and danced in his shows and played under his baton.

On February 13, 1961, the orchestra paid Bernstein a tribute with a special concert for him. The program displayed a red heart and a banner: "A Valentine for Leonard Bernstein." Copland conducted the *Candide* Overture, and Foss introduced the *Symphonic Dances* from *West Side Story* into the repertory. The performers included Jennie Tourel, Richard Tucker, Edie Adams, Barbara Cook, Carol Lawrence, Elaine Stritch, John Kriza, Anna Moffo, the Philharmonic musicians, and dancers from the American Ballet Theater. David Oppenheim, then director of artists and repertory at Columbia Records, where both Bernstein and the Philharmonic recorded, supervised the event.

The careers of music critics in New York profit from the attention generated by attacks on the conductor of the New York Philharmonic. The tradition extends back as far as the 1840s, when critic Henry Cood Watson battered away at Ureli Corelli Hill, the first conductor of the orchestra. As Taubman played a leading role in bringing down Mitropoulos, so Harold C. Schonberg set his sights on Bernstein.

When Taubman was setting the tone for the rest of the reviews at the *Times*, Schonberg's attacks on Bernstein were subtle. Generally they were couched in the quotes of anonymous musicians all of whom sounded remarkably like himself. In 1957, for an article in *The New York Times Magazine*, he quoted an unidentified musician in the orchestra on the incoming musical director:

> I've got to hand it to Bernstein. How does he do it? He has this big reputation as a composer and his serious music is almost never played. He'd never conducted opera, yet La Scala fell all over itself last year and wants him back. He never had a good press when he conducted the Symphony of the Air or when he made Philharmonic guest appearances. And what happens? He gets the Philharmonic. He's supposed to be this wonderful pianist and he's never given a New York recital. And how

many concertos has he in his repertory? Five? Six? How does
he do it?

If Schonberg had checked the files, he would have found that the
reviews of Bernstein's Symphony of the Air concerts had been largely
favorable and so had those for his Philharmonic guest appearances. As
for Bernstein and piano performance, even the least intelligent performing musician should have understood that Bernstein's many activities in music precluded the long hours of practice at the instrument
that a concertizing career demands.

In 1959, a year before Schonberg got the top job at the *Times*, he
wrote an article attacking Bernstein on the matter of a change in the
musicians' attire. Bernstein had ordered a more comfortable outfit for
the men to wear for the Thursday Preview concerts. It was modeled on
the one worn by Toscanini and Walter. Before the first of these events,
Schonberg wrote an article headed MUSICIANS STRIKE A SARTORIAL
NOTE IN THE NEW PHILHARMONIC UNIFORMS. He described
"off-black trousers and jackets of tropical basket weave ... the jacket
vented at the sides with white piping at the cuffs and a stiff bandmas-
terish collar secured with a hook at the Adam's apple." Again he quoted anonymous musicians trying on the outfits backstage: " 'You look like
a bellhop at the Astor,' 'Like a bandmaster,' 'A Field Marshal,' 'Like
Father O'Malley,' 'Like a space cadet,' 'Like Chiang Kai-shek.' The
room was filled with cries of 'Hey, Toscanini.' Some of the men felt the
urge to conduct and did so." The last sentence stated a crucial fact
grudgingly: "The men conceded that the costumes were comfortable."

All of this was enough for Schonberg. The day after the first
Preview concert he came back with still another story describing the
costumes in infinitely more detail and revealing what the men were told
to wear underneath them. Apparently the musicians did not enjoy
appearing on stage in attire that had been ridiculed in this way. A few
months later Bernstein returned to white tie and tails for the supposedly informal Previews, exactly what the men wore for their other public
performances, and suggested that the whole affair go down in history as
"Bernstein's Folly." Schonberg had won the first round.

During Bernstein's first two seasons in New York, Taubman consistently praised his performances with the orchestra. In his summary of

Bernstein's second year, published on May 16, 1960, he wrote, "The New York Philharmonic has had another good season. It has done excellent business. It has worked hard and persuasively." He added that Bernstein had planned the season as a whole, remained "curious and energetic," and "sought to be a modern man in a position that could easily tempt a musician into complacency." He also noted that the following fall he would retire, and Schonberg would take his place as chief music critic of *The New York Times*.

Once Schonberg got the top spot, he attacked Bernstein concert after concert. In the *New York Herald Tribune*, Paul Henry Lang, an academic who was never absolutely comfortable with the job, more often than not echoed Schonberg's fiercely held points of view a week or so later.

The first concert of the 1960–1961 season took place at Carnegie Hall on October 1. The program: Beethoven's *Leonore* Overture No. 3, Schumann's Symphony No. 4, and Beethoven's Piano Concerto No. 1 with Bernstein as soloist as well as conductor. Here is Schonberg:

> The tricky retards in the last movement of the Schumann were overdone. And throughout the symphony, there were too many shifts in tempo for comfort. In the Beethoven there were a couple of moments that were absolutely bizarre.
>
> On the cadenza, Bernstein sounded like a frustrated pianist…. With foot on the pedal, he whaled away at the keyboard, piling sonority on sonority. The results were disproportionate to say the least. Mr. Bernstein took a very romantic view of the finale. In the last movement there is a theme in A Minor that has jazz qualities, Here Mr. Bernstein went to town, all ten fingers and body shaking away…. On the whole it was a highly personal and rather vulgar performance, which also was a little rough pianistically. Perhaps the time has come to call a halt to the exhibitionism of pianist-conducting, for exhibitionism it is.

No need to call a halt. Nobody but Bernstein was doing it. Mitropoulos had done it, but no other conductor, except perhaps Foss, was capable of pulling off such a *tour de force*. In this attack Schonberg stood alone. Lang, while complaining about the inherent defects of the concerto itself, wrote that Bernstein had handled it well. In the *New York World Telegram and Sun*, Louis Biancolli wrote:

> The performance seemed to have a firmer unity of spirit and style because conductor and pianist were one and the same man.... My feeling has always been that Mr. Bernstein would have had a brilliant career as a concert pianist, had he not chosen the podium instead. All through the concerto the tone was strong and supple. Slow passages were pure poetry.

To single out Schonberg's attacks on Bernstein is not to imply that Bernstein was beyond attack. His performances could be erratic, sometimes his tempos could indeed be challenged with integrity, and he often underlined themes in a pedagogic way. But the nastiness of tone and the consistency of the negative reviews transcended the nature of the criticism in each instance.

Because it was the Friday afternoon concert that was reviewed, the judgment of the *Times* critic appeared in the Saturday morning paper. Bernstein has always unwound after concerts by staying up until the early morning, then sleeping until early afternoon. It was only a matter of hours, then, after reading Schonberg's assault that he had to mount the podium again for the Saturday evening concert. If Bernstein reacted to Kerr's review of *West Side Story* in the way that he did, one can only imagine how he felt on reading the first review of him that Schonberg had written as chief critic. He completed the Beethoven concerto and immediately walked out of the hall and went across the street to his own apartment, leaving the rest of the concert in the hands of the three assistant conductors—Gregory Millar, Elyakum Shapira, and Russell Stanger. The announcement to the public said that Bernstein would not return because of a "temporary indisposition." The next day he was back on the podium. From then on his reaction can be characterized as a combination of toughness and resignation. Alexander Bernstein remembers times his father came to the breakfast table, rubbed sleep from his eyes, and said, "Let's see what he's done to me today."

From time to time Schonberg had a kind word. On October 15, after harsh words about Bernstein's work in the traditional repertory, he remarked on the performance of Barber's Violin Concerto and Schuman's Symphony No. 3: "In the two contemporary works he sounded completely assured and the Philharmonic musicians played like demons...." But the traditional repertory is the meat and potatoes of the programming, and it was the performances of those pieces from the classic and romantic periods that interested the public and therefore the management. Here is Schonberg again, a few weeks into his first season:

> Mr. Bernstein did a pretty good job upstaging Mr. [Sviatoslav] Richter in Liszt's A Major Piano Concerto and Tchaikovsky's B Flat Major.... He made almost as much noise on the podium as his colleague did on the piano. Such foot stompings have not been heard since the Fifty-Fifth Division was on parade....
>
> Obviously Mr. Bernstein was exhilarated. In the "Battle of the Huns," he did everything but ride a horse to battle. Towards the end of the Liszt Concerto, he rose vertically into the air, á la Nijinsky, and hovered there a good fifteen seconds by the clock. His footwork was magnificent last night. But one did wish that there had been more music and less exhilaration.

In February 1961, the New York Philharmonic gave Bernstein a seven-year contract, the longest contract any of its conductors has had in this century. It required a minimum of twelve weeks a year in concert, but permitted him to continue with educational TV, recordings, and touring. The contract was celebrated by the valentine concert given to Bernstein by the orchestra and his friends.

It would have been unlikely for the Philharmonic to do anything else but give Bernstein this long-term arrangement. For one thing, Schonberg had been in his job only a few months, while Taubman had been extolling Bernstein for the better part of a decade. Even more important, Bernstein sold out the house.

One would have thought the contract, with its provision of only twelve weeks of concerts a year, would have delighted Schonberg because he clearly thought Bernstein such a pernicious influence. But that was not true. His wrap-up of the 1960–1961 season was so far removed in tone from the Taubman summary article of the year before that it is difficult to believe that both were written about the same man. First Schonberg noted the casualties that year. They were big ones, and it is important to note that many older conductors had not performed at the Philharmonic as scheduled. Reiner and Markevitch both canceled. Karl Boehm conducted only one week instead of two. Mitropoulos, who was to have conducted, died. The conductors who substituted for them were not at all in the same league. Two were composers—Chávez and Copland—while the others—Vladimir Golschmann, Paul Paray, and Stanislaw Skrowaczewski—had smaller reputations. Among the guest conductors in the 1960–1961 season, only Alfred Wallenstein, Thomas Schippers, and Hans Rosbaud conducted as scheduled.

Here is Schonberg on the new contract:

> Mr. Bernstein was not too much in evidence during the twenty-eight week subscription season. He conducted the first six weeks and the last six. That seems to be the pattern he will follow.... The Philharmonic is alive to the danger of this procedure: "As time goes on," David Keiser, the Philharmonic's President, said, "we hope that he may be able to conduct a longer period of the season.... If this is not feasible, the society will seek, in consultation with Mr. Bernstein, an additional principal conductor for a substantial part of the remainder of the season."
>
> In the meantime, even though the Philharmonic humbly hopes that Mr. Bernstein will grant more of his time to its Carnegie Hall activities, it has awarded him a 7-year contract. It was a gesture reminiscent of what happened some years back, when one of the television companies, afraid of losing Milton Berle, gave him a contract for a couple of billion dollars for the next hundred, or is it thousand years....

More than twenty years later, when Luciano Berio, the Italian composer who is a friend of Bernstein's, asked him what the most painful aspect of his long and apparently rich career had been, Bernstein said, "The New York critics." In *Facing the Music*, a collection of his Sunday essays published in 1981, Schonberg wrote in his introduction:

> Critics don't make careers. Artists make careers. A bad review in the *Times* may set a career back a season or two. That is about all…. For years, as an example, Leonard Bernstein could not get a favorable review in the *Times* or the *Herald Tribune*. What difference did an unfavorable review make to him except bruise his ego?

In one sense Harold Schonberg was right. Bernstein's ego was bruised, but not destroyed. Only months after Schonberg replaced Taubman at the *Times*, Bernstein found himself catapulted into a league of power and money that transcended anything he had known. He was the first American-born, American-trained musician

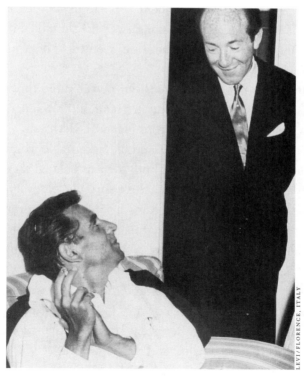

1953

Bernstein with longtime friend, composer David Diamond, in Florence after Bernstein had conducted a performance of Diamond's Music for Shakespeare's *"Romeo and Juliet." In a letter to Diamond in the summer of 1960, Bernstein wrote: "This winter I shall have nearly four months off from conducting, and I'm going to write a hell of a lot of music. I feel it. No shows, just music." He tried, not altogether successfully, for the next quarter of a century to remain true to his resolution.*

to be the director of a major orchestra, and the first American composer and conductor to have built a reputation abroad. It was a time of
ascendancy for American power and American culture, and Bernstein
became a prominent spokesman.

President Eisenhower maintained a cordial relationship with him,
and he was invited to the White House for evenings he has characterized as less than enchanting because no smoking was allowed in the dining room. In May 1958, the president appeared in New York for the
ground-breaking ceremonies at Lincoln Center for the Performing
Arts, one of whose parts would be a new hall for the Philharmonic.
Serving as master of ceremonies, Bernstein started the proceedings with
a performance of Copland's *Fanfare for the Common Man.* There was
nothing inappropriate about the work except perhaps its title.
Even with a Republican president and John D. Rockefeller III,
chairman of Lincoln Center, looking over his shoulder, Bernstein, in
choosing that piece, or at least that title, seemed to be proclaiming his
own political opposition.

Bernstein's closest link to American power came through John F.
Kennedy. In reality, they had little in common, but superficially they
seemed to. Both had graduated from Harvard, Bernstein a year before
Kennedy, and both had married beautiful, fashionable women who lent
grace to their husband's activities. Both men articulated their interest in
the poor while cultivating social circles that excluded everyone but the
talented, beautiful, and rich. Both came from families far removed from
the elegant enclaves in which they themselves moved. And both were
sons of fiercely competitive fathers. Neither was beloved by colleagues
older than he. On Kennedy's assumption of the presidency, Sir Harold
Macmillan is reported to have deplored the loss of Eisenhower and his
replacement by "this cocky Irish man." "Cocky" for Kennedy translated into "chutzpahdick" for Bernstein: the adjective most frequently
used to describe his personality and temperament.

During the summer of 1960, when Kennedy was campaigning
against Nixon, Bernstein was on a tour that covered thirty-four concerts in the United States, Canada, and West Berlin. In Vancouver five
thousand children sat in silence, then roared with approval. In Berlin,
on television, seven hundred students listened to Bernstein discourse
not on Ives or Gershwin, but on Beethoven. In Hawaii screaming audi-

ences hounded him wherever he went. To the press he attributed the magnitude of his reception to "the astounding power of TV." Bernstein was correct. Before the era of TV, a musician engaged in art music could never have behaved the way he did, talking to his audiences in a combination of slang expressions and homilies. When Bernstein took over the Young People's Concerts, by then a long and moribund affair—they extended back to 1885–1886 when Theodore Thomas conducted twenty-four such matinees—he did it only on condition that the events be televised. He says he presented that idea to William Paley, chairman of the Columbia Broadcasting System, who agreed to it fifteen minutes into the conversation.

After Hawaii, the tour went to San Francisco. In a letter to David Diamond, dated August 26, he wrote:

> I was 42 yesterday. What happened to time I no longer know but it must be six months since I last wrote to you. I've thought of you a lot and talked of you with Marc [Blitzstein] this summer. The months on the island [Martha's Vineyard] were lovely, but utterly unproductive. I was so fatigued that I never managed to switch off to composing at all. But I thought a lot and ideas have begun to germinate. This winter I shall have nearly four months off from conducting, and I'm going to write a hell of a lot of music. I feel it. No shows, just music.

Before the tour the Bernsteins had rented a house on Lagoon Pond in Vineyard Haven. It had five bedrooms, three baths, a three-car garage over which there was a large studio with a grand piano. According to Carly Kronig, the real estate agent who handled the rental of that house to the Bernsteins for three years, the family members were full of life. They boated, sunned themselves, enjoyed their summers, and left the house and grounds—one hundred acres, much of which was woodlot—in impeccable shape. No echo of Beatrice Fields's Tenth Street apartment here. Felicia Bernstein, according to her children, while being playful and ready to do virtually anything on a moment's notice, could also run a spectacularly smooth and gracious life.

After San Francisco, the orchestra went to the Hollywood Bowl. Murray Schumach, a reporter in the Los Angeles bureau of *The New*

York Times, sent back a piece that had Bernstein "getting as much attention as a film idol here." Autograph hunters besieged him and one evening, backstage, he began to receive in his dressing room wearing nothing more than a jockstrap. Goddard Lieberson, president of Columbia Records, who had signed Bernstein to an exclusive contract, told him to put on some clothes. But when Lieberson or Felicia was not around, Bernstein easily fell into his idiosyncratic, uninhibited ways. Just before San Francisco, when the musicians were in Hawaii, he had staged a party for them on Maui, where he was photographed in a slit-to-the-hip *malo*, wearing a rakish palm hat.

On September 2, a wire service sent out a report that Bernstein, now in California, was considering starring in a movie, *Diana at Midnight*, whose script was then making the rounds. Fame and money were not the only seductions for Bernstein where movies were concerned. Each time he was drawn to a role, it was one he perceived as an extension of himself, a fantasy he had of himself at the time. In his youth the part had been George Gershwin. After he met Felicia, it was Tchaikovsky, a homosexual composer protected by his beautiful patroness, Baroness von Meck. *Diana at Midnight* was described as the story of an "untalented composer who sells his soul to the Devil to write a great symphony."

Bernstein was not without talent as a composer. But because of his lack of success with his concert works, which few conductors ever programmed, he must have harbored a belief that he lacked talent. That may be why he continued to long to write "a great symphony." Nothing ever came of the movie or of Bernstein's prediction that during the coming year he would compose "no shows, just music." Bernstein had not composed a concert piece since 1954, when he had written *Serenade* for Isaac Stern.

Throughout his life, Bernstein was elated and excited when he was conducting and in the limelight and the center of the social action. Those were also the times when he expressed the desire to be free to compose. But whenever he took that time, according to his son, Alexander, he would enter the period depressed, more depressed, he would insist, than at any other time of his life. But, Alexander says, as soon as he started to compose he disappeared into his study for hours without any breaks at all, and when he did emerge he was filled with joy.

To report this is to imply that Bernstein's ambition does triumph over his creative drive. The most flagrant manifestation of this can be seen through an incident that occurred after Kennedy's inauguration. During the period he told Diamond he had set aside to compose, Bernstein wrote a short "Fanfare," which he conducted with the National Symphony Orchestra.

"I had emceed in the armory in Washington," Bernstein told a reporter in 1968, "and the President said as he was leaving: 'You are the only man I know I would never run against,' which was the greatest compliment I've ever had in my life from anybody. I was absolutely drop-jawed, and I thought to myself, gee, well, Lord, maybe these people have a point, but no. The idea of campaigning just turns me off, so I couldn't take it." When the reporter asked Bernstein if he would consider a post like minister of culture—which André Malraux then held in France—Bernstein said it would be "my idea of death." In answer to which position attracted him most: "President, or something modest like that." And he laughed.

The guest list of the inaugural ball was loaded with such show business personalities as Ethel Merman, Milton Berle, Nat "King" Cole, Mahalia Jackson, Juliet Prowse, Laurence Olivier, Jimmy Durante, Peter Lawford, and Leonard Bernstein. Bernstein enraged a few women that night when he cut in on the president while he was dancing with them. But the guest list was appropriate company for Bernstein, as far as the Kennedy staff was concerned: He invariably projected an image of show business personality, more than that of a cultivated Bruno Walter or Serge Koussevitzky.

On November 24, 1961, ten months after the inauguration, Bernstein was invited to the White House for an occasion more suited to his life's work. For a party honoring Luis Muñoz-Marín, the governor of Puerto Rico, the Kennedys had invited eighty-four year old Pablo Casals, the Spanish cellist, to perform. He had not performed in the United States in decades for political reasons. Playing with him were violinist Alexander Schneider and pianist Mieczyslaw Horszowski. This time the guests included members of the elite—such as journalist Walter Lippman as well as conductors Stokowski, Ormandy, and Bernstein. Probably the most striking fact of all was the inclusion of virtually every American composer of stature. The White House party for

Muñoz-Marín was highly publicized and served an important purpose: It managed to put a large dent in the uncultivated image of America. Eisenhower's favorites had been Hildegarde and Lawrence Welk. Harry Truman used to play the piano as accompaniment to his daughter's singing. Roosevelt had doted on Kate Smith. Here the shift was noticeable. Henry Cowell spoke for his colleagues when he told the press how much it meant to have the American composer honored in this way. Whatever the president's personal taste in music may have been, the public shift was noticeable.

In January 1962, when Stravinsky was in Washington conducting three performances of his own *Oedipus Rex*, a small dinner party was held at the White House in anticipation of his eightieth birthday. The guests included Jacqueline Kennedy's sister, Lee Radziwill, the composer Nicolas Nabokov, the Goddard Liebersons—like Bernstein, Stravinsky recorded with Columbia Records—and the Bernsteins. Stravinsky was accompanied by his wife Vera, Robert Craft, and Lillian Libman, who served Stravinsky as a combination friend, chauffeur, and secretary. Recalling this occasion in 1985, Jacqueline Kennedy Onassis speaking through Nancy Tuckerman, her secretary, said that, just as after the party with Casals, the Bernsteins had joined a few other guests in the family quarters of the White House after the guest of honor had gone.

During the winter of 1961–1962, the Soviets resumed a massive buildup of nuclear devices and nuclear testing. In the spring of 1962 President Kennedy responded with the announcement that the United States would react to this by starting a nuclear testing buildup of its own. The opposition was well organized, and managed to bring some twenty-five thousand people—most of them from the American Friends Service Committee and the Committee for a Sane Nuclear Policy—who converged in a march on Washington. Leading the activities were such celebrities as singer Harry Belafonte, Representative Helen Gahagan Douglas, pediatrician Benjamin Spock, and Bernstein. Not having felt obligated to the high brass in Moscow, even after they had given him lavish parties, Bernstein did not consider that he had any special political debt to the White House, even after being given preferential treatment there.

While the political news of the fall of 1962 was concerned with

Soviet-American relations, the cultural news dominating the country was the opening of Lincoln Center. Everywhere the event was heralded for being precisely what it was: by far the largest amount of money ever placed at the service of a temple for the performing arts in the United States. Everyone who participated in the planning expected the Kennedys to be there. Arrangements were made for the president to attend the performance and to appear at intermission on television with Bernstein. Yet on September 11, twelve days before the opening, the following news item appeared in *The New York Times*:

> Supporters of Lincoln Center expressed dismay that neither the President nor Mrs. Kennedy could attend the opening of Philharmonic Hall on September 23. One spokesman was "baffled" to learn that the Kennedys, actively espousing American culture, "could not find the time to participate in such a significant cultural occasion." Pamela Turnure, Press Secretary to Jacqueline Kennedy, said they would be resting in Newport on the 23rd, a Sunday, and that they have to be in Washington early the next morning to greet the President of Pakistan. The Lincoln Center opening was to be a white-tie event, and is expected to be one of the most impressive opening nights in the city's cultural history.

The Lincoln Center spokesman went on to note that the decision was particularly surprising in light of the fact that two evenings later the president and his wife were planning to attend the opening night performance of *Mr. President*, an Irving Berlin-Russel Crouse musical.

The day after this story appeared, Bernstein was supposed to be in Newport, Rhode Island, to launch a fund-raising drive for the National Cultural Center, the complex modeled after Lincoln Center to be built in Washington. Jacqueline Kennedy was to be there to display a revised model, and Bernstein was to introduce her. Here is Arthur Gelb in the *Times*, dateline September 12, Newport:

> The ceremonies were attended by celebrities from the arts, television cameramen and as many millionaires as could be packed into the ballroom of one of this nation's fabled estates.

Only Leonard Bernstein's last minute failure to appear sounded a disappointing note for the fund-raisers from thirty-nine cities to give the model their blessing. The conductor of the Philharmonic said he accidentally cut his lip and would be unable to deliver his speech.

If Bernstein was trying to flex his muscles to discover how far he could push the powers that be, he learned he could push them almost halfway. When Lincoln Center opened, Jacqueline Kennedy appeared, escorted by Chairman John D. Rockefeller III. Her husband was said to have remained in Newport. At intermission in the opening concert, the president's wife substituted for her husband in the conversation that was to have been televised between Kennedy and Bernstein.

During the first half of the concert, Bernstein had conducted parts of monumental works. (Playing excerpts is generally considered frivolous by people who are knowledgeable about music.) The pieces were the "Gloria" from Beethoven's *Missa Solemnis* and the first movement of Mahler's Symphony No. 8, also known as the *Symphony of a Thousand*. These were undoubtedly selected to show off the hall's technological facilities. The flexible stage was enlarged to its maximum to accommodate the hordes of performers, chorus, and orchestra. Even with less demanding fare than this, Bernstein loses pounds at each performance. This time, perspiring visibly, he greeted the first lady with "I'm all sweated up." Then he kissed her on the cheek.

The president's wife did not return to the concert after intermission, but drove back to the airport and flew to Newport. The incident of the evening that drew the most comment was not her rapid departure, but the kiss Bernstein had planted on her cheek, a repetition, incidentally, of his behavior at the Casals party. Under the headline MANNERS, *Time* magazine assessed the incident: "The moment, recorded on nationwide television, brought some cries of public outrage. 'Distasteful,' 'disgusting,' sniffed the proper to the polltakers." (In 1985, Jacqueline Kennedy Onassis said that she had not been irritated by the public kiss.)

After the Stravinsky party, the Bernsteins did not go to the White House again during Kennedy's tenure. Jacqueline Onassis insists that they "could" have been there, that nothing prevented them from being invited. The tone of her response suggests that if the president reacted to Bernstein's anti-nuclear public stance, she knew nothing of it.

If, in fact, Bernstein's politics played any role at all in keeping the president away from the opening ceremonies at Lincoln Center, the decision was probably made by his staff. Kennedy is unlikely to have placed much weight on the political pronouncements of someone in the arts.

More likely the president's absence that day indicates that in the late summer and early fall of 1962, he had enough on his mind to distract him from social and cultural events. For one thing, he was beginning to see the photographs of the Soviet missile buildup in Cuba.

Almost a year later, on August 24, 1963, Bernstein wrote to Diamond, "Best news is that I finished *Kaddish* this summer. That's all I did. I had virtually no vacation. My text still needs cleaning up— and a short section or two remains undecided: but actually, it's a piece! I can't wait for you to see it...."

Bernstein says he was finishing the orchestration of the work on November 22 when he learned of the president's death. Two weeks later he conducted the world premiere in Tel Aviv. Looking back at that event from a vantage point fifteen years later, Bernstein said:

> The assassination threw me for a loop. In fact, I don't think I've recovered from it yet. I think we're all still going through a very bitter period of loss and mourning....
>
> At that moment I realized that I had to dedicate the piece to the beloved memory of this man whom I did indeed love very much. And in whom I had great faith and hope and who I think was at that moment on the brink of becoming perhaps the greatest president we ever would have had. He, however, was not allowed this opportunity and we lost him. This brings up the whole problem of what music has to do with current affairs, with politics, with whatever, and it really has little if anything to do except to serve as a great time capsule—what is the word I'm looking for?—memento, no, more than that. A picture, a residue—oh, God—I can't find the words—an artistic incarnation of a given period in history. [3]

Leonard Bernstein was not the only child of Sam's
who was subjected to harsh buffeting in the early years of success.
Leonard's sister, Shirley, also endured much pain.

In the 1950s, Shirley worked for a film producer in New York,
then went to work for a producer of television game shows. In 1959

© WHITESTONE PHOTO / HEINZ H. WEISSENSTEIN

1963
The Bernstein children: Jamie, the oldest; Alexander; Nina.
"... at his seventieth birthday party, [Bernstein's father] Sam put his son in a class
that transcended even a Stravinsky or a Rubinstein: 'You don't expect,' he told
the guests, 'your child to be a Moses, a Maimonides,
or a Leonard Bernstein.'"
Bernstein's attractive, gifted children love him and he loves them, but his powerhouse
personality may have left them feeling they have a tough act to follow.

when she was called before a House of Representatives committee investigating game-show rigging, she found herself referred to as "Girl TV Fixer" in one newspaper. In an affidavit, she admitted she had tried to control the contestants' abilities to answer the questions but said she had done so on the instructions of Revlon, the cosmetics company sponsoring the show, *The $64,000 Challenge.*

From the time Shirley graduated from Mount Holyoke College, she had been in an unenviable position. She has said she could not find a man who compared with Leonard. Leaving her parents' home within months after finishing college, she moved to New York where she lived with Leonard, serving as a kind of secretary.

Soon the job became too complex. Bernstein had taken on so much that he needed a more experienced person, so he gave the job to Helen Coates. The two women did not get along; Coates apparently did not get along with any other woman in Bernstein's circle. But an accommodation was reached that made it possible for them to live—from time to time—under the same roof with Bernstein and his friends in the Berkshires.

When Felicia first entered Bernstein's life, a tense situation developed. Felicia told friends she did not enjoy going everywhere with her lover and his sister. Still, when Leonard broke the engagement, Felicia kept in close contact with Shirley, probably understanding that she had no chance at all of recapturing Leonard if Shirley worked against her.

In 1951 Leonard and Felicia married. They spent that first winter in Cuernavaca, the spring in Brookline working on *Trouble in Tahiti,* and they were at Brandeis in the fall. Then their first child was born. It was when her brother concentrated his attention on his growing family that Shirley went into the fiercely competitive game-show business.

One of the contestants on *The Big Surprise* was Nicolas Slonimsky, the writer and musician, who reflected on the episode in 1985: "Shirley Bernstein brainwashed me for thirty thousand dollars. Before every session, she would fire a lot of questions at me, fast and furiously, with a book in front of her. Some of those were the questions I was asked on the show. It is terrible that you can publish books, but the only thing that counts is making money in public. It made the front page when I decided not to go for the top prize of a hundred thousand dollars."

On January 5, 1962, Samuel J. Bernstein turned seventy. His birthday fell on a Friday, the eve of the Sabbath, so the celebration was postponed until Sunday. The dinner for eight hundred guests, held in the grand ballroom of Boston's Sheraton Plaza Hotel, was marked by a guest list that included not only Boston's prominent Jews but its influential Gentiles as well. Among them were Boston mayor John Collins, Massachusetts lieutenant governor Edward McLaughlin, state attorney general Edward J. McCormack. Because the whole Bernstein family was there, Burton Bernstein chose this particular event as the focus around which to center his family memoir. He writes that the party was as well attended as it was because the word was out that Sam's first son would be there.

At the time of Sam's seventieth birthday, Leonard was a celebrity. He was experiencing what William Schuman later described as the "most remarkable career in the history of music." Bernstein had been to the White House to honor Casals and for Stravinsky's birthday. He was the composer of the most celebrated musical in recent Broadway history, *West Side Story*. Virtually everything he did attracted public notice.

Bernstein's renown as a composer and as music director of the New York Philharmonic was nothing compared to what television broadcasts in the United States, Europe, Japan, Australia, and the Philippines gave him. The programs began with the Ford Foundation's historic *Omnibus* (1954–1958). Then came a pair of programs that ran between 1958 and 1972, *Leonard Bernstein and the New York Philharmonic* and *The Young People's Concerts*. Naturally the guests at Sam Bernstein's party hoped that the maestro would perform. Nor did he disappoint them. Bernstein went to the piano and played a variation of the same fragment of Jewish liturgical music on which he had set three variations for Rabbi Rubenovitz thirty years before. Recalling that occasion to the audience Bernstein said, "At the time I played variations of this song in the manner of Chopin, Liszt, and Gershwin. Now I will play it in the manner of Bernstein."

Burton Bernstein's story focuses on Sam, Jennie, Burton and Ellen (Burton's first wife), Shirley, and Leonard and Felicia. Photographs show Felicia, pregnant with her third child, almost as thin as ever. Not even under these conditions could she have been described as a voluptuous woman. According to Burton, she was "beautiful in her finely made white dress and simple jewelry, her eighth month of pregnancy hardly noticeable.... She gives the impression of aristocratic grandeur despite her small stature. She used to say that it was a trick she had learned as an actress, something to do with one's carriage and expression, the way the neck is extended...."

Like Leonard, Burton had moved far from his roots in his choice of a wife. He describes Ellen as "descended from Danish nobility." But he says that Sam and Jennie referred to her as their "other daughter," a description he writes they would never have used for Felicia. Apparently Felicia had treated Leonard's parents as she treated all the other people who had been a part of her husband's life before she married him: badly. This initially shy, frail, gentle woman had a reserve of strength she used to annihilate all of them. Rarely did she acknowledge their presence when they came into the Green Room. Nor did she invite them to the house, as her husband had done so often in the past. Ned Rorem points to the homosexuals, saying that Felicia "couldn't stand it when Lenny kissed them on the mouth." But the list exceeded homosexuals. It included Janice and Herschel Levit from Philadelphia; Jennie Tourel, who had first met Bernstein in Lenox in 1943; Irene Diamond, Hal Wallis's assistant when Bernstein had taken the Tchaikovsky screen test; Lester Cowan and Ann Ronell, in whose home in Canoga Park, Los Angeles, Leonard and Felicia had stayed.

One can understand why Felicia, reared by a strong mother who had married a Jew and brought her children up as strict Catholics, would echo some of her mother's ways. But in this instance there was a practical purpose as well: Her screening of her husband's friends helped him move up in his career. Bernstein was no longer, after all, a music student at Curtis or Tanglewood. Nor was he a composer looking for a Hollywood score. He was that singular celebrity so celebrated that he has never appeared on a television talk show. A bigger-than-life artist, with a talent to match his reputation, he was now the friend and confidant of the celebrated.

In 1960 Bernstein was given the Albert Einstein Award for furthering the cause of international understanding through the arts. The following year he was inducted into the National Institute of Arts and Letters along with historian Arthur M. Schlesinger, Jr., sculptor Jacques Lipchitz, architect Miles van der Rohe, and novelist Marchette Chute. Bernstein not only received encomiums on a regular basis, he was also the subject of several books. One, by David Ewen, was an inspirational story for children. Another, in German, by Arthur Holde, was a simple overview of Bernstein's life. A third, by music critic John Briggs, was an attempt at a bona fide biography. In the *New York Herald Tribune*, John Barkham wrote, "This biography suffers from the same defect as its subject—it is spread too thin over too wide an area."

The fact is that Briggs did what he could. Bernstein insisted on reviewing anything that went out about him. According to William Targ, the publisher, Bernstein did receive the galleys and covered them with "This is a lie," and "Absolutely wrong!" Targ says that the book had been based mostly on clippings and that everything was document-ed so nothing was changed on publication. Still, when an author knows he is obliged to submit galleys to his subject for review, a certain inhi-bition is bound to creep in.

Despite being hampered in this way, Briggs came forth with a few important new details. One involved Bernstein's having chosen the name "Nina" for his firstborn child and then suddenly changing it to "Jamie." "Nina" comes from *Reuben, Reuben,* the musical Blitzstein was working on when Felicia was pregnant in 1952. By 1962, that show was long dead, having failed in its out-of-town tryout. According to Jewish superstition, a child should not be named after a living person or, as far as Bernstein was concerned, a show that had not been closed. So in 1952 "Nina" was an inappropriate choice. In 1962 Bernstein seemed no longer intimidated by God in that superstitious way. The second daughter was named Nina Maria (after her maternal grandmother, then still living) Felicia. At that time Bernstein was writing *Kaddish*, a piece in which he not only assaults God but triumphs over Him.

By 1962, even Samuel Bernstein was persuaded that Leonard was some sort of deity. This was the father who, when his son was sixteen and in command of an impressive piano repertory, had forced him to spend the summer as a stock boy in his stock room. When his son was twenty-one and had been singled out by Copland, Mitropoulos, and Blitzstein, Sam told acquaintances he could not understand why Leonard would pursue music when he offered him a hundred dollars a week and free room and board and a chance to rise in the beauty supply business. When his son was twenty-three, playing for the first time in Town Hall Sam Bernstein reportedly said after Leonard had completed the piece,

"All this applause is very nice but where's the money?" Yet now, at his seventieth birthday party, Sam put his son in a class that transcended even a Stravinsky or a Rubinstein: "You don't expect," he told the guests, "your child to be a Moses, a Maimonides, or a Leonard Bernstein."

That acknowledgement came too late to effect a change in Leonard's character. If man's inhumanity to man is his vengeance for the abuse he received in his childhood, then Bernstein's explosions of cruelty to others can be interpreted as retribution for the scars he had received at the hands of his father. One example of such cruelty appears at the end of a letter to Diamond written on February 28, 1962, the day Nina was born:

At last, pen in hand. It seems to me that so much time has gone by since you were here, and that in all this time I haven't written, but there you are. I haven't. November went pfft with a bout of hepatitis, of all things, and I lost December recuperating therefrom. Then January went in preparing the Japan TV show, February has gone in writing and preparing a 90-minute TV on *Carmen*, which I just finished Monday night. It's been grueling beyond words, and I've learned my lesson about the television business: it eats up my life, and has absolutely stopped me cold as a composer. *Basta!* Now it's back to the scores—Bach, Bruckner, Mahler, & the Philharmonic again in three weeks. *Bref:* my 4½ months of composing time are down the drain. But I'm not depressed, I've learned a lesson. And the TV shows have been immensely satisfying and creatively rewarding. I think I'll spend the whole month of June at MacDowell or somewhere and finish my *Kaddish*.

At the moment, we are waiting breathlessly for the baby. I had predicted a date of March 1, & that's tomorrow. I'll let you know. We're all terribly excited.

One of my big disappointments was missing your Seventh with the Philly Orch. All reports were great—critical praise and colleague praise. I had so wanted to hear it, but I had just finished working on the Japan show, was exhausted, & took off for five days to go to Colorado to ski, which saved my life. But I missed the 7th—Forgive me.

Here we have one of Bernstein's closest friends, a man he had known since 1938, one to whom he had confided secrets, and one known among musicians to possess the most fragile of egos. This friend had composed a new symphony that was being given a world premiere by one of the greatest orchestras in the world under the direction of Eugene Ormandy—and at this moment Bernstein not only went off to ski, but later told Diamond he had gone off to ski. Not to compose or conduct—but to ski. The incident recalls the one told by Mitropoulos to his friends: that Bernstein had not only bad-mouthed him to the directors of the Boston Symphony, but then told Mitropoulos he had bad mouthed him because he wanted the post so much for himself.

Diamond says that Bernstein's behavior often "hurt me very much," particularly when it involved performing a work and then reneging on those promises. But Diamond is quick to add that he always believed Bernstein did the best that he could—had conducted the premieres of four Diamond symphonies—and that he, Diamond, was grateful. Regarding this particular incident, Bernstein's nonappearance at a Diamond's work premiere by Ormandy is probably attributable not only to his desire to ski, but to Bernstein's genuine distress when anyone other than he is in the spotlight. On this occasion he would have been eclipsed twice—by Diamond as composer and by Ormandy as conductor—and that was a circumstance he chose not to put himself in.

Diamond says Bernstein was always asking him how he managed to compose so much and that he always gave the same reply: that he did nothing but compose. The implication of Bernstein's question and Diamond's reply is that serious composition is the sine qua non of a contemporary musician's life. But if one looks with hindsight at just how these two musicians spent their time during the winter of 1961–62, one is led to challenge some long-accepted truths. Diamond's Symphony No. 7 was rarely performed after the Ormandy reading. A performance by the Juilliard Orchestra is the only one that could be tracked down. Nor is there a recording of the work. Therefore the symphony has had little opportunity to do what we expect a work of art to do: change the listener's perception of the world in even the least of ways. On the other hand, Bernstein's Japan and *Carmen* shows, preserved on videotape, have reached many millions of people in all parts of the world. Approaching each subject freshly, with questions he has yet to answer for himself, Bernstein still attracts viewers to these enlightening shows about his own art. Of his more that seventy television lecture-demonstrations, eleven received Emmy Awards.

Concerning the particular shows written and produced in 1961 and 1962: In Japan, Robert Saudek and his staff followed Bernstein into the Imperial Palace in Tokyo, where they televised a performance of Japanese *gagaku* music. Bernstein sat shoeless among the players. Then he introduced traditional *bugaku* dance, the *bunraku* puppet theater of Japan, the stringed instrument called *koto*, and fisherwomen singing Japanese folk songs. At the piano he accompanied a rehearsal of Japanese singers in *Trouble in Tahiti* and through all of this he chatted in Japanese. Bernstein had recently met Seiji Ozawa, the Japanese conductor, in Berlin. Bernstein was taken by Ozawa's talents and, in return, Ozawa wrote out for him in Japanese everything Bernstein wanted to say on this show. Bernstein also conducted the orchestra in the first movement of Beethoven's Seventh Symphony, an excerpt from Ravel's *Shéhérazade*, and the Japanese composer Toshiro Mayuzumi's Western-style work, *Bacchanale*.

With *Carmen* Bernstein anticipated by more that twenty years the most recent approach to the Bizet opera. In its original form, the one done at the Paris Opéra-Comique in 1875, the work contained spoken dialogue. But the world premiere was a disaster and Bizet died soon after, a broken man. After his death, his friend Ernest Guiraud substituted sung *recitative* for the dialogue. It was in this ultimately diluted form that the opera came to be known and was presented over the years.

On television Bernstein introduced the spoken dialogue and compared it with the sung *recitative*. For the former he used Broadway players; for the singers he turned to the Metropolitan Opera. He also concentrated on the drama, pointing out that, in the very beginning, Carmen's feelings are dominated by the contempt she feels for Don José a critical point rarely comprehended by the audience. Even Schonberg was moved to give credit. In the next-to-last paragraph of his review he wrote, "A few million people ended up knowing much more about 'Carmen' than when they turned the dial ninety minutes previously."

Still, Schonberg couldn't leave it at that. In the last paragraph he inserted the knife in the way of an Italian opera: "There was one funny moment, though. Mr. Bernstein was at the piano, tracing the course of the 'Seguidilla' from F Sharp to B Minor. 'Modulation, as we call it,' he explained, with the grave bedside manner of a physician diagnosing a case of disseminating lupus erythematosus, as we call it."

In 1984 Bernstein said that although he had been homosexual and heterosexual, he had never been both during the same period. There is another point to be made: During his homosexual periods, Bernstein made contact with a large number of men. During his heterosexual years, if he was unfaithful to Felicia, it was not with other women, but through an occasional encounter with a man.

In 1962 Phyllis Battelle, a syndicated columnist, wrote a long feature piece on Bernstein in which she noted that his first engagement had been "broken for reasons which they never revealed … after which he resumed his swift, women-free pursuit of superiority in all forms of music." After describing the encounter between Bernstein and Tallulah Bankhead in 1940, Battelle wrote that other than this, "there is no record of any escapade, however harmless, with the adoring sex. He is a devoted husband to his wife of eleven years, the beautiful ex-TV actress Felicia Montealegre who, incidentally, reacted as all women have…. 'Every now and then he just makes you want to cry, Oh. Thank you for loving me.' From a long-term wife this is glowing praise, if a bit hard to take at face value."

Apparently to illustrate Bernstein's prodigious memory, but perhaps to reveal a dark aspect of his personality, Battelle quotes Bernstein conjuring up some lyrics he had written during his teens to a so-called typical Cole Porter tune. The title: "You Stink."

> *I'm erethistic,*
> *You're Calvanistic,*
> *You think you're swell.*
> *You're so sadistic you smell.*
>
> *You little trollop,*
> *You need a wallop,*
> *I think*
> *To sum it all up,*
> *You stink.*

Battelle was correct when she said there was nothing on record about any escapade involving another woman in Bernstein's life. But almost as soon as the piece appeared, something did go on record involving another man. On December 11, the following item appeared in the *Philadelphia Bulletin*:

> Woodbine, Georgia, December 11 (UPI)—The chauffeur of composer conductor Leonard Bernstein was held here today on charges of car theft and desertion from the Marine Corps. The car, a new $8,000 convertible, allegedly was stolen from Bernstein by PFC Lucky Earl Beckwith, 20, of Hancock, New York, the musician's chauffeur, Sheriff W. E. Smith said. Beckwith was arrested Saturday with another serviceman, Marine PFC Kenneth Willard, 20, of Kalamazoo, Michigan, after they were stopped for speeding. The sheriff said Willard was driving the Lincoln Continental convertible, later traced to Bernstein.

The Continental had been a part of the deal with the Lincoln division of the Ford Motor Company, one of the sponsors of Bernstein's TV shows. The report, in the Philadelphia paper, would not have been cause for much alarm because the paper reached few New Yorkers. But when the same information was reported in *Time* magazine with racy overtones, Bernstein found himself in serious trouble, both at home and in his career. In 1962 it was still not possible for such a figure as Bernstein to be implicated in anything that even sounded remotely homosexual. *Time* quoted "absent-minded Bernstein, who apparently forgot to report the theft, 'All I know is that he let me out at a recital November 24 and never did pick me up.'"

Bernstein became angry enough at *Time* not to grant another long interview for more than five years. Whatever the details of the Beckwith story, they suggested that Paul Feigay's prediction to Ricky Leacock in 1957 turned out to be a prescient one: Bernstein had tried to go straight but he wasn't making it.

In 1963 Shirley wrote a book about her brother Leonard, *Making Music*, which was designed for children. She began by relating

Leonard's first memory. He had told her that when he was four, he had learned that man was made of dust. Collecting the whorls of dust from underneath his bed, little Lenny put them in the bathroom sink and turned on the water to make the whorls congeal. Once he had turned on the water he was unable to turn it off. When his mother entered the bathroom she found her son up to his knees in a flood. The water went through the floor to the apartment below where a tailor had his clothes laid out, and the Bernsteins were obliged to pay a large bill to compensate for the tailor's losses.

It is a memorable incident for a child and Bernstein later converted it into a piece of fiction for his composition class at Harvard. What he may have remembered most was his parents' rage, for in the story the protagonist redeems himself through a heroic act. But what is of interest to the observer now is that, at the age of four, Lenny reportedly played God and tried to make man.

After 1962, Bernstein's competition with God became the rule. He had competed with his father, with the Soviets, and with Kennedy. What mountain was there left to scale? Although all of Bernstein's concert works deal with what he calls "the problem of faith," it was only after the early 1960s that he set himself up in a confrontational posture with God.

The first of the works in which he did this was *Kaddish*, or Symphony No. 3.

A fifty-minute work originally, played without a break, *Kaddish* is more an oratorio than a symphony. Using the doxology mostly in Aramaic, with some Hebrew phrases, Bernstein also wrote a spoken text. The vocal parts are scored for mixed chorus, children's choir, and soprano soloist, with the text initially intended for a female Speaker. Now the work can be narrated by a performer of either sex. Bernstein says he submitted the work to Jewish scholars including his father to assure that religious sensibilities would not be hurt. But it is difficult to believe that they gave him the go-ahead. For the most part religious Jews find *Kaddish* blasphemous. Not accompanied by the cantor's cry, but by the chorus's hand clapping, it leaves the Hebrew prayer of sanctification far behind: Conjuring up the finger snapping of *West Side Story*, this *Kaddish* turns the Old Testament on its head.

Bernstein began working on *Kaddish* during the summer of 1961 at

Martha's Vineyard, continued to work on it at the MacDowell Colony in the summer of 1962, and finished it the following year in Fairfield, Connecticut. The Bernsteins had sold their home in nearby Redding and bought a large white New England-style house with spacious grounds and a swimming pool. Considering the luxury of his personal circumstances, it is difficult to understand the source of Bernstein's rage. In *Kaddish* he attributes it to man's development of the atom bomb. In the text he treats God as an equal, as one who needs to be comforted for His many mistakes as man needs to be comforted for his having made the bomb.

The central character identifies herself as Lily of Sharon, and in Bernstein's original version, opens the piece with "Oh Holy Father, ancient hallowed lonely disappointed Father, angry, wrinkled old Majesty: I want to pray." And then she does that publicly throughout the remainder of the work. Starting with a shout: "Listen, Almighty, with all your might," she follows that with a cry: "Amen, did you hear that, Father?" And still later, with remorse, the Speaker asks, "Have I hurt you, Father?" The words suggest a projection of Bernstein's own self, attacking all the unapproachable authorities in his life, and then begging their forgiveness for the hurt he had inflicted on them. (One must remember that Bernstein began this work, his first concert piece in nine years, almost immediately after the death of Mitropoulos.)

Then the Speaker offers to sing for God. Here the soprano appears and comes forth with a sweet lullaby. After the narrator describes a dream in which lambs are frisking about in heaven, she concludes: "We are in this thing together, you and I. You can no longer afford my death, I shall continue to create you and me." All of which suggests that in this particular creation, Bernstein emerges at the very least on a level with God, and bullies God in relation to his own death. The music parallels the text; a simple diatonic tonal language underlies all the expressions of faith while the twelve-tone principle, in all its accustomed angularity, informs the enraged and rebellious shouting.

Overall the score contains many striking moments. First there is the assertive energy, which comes from the skillful handling of jazz. Then there is the beauty of the slow movement, composed for soprano and women's voices, which Bernstein calls a "Pietà." Then there are the varied and inventive handlings of the settings of the "Amen." What is remarkable is the way seemingly simple popular melodies dissolve into rich contrapuntal texture within the chorus and orchestra. Finally there is the dramatic choral fugue at the climax, which rivals any number of such fugues in the romantic repertoire. The problems with this piece are twofold: One wishes the Speaker would disappear so the music could be properly heard. And when the music can be heard, as soon as one begins to hear its beauty, it often gets lost, because Bernstein has gone on to something else.

The first performance of *Kaddish* took place on December 9, 1963, in the Frederick Mann Auditorium in Tel Aviv. Bernstein conducted the Israeli Philharmonic, Hannah Rovina of the Habimah Theater performed the Speaker's role in what turned out to be her last public performance, Jennie Tourel was the soloist, and Abraham Kaplan led a combination of four choruses. Bernstein enjoyed prolonged applause and says that afterward "Golda [Meir] came around to see me. She lit up my cigarette declaring, 'Thank goodness, someone else smokes.'"

Some reporters claimed that Bernstein's choice of a Jewish theme and the gesture to the Jewish state affected the Israelis sentimentally. But there were probably more who agreed with the critic who wrote, "It's philosophy, it's dramatic, it may even be music. But it certainly is not *Kaddish*." Bringing this *Kaddish* to Tel Aviv was a little like kissing the first lady on TV.

Kaddish was the result of a commission from the Koussevitzky Foundation and the Boston Symphony to commemorate the symphony's seventy-fifth birthday Though it had been scheduled for the 1955–1956 season, Bernstein delivered the work eight years late. But the orchestra for which it had been written went ahead and presented the American premiere: In February 1964, Tourel repeated the performance and Felicia took the Speaker's role. Assembled on the stage of Symphony Hall in Boston were the Boston Symphony, the New England Conservatory Chorus, the Columbus *Boychoir*, and the soloists, all under the direction of Charles Munch.

To the consternation of many in New York, Bernstein absented himself that week, a week in which he was scheduled to conduct the Philharmonic, to oversee rehearsals of *Kaddish*. After listing the huge forces employed in the work, *Time* went on to describe what was going on in Boston: "With such an ensemble, the Boston was committed to

Kaddish up to its ears. Bernstein had come to town to cajole and kibbitz while poor Munch tried to lead rehearsals. '*Beaucoup mieux*, Charles,' Lenny called down from the balcony, then finally took the baton for one of the last run-throughs." Munch, after all, was not the leader of the Sanitation Department Band from whom, some years before, an ebullient Bernstein had taken his baton on his return from a big trip. It must have driven the French conductor out of his mind to have been humiliated by Bernstein in front of the musicians in this way. If one considers Bernstein calling Reiner "Fritz" when he entered Curtis at twenty-one, asking Rodzinski to turn pages for him at Tanglewood when he was twenty nine, now condescending to Munch with his "*Beaucoup mieux*, Charles," one can understand why a good many guest conductors during Bernstein's tenure at the New York Philharmonic may have gotten sick or died, or in any event did not show up. This repetitive pattern of subtle and not-so-subtle attack on older men with established reputations is another manifestation of the anger that was first apparent in his behavior toward his father and culminated in his rebellion against God.

Marc Blitzstein died on January 22, 1964, after a beating by some sailors on the waterfront in Martinique. Bernstein made this statement to the press: "Mr. Blitzstein was so close a personal friend that I cannot even begin to measure our loss of him as a composer. I can only think that I have lost a part of me; but I know

In 1970, Bernstein wrote of lifelong friend Aaron Copland: "The truth is that when the musical winds blew past him, he tried to catch up—with 12 tone music— just as it too was becoming old-fashioned to the young."

also that music has lost an invaluable servant. His special position in musical theater is irreplaceable."

On February 1, 120 people attended a memorial service for Blitzstein in New York. Lillian Hellman said that Bernstein was in Boston for the American premiere of *Kaddish*, that he regretted he could not attend. She added that a Blitzstein memorial concert, arranged by Bernstein, David Oppenheim, and herself, would be held in April.

In many ways the early 1960s were catastrophic for Bernstein. The loss of Mitropoulos and Blitzstein, the weekly attacks in the New York press, and the crystallization of the twelve-tone technique among composers young and old accentuated the distance between Bernstein, the hugging and kissing celebrity, and Bernstein, the interior man. Because Bernstein's primary view of himself has always been as a composer (he says that when he conducts he fantasizes he is composing the work in front of him), the shift to the twelve-tone system was probably the most debilitating of all. Not only had Stravinsky turned to it soon after Schoenberg's death, but now Copland was doing it, too. In 1957 Copland composed his twelve-tone *Piano Fantasy*. Then in 1962, at the opening concert at the new Philharmonic Hall in Lincoln Center, Bernstein conducted Copland's *Connotations for Orchestra*, another twelve-tone piece. It had been commissioned by the orchestra for the occasion. In addition to kissing Jacqueline Kennedy, Bernstein remarked to her on television about the density and the difficulty of the Copland score.

The elegantly dressed opening night audience certainly did not expect it would have to do any hard listening that night. Here is some typical press comment: "Twenty minutes of dissonance," Harriett Johnson wrote in the *New York Post*. "Nobody liked it." After *Connotations*, Copland wrote only one more work, *Inscape*, completed in 1967. It was also commissioned by the Philharmonic during Bernstein's tenure. It, too, was a twelve-tone piece. In an article in *High Fidelity* magazine commemorating Copland's seventieth birthday, Bernstein wrote:

> After the war, the Schoenberg syndrome took hold and was
> heartily embraced by the young, who gradually stopped flock-

ing to Aaron. The effect on him—and therefore on American music—was heartbreaking. He is, after all, one of the most important composers of our century. I am not thinking historically now, but musically. In fact, he became an impetus to subsequent American music only because his own music is so important. It contains a rare combination of spontaneity and care; his creative material is purely instinctive and his crafting of it extremely professional. Unlike much of the past decade's transient works, Aaron's music has always contained the basic values of art, not the least of which is comunicativeness.

As these virtues became unfashionable, so did Aaron's music. One of the sadnesses I recall in recent years occurred at the premiere of his *Inscape*, when he said to me, "Do you realize there isn't one composer here, there isn't one musician who seems to be at all interested in this piece—a brand new piece I've labored over?" The truth is that when the musical winds blew past him, he tried to catch up with 12-tone music just as it too was becoming old-fashioned to the young.[2]

Bernstein was not above responding to the musical winds himself. He experimented with the twelve-tone technique, especially in his *Kaddish*. Here is Bernstein on that work and the reaction it provoked:

Perhaps the most striking example of my nontonal music is *Kaddish*, my Third Symphony, which contains a great deal of highly complex, carefully worked out—according to the Schoenbergian system—twelve-tone music. As a matter of fact I remember when it was first played in Boston, the American premiere of the symphony with Charles Munch conducting. A whole group of young composers who were at the time considering themselves avant-garde artists, who had gotten wind of the fact that I had *finally* written a twelve-tone piece, came to the rehearsals in a body. Arthur Berger, Harold Shapero, Leon Kirchner, the Harvard group, the Brandeis group. And they seemed terribly excited until the midpoint of the symphony when the second kaddish, which is sung by a soprano (and which is a lullaby and completely tonal), appeared. And they all threw up their hands in despair and said, "oh, well, there it goes. That's the end of the piece."

And they didn't come to any more rehearsals as far as I know. It was that cut and dried and that simple-minded. Of course they didn't understand at all that one of the main points of the piece is that the agony expressed with the twelve-tone music has to give way—that is part of the form of the piece— to tonality and diatonicism, so that what triumphs in the end— the affirmation of faith—is tonal.[3]

But those composers probably did understand exactly that. The use of the twelve-tone language simply to create an effect must have disturbed them more than anything else. While Bernstein may have told a *Young People's* audience that music can express only itself, his own treatment of it is a far more literal one. Members of orchestras he conducts report that when Bernstein rehearses a work he will say: "Here are the bad people. Now come the good ones." The point is that Bernstein will use whatever he has to use to put across what is in his mind—and he does this in both conducting and composition. But the twelve-tone principle, particularly when it was fresh to these shores, was never conceived of by its proponents as a mere musical device. Rather it was seen as a language with its own particular grammar, a language that had displaced the tonality of the past three hundred years. Charting new territory, moving ahead into an unfamiliar terrain, was not taken lightly by those who followed this route. Such artists deplored the use of the twelve-tone method as a tool with which to convey rage, anguish, trauma, or tragedy. The general feeling was that if a composer was committed to tonality—as Bernstein surely was—he could write chromatically as Wagner had, compose a compelling melody, or indicate a rubato to convey what he wanted in a moment in his piece. But to use a whole language in a part of a work in order to contrast that part with a joyous tonal one is ultimately to trivialize the language.

Bernstein has said he tells the truth, just not all the truth. Often he exaggerates in order to dramatize a point. He will say, "Koussevitzky died in my arms," when in fact Bernstein left the hospital around midnight, after which Koussevitzky lapsed into a coma and died early the next afternoon with Bernstein absent. He will say he was orchestrating the very last measures of *Kaddish* the moment he heard of Kennedy's death, when something less neatly self-aggrandizing was probably the case. Similarly, in telling the story of the *Kaddish* rehearsal, Bernstein appears to have strained the facts a bit. His point was undoubtedly to emphasize the distance between himself and the twelve-tone composers. Fewer composers walked out than he later said. Arthur Berger did not; he was composing tonally himself. Then, too, one Bernstein named was not there at all. Leon Kirchner, who would come under Bernstein's heading of the Harvard group, for he was a professor there at the time and later came to occupy the Walter Bigelow Rosen Chair in music, did not attend any rehearsal of *Kaddish*.

Kirchner's first connection to Bernstein had been one of which Bernstein was unaware. Early in 1944, when Bernstein was conducting the world premier of *Jeremiah* in Pittsburgh, Kirchner was in the audience. In the army, stationed in Pittsburgh, he says he remembers two emotions that night. One was excitement that a man his own age who was also a Jew could be conducting the eminent Pittsburgh Symphony in a composition of his own. The second emotion was jealousy, and that was twofold. Kirchner was jealous that as gorgeous a woman and great an artist as Jennie Tourel would embrace Bernstein with the passion that she did after their performance. And he was envious that Bernstein was up there on the podium while he was stuck—Kirchner served for five years—in the army, unable to do his own work.

Between his discharge and the Boston performance of *Kaddish*, Kirchner pursued a career as composer and conductor within the protective world of the university, that haven for so many composers after World War II. He studied with Schoenberg in California, then moved to the Northeast, where the Ivy League schools solidified their commitment to composition by granting composers advanced degrees.

Kirchner says that at the party after the first performance, he told Bernstein "what was wrong with *Kaddish*. I specified that the only beautiful part of the work was the Mahler section, you know, the tonal lullaby." Tourel overheard the comments and attacked Kirchner for criticizing Bernstein. But, according to Kirchner, Bernstein listened attentively and then asked if he would like to "fix it up." Kirchner never did that. He says that a similar conversation, one in which Bernstein invited his help, took place after the first New York performance of *The Age of Anxiety*.

From the start of his career, Bernstein invited and accepted criticism when it came to his compositions. Such an attitude never characterized his life as conductor. In the early 1940s, he told people that Reiner could not handle the complex rhythms of *Jeremiah*. Later he ridiculed Koussevitzky, sometimes for his idiosyncratic locution, sometimes for his musical defects. Still later he condescended to Munch in front of a hall filled with people. There was no one to whom Bernstein deferred in the realm of conducting as he continued to defer to composers like Copland and Kirchner.

Bernstein told a television audience that he understood Mahler so well because, like Mahler, he felt himself to be two men locked up in the same body. The two men were, of course, a composer and a conductor. But, like Mahler, Bernstein finally is only one man. It follows that his preference for tonality in composition would also manifest itself in the works he chose to conduct. During his tenure at the New York Philharmonic, Bernstein did not concentrate on presenting works by those composers who had crystallized and developed the twelve-tone technique in Germany and Austria. But his programs were nevertheless adventurous. Even in his first months as co-conductor with Mitropoulos, he conducted a program that included pieces by Wallingford Riegger, Carl Ruggles, and John Becker, all pathbreaking Americans. The three of them attended the concerts and took bows from the stage.

In the spring of 1961 Bernstein went even further, conducting the American composer Henry Brant's Antiphony No. 1, a work that had had a profound effect on Karlheinz Stockhausen, then the leading figure of the European avant-garde. In the 1961–1962 season. Bernstein again programmed advanced pieces. Foss's *Time Cycle*, which he played through a second time for those in the audience who chose to stay, Gunther Schuller's *Spectra*, and Ben Weber's Piano Concerto. When Weber went to see Bernstein in his apartment to prepare for the piece, Bernstein asked him to sit down at the piano and play it. Timid, Weber said he could not do that. Then Bernstein lifted the score from the bottom of a pile of scores, and played the work from beginning to end with such style and precision that Weber spoke of the performance for years.

When he first assumed the post at the New York Philharmonic,

Bernstein supervised the commissioning of ten pieces for the orchestra's opening year at Lincoln Center. They included Copland's *Connotations for Orchestra*, William Schuman's Symphony No. 8, Milhaud's *Ouverture Philharmonique*, Barber's *Andromache's Farewell*, Poulenc's *Sept Répons de Ténèbres*, Hindemith's Concerto for Orchestra, Henze's Symphony No. 5, Ginastera's Concerto for Violin and Orchestra, Chávez's Symphony No. 6, and a new work by Bernstein himself. During the opening year he also conducted such rarely performed pieces as Janáček's Slavonic Mass, Roberto Gerhard's Symphony, Berg's Violin Concerto, Hindemith's Requiem, and Piston's Concerto No. 2 for Piano and Orchestra. After the Piston work, the composer rose to take a bow. Bernstein gesturing to him said, "My beloved teacher." In one instant all the complexities of the old student-teacher relationship were erased, as Bernstein refocused the event on himself.

Harold Schonberg characterized this 1962–1963 season in an article in the *Times* on April 26:

> To celebrate its new home, the Philharmonic commissioned ten works. Three of these—by Alberto Ginastera, Carlos Chávez and Mr. Bernstein—were not delivered. Contributing the large-scale works were Aaron Copland, William Schuman, Francis Poulenc, Paul Hindemith, and Hans Werner Henze. Shorter works were those by Darius Milhaud and Samuel Barber.
>
> Nearly all of these were safe commissions. Apart from the Henze score, they represent work from established composers whose style has long been performed. Thus there were no surprises in store; the Copland "Connotations" was predictably Copland; the Poulenc "Sept Répons" were predictably Poulenc and so on.... These commissions indicate a lack of adventure on the part of the New York Philharmonic.... As a result the entire season was somewhat gray and lacking in luster.

The Copland *Connotations* was the first big work by that composer to be written in the twelve-tone system, and the *Sept Répons* by Poulenc was so anti-Semitic in its text that many people walked out, and many others wrote letters of protests. "Predictable" was hardly the correct word to characterize these two new works.

There would be no point in quoting Schonberg in such detail if the administrators of the New York Philharmonic had not responded to him with such alacrity. As they had reacted to Taubman's attack on Mitropoulos in 1956 by removing the conductor from his post, so they now responded to Schonberg's remarks by intruding a schedule of avant-garde works into already fixed plans. The avant-garde festival would include works by John Cage, Earle Brown, Larry Austin, Morton Feldman, John La Montaine, György Ligeti, Witold Lutoslawski, Edgard Varèse, Stefan Wolpe, and Iannis Xenakis. On September 27, just after the announcement of this plan, Schonberg wrote:

> The adventurous part of the season comes in January and early February when Mr. Bernstein addresses himself to a series called 'The Avant-Garde.' In the past Philharmonic audiences have objected quite audibly to some of Mr. Bernstein's ideas about contemporary programs, and this time they are sugar-coated a bit. Thus for six weeks the Philharmonic will have its quota of Beethoven, Mendelssohn, Mozart, and Tchaikovsky. But sandwiched between these revered figures will be such revolutionaries as Stefan Wolpe, Pierre Boulez, Mario Davidovsky, and Edgard Varèse (both represented by electronic works). John Cage and Morton Feldman (representatives of aleatory or music of chance).... It is all part of the current scene and, as such, deserves some kind of representation by the Philharmonic.... Aside from this splurge, the Philharmonic programs are not very stimulating.

There were problems associated with the festival. Boulez did not complete his piece in time, Davidovsky's electronic work presented problems, and Bernstein spent a week in Boston helping Munch with *Kaddish*. Then Bernstein angered those committed to new music with his introductory remarks to virtually all of these concerts.

In the *New York Herald Tribune*, Alan Rich wrote:

> Bernstein tried everything short of a flit-gun to kill off the avant-garde movement in music. To describe the goings-on ...

as disgraceful is to give the word new depth. What the conductor accomplished on the podium ... was reasonable enough, but what he said as prefaces to the performances established the whole event as some sort of sour, cynical circus.

It was inevitable that Bernstein's antipathy to nontonal music would show through in his explanations. Still sometimes the concentration on one detail of a complex operation can illuminate a great deal. Here is Stefan Bauer-Mengelberg on the performance of the Wolpe symphony: "In the early 1950s, Wolpe received a commission from the Rodgers and Hammerstein Foundation for a symphonic work. The commission carried with it the promise of being played by nine symphony orchestras. The symphony, finished during the 1955–56 season, lay around. Bernstein saw it. He admired it but knew it could not be done as written. 'Would you consider,' he asked Wolpe, 'having it renotated?' Outraged, Wolpe said, 'Of course not.' Gently, Bernstein went on, 'We're not talking about what Rimsky did to Moussorgsky when he orchestrated *Boris Godunov*. We're talking about someone helping you to write it so it can sound precisely the way you wrote it the first time.' At that Wolpe calmed down.

"Bernstein suggested I do the job. By that time I was busy writing books and tending to other matters. I was no longer assistant conductor there. Still, everywhere I went I was told the Philharmonic wanted me to know that Wolpe was waiting for my call. So finally, early in 1962, I called. I was expecting an ogre. I remember getting off the elevator and seeing Wolpe, who extended his arms to me and said, 'Here comes my savior.'

"We did not even exchange courteous remarks. His score was on an easel-like drafting stand and we walked right over to it. 'What would you do about the first measure?' he asked. And I showed him. He accepted it with delight. Not so easy was the second measure or the many to follow but finally he agreed on all the changes in notation that I made. We spent twenty-two afternoons doing this. I would move the bar line by an eighth note—that kind of thing. The Bernstein Foundation paid for this work. It was a personal charitable contribution from Bernstein himself.

"When Bernstein saw the score he said it was 'obviously infinitely improved' and that he would program it. I remember running into him on MacDougal Street in Greenwich Village when I was working for IBM. I was with another IBM employee and Bernstein was extremely friendly and cordial. It was then he said to me, 'You probably know the Wolpe symphony better than anyone else. So will you conduct it?' As always with Wolpe, things went badly. He had had the parts copied in Italy and the job was terrible. Nothing was correct. It made *Wozzeck* look like a bagatelle. Then David Oppenheim raised the money to get Arnie Arnstein to copy the parts. Arnstein is just about the best copyist in the world.

"There is nothing that matches Bernstein's behavior during that difficult week. I had anticipated trouble at the beginning of the season so I asked management if we could set aside a half hour each week during rehearsals throughout the fall and early winter so that the musicians could be familiar with the piece by January. That was turned down. The players saw this incredibly complex work on the Tuesday before the Thursday night performance for the very first time. The other pieces on the program were the Beethoven Symphony Number One and the Beethoven Piano Concerto Number Three with Rudolf Serkin. Both were scheduled to be recorded the following Monday. A recording is for eternity. Still Bernstein gave me both the Tuesday rehearsals, all of them. Then he called and asked how it was going. I said, 'We have a problem.' Bernstein said he would be right over. Together we decided that we could bring off the first and second movements with some degree of success but not the third.

"During this festival Bernstein made a practice of speaking to the audience in advance. The morning of the first performance Helen Coates came to me with Bernstein's typescript and said he would like Wolpe and me to read it through and tell him if there is anything there either of us wanted changed. I found nothing wrong. Neither did Wolpe. In his remarks Bernstein gave the audience a glimpse of what goes on behind the scenes and neither of us saw anything wrong with that.

"There was a lot of confusion with this concert. Because it had been canceled once and rescheduled, there were no tickets for the contingent of personal friends and composers that usually exist. Coates was instructed to ask some of the ticket holders to move so that Wolpe could be in the right seat, the one on which the spotlight shines after the performance. All of this takes unbelievable planning—like the Normandy invasion. Suddenly a member of the administrative stall came backstage in a panic and said there had been a mistake. Someone would have to change Wolpe's present seat with the seat of a lady sitting nearby. Here I am, trying to keep my mind on how to beat those five 32nd beats, and I am bothered with such details as seating. Then, when I did come out on stage, I found the podium pitching underneath me. Apparently the elevator bringing up the piano to the stage had not leveled off exactly and I went through the whole performance with this pitching podium beneath me. Remarkably, when the performance was over, there was a large round of applause. I turned around, gestured to the terrace, and the light went onto the lady who had been in the right seat before she was asked to change, and who happened to be my mother. Wolpe was entirely in the shadows. By the Sunday performance the lights and Wolpe were synchronized and he got the applause that he deserved."

In his review Schonberg wrote that Wolpe had gone beyond Schoenberg and Webern and that his program notes referred to Einstein, Planck, Bohr, and Cantor. He quoted Wolpe as saying that his "structured field of pitches" was analogous to "those of physical bodies in a force field." Schonberg described Bernstein's preconcert talk and his remark that the work was so difficult it had proved impossible to do in its entirety. "Bernstein said he first saw the score several years before and asked Wolpe to rescore it and rebar it in the interests of practicality." At the time, Schonberg went on, "Bauer-Mengelberg was picked 'because he is a mathematician as well as a conductor.' (Mr. Bernstein did not intend this in the pejorative sense, but the idea of a symphony's needing a mathematician to conduct it drew a good laugh from the audience.)"

Concerning the reaction backstage to the laugh, here is Bauer-Mengelberg: "When Bernstein said he had chosen a mathematician to conduct the work, there was a tittering in the audience. Afterwards there was a conference. Should he take that out? No, he decided. It's entirely appropriate that one should rescue this score with the help of a mathematician. 'What I will change will be my delivery of the sentence and that will make a difference.' He did, and after that, there was no tittering."

In assessing the work, Schonberg wrote, "Tremendously dense, complex work, finally an exercise.... One that is bigger than most serial works and hence more impressive, but fundamentally differing very little from any of them."

This story may shed some light on far more publicized events that took place in April 1962, when Glenn Gould was the piano soloist in the Brahms D Minor Concerto. As with the Wolpe, Bernstein made a preconcert speech. He said there had been considerable disagreement between him and Gould about tempos, dynamics, and so on, but that because Gould was such a serious artist, he would defend to the death Gould's right to experiment in this way. "Who's the boss in a concerto—the conductor or the soloist?" was the rhetorical question Bernstein put to the audience.

A tape exists of that performance. It includes Bernstein's oral renunciation of Gould's ideas as well as an interpretation that Alan Rich, in *Keynote* magazine, July 1985, describes as "pretty spectacular Brahms playing, technically flawless ... shaped with an impressive imagination, a few minor details worth raising an eyebrow at ... and on the whole a fascinating example of a persuasive mind at work on music that doesn't give up its secrets easily." At the end of the tape there is an ovation that suggests that Bernstein's apprehensions had been misplaced.

But Harold Schonberg delivered a scathing review. He wrote one of his "Dear Ossip" letters. (Ossip Gabrilówitsch was a renowned pianist and conductor in the first half of this century.) It went like this:

> I mean this, Ossip. Glenn Gould is waiting in the wings ...
> and has to listen to Bernstein saying that this was a Brahms he
> never dreamed of. He washes his hands of it. He says, believe
> me. Ossip, the discrepancy between what he thinks of the con-
> certo and what this Gould boy thinks of the concerto is so great
> that he must make clear this disclaimer.... So then the Gould
> boy comes out, and you know what, Ossip? ... He played the
> Brahms D minor Concerto slower than the way we used to

practice it. (And between you, me, and the corner lamppost, Ossip, maybe the reason he plays it so slow is maybe his technique is not so good.)

At this time Gould was at the height of his popularity and enjoyed stirring up some controversy. But this review was not just controversial. It humiliated him as an artist and as a man. Shortly before his death, Gould told Tim Page, who later compiled an extensive collection of Gould's prose writings in *The Glenn Gould Reader*, that he had been charmed by Bernstein's words and had seen them in a sporting spirit. He also said he had been upset by Schonberg's review.

Gould retired from the concert stage within two years of this event. Scheduled to play under Bernstein with the New York Philharmonic the following February, in 1963, Gould called in sick. This particular cancellation had felicitous consequences: Bernstein used the opportunity to introduce André Watts, the brilliant sixteen-year-old pianist, at a subscription concert. Only two weeks before, Watts had played the Liszt Piano Concerto No. 1 at a *Young People's Concert*, alerting Bernstein to his talent. So Gould's canceling this particular date led directly to the launching of another career.

In 1983 still another book devoted to the Canadian pianist, *Glenn Gould Variations*, was published. Bernstein wrote the introduction, concentrating his attention on that event of April 1962. But all the facts are distorted. Although he writes with apparent affection about the artist who had just died at the age of fifty, Gould does not come out ahead. While the tape of that performance consumes a playing time of fifty-three minutes and fifty-one seconds—which, as Rich points out, is twenty-three seconds *faster* than Bernstein's most recent recording of the same work with the pianist Krystian Zimerman—Bernstein writes that the Gould performance lasted "well over an hour."

Bernstein's revisionist portrait of Gould is much like his revisionist portrait of his father as poor and Boston Latin School as remiss in music. He begins by being full of sweetness and love for people or institutions. But then, almost instinctively, he is driven to reduce them in some way.

Throughout the 1960s Bernstein was well aware of the large number of talented, strong-minded, intelligent composers who had chosen to leave tonality. Stravinsky and Copland, his mentors from his earliest days, were now among them. Bernstein said in 1977:

> This so called conflict between tonality and nontonality is not a conflict at all, but really a marriage of musical elements. Not even of styles, because style is something that cannot be conceived and prepared unless you are a bad composer. I mean a bad composer can sit down and consciously decided to write in a certain style and most bad composers do. But to write what is really inside you can very often cause you to write eclectically. Now this is a word that is usually used in a pejorative sense, even in a derogatory sense, and it's a word of which I'm very proud because I find that every good composer in the history of music is eclectic in one sense or another....
>
> The artist in America is in a particularly eclectic position, much more than Bach, Beethoven, the others that I mentioned, because he signifies and stands for a highly eclectic and pluralistic country. After all, there is no such thing as an "American." Americans, if you want to go down to the roots, are red Indians and with the exception of them, everyone else is an immigrant. We are immigrants or sons or grandsons or great-great-grandsons of immigrants and these immigrants are of all kinds. Some were slaves when they came here and we tend to forget that when we speak of Americans as types. Some were Poles and some were Hungarians and some were Jews and some were Spanish and many of course now are Latin Americans.
>
> But they're all Americans. And anybody who has his ear to the ground, and who is sensitive to the country in which he lives reflects that country; and being a melting pot and such a pluralistic kind of country, it would naturally cause a reflection to take place which is in itself eclectic....
>
> In the case of my own music, I would have to say that it has its roots everywhere. In jazz, in Hebrew liturgical music, in Bach and Beethoven and Schumann and Chopin and Mahler and the rest. In the musicians of my own country like Copland and Harris and Schuman. It also has roots in Schoenberg and

in the various movements that have revolutionized music in our century....

As a matter of fact, in 1964 and 1965 I was given a sabbatical from the Philharmonic and decided to use that year only to compose. In the course of that year I made many experiments because I had the luxury of a whole year to do nothing but experiment. And part of my experimentation was to try—it was the only time in my life I *tried* to write a specific kind of music—to try to write some pieces which, shall we say, were less old fashioned. And I wrote a lot of music, twelve-tone music and avant-garde music of various kinds, and a lot of it was very good, and I threw it all away. And what I came out with at the end of the year was a piece called *Chichester Psalms*, which is simple and tonal and tuneful and pure B flat as any piece you can think of. I don't mean that it was all in B flat but I'm sure you get my point. Because that was what I honestly wished to write.[3]

On the surface *Chichester Psalms* seems almost a parody of a tonal piece: Its pitch relations are simple. Nevertheless it is difficult to perform. That is because of the presence of so many irregular meters of fives and sevens. Although there is no sustained syncopation in this apparently sacred piece, the prevalence of irregular meters contribute to a feeling of suppressed jazz. Unlike *Kaddish*, this work has no presumptuous text. Still one may well consider the use of Hebrew for the psalms to be something of a slap in the face to the man who commissioned it, the Reverend Walter Hussey, who presides over Chichester Cathedral in England, for which the work was named. Charles Solomon, Bernstein's physician and a friend of Hussey's, had served as go-between in arranging the commission.

The piece as a whole suggests a Bernstein more at ease with himself than when he wrote *Kaddish*. There is no railing against God here. The first movement ends with a joyous chorus in the kind of rhythmical singing that calls to mind the sounds of Broadway. The slow movement presents a touching melody delivered by a boy alto, Bernstein's slow music at its haunting best. The boy's sweet sound is suddenly interrupted by a men's chorus, which presents rapid, staccato, harsh passages. The men's aggressive sound is diffused by the reentrance of the young boy, whose slow, sensuous melody prevails over their agitated whispers. A string orchestra begins the last movement with a rising melody, which is picked up by the remaining instruments. The complicated, not always wise God that had hovered over every thing in *Kaddish* has been replaced by a boy whose slate is still unmarked by life's blows.

In 1977, when Bernstein recorded *Kaddish* and *Chichester Psalms* in Berlin, he said.

> If one is trying to find optimism versus pessimism in my music, the closest musical equivalent is tonality versus non-tonality. I believe very deeply in tonality, that one can always write fresh sounds, really new melodies and harmonies with tonality as the basis. This does not mean, however, that I disbelieve in non-tonal music. Any kind of music that is a genuine human expression is valid for me. What's more, I don't think there is one large piece I have ever written that does not use dodecaphony in some way or another. In most cases, I use tone rows, manipulating them with some pessimistic or disturbing element in my mind.

When Bernstein rehearses Mozart's Symphony No. 40, he points out what he calls a tone row in the first movement. All the notes of the chromatic scale except the G are there. But what he is pointing out is a chromatic passage, not a tone row. Factors altogether independent of it determine the structure of the movement.

Bernstein uses this illustration to gain support for his own practices. If Mozart makes use of the twelve notes in this way, who would dare suggest anything unmusical about it?

Nobody, of course. But the Mozart symphony is not twelve-tone, any more than *Kaddish* can be considered twelve-tone. As jazz musicians deny Bernstein is a jazz musician, so twelve-tone composers deny Bernstein is a twelve-tone composer.

In 1985 Nina Bernstein, twenty-three, said, "When
I look at the home movies taken then, I wonder where all of that was
for me. There were all these beautiful people—my mother and dad
were gorgeous, too—they were all thin, tanned, running joyfully
around the beach, but it was never like that for me." Nina's own

© WHITESTONE PHOTO / HEINZ H. WEISSENSTEIN

Bernstein is as unsparing of himself as of his associates. They do not always appreciate
his demanding ways. Recalls Herman Krawitz, then assistant manager
of the Metropolitan Opera: "... Lenny told us he needed more time [for rehearsal].
He begged us to give him an extra half hour....
Still, when he completed the time, Lenny would not leave the pit. It was as though it
had become his own terrain and he could not be moved from it."

childhood was more austere. She says she was often left in the care of an authoritarian housekeeper. Nina adds that if there was any fighting between her parents, none of the children knew. Her mother, whom she characterized as possessing a "stiff upper lip" kind of personality, would invariably excuse herself from the family quarters, saying she was going to the studio to have a talk with their father.

"I was a mistake," she says. "My mother awakened one day in great pain, and thought she was experiencing an ectopic pregnancy. But she went to the doctor and found that she was healthily pregnant."

Nina's birth was not, of course, the precipitating event for the tensions between the Bernsteins in the following years. The period of her childhood coincided with several events that caused Bernstein distress. All of them, including Kennedy's assassination, occurred during the first five years of Bernstein's appointment as director of the New York Philharmonic.

Bernstein says that when he was in grade school, he was attacked by the Catholics in the neighborhood because he was a "skinny Jewish kid." Later he was maligned by his father for his pursuit of music as a career. Bernstein developed a protective hardness necessary to get and hold on to power. Laurence Olivier has said that his mother's death, when he was twelve, "paid off, in a way. It does something for your character, your courage, your guts." Others develop the same quality through the effects of a debilitating disease. In a 1985 biography of Franklin Delano Roosevelt, author Ted Morgan identifies the polio Roosevelt contracted in 1921 as the turning point in his life. It was because of Bernstein's ability to learn—as Roosevelt did—from genuine adversity, to refuse to accept defeat, that he appeared through the difficult years of the early 1960s to be the resilient, triumphant man he had always seemed.

The members of the orchestra were generally pleased with the change to Bernstein. They had not enjoyed playing the twelve-tone works that Mitropoulos had programmed. Nor had the majority found him to be the good disciplinarian that any orchestra needs. "Mitropoulos was very popular as a man," two former Philharmonic musicians say. "And he would give you the shirt off his back. But he had no stick technique and the men finally walked all over him." These musicians recall that Mitropoulos seemed to them "neuter," and that he spent his time studying scores and going to the movies. They also recall a scandal he caused when he allowed himself to appear in *Life* magazine wearing nothing more than bathing trunks. There was another scandal to which the men did not allude. In his column in the *New York Daily Mirror*, Walter Winchell asked "what New York conductor" had been found in a compromising sexual situation.

Martin Eshelman, a violinist who still plays with the Philharmonic, says, "When Bernstein came in, there was suddenly so much to do: television, recording, extra concerts, all of it exciting. Usually the musicians are scheduled for eight or nine services a week. A service is a rehearsal or a performance. This meant that in general we had five rehearsals and four performances. With Bernstein the number of services escalated almost right away to seventeen, eighteen, and nineteen. And nobody complained about being overworked. On tour we were white-hot. Before we went to the Soviet Union, Bernstein studied Russian. He addressed the audiences in their own language. That made a big impression. Pasternak came to the concerts. So did Shostakovich. Once, when we did his Symphony Number Five, Shostakovich came running back after the performance and embraced the musicians with tears streaming down his face."

The difficulties that Bernstein's imprudent statements created between him and officials in the Soviet Union were unknown to the public at large or to the musicians in the orchestra. All they experienced was the excitement of the visit and the heat Bernstein generates whenever he goes anywhere. In fact they were guests at one party during which the violinist Leonid Kogan played for them. Eshelman speaks of Bernstein's humor, of his regaling the musicians with stories that still make the rounds today. Most of them deal with Koussevitzky.

"In one," Eshelman says, "he told how Irving Fine had conducted a rehearsal at Tanglewood, after which Koussevitzky came running down the aisle shouting, 'Fine. Fine. That was awful.'" Others mimicked Koussevitzky's English, most particularly the often repeated command "Took it at a tempo und kept it!"

The musicians remark on Bernstein's need to be loved. "If one of us did not say hello one day, he would inevitably ask, 'What's the matter? Are you mad at me?'" Disappointed during a rehearsal, Bernstein would never behave in the usual authoritarian way, insulting the musicians in front of their colleagues. Instead he would explode in what was more a child's tantrum, then hang his head and sulk, "It's no fun for me anymore."

Bernstein's hunger for love was probably the most important factor in the remarkable record maintained during his eleven years at the New York Philharmonic: Not a single musician was fired. Bernstein never personally hires or fires, apparently unwilling to take control of people's lives in this way. In fact his identification with the men and his refusal to be publicly allied with management lay behind several incidents that characterized his relations with the Metropolitan Opera, a company often plagued with serious union troubles. According to Herman Krawitz, assistant manager of the Met during most of Rudolf Bing's tenure, "Bernstein could never make up his mind that he was senior management. In the labor disputes he always wanted to be a good boy. When he complained to us about a particular member of the orchestra, he would never stand up and be counted. We, on the other hand, would be obliged to act on his complaints in a public way. In 1964, our first experience with him, it was Felicia who would always be helpful. She would invariably get to him in the right context. But later all that changed."

Bernstein's resolve never to conduct another orchestra as long as he was music director of the New York Philharmonic lasted until he agreed to conduct Verdi's *Falstaff* at the Met. It was this assignment that led to Bernstein's conducting *Falstaff* at the Vienna State Opera only a few years later. That led to his arrangement with the Vienna Philharmonic, which is also the Vienna State Opera orchestra.

When Bernstein returned home after his first concert engagement with the Vienna Philharmonic, he deeply wounded his New York musicians by telling them that they had never played as well as the musicians in Vienna.

Bernstein first conducted *Falstaff* on March 6, 1964. It was the first time he had been in the pit of an opera house since 1955, when he had directed Callas at La Scala. After his success in Milan in 1955, the Met did not invite him there right away. Here is Krawitz on the matter of Bernstein and the Met: "Bernstein was wanted at the Met. Bing reached for the best so naturally he wanted him. Lenny was always in demand. Bing was probably looking for the right moment. Lenny was special and Bing knew it.

"*Falstaff* had a special meaning to the Bing management. For one thing it had not been done since Toscanini in the nineteen-forties, when it was broadcast over NBC. For another there was a special passion for it. Leonard Warren wanted to do it and Bing thought that would have been a disaster. So only when Warren died did the opera open up.

"I was in charge of *Falstaff*," Krawitz says. "Because it had never been a popular opera, it presented a professional challenge. It could not be approached routinely. The Met had often been faulted for not being an ensemble company, for operating on the premise of the star system. Our ensemble productions of *Don Giovanni* and *Madame Butterfly* should have given the lie to that. Still, it was not until *Falstaff* that the public's perception of the Met as an ensemble group took life. As soon as we decided to do it, we engaged first Zeffirelli, then Bernstein. Then a budget had to be made. The arrangement of moneys for a work generally happens about eighteen months before that work's debut.

"In the spring of 1962 a social evening was set up to celebrate the plans for *Falstaff*. Mrs. Kennedy was invited. She had just had a miscarriage and I remember it being her first evening out. The performance was the Royal Ballet with Margot Fonteyn and Rudolf Nureyev. The plan was for the party to take place during intermission. Because my office was just opposite the general manager's box, it was decided to have it there. That meant that in the short walk between the box to my office, no one would be able to see Bernstein or Mrs. Kennedy. And no one did. I remember Jackie and Lenny being upset by this. They wanted to know why they had been brought there if no one in the audience was going to be able to see them. So we moved the intermission party upstairs during the next break where everyone could see them—and everyone did.

"We got off to a gorgeous start," Krawitz recalls. "There was no panic. Everything was as smooth as it could be. Just before the last orchestra rehearsal, on the Friday before the opening, Lenny told us he needed more time. He begged us to give him an extra half hour. In our estimation, the musicians were perfect and the extra time unnecessary. But we gave him what he asked, to serve as a gesture of our cooperation. Still, when he completed the time, Lenny would not leave the pit. It was as though it had become his own terrain and he could not be moved from it. I was forced—a very unpleasant situation—to go down into the pit myself and tell him in front of all the musicians that he would have to leave.... This was a peculiar moment. Lenny acted like a spoiled child. It was as though he had taken possession of the space and nothing would persuade him to let go of it."

Bernstein's refusal to get out of the Metropolitan Opera pit preceded many similar incidents—both in the United States and abroad—when he is reported to have behaved in precisely the same way: demanding more than had been agreed upon, testing how far others could be pushed. The scenes he began making were merely the beginnings of the self-indulgent public personality he was to become.

Bernstein of course finally got out of the pit and conducted a series of magnificent performances. "Franco [Zeffirelli] can't read a note of music," Krawitz says. "But he and Lenny were so in tune. The cast was made in heaven. Not only great singers but great actors as well, Zeffirelli was not then as well known as Lenny. He had directed the Old Vic's *Romeo and Juliet*, which had played in New York, but he had not made any movies at that time. He was a marvel. He knew exactly what he needed and didn't ask for anything more."

The extra time appears to have cost the Met both money and discomfort. Almost twenty-five years later, it still looms large in Krawitz's recollections of that *Falstaff*. "In his display," Krawitz says, "Lenny revealed he was not an ensemble player but a star performer and that is entirely different. It is not as though a star cannot be an ensemble performer. Regina Resnik was in that production and she certainly is a star. Yet she consistently behaved in such a cooperative way that she helped the production as a whole. Lenny's difficult behavior was to lay behind a rift that occurred almost immediately."

Bernstein had entered the first rehearsal knowing every word of the libretto and every note in the score completely by memory. When the singers spoke to the press about Bernstein, they talked about having "fallen in love with him." He created such a convincing production that even Harold Schonberg of the *Times* had praise: "From the second act he was a different conductor and 'Falstaff' a different opera. Color, clarity, precision and strong rhythm marked his work. And charm, too." *Life* magazine quoted a critic: "Opera at its peak!"

Virtually every review reflected this judgment, and Bernstein assumed the accolades would be translated into an offer to conduct the opening performance of the new Met at Lincoln Center. But he was wrong. Here is Krawitz: "One of the things we had determined internally was that Leontyne Price, a leading lady of ours for years, would star in this opening night. Another was that Thomas Schippers, also a regular member of the Met, and one who had been conducting there since 1952, would be the conductor for whatever that would be. Lenny, who had recently opened Philharmonic Hall, the first of the houses at Lincoln Center, had done nothing for the Met other than ten performances of *Falstaff*.

"Suddenly I hear Lenny's nose is out of joint. Originally we had thought we would do a new production of *Carmen* for the opening. But then we decided to do something special: to commission a new work by an American composer, and we gave that commission to Samuel Barber. That meant that Schippers was particularly suitable as conductor because he had long been closely identified with Barber's music. Lenny was astounded that after his success with *Falstaff* he was being ignored for the Met's big opening in 1966. It caused a coolness between us and we didn't get Lenny at all for our first season at Lincoln Center. As far as he was concerned, it was opening night or nothing."

Apart from his disappointment that he would not be at the center of this high-powered social evening, Bernstein had other reasons to be upset. First he probably felt regret that he was being denied the chance to conduct *Carmen*, Koussevitzky's favorite opera and one he had loved since he produced it as an adolescent, also one to which he had given enough thought to justify a star-studded and costly ninety-minute exploration that appeared on coast-to-coast TV.

But that wasn't all. Sam Barber was as tied to tonality as Bernstein had ever been. And he didn't try to break from it. There is no experimenting with twelve-tone notions in Barber's early, middle, or late works. He was adored by Mary Louise Bok when he entered the Curtis Institute, and then moved along, saying little to the press, composing beautiful music until the last years of his life. And he was amply rewarded. Toscanini discovered him and conducted the First Essay for Orchestra and the *Adagio for Strings* when Barber was only twenty-eight. Walter, Reiner, Szell, Mitropoulos, Munch, Koussevitzky, Leinsdorf, and Ormandy all conducted Barber. Virtuoso performers also championed his music. Vladimir Horowitz gave the first performance of the Piano Sonata; Martha Graham danced *Medea*; Eleanor Steber programmed *Knoxville: Summer of 1915*; Leontyne Price introduced the *Hermit Songs*. In 1962, just before Bernstein's *Falstaff* at the Met, Barber won his second Pulitzer Prize for his Piano Concerto.

A few years before Barber's second Pulitzer, Bernstein had written a letter to Diamond dated August 15, 1958, in which he described his plans for what was to be his first real season as director in New York. The previous season he had served as co-conductor.

> The Philharmonic looms large and exciting and frightening. There will be much more television, more difficult programs, more "points" being made, more Handel, more Vivaldi. [Varèse's] *Arcaria*, at last, and all kinds of Ruggles & Riegger, & the Sessions [Violin] Concerto, & Ives No. 2, & Aaron *Variations* & Ned Rorem & Bill Russo & Ken Gaburo and and and. A sort of overall look at the whole picture. Not the whole picture, of course: that's impossible: and I have to leave out all kinds of important fellers like Virgil & you and Marc & Dello Joio ... and Creston ... & Ben Weber & Imbrie & Kirchner...

In this handwritten letter, Bernstein inserted composers Blitzstein and Kirchner, suggesting they were afterthoughts. But one man he didn't mention at all was Samuel Barber, who was to walk off with the most coveted commission of the decade when the Met gave him the go-ahead to compose *Antony and Cleopatra*.

Bernstein and Barber were strikingly different men. Always theatrical, Bernstein was a hurly-burly, rough-and-tumble kind of person. Barber was always something of a snob. A progressive thinker, who supported all manner of causes, Bernstein had been associated with the Left. Barber avoided all things political.

Bernstein found his music-theater roots in Weill, Blitzstein, and Gershwin. Barber was European in his tastes: Among the composers he loved, Chopin, Fauré, Richard Strauss, Debussy, and Bach stood at the top of the list. Often undermining those who helped him move ahead in his career, Bernstein did not show gratitude. Barber thanked anyone for the most modest help. He was always the perfect gentleman.

Each composer recognized the other's talent. But Barber did not like Bernstein and would not pretend he did. Bernstein could not bear this, any more than he could stand a negative assessment of his achievements by a youthful guest at a Manhattan party.

Charles Turner was Barber's close friend during the later years of his life. He also taught Alexander Bernstein composition. Turner tells the following story. In the 1960s Bernstein confronted Barber: "You don't like me, do you?"

Barber replied, "I like Felicia one hundred percent."

Bernstein then said, "I must know why you don't like me."

Barber said, "I like you seventy-five percent." Then, according to Turner, Barber added, "Twenty-five years ago, when Koussevitzky conducted my Violin Concerto with the Boston Symphony, there was an after-concert party. You sat down at the piano and played through the first measures and you made some mistakes."

With that Bernstein, who had not heard the work since, sat down and played the beginning of the piece again, this time without a single mistake. Then he asked, "Does that make things better?"

Barber replied, "Now I like you seventy-six percent."

Bernstein had never been an advocate for Barber as he had for Copland, Harris, and William Schuman. In 1959, when Bernstein learned from Diamond that a Diamond piece he had programmed to be conducted by Thomas Schippers was going to be replaced by a Barber piece, he wrote to Diamond that while he could not ensure that his *World of Paul Klee* would be restored, he would do something about the performance of "yet another Barber piece." Bernstein succeeded. The Diamond work remained on the program, and also was performed during the Philharmonic tour of the Soviet Union the following fall.

Barber's wide recognition as what Slonimsky calls "an American composer of superlative gifts" was probably not the only reason Bernstein felt envious. Barber had served in the Air Corps during World War II. He also lived the life of a homosexual with openness and grace. In 1943, he and Gian Carlo Menotti, together since their days at Curtis, bought a house in Mount Kisco, New York, and lived there for what turned out to be the most productive years of their lives. If Bernstein's primary identity was as a conductor, he would not have had the problem he did when confronting Barber. But at least part of his identity, even during those years when he was the conductor of one of the greatest orchestras in the world, was as a composer and as a homo-sexual, and in both of these arenas Barber seemed to do better than he. Probably as an unconscious act of revenge, Bernstein gave the thankless job of guest-conducting Poulenc's anti-Semitic *Ténèbres* to Thomas Schippers, who had always been identified as the most visible of the young conductors promoting Sam Barber's music. Probably also an unconscious act of revenge was Mitropoulos's conducting of Barber's *Vanessa* at the Met during the 1958–1959 season, just after Bernstein had displaced him as music director of the New York Philharmonic.

Many composers who were not programmed much during Bernstein's time at the Philharmonic, or were not conducted by him in his hundreds of guest engagements over the years, attribute his rejection either to their heterosexuality or to their adoption of the serial technique. But Bernstein's reluctance to play Barber or, for that matter, Virgil Thomson indicates that these speculations are simplistic. More complex considerations invariably prevail.

In 1960 Bernstein moved out of the Osborne and into a large Park Avenue building in which his family occupied the two top floors. From the terrace they could see all of Central Park. Everything was decorat-ed elegantly. Even the children's rooms appeared in designer maga-zines. Felicia Bernstein used the services of a professional decorator but her personal choices set the tone.

Felicia was a size six, and generally wore trousers during the day-time. She had changed from a girl whose blooming freshness had been her most striking attribute to a woman whose fine features were set in a tight, controlled look. Entertaining frequently, she would receive guests after the concerts, generally serving them herself. During those evenings when there were no concerts, the couple would have four or six to dinner. In the 1950s, when they had gone out to parties, Felicia invariably led her husband to the most comfortable chair in the room, after which she would escort musicians, one at a time, to him so they could converse quietly. In the 1960s, his behavior changed. He seemed no longer to care how he appeared in public. Several friends recall that once, at a party at Tourel's, "Lenny disappeared—no one knew where he had gone. Two hours later he reappeared with a well-known screen actor. Lenny was ruffled and tousled, looking like the wrath of God. Everyone gasped. Felicia, chin up, led him out and they went home."

Felicia's life with Bernstein, difficult in the beginning, grew humil-
iating. At Tanglewood, it was Arthur Weinstein. During her pregnancy,
she faced John Mehegan. At the start of his Philharmonic career, she
shared Bernstein's attention with a number of Chilean men when they
were away on tour. Even then, she could not have anticipated the accel-
eration of such incidents once gay liberation took hold. By the mid-
1960s, Felicia, in need of some antidote to help her preserve some sense
of identity without losing her marriage, took refuge in painting.

By this time she was rarely acting—she did appear in a 1968 revival
of Hellman's *The Little Foxes*—except to recite the narrator's role in
Bernstein's works or in those oratorios he conducted. Jane Wilson, the
wife of journalist John Gruen and an American painter whose works
still hang on Bernstein's walls, became her teacher. "I took up painting
and went to class," Felicia told the press, "like a proper Victorian lady."
Always prim, always under control, this proper Victorian lady was living in an unholy alliance with an apparently insatiable man.
Koussevitzky had intuited the gargantuan nature of Bernstein's
appetites from the earliest days of their connection. The elder conductor told his barber in Lenox that he had two spectacularly gifted students. One, he said, was Apollonian, one Dionysian. Lukas Foss tells
this story, spelling out that of course he was the Apollonian. The
Dionysian aspects of Bernstein's temperament grew. His appetites, his
sexual compulsions, enlarged over the years. Those who have lived with
him describe the way he eats fowl. Picking the bird up with both hands,
he devours every particle of skin and meat until there is only a pile of
bones left on his plate.

By the mid-1960s, Bernstein was entertaining at his estate in Fairfield,
Connecticut. In New York, the older children attended private schools,
and the youngest one was in the care of Julia, the governess who had
been a servant in Felicia's earlier years, having worked for her parents
in Chile. To maintain their country house and the duplex apartment in
Manhattan, to pay tuition at the Brearley and Collegiate schools in
New York, the salaries of his assistants and servants, and the fees of his
psychoanalysts, Bernstein needed a lot of money. He set up a management company staffed by his lawyer, Abraham Friedman, and his
accountant, Gordon Freeman. He revived the name "Amber," which he

had used in 1942 when he was arranging popular songs for Harms, and called the company Amberson. In the early 1960s, the royalties from *West Side Story* burgeoned because of the movie, and Amberson succeeded in negotiating a new deal with G. Schirmer, Bernstein's publisher, to gain rights it had not controlled before.

Looking at this, one might think that Bernstein would retire and depend on the skillful investing of money and successful exploitation of what he had already done. This is the pattern many people follow after achieving a resounding success in their early years. But instead of thinning out in texture, Bernstein's life has thickened. He always made risky choices. Often those choices led to despair. In *Trouble in Tahiti*, after Sam sings his big aria about the God-given qualities of the "winner," he continues with the morose reflection that "there's a law.... There's a moment when the payment begins." Bernstein wrote this line in 1952. From the start of his career he seemed to know that he would pay the price.

Even when he was on a course that could not be characterized as a winning one, Bernstein at the least endured. He didn't pack up his bags and flee or climb under the covers and hide. It was in fact in 1961, when Harold Schonberg was hammering away at him, that he signed the seven-year contract that kept him at the Philharmonic, while he continued to undertake projects besides conducting and composing. In the fall of 1962, Bernstein followed *The Joy of Music* with *The Young People's Concerts*, which encompassed five LP records and a book adapted from eight of the sixteen TV shows of that name. He edited the text himself.

The following year, he conducted *The Martyrdom of Saint Sebastian* to commemorate Debussy's centenary. The sung parts were in German, the dialogue in English. Fritz Weaver, the actor, was the narrator and Felicia appeared as the male saint. Bernstein probably thought of her as at least a saint. If he tested orchestra managements and presidents to see how far he could push them, he repeatedly tested Felicia, too. She seemed to pass all his tests right up to the end of her life. As for the Debussy, critics remarked on the clean articulation of the text. One even questioned whether this was at all valuable: "Does it really help to have the play so intelligible? It has so many Oscar Wildean overtones and presents a view of Christianity in which

Jesus, Sebastian and Adonis get all mixed up together."

As *Les Mamelles de Tirésias,* Poulenc's opera about a man who bears children, gave a clue to Bernstein's fantasies during Felicia's pregnancy, perhaps *The Martyrdom of Saint Sebastian* suggested what was on his mind during the period when he brought home a marine deserter.

From the start Bernstein surrounded himself with
people who could be counted on to say yes to him. His father,
of course, was not one of them. But his mother certainly was,
and Helen Coates followed in her path. Bernstein could behave
abusively to Coates, often firing her, yet knowing that the next

*Bernstein behaved cruelly toward other composers, particularly those who were
successful. Morton Gould remembers that in the late 1940s he was playing one of his
own pieces for Bernstein: "As I played, Lenny was calling out all the
different influences. By that time I had had my work conducted by Stokowski, Reiner,
and Mitropoulos. As he was shouting out the influences, he had the nerve
to add his own name to the list. The fact is that the work I was playing had been
composed before the one of his that he named. I never sent him another score."*

morning she would be there ready to serve.

In 1959 Bernstein met Schuyler Chapin for the first time. Chapin had just replaced David Oppenheim as head of Artists and Repertoire at Columbia Records. Oppenheim had moved on to Robert Saudek Associates, the producer of the *Omnibus* shows. When the New York Philharmonic returned from its tour of the Soviet Union in the fall of 1959, Chapin was at the Washington airport. In *Musical Chairs*, a memoir, Chapin writes:

> Over the years the company had been taking an affectionate but paternal approach to Bernstein, and he must have begun to resent this attitude. Overlooked, of course, was the fact that he had become the number one figure of classical music in America and one of the major stars of the lyric theater and television as well and, wunderkind or not, he was bound to want to burst out of restrictive obligations.

Chapin gave him the go-ahead to do that. He agreed to everything Bernstein asked. Chapin quotes Bernstein: "I want to be free to record whatever I wish. I don't want anyone telling me such-and-such cannot be done. Right now I want to make certain we record the Shostakovich Fifth before we open our New York season. We have some dates in the South next week and then perform at Symphony Hall in Boston. I want to record the work there." Bernstein wanted Symphony Hall because of the quality of its sound, but the hall was the official home of the Boston Symphony Orchestra, which was under contract to RCA, Columbia's competitor. Several Bernstein associates acknowledge that despite his not getting the Boston Symphony, he always behaved as though he had. This time, too, he had his way. The New York Philharmonic under Bernstein recorded the work in Symphony Hall, much to the despair of Munch, says Chapin. It apparently was worth the effort. On January 9, 1986, visiting Russian conductor Yuri Temirkanov told *The New York Times*, "I don't know a better recording of the Shostakovich Fifth Symphony than the one by Leonard Bernstein and the New York Philharmonic."

By the 1960s the classical music market represented only a small fraction of the recording industry's output. Clive Davis, who replaced

Goddard Lieberson as president of Columbia, has written that classical music barely broke even for the major record companies, while popular music was producing just about all their profits. But for a time the record companies had the vestiges of a cultural superego and felt a moral obligation to keep their classical departments alive. Since Bernstein was about as big a seller as there was in that segment of the industry, he could pretty much write his own ticket.

John McClure, then music director of the Columbia Masterworks division, said that "in addition to determining repertory, he did an incredible amount of recording. In the spring of each year, we would meet to decide what should be done. During the following year Bernstein would record each week. He received a payment as an advance against royalties of from three thousand dollars to five thousand dollars for each record, which would then be split with the orchestra. Abraham Friedman, Bernstein's lawyer, negotiated a contract that allowed Bernstein to record whatever he chose. He chose some works that at the time seemed unlikely to pay their way—Mahler, Nielsen, and Ives among them. But in the end they reportedly have produced profits for CBS."

In the early 1960s Bernstein recorded Eileen Farrell in Wagner's *Wesendonck Songs* and the Immolation Scene from *Götterdämmerung*, Beethoven's First Piano Concerto with Bernstein as conductor and soloist, the Beethoven *Missa Solemnis*, the Bach Magnificat, all the Beethoven and Brahms symphonies, the score from *On the Waterfront*, the *Symphonic Dances* from *West Side Story*, and a remake of *On the Town* with Comden and Green re-creating their original roles.

Bernstein's fame and financial success as a conductor did not keep him from behaving cruelly toward other composers, particularly those who were successful. Charles Turner reports an incident that occurred during the summer of 1959 when he and Sam Barber had a house on Martha's Vineyard: "Sam was writing an orchestral work, and invited Lenny and Felicia to dinner after he had nearly finished it. The work used a four-note motif: D, B flat, F sharp, and G. Before he played to the bottom of the page Lenny cried, 'Stop! You can't use that motif. It's the same one as in *Daphnis and Chloé*.' He was right, and neither Sam nor I had noticed it before. Sam threw the piece away."

Barber told Morton Gould the story, saying there had been a

terrible confrontation and that Bernstein called the score "pure Ravel." Gould says the same thing had happened to him more than ten years before when he was playing one of his own pieces for Bernstein. "As I played, Lenny was calling out all the different influences. By that time I had had my work conducted by Stokowski, Reiner, and Mitropoulos. As he was shouting out the influences, he had the nerve to add his own name to the list. The fact is that the work I was playing had been composed before the one of his that he named. I never sent him another score."

Bernstein's memory obviously is formidable. But the force with which he has attacked composers for their borrowings, going back at least as far as 1938 when he told Schuman that there was much Sibelius in his Second Symphony, seems to stem from his fiercely competitive nature. He has caught them out doing something that he himself and other composers often do, sometimes without realizing it, other times without hesitating. Bernstein's later works would not have been possible without Copland's 1926 Piano Concerto. The romantic songs in his Broadway scores are heavily indebted to others. Not only was "Maria" taken from Blitzstein, "Tonight" was derived from Benjamin Britten. Here is how the Britten connection was made: In 1946, after conducting *Peter Grimes* at Tanglewood, Bernstein made a trip to England and attended rehearsals of Britten's *The Rape of Lucretia*. The next year at a dinner party in London, reports the host, Peter Gradenwitz, an Israeli music critic, Bernstein went to the piano where he found Britten's score. He played through a song called "Goodnight."

In a 1984 book on Bernstein, written in German and published in Switzerland, Gradenwitz describes how the structure, melody, and dynamics of Bernstein's "Tonight" echo Britten's "Goodnight." In addition to this borrowing, a lyrical line from the second movement of Beethoven's Piano Concerto No. 5 turns out to be the source for "Somewhere," another song from *West Side Story*. Whether Bernstein actually created them or not, it was unquestionably he who put those obscure tunes by Blitzstein and Britten and the secondary theme by Beethoven into the hearts and minds of the world. Bernstein transformed his borrowings into memorable music.

Roger Sessions said that after listening to one of Bernstein's works, he, told Bernstein "to go off into the woods for at least six months until the music you hear is your own." Sessions also said, though perhaps not to Bernstein, that "the only alternative an artist has to being himself is being nobody." In the mid-1960s, Bernstein may well have feared that he had chosen the wrong alternative.

In June 1963, Bernstein announced he was taking a sabbatical leave during the 1964–1965 season; it had been written into his 1961 contract. This turned out to be the year he later characterized as one filled with experimentation with various avant-garde modes and the one from which he emerged with the sweetly tonal *Chichester Psalms*. But as he started on his sabbatical, Bernstein was also working on a musical version of Thornton Wilder's *The Skin of Our Teeth*. He had first seen the Wilder play in 1942 with Comden, Green, and Robbins. The three of them were slated to work on it with him, Comden and Green doing the book and lyrics, Robbins the direction and choreography. Leland Hayward was the producer, and Columbia, which was to produce the album, invested $400,000 plus a 20 percent overcall if more funds proved necessary.

Columbia had already financed *My Fair Lady* and *Camelot*, both hugely successful musicals by Alan Jay Lerner and Frederick Loewe. Hayward had produced a string of hits including *Call Me Madam, The Sound of Music, South Pacific*, and *Gypsy*. Despite the talent involved in the Wilder project, it collapsed in about six months. At the time Bernstein told the press that he didn't want to go into the reasons for it, that "personalities were involved." But there can be no doubt that the inability of his good friends who had worked together so productively in the past to work productively again was a singularly disquieting one.

At a time when Columbia was recording Bernstein as conductor and underwriting him as composer, it also put twenty-five thousand dollars into a new production of Blitzstein's *The Cradle Will Rock*, in which Bernstein was music consultant. Howard da Silva directed, Jerry Orbach played Larry Foreman, and musical director Gershon Kingsley accompanied on a lone piano, as Blitzstein had done at the Venice Theater on Broadway and Bernstein had done in the Sanders Theater in Cambridge. But the record company did not come close to recovering its investment. *Cradle* was out of date and could not have been expected to generate much interest.

It may not be immediately obvious why Bernstein would involve himself in what inevitably would prove to be a losing proposition. At least one answer is that this project might help extricate him from another Blitzstein project that would have proved even costlier for him. In January 1964, when Blitzstein was killed in Martinique, he had been visiting the island supposedly to work on an opera based on the Sacco and Vanzetti case funded by the Ford Foundation and slated for performance at the Met. Before he left for the Caribbean, there had been a number of phone calls between John Gutman of the Met staff and Blitzstein. To have such proper institutions as the Ford Foundation and the Metropolitan Opera support an opera about Sacco and Vanzetti by Blitzstein was either a joke—the revolutionists exploiting the capitalists for their own purposes—or a most peculiar turn of events. In any case it was natural for everyone to be uneasy about it. Blitzstein certainly was. Instead of bringing his work with him to Martinique, he left the incomplete score in the trunk of his car, which he stored in a friend's garage in New York. In the spring of 1964, the car was put up for sale and the fragments of the work were found. Bernstein then came under considerable pressure from Blitzstein's circle of friends to complete the Sacco and Vanzetti work and another, almost completed opera, *Idiots First*.

There were good reasons for him not to. For one thing, the Met's Rudolf Bing had told Bernstein how little he thought of Blitzstein as a composer. According to Bernstein's account, he showed the Met director to the door. Second, Bernstein had real reservations about one person completing another one's work. His resistance to performing any of the reconstituted versions of Mahler's Tenth Symphony testifies to that. Finally, he was having enough trouble making his own music-theater pieces—the Wilder work had been signed in 1962—so there was little motive for him to compose what would turn out to be somebody else's opera. It is reasonable to assume that Bernstein welcomed the opportunity to pay his respects to his mentor in the music-theater field by supervising the performance of the music in a new production of *The Cradle Will Rock*.

To chart an incident like this one is not to suggest that Bernstein gave conscious thought to the pros and cons of every step he took. Rather is it to imply the multiplicity of matters on his mind at any given moment. This new *Cradle* was something he did not do for the money.

He did it because it seemed to be a decent memorial for a man to whom he owed a great deal. And the price he paid for doing it was not nearly so great as the one he would have had to pay if he had taken on the Sacco and Vanzetti score.

On July 18, 1965, *The New York Times Magazine* ran an article, "The In Crowd and the Out Crowd" by Sherman L. Morrow, that said:

> Everyone in the Social Register is Out, while Leonard Bernstein, who is the decidedly non-Social Register son of a Brookline, Massachusetts, beauty supply dealer, is one of the most In of the In Crowd. And in describing Bernstein, one describes exactly what it takes to be in: he is egregiously successful in several creative fields, he possesses immense personal charm and wit, and he is unquestionably a genius. Moreover it doesn't hurt at all that entirely through his own creative efforts, Bernstein has become a millionaire, for the In Crowd does not exactly sneer at money—after all, there has to be some on hand....

A few weeks later Russell Baker, a humor columnist in *The New York Times*, picked up on the theme in a column in which he described how a list maker works: "If he hasn't a newspaper handy when composing the list, he can always throw in Leonard Bernstein. Like Albert Schweitzer and nine or ten Kennedys, Bernstein is safe on any list." Bernstein was now more than ever publicly tied to the Kennedys. He actively supported the candidacy of Robert Kennedy and, in 1967, Jacqueline Kennedy invited him to be the head of the Kennedy Center in Washington. Because Bernstein has difficulty saying no, he said yes and then sent Felicia to Washington to extricate him from the primarily administrative post.

Bernstein was seen with Jacqueline Kennedy on numerous occasions. There was the time in the spring of 1962 when they had partied at Sherry's restaurant in the Metropolitan Opera. Sometimes he would attend a dinner party at Lee Radziwill's with other notable guests. On opening night of a Bernstein evening put together by Comden and Green and friends, the Bernsteins pulled up to the Theater de Lys in

Greenwich Village in a limousine with their family and some Kennedys. Bernstein used a stretch limousine to get to this tiny Greenwich Village theater where the anticapitalist *Threepenny Opera* had had its American premiere. Several explanations for this kind of behavior present themselves: His friends speak of his need to "have it all"; others less loyal draw on his own application to himself of the adjective "schizophrenic"; still others see it as an expression of the crudest kind of cynicism.

In the mid-1960s, Bernstein sent Alex, his son, to the psychiatrist Milton Horowitz. Like many adolescents of the period, Alex had become involved with drugs. Alex recalls the single session, in which he did not open his mouth except to smoke four cigarettes. He was, therefore, not made to go again. If communication was difficult between Alex and analyst, it was even more of a problem between son and father. Alex says Bernstein remembers a two-year period when the two did not exchange a word. In public Bernstein was still pretty voluble but in private he was often preoccupied and depressed.

Bernstein's tendency to be drawn to both sides of every issue (his difficulty with saying no is one manifestation) was apparent in his earliest adult years. This aspect of his personality re-emerged during the years now commonly identified as those of the midlife crisis. In 1965 Bernstein was forty-seven years old. The chasm between his public success and his private despair led to a reassessment of values. Always haunted by the specter of time, Bernstein, even earlier, would banter with friends about his fear of birthdays, the terror of a receding hair line, the need to finish a project by a particular date. Time, he said, was his "worst enemy." For a man who invested numbers with magical significance, fifty was a critical year. Bernstein would be fifty in 1968. The year not only marked his first half century, it was also his tenth as music director of the Philharmonic and his twenty-fifth as a conductor in the public eye. Whatever changes there were to be made, they should be made then. Bernstein set about planning. He even hoped out loud that his last performance as music director of the Philharmonic would turn out to be precisely his one thousandth performance. But his last performance fell a little more than fifty short of the mark.

In the spring of 1966 Bernstein solidified his relationship with Vienna by conducting a performance of *Falstaff* at the Vienna State Opera. The reviews were so different from the harsh ones he had been receiving from Harold Schonberg in *The New York Times* that it is not surprising Bernstein turned his attentions to a foreign country. Here is Rudolf Klein in a review from Vienna that appeared in the *Times*:

> Since the departure of Herbert von Karajan from the Vienna State Opera, no conductor has been so extolled in this house as was Leonard Bernstein for the premiere of his production of the opera "Falstaff."
>
> He certainly deserved the ovations: his work achieved the maximum both on stage and in the orchestra. Moreover, one never had the impression that here was dictator issuing commands with an iron will. Quite the contrary, each musical phrase came forth as improvised, as if of itself, without any compulsion...
>
> A unison of praise followed—and in the very papers that have found nothing right with the State Opera since Mr. Karajan left [in 1964]. A comparable production of "Falstaff" has not been seen since the already legendary performances under Toscanini....

The reaction suggested that whatever risks might be involved in Bernstein's leaving the New York orchestra, they would be slight. The time had come to move. During the early and middle 1960s Bernstein was recording all of the Mahler symphonies, the first time any conductor had set himself this particular goal. He believed the public was ready for it. More than ever before, he was gripped with a sense of identification between himself and the tormented Jewish composer and conductor. Really to be Mahler, in the same sense that he had been both Blitzstein and Koussevitzky, to incorporate within himself all the various stimuli that had made Mahler compose as he did, what better city to be in than Mahler's own, and what better orchestra to conduct than the Vienna State Opera, the one Mahler had sought so much that he converted to Christianity to get it?

In November 1966, a press conference was held that looked as if a chief of state were about to step down before his time. The directors and executive staff of the New York Philharmonic were there. Reporters jammed the room. Bernstein had written a statement that was distributed to the press. The big news was that Bernstein would leave his post at the end of the 1968–1969 season.

Management appears not to have fought his decision. Always sensitive to the press, the management of the orchestra probably breathed a collective sigh of relief that Schonberg would be losing his favorite target. Besides, Bernstein had been pressing the orchestra with increasing demands. The attitude reflected the disdain for trade that he felt for his father and Mister Mister and all the corporations with which he dealt. A colleague recalls a *Young People's Concert* that called for the presence of one harp. Bernstein wanted the camera to pick up harps on both the right and the left sides of the stage, so he put in a call for two harps and two harpists. This provoked complaints, but he didn't yield. The colleague says he told Bernstein how much the additional harp would cost and how it seemed unjustified when only one harp was called for in the score. To which Bernstein confided, "Don't worry. They respect you more when you make such demands." Still, there comes a time when anxiety displaces respect and they finally say no and let you go.

It was natural for the administration to believe that the orchestra's success at the time was the Philharmonic's own and that Bernstein's contribution was only incidental. By this time Bernstein and the Philharmonic had been so entwined that it was hard to determine exactly where the one's achievements ended and the other's began. Finally, Bernstein was not in high repute during this period. According to Maurice Peress, "Nobody had a good word for Lenny in those days."

After losing the heavyweight title to challenger Michael Spinks, Larry Holmes said, "After you hold the title for seven years, you don't make a lot of friends." He might have added that once you let it go, you may just uncover an old enemy or two.

On Sunday, November 13, eleven days after Bernstein's resignation was announced, Schonberg wrote a Sunday essay: BERNSTEIN: WRONG TIME TO LEAVE? He discussed what he considered the recent improvement in Bernstein's conducting style, noting that it "now seems more intent on substance and less on flashiness.... In short he is threatening to turn into the kind of conductor that his talent originally indicated. Therefore—a typically Bernstein gesture—he is leaving. The Muse across the river is calling."

The Muse across the river was Mahler. By the summer of 1967

Bernstein had recorded the nine symphonies and *Das Lied von der Erde* for CBS,* which, according to McClure, was never disconcerted by Schonberg's reviews: "We knew how good Lenny was. We knew all this was bullshit. That seems to be the way the *Times* works. It has to present a strong position in order to get read."

By November, Bernstein's Mahler was available in a leather-bound set that was selling well at one hundred dollars. Dietrich Fischer-Dieskau sang a solo in *Das Lied von der Erde*. Virtually all the critics agreed that the package was a formidable cultural product, which made Bernstein a hero. *Life* magazine said:

> Mahler was a man split in halves, a vain, insecure man, a Jew who converted to Catholicism, an orchestra conductor who yearned to be conducted, and a creature of delicate health who died, depleted, his tenth symphony unfinished, at 50. In everything he wrote these conflicts make themselves felt as he stretches German music on the rack and pulls until it feels as if at times Mahler himself must break. In his superb recordings, Bernstein restates them and spares nothing, not himself, Mahler, nor the listener.

Almost every characteristic *Life* attributes to Mahler was also attributable to Bernstein. Bernstein also saw a point of identification in the length of time both men stayed at major posts; Mahler had had ten years with the Vienna State Opera, Bernstein ten with the Philharmonic. Because of all the similarities, apparent and subtle ones, Bernstein was probably haunted by the possibility that as Mahler had died at fifty, he might, too.

He did not, of course, and the Viennese experience took off in an unimaginable way. When he walked down a street in Vienna, crowds surrounded him almost as they surrounded the Beatles in other cities. Bernstein thinks that the Viennese adore him because of the guilt they feel over their heinous treatment of the Jews. He is particularly pleased that he was able to restore the bust of Mahler—which had been removed by Hitler—to its place in the opera house. But Bernstein, with this formulation, is not entirely fair to himself. He was only in his teens

---

* *The company gradually changed the name of its record division from Columbia to CBS.*

when a music teacher at Boston Latin asked him where he had learned to hold the second beat just a little bit longer in Viennese music the way he did. He said that he did it by instinct, suggesting a Viennese soul. Some Viennese seemed to believe that. In any event, Mahler's city was moved to embrace Bernstein in an unprecedented way, and to give him all the things that the Met and CBS Records were now beginning to deny him.

In June 1967, a year after *Falstaff*, Bernstein conducted the Mahler *Resurrection* Symphony with the Vienna Philharmonic, the State Opera Chorus, Hilde Gueden, and Christa Ludwig. It was the high point of an important music festival. The opera house was used as a concert hall, a rare occurrence, one that indicated the importance the Viennese gave to the event. Bernstein dealt with whatever guilt he may have felt at performing in this anti-Semitic city by donating his entire fee to Israel. Gueden and Ludwig did the same. The orchestra then gave part of its own fee to the Red Cross for Israeli casualties. The Viennese evening turned out to be a virtual benefit for Israel, almost like making the Ford Foundation and the Metropolitan Opera pay for a celebration of Sacco, Vanzetti, and Blitzstein. According to reports reaching New York the house was spellbound. The Vienna State Opera and the Gustav Mahler Society honored Bernstein with the Gustav Mahler Medal. In acknowledging it he said, "I have always felt close to Mahler but now my relation to him is different. I have become more Viennese."

In October 1967, the Vienna Philharmonic gave a concert at Philharmonic Hall in New York for the benefit of the Pension Fund of the New York Philharmonic. Both of the orchestras were celebrating their 125th anniversaries. In an all-German evening, Karl Boehm conducted Schubert's Eighth Symphony and Strauss's *Ein Heldenleben*, Bernstein conducted Beethoven's *Leonore* Overture No. 3. After the performance Bernstein warmly embraced Boehm on stage. Anyone who has ever attended a Bernstein performance knows he kisses anyone near him at the end. The problem here was Boehm's past involvement with the Nazi party. It had been considerable enough to move the Allied authorities to forbid him to perform after the war. In 1947 Boehm was permitted to resume his career. In 1967, he was conducting music by Richard Strauss, who had worked with the Nazis in his last years, before an audience that inevitably included many New York Jews while a

Jewish conductor shared the podium with him. Soon after this, in September, 1968, Bernstein took the New York Philharmonic to Bonn, the West German capital and the birthplace of Beethoven. One of the remarkable things about this visit was what he did not do; he did not conduct Beethoven. But the most remarkable thing of all was his presence there. William Lincer, the violist, was quoted in this remark: "They gave flowers to Mr. Bernstein today. Twenty-five years ago they probably killed fifty of his relatives. I can't wait to leave."

Visibility always has been a critical issue to Bernstein. He was highly visible in Marson's class at Boston Latin; thirty years later Marson remembered exactly where he had sat. He was highly visible at the parties around Boston, entertaining other guests as he played the piano standing up. Bernstein was highly visible at Curtis, where he played jazz piano and talked so much that Persichetti, one year ahead of him, noticed him enough to recommend him as composer for *Fancy Free*. Touching on this characteristic, Charles Turner says, "In public Lenny enjoyed his celebrity and liked being recognized. The Bernsteins often played games, at which they were whizzes, and sometimes they played games in restaurants because, one felt, Lenny liked having people see him having a good time with his family." As Bernstein enjoyed being seen playing games with his family, so he enjoyed being seen as he moved around Israel or anywhere else, and he arranged to have those visits filmed. He needs people to watch what he does.

Getting the post at the New York Philharmonic certainly heightened his visibility. But there is no reason to think that because he now planned to leave it, he could also leave his exhibitionism behind. During the summer of 1967 the Bernsteins went on a holiday to Ansedonia, a small fishing village in Italy on the Tyrrhenian Sea, which had become a very popular resort with the international set. This summer Charlie Chaplin was there. In addition to his own family, Bernstein had with him Ken Heyman, a photographer, and John Gruen, both of whom had their own quarters nearby. The understanding was that the summer would produce a book on Bernstein that would be far more revelatory than any of those then in print.

With photographs by Heyman and a text by Gruen, *The Private World of Leonard Bernstein* was published by Viking Press. The book was oversized, appropriate for the coffee table. The cover, a close-up of Bernstein's face, revealed every pore. With such a photograph the subject appeared to be telling the public that he would reveal himself here as he had never done before. In some ways this turned out to be true. Gruen writes about Bernstein's combative times with Rodzinski, reporting a physical attack the older man made on the younger one the morning after the barbershop incident. When the book was reviewed in the *Times* with that incident duly noted, Richard Rodzinski, the conductor's son, wrote a letter to the editor attacking Bernstein for his ungracious behavior toward a man who had opened a professional world to him. Bernstein replied with a letter to the *Times* in which he agreed with young Rodzinski, stating that he had not intended the story for publication. That is, he was still choosing then to be quoted in only the nicest remarks about everyone.

In the Gruen book Bernstein treated his own family in the most complimentary, even grandiose terms. Photographs show them relaxing on a terrace. Husband and wife have arms around one another. Wife cuts husband's hair. Husband looks over wife's shoulder as she works on canvas. Nina Bernstein says that when the book appeared, the whole family was stunned. They did not recognize themselves. Inevitably they had become a piece of fiction.

In reviewing the book, Donal Henahan wrote that it

> fastened on profoundly trivial things. "Look!" we whisper, "Lenny doing pushups. Imagine!" Or Lenny scuba-diving, or making funny faces, or having his hair cut by his wife. Of course both text and pictures depict Mr. Bernstein in more important moments, clowning with Charlie Chaplin, reading musical scores (seeing a man gazing at all those arcane squiggles never fails to amaze the public), and conducting his men....
>
> And before long we know as much about Mr. Bernstein as we ever learn about a public figure, that, for instance, he eats his eggs raw, right out of the shell

That last piece of information would have told more about the subject if Gruen had known that eating eggs raw, out of the shell, was exactly how Mitropoulos had eaten his breakfast each day.

In 1965 Bernstein said he was interested in

exploring the reconstituted Mahler Tenth Symphony and would in-
vestigate the version by Joseph Wheeler as well as the better-known
one by Deryck Cooke. The Wheeler edition, which, at that time,
had been performed only nonprofessionally in England, was being

"Bernstein asked him if he should conduct the work. Bloom said that he could not answer that, that such a decision was for Bernstein to make alone. According to Bloom, Bernstein said, 'I have one criterion. Will it give me an orgasm?'"

rehearsed by the Caecilian Symphony in New York under the direction of Arthur Bloom. Some time after that performance, Bloom visited Bernstein in the Green Room of Philharmonic Hall. Bernstein asked him if he should conduct the work. Bloom said that he could not answer that, that such a decision was for Bernstein to make alone. According to Bloom, Bernstein said, "I have one criterion. Will it give me an orgasm?"

During a conversation in 1983 at Tanglewood, Bernstein discussed Freud's theory of sublimation, an idea that holds that a person makes art to the degree that he can suppress his sex drive and redirect it into his work. Bernstein said he did not believe this to be valid. "If there were anything to it," he went on, "Wagner could not have fucked as many women as he did and put on paper all the notes that he did."

Artists' experiences vary. Some say that as long as they are at work on a particular project, they do not participate in sex at all, that their responses range from lack of interest to total impotence. Ricky Leacock says that while he is making a film, he is completely abstinent. Others report that the more sexually active they are, the more and the better art they think they produce. Vera Stravinsky maintained that "Stravinsky was always very sexually active." In her late eighties when she made the remark, she may not have been capable of recalling with accuracy the various patterns of her husband's life. Still, if her memory did serve her, Freud's theory of sublimation finds contradiction in Stravinsky.

One fact seems to emerge: the greater the artist, the more powerful the sexual drive, whether suppressed or not. As for the details— whether one is homosexual or heterosexual and the particular practices that excite—the same profile can probably be found in the most sophisticated of artists and the most unsophisticated of laborers. The point then is not whether Bernstein was homosexual or heterosexual and why, but rather how the choices he made affected his life and his art.

Except for the period when he was engaged to Felicia the immediate post-World War II years were homosexual ones for Bernstein. It was then he composed *The Age of Anxiety*, which had as its program a poem by W. H. Auden, a homosexual, and which reflected Bernstein's own anxiety. *The Age of Anxiety* was the only major work Bernstein composed between 1944, when he completed *On the Town*, and 1952, when he wrote *Trouble in Tahiti*.

By that time Bernstein had married. Later he characterized himself at the time he made this move as a "well-behaviorized chimpanzee," and incorporated his bitterness into *Trouble in Tahiti*, an ironic opera about a cute little couple living in a neat little house. He followed that with *Wonderful Town, On the Waterfront, Serenade*—which, he writes, "some people think is my best [concert] piece—*Candide*, and *West Side Story*, a significant list of achievements in a five-year period.

Despite Bernstein's belief that there is nothing to sublimation, there does seem to be something to it for him. Whether Bernstein's partners were men or women is not the issue. What seems to matter more is that during the early years of his marriage, he inhibited his formerly licentious ways in favor of an ordered family life. The promiscuity that had characterized his activity during the composing of *The Age of Anxiety* and his visits to Key West dives now seemed to be under control. In its place was a string of works that have endured. Thomas Mann and Oscar Wilde were other artists who went through similar experiences. It was during their marriages that these artists, sexually ambivalent, did their best work.

In the spring of 1968, only months before Bernstein's fiftieth birthday and during a time when he was attenuating his ties both to New York and to his wife, he conducted Richard Strauss's *Der Rosenkavalier* at the Vienna State Opera. According to English critic Peter Heyworth, "Bernstein's arrival at the State Opera has evoked not resentment, but enthusiasm. Since von Karajan stormed out of it some years before, the great building … has been becalmed and rudderless…. With the arrival of the composer of *West Side Story*, the Viennese have sensed the fresh air their opera so desperately needs, and for that they are grateful."

When Heyworth identifies Bernstein as "the composer of *West Side Story*" in writing of his Viennese activities, he knows what he is doing. The initial adoration of Bernstein by the Viennese may have come in part from their love of this Broadway show, which they presumably saw as a variant of the pop music theater that had a special place in Vienna's cultural life at least as far back as Mozart. That always irritated Bernstein. Before he made conducting trips abroad, he would tell those in charge of publicity at Columbia Records to make certain never to identify him that way. Throughout his life Bernstein downplayed his music-theater achievements. The subject came up even on a fishing trip to Florida in 1949: "Lenny and I discussed opera versus musical comedy," Harvey Probber says, "and I took the position that musical comedy was the opera of our time. Opera, in my mind, was in the category of the museum. But Lenny never saw it that way. With Broadway he thought he had done nothing of importance and used to say all the time that to achieve immortality he would have to compose serious music that would last."

As for *Der Rosenkavalier*, Heyworth in his remarks noted that for years it had been performed in Vienna "as though in a somnambulistic trance, with singers and orchestra going through their rituals as automatically as a lazy priest saying Mass. To critics and public alike, Bernstein's interpretation has had the impact of a newly cleaned picture. Detail ... lain buried under a patina of dirt and varnish (in this case a brown soup of string tone) has emerged with startling clarity."

Just as Bernstein had dared to conduct the Mahler *Resurrection* Symphony in Willem Mengelberg's country some years before, he now had the courage to conduct *Der Rosenkavalier* in the city that had seen productions under such conductors as Clemens Krauss, Karl Boehm, Hans Knappertsbusch, and Herbert von Karajan. The result was controversial but apparently exhilarating. Karl Lobl, music critic of Vienna's *Express Today*, wrote, "From the orchestral point of view it was a sometimes fascinating, always unusual, often exciting evening."

In June 1968 Robert Kennedy was killed. Bernstein says that after the murder, he was unable to work at all for at least a week. But he did participate in the requiem mass for Kennedy at St. Patrick's Cathedral celebrated by Angelo Cardinal Dell'Acqua. President Lyndon Johnson, Princess Grace of Monaco, Prime Minister Pierre Trudeau of Canada, and other high-ranking emissaries were present for this televised service. Virtually all the reports of the event centered on Bernstein, who wore white suit and white shoes as he conducted the slow movement of the Mahler Symphony No. 5 at the request of the Kennedy family.

On August 25, Bernstein turned fifty. The official celebration started in Philharmonic Hall with a concert version of *Candide*. Afterward there were the parties. One was hosted by Beni Montresor, the illustrator and stage designer, and another by Earl Blackwell, the publicist, in his private ballroom with a scattering of dukes and duchesses among the guests. Felicia, who, by that time, rarely accompanied Bernstein when he went out on the town, appeared in a Givenchy gown.

An unofficial celebration came in the form of a skit written and performed by the two older Bernstein children. Alex played his father. He awakened to a report of the various messages that had come in while he slept. Jamie, playing the secretary, said, "The president called, wants you to come to the White House. Governor Rockefeller invites you to dinner. Neil Armstrong called, wants to fly you to dinner with Garbo in Paris. Colonel Lindbergh and Picasso called." Mimicking his father, Alex then wrung his hands: "I'm a forgotten man." Bernstein's son had apparently learned a lesson from his father: that a good joke contains a kernel of reality. The reality in this instance was that Bernstein's need for love was a bottomless pit. Despite hobnobbing with the Kennedys, entering a reception after a concert in Monte Carlo with Princess Grace on his arm, being feted by heads of state everywhere, Bernstein never had enough adulation from the greats.

Bernstein's last season with the New York Philharmonic was a celebratory one. Under his leadership every aspect of the orchestra had grown remarkably. His popularity had made it possible for the orchestra to record more than two hundred albums. In a typical Bernstein year, record sales ran about four hundred thousand, which brought royalties of between $150,000 and $175,000 to the Philharmonic Society. The success of the Bernstein Philharmonic recordings, together with the even more widely heard and seen TV programs, encouraged innovation and enlarged the orchestra's influence.

On his programs Bernstein used old instruments—the viola da gamba and the oboe d'amore—and he introduced newer ones—the ondes martenot and the tape recorder. He included jazz groups—Dave Brubeck's was one—as well as dramatic pieces with narrators, military bands, pantomimists, and musical comedy performers. He also encouraged young conductors in a way they had not been encouraged before: He took on not one but three assistants, helping to cover the costs with his own foundation. In 1963, he initiated an international competition for conductors in memory of Mitropoulos.

But what is probably most tangible of all is the advance he oversaw in the economic stability of the musicians under him. Halfway through his tenure, Bernstein was the guest of honor at a party at the Tavern on

the Green in Manhattan's Central Park. He was about to go off on a
sabbatical leave and started to compose what he called an ode, which he
recited to the orchestra:

> *Love one another, and sing while you play,*
> *And be good to Mother while Daddy's away.*
> *And so forward, my hearties, with courage and cheer,*
> *To a season with 98 weeks in the year.*

Bernstein was pointing out that under his dominion, the season had
increased in length between 1957 and 1964 from thirty-two to forty-
two weeks. Then a one-week strike brought the musicians a year-round
contract, the first for an American orchestra.

During Bernstein's time as the conductor, Philharmonic performances of American works rose from about four percent to fifteen percent of all performances. For his own concerts, close to thirty percent
of the programming was American: European guest conductors
brought the average down. There was also a dramatic increase in the
number of American soloists. The same cannot be said, however, for
the number of American conductors. Here the conductors who had
been important when Bernstein arrived were still the important ones:
Alfred Wallenstein, Thomas Schippers, and Lorin Maazel. American
conductors slightly younger than Bernstein say he was more a
hindrance than a help in increasing the number of American conductors, because he became the standard against which other Americans
were judged.

But if Bernstein's success did not immediately rub off on other conductors, it propelled him into a significant television career. Television
and Bernstein have been more than generous to each other. According
to Burton Bernstein, "Television made an enormous difference in our
lives. As famous as Lenny was before *Omnibus*, we could still go to the
movies and stand in line. Once he appeared on TV that was no longer
possible. We would be besieged. It was like being with Muhammed Ali.
Television changed everything. He was now a living room figure.
Everyone knew him. Kids. Old people. It got to a point very quickly
when, if we wanted to go to a movie, we would have to call ahead so the
management would open back doors for us."

Despite all of his contributions, Bernstein, in the late 1960s, was
still a target for criticism. There was criticism of his excessively theatri-

cal ways, his upstaging of soloists, and maybe especially his refusal to participate in the development of the twelve-tone musical language. In January 1969, during his last months as director of the orchestra, he conducted Milton Babbitt's *Relata II*. Commissioned by the Philharmonic for its 125th anniversary season, the work was postponed for months because of the copyist's errors in the musicians' parts. All the conflicts inherent in the purposes of the mainstream modernist movement of the time and the talents and tastes of Bernstein came to the surface in this event. The present writer contributed an article to *The New York Times* of Sunday, January 12, 1969. Devoted to the Philharmonic performance of *Relata II*, the piece may shed light on the multiplicity of causes behind the friction between Babbitt and his art and Bernstein and his. It is reprinted here in its entirety:

I expected Milton Babbitt to be serving champagne. The New York Philharmonic, under the helm of the lionized Bernstein, is about to perform his latest work, *Relata II*. It will have its world premiere Thursday night at Philharmonic Hall. Only once before—in 1955—when the Cleveland Orchestra played his *Relata I*, written under a Koussevitzky commission, did the composer receive a comparable honor. But Babbitt, the leader of the academic school of composition that has flourished in the United States since World War II, did not appear to be in a celebratory mood. In fact, the interview was distinctly low key.

After defining "relata" as the traditional word used in logic and philosophy for interrelationships, the composer told the following story: *Relata I* started as one work but grew into two large, related movements. I spent fifteen months writing *Relata II*, finishing it a full two months before rehearsals, which were scheduled for this past October. The premiere was to have been on October seventeenth. But on the occasion of the first rehearsal, Bernstein introduced it to the musicians with these surprising words: 'Gentlemen, you've probably never played a piece like this before.'

"If this is true—if this is an unfamiliar language to the musicians, look at what the composer is up against: The men could not see the serious mistakes that the copyist had made in writing out their parts. Because of the errors, Bernstein had to stop the rehearsal many times and make the necessary corrections.

"He was afraid, under the circumstances, that he would be unable to bring the piece up to tempo and asked me, 'Dare we go ahead?' I agreed, of course, that we could not and we decided to postpone further work—and the premiere—until all the parts could be properly checked. I have spent nine weeks doing just that, but I still view rehearsals with trepidation. There are six hundred measures in *Relata II*, no two of which are alike. If each measure were to be practiced for only five minutes— a minimal requirement for a Chopin piano piece—we would need fifty hours to rehearse this composition. Instead, with luck, we'll manage to find six! So we bang bang, we plow through it, we do it. It's all over within one week—from the first rehearsal to the last performance.

"The piece, of course, is a difficult one. I treat the orchestra as a large ensemble with many octave doublings creating problems of intonation because they occur in intricate rhythmic combinations. There are also questions of relative dynamic projection. With *Relata II* I have tried to exploit the most subtle resources of a most sophisticated orchestra, but rather than flattering the musicians by giving them a challenging score, I managed only to anger them considerably.

"Finally there's the question: Who will hear this piece? No one is concerned about my interested musical colleagues, those for whom I really offer it. There will not be a broadcast, a tape, a recording. There won't even be a published score. My associates across the country will not have any opportunity to hear it unless they get to Philharmonic Hall next week.

"On the other hand, the regular Philharmonic audience does not want to hear this piece. And why should they have to? How can it be coherent for them? It's as though a colleague of mine in the field of philosophy were to read his paper on the Johnny Carson show. The milieu is inappropriate for the event.

"Steuermann, Schoenberg's friend and disciple, told me many years ago that music, as we know it, is altogether finished.

I did not agree with him at the time but now I think he was quite correct. I am unable to see who will provide the necessary support. In order for serious music to survive, the people who make it have to survive and the music itself has to survive. Its survival, under the present conditions, appears to me to be highly unlikely."

Like Webern and Varèse—the two most crucial figures to the current generation—Milton Babbitt is the son of a mathematician. From his earliest years in Jackson, Mississippi, Babbitt not only studied mathematics and science but classical Latin and music as well. In 1932, when he was sixteen, he saw his first Schoenberg scores, which an uncommonly cultivated uncle brought back from a trip abroad; this precipitated his decision to compose. After graduating from NYU in 1935, Babbitt studied privately with Roger Sessions. As early as 1939, when Schoenberg was still the object of intense humiliation— "He was considered more a musical freak than a celebrity," Babbitt recalls—and even the cerebral Sessions opposed the twelve-tone technique, Babbitt adopted it for his own use.

"If it had not been for Schoenberg's music and Roger's teaching," Babbitt said the other day, "I never would have stayed in the field." But stay he did and now the fifty-seven-year-old musician is the high priest of what remains in this country of the Schoenberg-Webern serial tradition. Babbitt not only inspired the school's technique, he also determined its academic tone and, in doing so, found composers a home. For over fifteen years, against bitter opposition, Babbitt fought for a composer's Ph.D. Today Princeton and Harvard are among the universities offering it.

But for Babbitt that is not enough. He claims much can still be done with the large orchestra. He admits that he "jumped at the chance to compose for the New York Philharmonic." But he emphasizes the need for more rehearsal time as well as a chance for a new work to reach everyone.

Babbitt explained why *Relata II* will not reach interested ears and minds: "The performance won't be taped; because it is not being broadcast, taping is against union regulations. It won't be recorded; recording it would cost at least twenty thousand dollars. *Relata II* won't even be published. The university presses are not publishing music. I have a chair at Princeton, and no one there thinks of me as a second-class academic, yet Princeton publishes in all other fields, persistently ignoring that of music. My own publisher—a subsidiary of Schirmer—has not published any one of the eight works that I've written for conventional instruments and voice since 1957. Computers can be used for music publication; the process was offered to publishers at least four years ago. But nobody picked it up because nobody regards the propagation of music as being at all consequential.

"The university, the composer's last hope, turns with delight to the electronic field because it is self-contained, requiring neither performance nor publication. The medium provides a kind of full satisfaction for the composer, too. I love going to the studio with my work in my head, realizing it while I am there, and walking out with the tape under my arm. I can then send it anywhere in the world, knowing exactly how it will sound. My last electronic work, *Ensembles for Synthesizer,* recorded by Columbia Records, has been played hundreds of times in universities. These are the people—the university people—whom we regard as our appropriate colleagues. I feel closer to members of my philosophy department than to many who regard themselves as musicians."

In Babbitt's frame of reference there are two kinds of composers: "academic" (his kind) and "theater" (those who write for audiences). In his less charitable moments, he dismisses the latter as the "show biz crowd." By thus separating himself from any responsibility to please an audience, he feels he can demand that the world meet him on his own terms, rather than give the world the music it wants.

Such an attitude is not as new as it seems. It is reminiscent of the medieval approach in which music, mathematics, geometry, and astronomy all were intellectual disciplines in the university, having nothing to do with the public at large. But this attitude creates a problem today: Hardly anyone will subsidize

academic music sufficiently. *Relata II*, for which Babbitt collected a scarcely compensatory three thousand dollars, not only
fails to reach the academic community for whom it was intended; it also earns Babbitt the performing musicians' antagonism,
and probably the hostility of the ticket holder, too.

Despite the best intentions of both Babbitt and the New
York Philharmonic, the potentially exciting liaison between
them has turned into a somewhat traumatic affair.

Julius Baker, the first flutist with the New York Philharmonic dur-
ing most of Bernstein's tenure, remembers that "the men hated *Relata
II*. They were furious and did not want to do the piece." To cajole them,
Bernstein set up a competition with prizes ranging from twenty-five to
one hundred dollars. The contest involved completing a limerick that
Bernstein had begun. These are the two lines Bernstein provided:

> *There was a composer named Babbitt,*
> *Who had a peculiar habit.*

Martin Eshelman, the violinist, won first prize. His winning lines:

> *Each day around noon,*
> *He'd go into a swoon,*
> *Scoring piece after piece like a rabbit.*

On April 30, 1969, Samuel J. Bernstein died.

Those at the funeral recall Leonard as being uncharacteristically quiet. Diamond says the death devastated him. Bernstein took a week off from the New York Philharmonic during which his assistants took over. When he returned on May 9, he conducted *Jeremiah*, with

© WHITESTONE PHOTO / HEINZ H. WEISSENSTEIN

Karl Boehm's performances were cultural highlights of the war years in Nazi Germany. Years later, Bernstein was offered a lucrative contract by the Munich entertainment conglomerate Unitel. "Bernstein said, 'I feel awkward signing a German contract.' Then he signed it."

Tourel as his soloist. It was the work he had dedicated to his father almost thirty years before. In the *New York Post*, Harriett Johnson used the words "depth" and "beauty." In the *Times* Allen Hughes claimed that this early work "held up." On the same program, Bernstein conducted the Schumann Symphony No. 2, the first work he had heard Mitropoulos conduct.

The deaths of fathers may have been on his mind. For his last performance as director of the New York Philharmonic, the orchestra he had conducted more times than any other conductor in its history, Bernstein led a performance of the Mahler Symphony No. 3, that massive, powerful symphony he had selected in the spring of 1961 as a memorial to Mitropoulos. This time there was only praise. "A shade too much rubato and the music sounds vulgar," Schonberg wrote. "A shade too little and it sounds mechanical. Mr. Bernstein hit a happy mean and he entered completely the spirit of the music." At the end there was a standing ovation.

Later at a private party, the musicians presented him with a silver and gold *mezuzah*—a container for religious texts that Jews fix to their doorposts—that they had had made for him. The management, taking a less spiritual approach, gave him a speedboat for water-skiing on Long Island Sound. Bernstein exchanged it for something else.

Freud claimed that the death of a father is "the most important event, the most poignant loss, of a man's life." While Bernstein speaks freely about many of those who have been close to him and have died, he rarely goes into any detail about Sam Bernstein, or, for that matter, about Mitropoulos. For all his exhibitionism, there are parts of his interior life that he withholds from the world. They deal with the love of his father, and with the father figures who followed, and with his convoluted, destructive connections with them.

On May 25, 1969 with Christa Ludwig and Walter Berry as soloists, Bernstein led the Vienna Philharmonic in a performance of Beethoven's *Missa Solemnis* to commemorate the one hundredth anniversary of the Vienna State Opera. It was a singular honor for him. The Viennese press and public went wild. Then he returned to the United States, intent on doing nothing but composing.

The first interruption came with a request from the Metropolitan

Opera to conduct Mascagni's *Cavalleria Rusticana*. After its opening performance Bernstein was interviewed by John Gruen, author of *The Private World of Leonard Bernstein*, for *The New York Times*. Gruen asked how his composition had been coming along, referring specifically to the Jerome Robbins project he had been working on called *The Exception and the Rule*. Based on a Brecht work, it had involved the efforts of lyricist Jerry Leiber, playwright John Guare, and Stephen Sondheim.

Bernstein said that was ancient history going back to 1965. "Actually," he said,

> we had gotten close to a solution, but we just couldn't bring it off. It was a question of our all seeing it in the same way. We finally lost heart. It would have been a very thrilling show and I have a very large score for it. Finally, however, there was a moment when we all looked at each other and said, "We cannot go on. We cannot bear to talk about these problems one more second." The problems were so dogged—they stayed there no matter how long we talked about them, in meetings, investigations, arguments.

Bernstein went on to describe his frustration with *Brother Sun, Sister Moon*, a film project with Italian director Franco Zeffirelli. He said that it

> dealt with the conversion of St. Francis of Assisi in very contemporary terms.... I made two visits to Rome and Zeffirelli visited me in Connecticut. We worked very hard on it. But there came a point when the same thing happened as with the Brecht. It just wouldn't budge and the problems couldn't be solved. Also I think that Zeffirelli changed his point of view, while I was more than ever convinced of the validity of the original approach. Again a divergence, and it seemed insoluble.

Bernstein told Gruen that there had been a revival of interest in *The Skin of Our Teeth*:

For a whole month I was excited about it and convinced that this time it would work. But that petered out too. The reasons are too complicated to go into. Yet another disappointment! By now my composing time was quickly coming to an end. It was already December, and I became extremely depressed because all this time had gone by, and I had these piles of music which I could never use for anything else.

Bernstein is a phenomenally fast worker. Not only had he composed *Wonderful Town* in less than five weeks, when he first postponed the performance of *Relata II*, he told Babbitt he was upset because he had spent "a whole Saturday learning it." Even for a specialist in new music, *Relata II* would require at least a few months' study.

In the late fall of 1969 Topol, the Israeli actor, approached Bernstein with yet another Brecht idea. He had prepared a film treatment of *The Caucasian Chalk Circle*. "I was immediately at the piano," Bernstein told Gruen,

and found myself writing music and readapting the original Brecht lyrics. I liked Topol very much and was excited by the project. I must have written five or six songs when the phone rang and there was Rudolf Bing saying the Met strike had been settled and "please we need you ... save our lives ... do 'Cavalleria,'" and Zeffirelli on the other extension saying "please ... please ... do 'Cavalleria.'"

Bernstein put aside *The Caucasian Chalk Circle* and the other composition projects to conduct *Cavalleria* at the Met. He may have had some regrets. "Have you ever read," he asked Gruen after the first performance, "such a collection of put-downs? When I read those reviews I suddenly realized why I do opera so rarely. Every time I do I swear, Never again! Because I forget that the best you can hope for is an approximation."

Approximation and some bedlam. Michael Tilson Thomas, then at the start of his conducting career, was backstage visiting Bernstein before a matinee performance. "[Franco] Corelli came in gasping," Thomas says, "saying he couldn't possibly sing. He was not well. He hadn't slept and so on. Lenny spoke to him in a calming, hypnoticlike, litany voice. 'Franco,' he said, 'your whole public is here. If you could just be calm and let your throat relax.' Corelli left the room a little calmer but still saying no, he could not go on. At that point someone told Bernstein that Domingo was on his way over. Lenny whispered this into Corelli's ear. In a booming voice Corelli shouted, 'Domingo!' A minute later Lenny turned to me. 'Corelli is singing,' he said. 'Now you understand why the Metropolitan Opera is the biggest psychiatric institution in New York.'"

But if Bernstein's implication was that Corelli was a patient in that institution, there are at least a few people at the Met who might think that Bernstein could have kept him company there. By this time Schuyler Chapin was executive director of Amberson Productions, a subsidiary of Amberson Enterprises, a firm set up by Bernstein in 1969 to produce films, television specials, filmed operas, and home videocassettes of Bernstein performances. Here is Krawitz on what happened during the 1969–1970 season between Chapin and Bernstein: "There had been a labor dispute and the performances had been postponed. When Bing and Zeffirelli reached for Lenny, Lenny said he didn't know *Pag* but would do *Cav*. [Leoncavallo's *Pagliacci*, another short opera, is usually performed following *Cavalleria Rusticana*].

"Then Chapin entered the picture. He was the worst influence Lenny could have had. He asked us to reverse the order of the operas, saying that they wanted to change it because it was not fair to Fausto Cleva, the old-time conductor [who would be leading *Pagliacci*], to come after Lenny, the big star. I explained to Chapin that if we switched the order so that Lenny could have the final curtain—which is what the request was all about—we would have to have an intermission of between forty-five minutes and an hour in order to make all the necessary scenery changes. Chapin came back again. He said he couldn't return to Lenny without getting his request granted. 'Don't force my hand, Schuyler,' I said. 'Don't let Lenny turn you into a messenger boy.' I reminded him that we had offered both operas to Lenny and that he had agreed to do only *Cav*. I had discussed Bernstein's request with Franco [Zeffirelli] and Bing, and both agreed with me that it was an impossible one to grant. All the rigamarole was getting us more than annoyed. It was wasting everyone's time. There were bad feelings everywhere.

"On opening night Bernstein took the opera very slowly. The public and the critics thought it was bad conducting. Cleva had a big success with *Pag*. The evening was Franco's anyway, because he had designed and staged both works.

"It was a big night," Krawitz says, "with Corelli, Tucker, and Bumbry. In the hierarchy of the evening Lenny was in about the number six spot. Franco was a big name. By then his *Romeo and Juliet* movie was out. I noticed that Lenny's public posture was not nice. In the viewing room he was muttering to himself and the people in the house could see that. Among us Lenny did not behave properly. He resented the people—Franco and me—who had made *Pag* the success it was. Lenny left a sour taste. There was no longer the good feeling of the *Falstaff* days when Felicia could get to him in exactly the right way. Cleva and Zeffirelli came out of this big in the press. It was not one of the great evenings for Bernstein."

Bernstein's use of Chapin was not as effective with Chapin on his own staff as it had been when Chapin was on the other side of the fence. In his book Chapin reports several incidents at Columbia Records when he allowed Bernstein his way and cost the company in the process. Chapin's tone is always one of complete forgiveness for these excessive demands. Here are only three examples Chapin himself reports:

1. After Bernstein's *Symphonic Dances* from *West Side Story* were played at the Philharmonic under Maurice Peress, plans were made for a recording of the work but Bernstein insisted on conducting himself. He promised Chapin there would be no extra time spent in the studio rehearsing. Yet he spent so much extra time that it cost the company an additional twenty-five thousand dollars, a large sum in 1961.

2. At the start of his recording contract in 1959, Bernstein told Chapin he wanted to record Liszt's *Faust* Symphony. Columbia executives told him it would never begin to make back the money it would cost. Bernstein demanded they adhere to the conditions of the contract, which gave him the right to record anything he wished. The record, although well

reviewed, was the financial disaster Columbia had predicted it would be. That of course was a risk—a virtual certainty—that Columbia had accepted when it agreed to Bernstein's demand in the first place.

3.   In 1970, while he was in Europe to record, Bernstein took off a few days to ski in Switzerland. He told Chapin he would send a telegram letting him know when he would get back. No wire arrived. Instead Bernstein alighted somewhere in the middle of Vienna in a helicopter he had chartered at a cost to Columbia of about five thousand dollars.

Chapin had been the middleman between Bernstein and Goddard Lieberson. Lieberson was a friend to Bernstein, and generally things were smoothed out. In 1970 Chapin, then Bernstein's manager, found he could not work with Rudolf Bing the way he had with Lieberson when Lieberson was president of Columbia Records. Bing was not the friend to Bernstein that Lieberson had initially been.

Looking at the outcome of the *Cavalleria* struggle, one could conclude that Bernstein was the loser. But Bernstein has an uncanny ability to make defeat appear to be victory. He certainly did that in this incident. For one thing he got out of *Brother Sun, Sister Moon*, the Zeffirelli film, and used some of the music for *Mass*, his own project. For another he told John Gruen that he had managed to make the critics seem stupid: "As usual," Bernstein said,

they wrote a lot of nonsense about why "Cavalleria" didn't work, about the tempi being so slow. My conception of "Cavalleria" is that it's a very different opera from "Pagliacci." "Pagliacci" is a "number" opera. It has one surefire number after another, although, God knows, there are lean stretches between them.

But "Cavalleria" is more like a music drama, and I tried to make it just that. To make a big arch from beginning to end, discouraging applause. As for the slowness of the tempi, they are actually not as slow as Mascagni's own, which I've heard on a recording with Mascagni himself conducting. The official timing of the Met "Cavalleria" is 77 minutes. Mine was 80, that's all. I set tempi that attempt to give the work a stature and nobility it customarily lacks in performance.

In an autobiography published in 1986, Zeffirelli wrote that Bernstein's tempos leaned "dangerously toward self-indulgence, which was fortunately abandoned at later performances."

Despite the disappointment he may have felt about the *Cavalleria* affair, Bernstein was remarkably resilient. Michael Tilson Thomas attended a matinee a few days after the opening. Here is Thomas's description of that afternoon: "Lenny had another performance that evening with the New York Philharmonic doing the Elliott Carter Concerto for Orchestra. He wanted me to go back with him to the apartment to go over the Sibelius Fourth, which I was doing at that time. He was then living on Seventy-ninth Street and Park Avenue. In the apartment he said, 'I'm too tired.' He looked utterly finished, physically and emotionally spent, literally at the end of his rope. He went upstairs and washed up. Forty-five minutes later he reappeared washed, combed, half-dressed. Then we had a light supper. I think it was bouillon. As we sat there I watched the lines smooth out in his face. 'Excuse me,' he said. He went to look at the Carter piece again. The car was in front of the apartment house. He put on his frock coat. We drove across the park to Philharmonic Hall. I got out of the car first, and was able to see him get out of the car. There he was completely reborn. I was absolutely astonished by this pulling together. It was the first time I had ever observed the phoenix syndrome, rising from the ashes, so to speak. He had used up everything. Then he rose again: From physical and mental ruin he rose again."

A few weeks later, with Chapin on hand, Bernstein began to film the Verdi Requiem in London. This was the first project in what was to begin a virtually new career for him. In 1968 Bernstein added Robert Lantz, a theatrical and literary agent, to his group of advisers. In 1986 Lantz said, "It struck me as totally insane that an artist spends weeks doing *Rosenkavalier*, conducting six sold-out performances, and that if there is any record at all, it is a phonograph record. That is immensely wasteful. Wouldn't we be thrilled with even a flawed reproduction of

Duse, Bernhardt, or Paganini? With the progress we have seen in sound and tape, my conviction was, and I told this to Lenny, that concerts, opera, and theater should take on whole other forms that will make it possible for them to be seen and heard on cable television and cassettes." In a memo Lantz advised Bernstein that he should rarely conduct unless there was a recording involved, and he went even further: that a film should also be part of any project he undertook. People in the classical music world explain that this arrangement meant that every time Bernstein brought down his baton, he would get paid three ways: for the concert, the recording, and the film. Chapin says that Bernstein was motivated, at least in part, by the desire to have continue the security he had enjoyed with the Philharmonic post. Lantz impressed Bernstein with the need to make inroads into the videocassette market, which he correctly predicted would burgeon.

Financing the Requiem became Chapin's first order of business as director of Amberson Productions. He went to Roger Stevens and Robert Whitehead, two theatrical producers who had put money into *West Side Story*. He told them that the singers were to include Martina Arroyo, Franco Corelli, and Ruggero Raimondi and that the setting would be St. Paul's Cathedral in London. Humphrey Burton would be brought in from the BBC to direct the project, which would cost somewhere between eighty-five thousand and ninety-five thousand dollars. After some difficult negotiations with a British union, the principal figures signed a contract that filled fewer than two pages, partly because no lawyers were involved in the negotiations.

The Verdi Requiem film began an annual series of films of Bernstein conducting orchestras all over the world. He recorded Mahler's Second Symphony with the London Symphony Orchestra in Ely Cathedral and *Das Lied von der Erde* with the Israel Philharmonic in Tel Aviv. But most of his activity centered in Vienna with the Vienna Philharmonic. There he recorded all the other Mahler symphonies, the Beethoven, Brahms, and Schumann symphonies, and more.

What this activity translated into was Bernstein's partial ownership of the rights to all his musical activities. In fact Krawitz believes that one of the reasons he walked out on Zeffirelli's film project was because be couldn't own it. Krawitz does not criticize Bernstein for this: "It is the only genuine defense that an artist has in a tough world. Charlie Chaplin and Irving Berlin set up their own companies. They were doing their families a good turn."

Bernstein did his family a good turn, too. Eventually he even set up a corporation called JALNI (an acronym composed of his children's initials) to give them a certain percentage of the profits his ventures earned. Emotionally Bernstein's life was more complicated. Felicia accompanied Bernstein on his 1970 trip to London. It was then that he told a group of friends that he loved his wife so much that he didn't know how he could get along without her. Then he spent two and a half weeks in Rome without her. While there, he participated in a homosexual orgy arranged by an American. During his stay in Rome, Bernstein was pursued by Edmund Purdom's girlfriend. Her pursuit proved fruitless.

In Rome Bernstein was joined by BBC director Humphrey Burton, who brought the Requiem film with him. Bernstein watched it with a group of friends that included Elsa Respighi, widow of composer Ottorino Respighi, and Phillip Ramey, a composer who was then working for him. Ramey says that as he watched the movie, Bernstein put his head in his hands, buried it in Ramey's shoulder, and actually used the word "grotesque" to describe "the way I carry on up there." Whether or not Bernstein is aware of what he is doing on the podium, it was this translation of feelings into gestures that attracted many of the Viennese musicians who played with him. Hans Novak, a first violinist with the Vienna Philharmonic, has said that this trait above all else "opened all the doors with us."

Amberson's second project was to be a film made in commemoration of the two hundredth anniversary of Beethoven's birth. The Vienna State Opera had invited Bernstein to conduct *Fidelio* in the Theater an der Wein, where Beethoven had conducted its premiere. Conducting this opera, Bernstein stood on the very same spot where Beethoven had stood when *he* had conducted his only opera. That fact provoked an emotional reaction. Lantz was there. He says on opening night Bernstein experienced the worst case of what seemed to be emphysema he had ever witnessed. "His wheezing was louder than the music," Lantz recalls.

Nevertheless the music was heard, and while some Viennese critics pointed out the ways in which Bernstein had departed from tradition, most of them celebrated those departures. One wrote, "All at once the entire opera came alive with human values." Several American critics were there. In 1986, Leighton Kerner of *The Village Voice* remembered Bernstein's 1970 *Fidelio* as one of the "most remarkable performances I have ever heard. A lot of the dialogue was cut and the score swept swiftly along. It was a most glorious event." Ten days later, on June 30, 1970, Bernstein received the Gold Medal for services rendered to the republic, one of the highest Austrian civilian decorations.

At this time Bernstein was also planning concerts with the Vienna Philharmonic and thought he could put everything together in a ninety-minute television biography. What he produced combined parts of *Fidelio*, the Ninth Symphony, and the First Piano Concerto with himself as conductor and piano soloist. *Times* critic Harold Schonberg's attack on him ten years before for doing both in this concerto apparently did not inhibit him then. Peter Gradenwitz writes, "The European critics were full of admiration and appreciation of Bernstein, unlike Schonberg and the American critics," and goes on to say that these European writers particularly held him in awe "as an interpreter of the classical and romantic repertory which the American critics have always denied him."

Biographical material was woven into the movie. The film showed the many houses in which Beethoven had lived, as well as the parks, the woods, and the streets in his neighborhoods. It also showed the stage and rehearsal rooms for *Fidelio*, the Vienna Philharmonic in the Musikverein with Bernstein conducting and playing, and the Ninth Symphony being performed in the Konzerthaus in a special set designed by Oliver Smith, whose association with Bernstein went back to *Fancy Free*. Smith also designed and lit the Requiem at St. Paul's.

Chapin tried to get CBS to pay for this film. When CBS did nothing, despite indications that it might be interested in the project, Bernstein was pushed into calling CBS's boss, William Paley, himself, a kind of confrontation he has always been reluctant to engage in. The money did come through but the film still didn't get on the air during the Beethoven anniversary year.

Besides the Beethoven goings-on, the general pandemonium that accompanies Bernstein everywhere was of course present then, too. Wolfgang Wagner showed up to try to persuade him to conduct a new

Tristan und Isolde at Bayreuth. Topol arrived to try to reactivate Bernstein's interest in his plan to do an opera based on Brecht's *Caucasian Chalk Circle.* Directors of La Scala came to tell Bernstein he could conduct anything he wished at the Milan opera house. Chapin reports Zeffirelli sent a variety of emissaries to "keep up a relentless attack about *Brother Sun, Sister Moon.*" Marcel Prawy, artistic director of the Vienna Volksoper; Peter Weiser, director of the Konzerthaus; Rudolf Gamsjaeger of the Musikverein; Rolf Gintel of the Vienna State Opera; representatives of any number of government ministries—all came hoping that Bernstein would do something for them.

While Bernstein was juggling all of these people, his lawyer, Abraham Friedman, was working out a contract with Leo Kirch, head of an entertainment conglomerate called Unitel, based in Munich, so Bernstein would never have to ask for money again the way he had importuned Paley for the Beethoven film. Chapin reports that Bernstein showed him the contract and asked him if "it is all right." Chapin said he thought it was a good deal. Bernstein said, "I feel awkward signing a German contract." Then he signed it. The relationship still exists, and the collaboration has produced at least thirty films.

In a brochure published in 1985 called "Leonard Bernstein: The Television Work," director Humphrey Burton wrote:

> The Unitel production company in Munich has invested substantial sums in these productions. Each public concert in Vienna is filmed twice, with Deutsche Grammophon recording the sound digitally. Bernstein insists on doing everything live, so even the retakes are done with an audience. Each concert uses as much film stock as a feature film, with as many as six blimped [silenced] Arriflex cameras running through all the concert.
>
> Quite apart from deciding what to look at with the six cameras placed startegically in and around the orchestra, the director has the mind-boggling task of organizing the script so that each camera can change film magazines in turn three or four times in each symphony. By comparison, television production seems like child's play, and much less intrusive for the public in the hall; but the wider range of the camera

angles and the precision of cutting offered by the film make it our preferred method, despite the heat of the film lights and the occasional clink of soundproofed cameras being unlocked, preparatory to reloading.

The Unitel contract gave Bernstein what he wanted both in financial gain and in technological excellence. But it probably also provided a less quantifiable but nevertheless crucial gratification. Remarks he made to Peter Gradenwitz about experiences in Germany in 1948 illuminate this aspect of his business deal in Munich.

Bernstein told Gradenwitz that a few years after the war, he had wanted to visit two displaced persons camps, Feldafing and Landsberg. He said that in order to do so, he had been required to "follow the direction of the American military, under whose command everything had to go, and conduct a concert with the State Opera Orchestra in Munich."

The concert Bernstein conducted took place on May 11, 1948, in the Prince Regenten Theater and included Robert Schumann's Symphony No. 2, which he had first heard conducted by Mitropoulos, Roy Harris's Symphony No. 3, which Koussevitzky had introduced him to, and Ravel's Piano Concerto in G, which Mitropoulos had conducted and played while Bernstein was still at Harvard.

Bernstein said that after conducting the State Opera Orchestra in Munich as payment, he was allowed to visit the two camps. "In 1948," he told Gradenwitz,

> I went to Landsberg and directed a small orchestra of 16 musicians, all that was left of an orchestra of 65 musicians. All the others had been killed. They had kept the name Dachau Symphony Orchestra. The survivors played for the people in the camp. One cannot imagine how moving that was. Of course I could only conduct music they had managed to save. Strangely enough, among these works was Gershwin's *Rhapsody in Blue.* I played it twice in one day on a piano that was out of tune. One performance was for 5,000 people in Feldafing; the other for 5,000 in Landsberg.

It was incredible but in both concerts the first three rows

were filled with members of the former Nazi orchestra from Munich. This whole orchestra—about 100 people—had come with their director, a woman, who had conducted the orchestra throughout the whole Nazi period. They almost went down on their knees. They brought flowers and put roses on the podium. [The conductor] herself kneeled down, a robust woman who had lived through the Hitler era. She said such a Schumann she had never heard as the Schumann I conducted in Munich. "Oh, the days of Bruno Walter have returned."

This was a kind of expiation for them—like Yom Kippur. They had become my slaves and wanted to show their regrets. And you have to understand they had come to listen to a small orchestra whose membership included only one viola, one clarinet, no bassoons…

This was May 1948. The State of Israel had just been formed. When I told the musicians I was on my way to Israel they called out, "Take us with you." These poor people sat in those detention camps and it went to my heart. I succeeded in placing three of the musicians; one of them, Ein Chaim, then 16, is still with the Philadelphia Orchestra. I was given a gift— a very moving present—of the clothing of a concentration camp inmate, one with the typical prisoner's stripes. It had a number on it of the man who had organized the orchestra. I can only remember that his first name was Walter. He played the flute. They had killed him. His uniform lay around for years and had a strong unpleasant smell, but the gesture touched my heart and I took it with me to New York. I had it cleaned five times but the stench wouldn't go out of it. It was an invaluable present but someone threw it away. I wanted to keep it because it came out of the guts of the people.

One of Bernstein's children says that their mother did indeed throw out an old uniform their father had brought back from a concentration camp.

In 1969 two black musicians filed a complaint
with the New York State Commission on Human Rights that appeared
incomprehensible to those aware of Bernstein's leftish political posture.
Earl Madison, cellist, and Arthur Davis, bassist, charged him and the
New York Philharmonic with discriminatory practices against blacks.

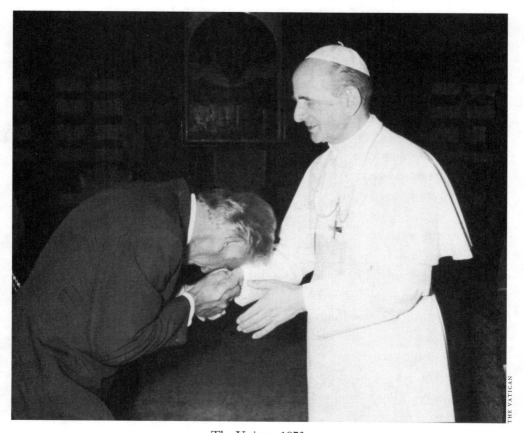

THE VATICAN

The Vatican, 1973
*In 1971, conductor Maurice Peress visited Bernstein in Vienna. "It was Passover.
I asked, 'What's a Jewish boy like you doing writing a mass?'
'We have to educate ourselves,' he said. 'We have to learn more about it.'"*

This complaint reverberated back to 1956. In that year, Douglas Pugh, a black man who had graduated from Columbia University in 1951 and who was then serving as industrial relations secretary to the New York chapter of the Urban League, headed an investigation into the job status of black professional musicians. A questionnaire was sent to black musicians in the metropolitan area to secure information on their education, professional training, experience, and employment. Interviews were held not only with black musicians but with whites who were performers, conductors, and union officials. In a twenty-one page survey issued in May 1958, Pugh described rampant discrimination in everything from symphony orchestras to studio bands in radio and television. "The most glaring examples of job exclusion based on race and color exist," the report began, "in New York's five major orchestras. (1) The Philharmonic Symphony Society of New York has never employed a Negro professional musician. (2) The Metropolitan Opera Orchestra has never employed a Negro professional musician...."

The report condemned the commercial world, too. From 1956 to 1958, the period when the industry had been under investigation, 26 Broadway musicals employed 650 musicians, only 14 of whom were black. Those 14 were hired when the principal performer was a celebrated black, such as Lena Horne, or Sammy Davis, Jr., who insisted on an integrated backup. In other words the entire picture was a racist one; it wasn't just in art music.

The Pugh report noted that the Symphony of the Air had been something of an exception in 1956, the year when its conductor was Bernstein. It then had on its roster three black players: a violist, a flutist, and a timpanist. Pugh wrote that this had come about at the instigation of Howard Taubman, who had pressed for the hiring of blacks in an article in the *Times*. Pugh went on to say that these blacks had been let go the following year because of the strong objections of some members of the orchestra.

The report was first leaked to the press in the fall of 1958 when *Jet*, a black magazine, ran this opening paragraph: "The long-hidden Urban League study of the status of Negro musicians in the New York metropolitan area charges that they are jimcrowed out of lucrative jobs in symphony, philharmonic, pit orchestras and in the radio and television industry." Other papers picked up the story and pressure was placed on orchestras to begin to hire black musicians.

New York was not alone in its bias, but its record was worse than some other cities': In 1958 the Boston Symphony Orchestra had on its roster Ortiz Walton, bass; the Cleveland Orchestra, Donald White, cello; and the Los Angeles Philharmonic, Henry Lewis, bass. When Bernstein assumed his post in New York, he invited Sanford Allen, a black violinist, to play in the summer stadium concerts. Allen said yes and did that a second year. During this period he auditioned twice for a place in the orchestra itself, but when a third audition was offered, Allen turned it down. Then the Philharmonic invited him to become a regular member. At the time the complaint was filed by Earl Madison and Arthur Davis, Allen was still the only black in the New York Philharmonic, and he was still playing in the second violin section.

Perhaps the most provocative statement Pugh made in his report came at the bottom of page four:

> Red baiting or using the communist smear technique is one of the most onerous means used against liberal white conductors who are willing to employ qualified musicians in pit orchestras of Broadway musicals.... The Industrial Relations Department interviewed several white conductors who stated that this red smear campaign ensued after they hired Negro musicians.

If this was true of pit ensembles, it would surely have applied to symphony orchestras. The troubles the Symphony of the Air experienced with the House Committee on Un-American Activities in the mid-1950s may have been exacerbated by the orchestra's employment of three black musicians. In light of this it is understandable that any number of white conductors who might have preferred to behave differently thought twice about hiring blacks, for fear of jeopardizing their careers.

In the 1969 hearings before the state commission, Bernstein said that at auditions for Madison and Davis, the orchestra had permitted both musicians to play in final auditions though they had not passed preliminaries. He said this privilege had been granted precisely because of their race. It does seem peculiar to have encouraged these musicians by letting them compete until the bitter end knowing they had no chance at all.

Madison and Davis offered to play behind a screen against any or all of the orchestra's cellists and bassists; all they wanted was their anonymity. "We have everything to lose," Madison said. "They have nothing." Yet that opportunity was denied them. Bernstein told the commission that no one to whom he had ever spoken had been satisfied with the behind-the-screen method. He said that an audition provided an opportunity not only to hear the music but to observe the musician's "physical technique." He cited as an example a violinist's bowing technique, which could reveal a lack of endurance not apparent if the musician could not be seen as well as heard.

The *New York Law Journal* story of the commission's decision ran under this headline: PHILHARMONIC ORDERED TO END RACIAL BIAS. The subhead of the commission's report was specific: "Pattern of bias found in hiring of substitutes." But *The New York Times* defended the orchestra, quoting its manager Carlos Moseley as being "gratified that the hearings had confirmed that the Philharmonic had not discriminated in its audition and hiring procedures."

The complainants, Madison and Davis, actually lost their case. Bernstein had contended that there was no objective system for scoring artists, that the qualities looked for were elusive. He said that they involved the musician's "sense of phrase, his sense of articulation, where he breathes, how he grasps the constellation of notes, the warmth that emanates from him, the rhythmic understanding that emanates from him, plus many things that are indescribable."

Bernstein's words are unarguable, but they do not explain why so few blacks have made it in music performance in New York. Whitney M. Young, then director of the National Urban League, remarked:

> It is shameful for a major cultural institution, one that gives concerts in a beautiful new hall financed by public subscription, to cling to a color bar while other fields are in the process of discarding it.... Behind the red and gold facade of our major cultural institutions is the rotten stench of racism.

Bernstein did not cover himself with glory in this case. Insensitivity characterized his manner. He arrived very tanned in a blue blazer, telling anyone who would listen that he had interrupted his work with Zeffirelli on a film just to appear there that day. Then Martin Oppenheimer, counsel for the Philharmonic, said in what was reported to be the most unctuous of tones that the complainants accused "not only the institution itself but the musical director … one of the country's renowned humanitarians … a man who had written eloquently about it." Bernstein was excused from the proceedings on the first day.

The complainants and some of those who testified in their behalf suffered later. Most of them left New York. Arthur Davis is probably the angriest—he started over from scratch and now has a doctorate in psychology. Davis attributes his difficulties in finding a post in music after the hearings to Bernstein's vindictiveness, to the conductor's "wanting to make an example of me and show any black man that if he were to do what I did, he would suffer in exactly the same way." It is hard to believe that this is true. More likely the people who control the jobs in symphony and Broadway theater orchestras reacted in a predictable way to protect their power.

In any event the experience probably caused Bernstein some pain, for in addition to the conflicts it posed between humanitarian and pragmatic considerations, there were also his friendships with such celebrated blacks as entertainer Sammy Davis, Jr., and author James Baldwin, as well as his personal involvements with black musicians who were less well known. In *Philharmonic*, the 1970 *roman à clef* that Bernstein has cited as a key to aspects of his life, the climax comes in a 1969 hearing before the Commission on Human Rights that is obviously based on the Madison-Davis case. In the novel the crisis is heightened when the conductor's wife tries to bribe a black former lover of her husband's who wanted a post in the orchestra by offering him a job in another orchestra providing he keeps silent about the sexual liaison between them.

In the 1930s and 1940s, Bernstein was involved in all kinds of left-wing political activities that would have been compatible with a strongly pro-black position. But in 1958, when he took over the Philharmonic, he became an employee of an elitist organization where policies were firmly controlled by George E. Judd, associate managing director, and Joseph De Angelis, orchestra manager, neither of whom was a compassionate man. So Bernstein's humanitarian impulses were muzzled for the next ten years. The extent of his muzzling can, to some degree, be illuminated by looking at what he did during his only sabbatical year.

On July 13, 1964, almost as soon as he was free, Bernstein gave a fund-raising party for the Legal Defense Fund of the National Association for the Advancement of Colored People. Some 600 people came to a jazz concert on the lawn of his Dunham Road estate in Fairfield, Connecticut, and 120 children from a nearby summer camp were also invited. Dizzy Gillespie played. So did John Mehegan, the jazz musician who taught at Juilliard and to whom Bernstein had been attached in the mid-1940s. Alex Bernstein, then nine, identifies the party as a wonderful and memorable event in a rich and complicated childhood. In 1985 Gay Mehegan talked about the day: "The house was on the top of Greenfield Hill, a beautiful neighborhood. It was a big white colonial with porticos in southern plantation style. A Ping-Pong table was on the lawn. Everything looked lovely. All the surroundings showed Felicia's touch. She was thin, quiet, shy, the prototype of the long-suffering, supportive wife. John and I played duo piano. We had to learn all the songs from *West Side Story*, even those that were hardly known.

"The party took place entirely in the garden. Leonard received in a red bikini. Felicia did not join us. She appeared only once on the top of the hill, then went back into the house. I could not understand why she didn't come down, why I wasn't even introduced to her. But now that I know more, I assume it was because John was there."

On March 25, 1965, the night before Martin Luther King, Jr., led a march of ten thousand people to Montgomery, Alabama, a show there featured such personalities as Sammy Davis, Jr., Harry Belafonte, Ossie Davis, Billy Eckstine, Leon Bibb, Anthony Perkins, Shelley Winters, Mike Nichols and Elaine May, and Peter, Paul and Mary singing "Blowing in the Wind." Bernstein talked to the crowd. He apologized for not bringing the entire Philharmonic with him but explained that "there isn't room for them."

"Enough room" was not what kept the Philharmonic away that night. Bernstein was the music director of an organization whose priorities had nothing to do with the rights of blacks. Clearly between 1958 and 1969, Bernstein's personal ideology came into conflict with career demands, and the career demands won.

Right after the state commission hearings, Bernstein was host for a fund-raising party for a group of members of the militant Black Panther organization. It was a source of great controversy at the time and was the subject of a renowned article by Tom Wolfe in *New York* magazine, in which Wolfe coined the term "radical chic" as the title and the operating idea of the article. If what Bernstein's friends say is true—that his promiscuous homosexuality of the late years was a reaction to the inhibitions he imposed on himself during much of his marriage—then perhaps this party was a reaction to the inhibitions imposed on him during the Philharmonic years.

For nine months a group of Panthers had been held on such charges as plotting to kill policemen and conspiring to dynamite department stores, police precinct houses, railroad facilities, and the New York Botanical Gardens. Later arson and possession of weapons were added to the original charges. All of the accused were destitute. Ten were held on $100,000 bail, two on $50,000, and one on $25,000.

In January 1970, coincident with his performances of *Cavalleria Rusticana* and just before a guest engagement conducting the New York Philharmonic, Bernstein held what he later called a "meeting" to raise money for the Panther defense fund. A number of modest contributions, plus his own pledge of the "four-figure fee" he was to get from his next concert, plus an anonymous donation of seventy-five hundred dollars brought the total raised to ten thousand. The smaller contributors included film director Otto Preminger, lyricist Sheldon Harnick, and Broadway composer Burton Lane.

In an introduction to *The Purple Decade*, a collection of Wolfe's essays published by Farrar, Straus and Giroux in 1982, Joe David Bellamy claims that the purpose of "Radical Chic" was to put forth the notion that "the ostensible desire for social justice and the display of generosity involved had somewhat less to do with the proceedings than had the secret motive, which was the longing for the aristocrats to feel in its fullest degree the heady sensation of 'How chic we are!'"

More than likely, at least part of Bernstein's motive was to obliterate the impression he had given by his behavior at the commission's hearings and to regain his earlier liberal image. At the time of all the excitement about the party and the article, Bernstein told friends that the idea had, in fact, been Felicia's, but that, because he agreed with it, he didn't want to redirect any blame onto his wife. Felicia's friends recall that she had been aroused by a story that held that Panther Lee Berry, an epileptic, had been beaten and denied medication by the police. There is no reason to doubt Felicia's motives.

Bernstein explained to the press that he was engaged in a fight for civil rights, not for the philosophy held by the Panthers. Still he became the object of a severe attack. On January 15, Charlotte Curtis ridiculed the event in a story in *The New York Times*. The next day the *Times* published an editorial taking Bernstein to task for doing what he had done. A week later Curtis ran still another story. By this time it had been picked up by publications all over the country.

In 1970, blacks and Jews were pitted against each other as they had never been before. In the 1930s and 1940s, there had been something of a communal feeling between them that derived from their shared status as minority groups. But by the late 1960s, blacks and Jews often were seen more as enemies than friends. Bernstein's multitude of Jewish fans were incredulous. Many felt betrayed. The Panthers were not like Martin Luther King, Ralph Bunche, or Whitney Young, who were nonviolent. The Panther movement talked violence, and occasionally used it. It was probably inevitable for Bernstein to find resentment against him not only in New York but abroad; when he went to Israel and London in the months that followed, he was assailed by the press in both places.

A few days after the party, Bernstein invited Michael Tilson Thomas, then in Boston, to a performance of an all-Wagner program he was conducting with the New York Philharmonic. Here is Thomas's description of that evening: "There was all this furor. Pickets were all around the hall. There was CORE, the NAACP, the JDL, B'nai B'rith, and so on. Everyone had problems with what he did. Bernstein had not been Jewish enough. He had been too liberal. He was not black enough. When he came on stage there was a great cheering from the audience. It was a great concert. There was a huge ovation. We went out to dinner afterwards: some friends, Lenny and Felicia, Nina and myself. We were surrounded by motorcycle cops. It looked like something from *Mission Impossible*. We waited in the car on the loading docks. Then iron bars lifted and we sailed away. We went to Trader Vic's. At the restaurant Lenny began to expound on the party. 'I was just trying to get people to talk to one another about their concept of justice, to air their gripes. It was so misunderstood. I've been threatened and the children can't go to school.' He was going on and on like this. Then he opened a fortune cookie and read, 'It takes brains to be a real fool.' We all roared with laughter."

Whoever wrote the fortune in that cookie and pointed it in Bernstein's direction should stay in the business, for any number of remarks he made during the party seemed to have been pretty foolish indeed. Here is some of the dialogue:

> PANTHER "FIELD MARSHAL" DONALD COX: If business won't give full employment, then we must take the means of production into our own hands.
> BERNSTEIN: I dig absolutely.
> COX: I can't blueprint social change for you. The resistance put to us dictates strategy.
> BERNSTEIN: You mean you've got to wing it.

Bernstein claims he was misquoted a great deal in relation to this event, but the exchange between him and Cox appeared in both the *New York Post* and the *Times* on January 15, although they may have had a single source. The aftermath of the Black Panther event brought pro and con arguments that continued in the press for many months. On January 22, James A. Wechsler complained in an editorial in the *Post* about the caricatures that were proliferating: "It did not take long for [William F. Buckley, Jr.] to review with joyous malice this encounter between the two worlds as further proof of the incurable masochism of a certain species of white who bids the Panther to devour him in his luxurious lair."

As late as September 1970 Jack Anderson wrote in *The Washington Post* of the grand contempt felt by the Panthers for those white liberals who raise money for them. Anderson claimed that Panther leaders had by then met with Arab guerrillas and

> made common cause with them. Coincidentally, Panther
> rhetoric has become increasingly anti-Semitic. A favorite
> Panther slogan: "Off (meaning Kill) the Zionist imperialists."
> They have joked roguishly that they will use the contributions
> of such eminent Jews as Leonard Bernstein to do the work of
> Al Fatah in this country.

One would think that after causing what he described as a crucial misunderstanding here, particularly in relation to the Jews, Bernstein would have approached his next big project with a great deal of care. Yet what that project turned out to be was the composition of a Roman Catholic mass. As his departure from the New York Philharmonic liberated him to become a radical, so the death of his father liberated him enough from his Jewish roots to permit him to compose a Catholic mass. Later he apologized to an audience at Brandeis for doing precisely that. In any event the stir he created by the choice of his next work, and the way he carried out that choice, caused him to be misunderstood yet again. In 1971 Bernstein no longer had access to the press department of the New York Philharmonic, and his worsening relations with CBS Records made it impossible for him to ask it for help. So he called on publicist Margaret Carson to answer all the questions that poured in and to assure all who doubted it that he was a profoundly religious man.

Bernstein's *Mass*, subtitled "A Theater Piece for Singers, Players and Dancers," was commissioned to open the Opera House at the Kennedy Center in Washington. For this occasion, Bernstein composed a work for more than two hundred performers. The orchestra was divided in two: One part was in the pit and consisted of strings, percussion, and two organs. On the stage there were the other instruments including brass, woodwinds, electric guitars, and a variety of keyboards. A chorus of "street people" was made up of singers and dancers while the choir pews were filled with a sixty-member chorus dressed in robes and placed upstage on both sides of the house. Dancers in hooded robes played acolytes assisting the key figure of the Celebrant.

Bernstein's *Mass* takes its exterior form from the Catholic mass and moves from the "Kyrie Eleison" to the "Agnus Dei." Between the traditional sections, the composer has interpolated music that runs the gamut from echoes of Shostakovich and Orff to rock, folk, and blues. *Mass* was staged by top Broadway people: Sets were by Oliver Smith, choreography by Alvin Ailey, costumes by Frank Thompson, lighting by Gilbert V. Hemsley, Jr. Roger Stevens, then director of the Kennedy Center, was also the producer of *Mass*. He negotiated a contract in which there were no fees to Bernstein. The composer, however, retained all the rights.

Mass was conducted by Maurice Peress, who had been an assistant conductor to Bernstein at the Philharmonic. In 1971, the year of the world premiere of *Mass*, Peress was conductor of both the Austin and the Corpus Christi, Texas, symphony orchestras. "When I came into music," Peress said, "a conductor was a European who played the piano and didn't have a Jewish name. My early experience was in jazz and with the violin. I was an excellent trumpet player and, until I was thirty, I supported my family playing trumpet. When Bernstein was appointed musical director of the New York Philharmonic, it was like a shot of lightning to me. Here was an American who did popular music, here was a Jew. Suddenly a path I thought had been closed forever became available. That fact was brought home dramatically when Stefan Bauer-Mengelberg, who lived above me in a little house in Sullivan Street in Greenwich Village, was given the post of assistant conductor. It was then I wrote a letter to the Philharmonic and one year later I was given the same post."

Almost ten years after that Peress visited Bernstein in Vienna. "In the spring of 1971 I was conducting at Regensburg, Germany. Lenny was staying in an apartment at the back of the Sacher Hotel in Vienna, the same apartment in which [Richard] Strauss and Mahler had stayed. On the piano was a piece called 'Thank You.' This was the first time I heard anything at all about *Mass*. I had no concept of what the piece was in the context of the whole work. 'What is it?" I asked. Lenny said, 'It doesn't exist yet.' What he meant was that we shouldn't say anything at all lest something should go wrong. The work was so beautiful. Yet Lenny was so shy. That is the vulnerable side of him.

"It was Passover. I asked. 'What's a Jewish boy like you doing writing a mass?' 'We have to educate ourselves,' he said. 'We have to learn more about it.' That summer Lenny did study with some Jesuits in Los

Angeles. Later on, when I became involved with the work, I found Hebraic and Greek traditions in it. Gordon Davidson, who directed, and I both went to mass school. That was to be comfortable with it. I had conducted Mozart masses and so on. But I had no idea of how theatrical this work would be. Lenny chose to do a mass because of its connection to the Kennedy family and its universality. The magic of this particular mass is best felt in the theater; it exerts a tremendous effect on everyone on stage and in the audience. It is such a complex work. It is one of the most important works of the twentieth century and this is said by someone who has conducted the Mahler Eighth any number of times."

The story line was devised by Bernstein and the manner of collaboration echoed what had gone on with *West Side Story*, in that Bernstein first thought he could compose both music and lyrics and then sought for help. This time he approached Stephen Schwartz, composer and lyricist of *Godspell*, a hit Broadway rock musical, and Schwartz helped him write the words of some songs. The plot begins with a young guitarist making his entrance singing "A Simple Song":

> *Sing God a simple song*
> *Lauda, laudē…*
> *Make it up as you go along*
> *Lauda, laudē…*
> *Sing like you like to sing*
> *God loves all simple things*
> *For God is the simplest of all.**

Gradually the guitar strummer becomes a priestly Celebrant by virtue of the sacred vestments that are placed on him. When he tries to give holy communion, the people shout out against him, attacking God for not preventing war. In response the Celebrant smashes the holy vessels, and in doing so, releases the symbolic body and blood of Christ. Surprised that the color is not red, the Celebrant describes it as a "sort of dirty brown." What follows is a Bernstein operatic "mad scene" in which the Celebrant dances, according to *Time* magazine, "on the altar like a curate on a bad LSD trip." Lashing out at the people, he tears off his vestments, giving up his authority and turning it back on the people themselves.

---

* © *Amberson Enterprises (G. Schirmer).*

Bernstein began to conceive his *Mass* in the late 1960s, when young people believed that drugs, sex, and rock-and-roll music would save the world. The four-day drugs-and-music festival at Woodstock in 1969 came to be viewed as the symbol of the period. That was also the time when some fifty thousand people protesting the Vietnam War marched on the Pentagon. It was also when Nixon ordered the invasion of Cambodia, provoking rioting on college campuses and the shootings at Kent State University. In its most apparent meaning, Bernstein's *Mass* supported the demonstrators and rioters, telling them that they were right and should take matters into their own hands when the authorities were evil and didn't agree with what they thought.

To agree with Bernstein on such issues is a sine qua non for having anything at all to do with him, professionally or socially. In his last formal words as president of Yale University, A. Bartlett Giamatti deplored the tyranny of group self-righteousness and called those who practiced it "terrorists of the mind." Bernstein is just such a terrorist of the mind.

In 1986 Peress talked about the Celebrant: "At first he is an innocent. He is Everyman. Then he becomes the Priest. Ultimately he faces the people. He tears his clothes off and has a midlife crisis. The people all lie there as he pours his guts out. Then he slams the door. He says, 'Fuck you!' That was the plan Lenny had and one he told us about while we were working on the show. He had a vision of Nixon and Congress sitting out there absolutely dumbstruck. The point of the piece is that the Celebrant suddenly abandons us, leaving us to bring peace to ourselves and to the world. I wanted to tell Lenny he couldn't do that. It was an antiwar piece. Nixon was in the White House. People were scared."

But Peress didn't have to worry about Nixon because J. Edgar Hoover sent Attorney General John Mitchell and presidential assistant Robert Haldeman a memo on July 12, 1971, telling them what Bernstein had in his mind. The memo appears in *The Anderson Papers*, published by Random House in 1973. Hoover wrote that this mass would include antiwar elements and that Daniel Berrigan had been asked to write the Latin verse. Bernstein had, in fact, consulted with Berrigan on the text. Hoover warned that "important government officials, perhaps even the President, are expected to attend this ceremony and it is anticipated that they will applaud the composition without recognizing the true meaning of the words."

The Black Panther episode had alerted Hoover to Bernstein's ways. A little more than a year before this memo, just after the Panther meeting, the FBI director issued a report in which Bernstein was criticized: "An organization which stockpiles illegal weapons," he wrote on March 5, 1970,

> trains in guerrilla warfare and seeks confrontation with enforcement officers for the expressed purpose of killing them is certainly in violation of the law. Yet, when lawful process is applied to bring the Panthers under control, their cries of genocide and harassment are seemingly accepted without question.

Nixon did not attend *Mass*. In absenting himself he was spared not only an attack on himself, but on the authority of the church, any church. Take, for example, only two of the verses that come between the "Mea Culpa," accompanied by finger snapping like that of *West Side Story*, and the "Gloria":

> *If you asked me to love you on a bed of spice*
> *Now that might be nice*
> *Once or twice*
> *But don't look for sacraments or sacrifice*
> *They're not worth the price*
>
> *It's easy to keep the flair in your affair*
> *Your body's always ready, but your soul's not there*
> *Don't be nonplussed*
> *Come love, come lust*
> *It's so easy when you just don't care …*[*]

It is hard to believe Bernstein's attack was directed solely at Nixon and not also at the God John Kennedy had worshiped—in other words, Jesus Christ. As he had railed against the God of the Jews in *Kaddish*, so he railed against Jesus Christ in *Mass*. The composer himself has said the one work led directly to the other.

---

[*] © *Amberson Enterprises (G. Schirmer).*

Bernstein is reported to have kissed each of the two hundred participants, and while he was doing this, the applause did continue. But there can be little doubt that there were some in the hall who did understand the words as well as the highly secular music that accompanied this *Mass* and preferred to sit on their hands. Maria DePasquale attended the congressional performance the night before the public opening. "The audience was in a state of shock," she recalled in 1985. "My aunt, Olga Koussevitzky, was good friends with the Kennedys. She had always been prejudiced in favor of Leonard but she was more than a little stunned by the harshness, the sacrilegious aspects of the work. We were sitting with Margaret Heckler [then a member of Congress from Massachusetts], and she found the piece sacrilegious, too. What Bernstein said with his *Mass* was that love and friendship were all that was necessary to solve the problems of the world."

In addition to being an attack on all authority, the work is also an attack on the authority the composer-conductor himself had become. Bernstein talked to Peter Davis about this in an interview that appeared in *High Fidelity* magazine. He spoke of the moment when the Celebrant smashes the holy vessels and there is only silence on stage:

> There are 160 people sitting there, none of whom can breathe, make a move, or take the next step in life because of the fraction that occurred. There has been a fraction of many things, of the vessels of the psyche, of this character, and of faith itself. At that point everyone has to look very deeply into himself to find that very thing he has destroyed.

When Davis asked what it is that finally heals them, Bernstein replied that it lies in the act of finding within one that part of oneself that has been destroyed.

> In other words, you cannot have a relationship with another person unless you have some kind of relationship with yourself, and with that indefinable "divine" element in yourself that we've been talking about—the quality the Celebrant possessed before he became priestly, gorgeously clad, powerful...."

Bernstein was talking about the qualities he believed he had had before he was clad with all the priestly vestments that Establishment music had imposed on him, while he was still singing "A Simple Song." Peress's remark about the Celebrant's experiencing a midlife crisis may be vulgar in the context of a sacred work, but it is psychologically astute. Once one sees the underpinnings of the piece to be autobiographical, many mysteries are solved. Through both music and text Bernstein traces the course of his life from the Greek, that is, the Mitropoulos influences Peress heard, through the composition of Broadway shows, to the inclusion of a kaddish. Then he moves on to his assumption of the robes of authority the New York Philharmonic conferred on him. By 1969 Bernstein felt he had lost the qualities that he himself had possessed before he came to be "priestly, gorgeously clad, powerful."

Virtually all the songs from *Mass* seem to be about his feelings. Here is one:

> *I don't know where to start*
> *There are scars I could show*
> *If I opened my heart*
> *But how far, Lord, but how far can I go?*
> *I don't know.* *

And another:

> *What I say I don't feel*
> *What I feel I don't show*
> *What I show isn't real*
> *What is real, Lord—I don't know*
> *No, no, no—I don't know.* *

---

* © *Amberson Enterprises (G. Schirmer).*

In 1986 Robert Lantz said, "When you are an
artist with a great success in New York you have conquered the
world. The same is not true of the artist in London, Paris, or Rome.
Here you are immediately on television. You become larger than life
to everyone around you, and that includes collaborators. American

"Through the years Bernstein has aroused controversy, though in the last decade
there has been little argument about his growth as a conductor,"
Harold Schonberg wrote in The New York Times *in 1971 on the occasion of*
Bernstein's one thousandth performance with the New York Philharmonic.
"...At this time it is only right to put reservations aside
and salute Bernstein for what he did and even for what he tried to do.
Bernstein was a figure that no conductor in history has matched."

success—the fame, money and power it brings—elevates people in such a way that it crushes those around them. Lenny is the sweetest, warmest man, but he is a conductor and therefore an autocrat. You can pretty well assume that he gets what he wants."

Over the years, what Bernstein wants has changed. When he composed *On the Town*, he wanted fun. With *Wonderful Town*, he wanted fun and money; he was then raising a family and had no steady conducting post. With *West Side Story*, he wanted fun, money, and Shakespeare in a work that would reflect leftist values, with its emphasis on oppressed youth in the United States. With *Candide* it was more complicated than the rest; here he was engaged in attacking McCarthy, thwarting Hellman, and distorting Voltaire's message so that it changed from a cynical one to the celebration of Bernstein's own solution: love.

Once Bernstein had the Philharmonic post, his priorities altered dramatically. He did not need the theater for fun or money. His new position gave him both. As he moved away from entertainment and toward pontification, Bernstein's failures grew, for he used his creativity more as an outlet for his ego than as a source for cash. That proved to be dangerous.

Mass was designed to launch the John F. Kennedy Center for the Performing Arts. The work was expected to celebrate the mass as Catholic ritual, John F. Kennedy as a president, and the Kennedy Center itself as a performance complex. Architect Edward Durell Stone had designed the sixty-eight-million-dollar center, and Jacqueline Kennedy Onassis had requested Bernstein to compose the opening piece, but she did not attend any performance of *Mass* during that first season. She said that a recent jostling in Poland, where she had gone to attend the funeral of her sister's husband, had made her reluctant to expose herself in public again. She did attend *Mass* the following year in Washington. If President Nixon or Mrs. Onassis had attended the opening night in 1971, Bernstein would have had to share the limelight. But because neither of them appeared and because the performers were all young and unknown, Bernstein was the central figure that night.

None of Bernstein's collaborators on *Mass* had the stature of Stephen Sondheim, who had written the lyrics for *West Side Story*, or of Max Goberman, who had conducted *West Side Story*, or Barbara Cook and Robert Rounseville, who had played the leading roles in *Candide*.

Stephen Schwartz, the lyricist, was twenty-three, and Bernstein came to him through Shirley Bernstein, who was Schwartz's agent. Alan Titus, who played the Celebrant, was twenty-five and a newcomer. Maurice Peress, the conductor, had been Bernstein's assistant at the Philharmonic ten years before and therefore in the position of something like a supplicant. Peress was conducting *Candide* on the west coast when Bernstein asked him to fill in for him in *Mass*. Bernstein had intended to conduct *Mass* himself, but because he was writing up to the last day he knew he needed someone to take over the conducting responsibilities and leave him time to finish.

To say Peress was in a position of some dependency does not suggest that he accepted Bernstein's behavior. Here is an incident that occurred in Manhattan's Ansonia Hotel during a rehearsal. "Lenny came down drunk," Peress says. "By this time the show was mine. It was in my body. I had two hundred fifty people under terrific control. Lenny started to put me down in front of the whole company. My reaction was 'If you have anything to say, say it to me, not to the whole company.' With that everyone applauded. Then Lenny came down into the pit, put his arms around me with 'Maurice, Maurice …' "

This was probably the first theater work in which Bernstein maintained total control. Before the last rehearsal he did capitulate to all those people who wanted considerable deletions to be made. But immediately afterward he said, "OK. You've had your fun. Now everything will be restored." Virtually all the critics annihilated him. Schonberg wrote a harsh review. " 'Mass' was a combination," he wrote, "of superficiality and pretentiousness, and the greatest melange of styles since the ladies magazine recipe for steak fried in peanut butter and marshmallow sauce."

Many Catholics found the work blasphemous. When it was performed in Cincinnati the city's archbishop, Paul F. Leibold, proclaimed:

> The main issue is that this production is a blatant sacrilege against all we hold sacred. Does any artist have the right to use elements of our central act of worship as a vehicle to present his theme? Indeed we may strongly disagree with his using our sacred instruments, prayers and rituals in any crude manner for any purpose. It seems to me that here is the real issue. I believe

that from this point of view the production is offensive to our Catholic sense and belief.

Important secular organizations registered disapproval. The Vienna State Opera, which had scheduled *Mass* for production, canceled its plans. But as with *Cavalleria Rusticana*, once the smoke cleared, Bernstein came out reasonably well. Rose F. Kennedy, a devout Catholic, signed a statement read at the National Press Club saying that after the initial shock, she supported what Bernstein had done. Even more important, Marcel Prawy booked *Mass* for the Vienna Volksoper and issued this statement: "We, in Vienna, where Beethoven, Brahms and Richard Strauss worked, consider Leonard Bernstein the greatest musician alive." If that were not enough, Pope Paul VI invited Bernstein to conduct for the commemoration of his tenth anniversary as pontiff, at the Vatican in 1973. Arrangements were made for Bernstein to lead the Newark Boys' Choir, a predominantly black ensemble, in Bach's Magnificat and his own *Chichester Psalms*. Bernstein brought his entire family, the maid Julia, his manager Harry Kraut, his publicist Margaret Carson, and Helen Coates with him on his visit to the pope. Finally, in 1981, in what seemed to be total vindication of the work, *Mass* became the first theater piece by an American-born composer to be produced at the Vienna State Opera.

A year after its world premiere, *Mass* was presented at the Met in New York. This time Donal Henahan reviewed it, and while he did not claim it was an enduring work of art, he did articulate a position somewhat removed from Schonberg's of the year before. " 'Mass' is one of those rare theatrical works," he wrote,

> that sum up their time and place, like it or not, and that is never a simple or useless thing to do…. The score is a minor miracle of skillful mixing, mortising together folksy ballads, blues, rock, Broadway style song and dance numbers, Lutheran chorales, plain chant and bits of 12-tone music. Orff's "Carmina Burana" makes what may be a parody appearance, "West Side Story" comes and goes, and even for this listener, hints of "Guys and Dolls" and other lovable, unpretentious shows….

Bernstein's *Mass* is above all else a theatrical work. Virtually every-one who has seen it in the theater says that this experience far transcends listening to it on records or watching the work on television. As in virtually every Bernstein score, there is much beautiful music: "Fraction" is just such a piece. What problems there are lie in the transitions between these pieces, and most of all in the words. Like a child playing a naughty game, Bernstein says what he is bursting to say, then covers his words with music, testing how much of the forbidden will be understood.

One message does come through clearly: Peace! At the end of the performance, the boys in the cast move out into the audience and squeeze the hands of those sitting on the aisles, whispering, "Pass it on."

One might reasonably question how to reconcile Bernstein's persis-tent pressure for peace with his often abrasive behavior and his gen-uinely aggressive temperament when it comes to his career. In *Freud for Historians*, Peter Gay refers to what Freud had called "the excessive measure and compulsive character" of an emotion and "the defensive maneuver of reaction formation" that is commonly associated with it. Gay describes this unconscious stratagem as one in which "an imper-missible aggressive or erotic wish has been covered over by exaggerat-ed conduct pointing in the opposite direction. It is harmless enough to feel compassion for animals, but the furious antivivisectionist arouses the suspicion that he once harbored the most cruel infantile sadism. The bellicose pacifist displays, with his single-mindedness, the traces of a very similar early past."

In *Style and Idea*, Arnold Schoenberg refers to music as a language "in which a musician unconsciously gives himself away." He predicts that one day,

> the children's children of our psychologists will have deciphered
> the language of music. Woe, then, to the incautious who thought
> his innermost secrets carefully hidden and who must allow tact-
> less men to besmirch his personal possessions with their own
> impurities. Woe, then, to Beethoven, Brahms, Schumann—
> when they fall into such hands—these men who used their
> human right of free speech in order to conceal their true
> thoughts. Is the right to keep silent not worthy of protection?

Schoenberg's statement illuminates more than anything else the philosophical and aesthetic distance between himself and Bernstein. While the Viennese composer devoted all his artistic energy to concealing every thought and feeling, Bernstein directs his to revealing everything. In order to take no chance at all that anything be missed, Bernstein even bypasses music and goes directly to words. One need only recall his anger when the Soviet authorities did not print his program notes to *The Age of Anxiety*. He believed the audiences could not "understand" precisely what he had had in mind. His reaction to the absence of those notes reveals the importance of the role that words play in each creation.

Early in *Mass* the protagonist sings:

> *If I could confess*
> *Good and loud, nice and slow*
> *Get this load off my chest*
> *Yes, but how, Lord—I don't know.* *

In 1968 Zubin Mehta, the conductor born in Bombay, India, whose family is descended from Parsi nobles, was named musical adviser to the Israel Philharmonic, the first conductor to have such a title there. Bernstein would not have taken on such a post; he had given notice to the New York Philharmonic to be free to compose. Still, for a man as emotionally demanding as he, one who surrounds himself with people who have no other ties, it must have come as something of a blow. Perhaps it even played a role in his hosting the Black Panther party a short time after that and coincidentally conducting the New York Philharmonic in an all-Wagner program. If the Israeli musicians, after being without such a leader for so long, would choose to select one at this time, then they couldn't expect absolute loyalty from Bernstein.

In any event, on May 12, 1971, just a little more than a year after the Black Panther party, the Bernsteins gave another civil liberties party, this time for Father Philip Berrigan and five co-defendants who were charged with conspiring to kidnap Henry Kissinger, Nixon's national security adviser, and plotting to destroy the heating systems in federal buildings. More than one hundred people came to the party, and the defense fund raised thirty-five

---

* © *Amberson Enterprises (G. Schirmer).*

thousand dollars. This time the press was not invited.

The right-wing Jewish Defense League picketed in front of the Park Avenue building where the Bernsteins lived. Signs attacked Bernstein for being silent on Jewish civil rights and for supporting the Berrigans. Stanley S. Cohen, a lawyer for the JDL, told reporters that Bernstein was "an ornament in the Jewish world but had made no move to help Jews obtain their rights." In allying himself with Berrigan, Bernstein supported a radical priest who had married a nun, who was known to be in favor of drugs, and who flouted Christian authority much as Bernstein attacked any authority he confronted.

Whatever Bernstein's relationship to the Catholic Church was in *Mass*, it cannot be considered either traditional or devout. In fact, in November 1971, when Bernstein was in Washington for a *Candide* production that had traveled from the west coast, he spoke about *Mass* to a reporter, talking about an experience he had had at a Greek belly-dancing club: "I danced with the belly dancer and she had been to *Mass* several times and loved it. It was sort of a merging of the cultures. I like that." Soon after the publication of this remark Bernstein said, "I keep reading about myself and not recognizing myself. Not only am I misquoted by the yard, but also misrepresented. A certain segment of journalists have this image of me, a sort of Broadway jazzy Joe showman fellow. I keep saying there must be something to this. I do some soul searching, and I can't find it in me. Maybe I talk too much and say the wrong things."

Bernstein could not stay away from conducting, no matter how much he thought he should. The demand for him was constant—as usual—and he loved to conduct. On December 15, 1971, he led his one thousandth performance with the New York Philharmonic, a number not reached by any conductor before or since. Schonberg wrote:

> Through the years Bernstein has aroused controversy, though in the last decade there has been little argument about his growth as a conductor. But no matter what one thinks of his conducting, or his creative work, or his podium mannerisms or anything, an observer would have to be blind to ignore Bernstein's importance to the New York Philharmonic and to

New York musical life. His years with the orchestra were a succession of sold out houses and contented audiences, and he covered a good deal of music of every description during his tenure. At this time it is only right to put reservations aside and salute Bernstein for what he did and even for what he tried to do. Bernstein was a figure that no conductor in history has matched.

In June 1972, nine months after the world premiere of *Mass*, Bernstein despaired at how little composing he had accomplished since leaving his orchestra. To rectify that he announced that he was canceling everything he had contracted to do beginning in September 1973 through July 1974. Commitments he would honor before this sabbatical began included a conducting stint with the Boston Symphony at Tanglewood, taking over the podium of the New York Philharmonic for five weeks early in 1973, and the preparation of the Charles Eliot Norton Lectures he would deliver at Harvard. This last assignment held a special place in a career filled with prizes and tributes because it conferred on him credentials as a creative artist. T. S. Eliot, e. e. cummings, Robert Frost, and Stravinsky were among the figures who had preceded him, and credentials as a creative artist were what still eluded him. In fact, in 1971, Copland asked his colleagues on the Pulitzer committee to give Bernstein the prize for his *Mass*. Copland said it would mean so much to him. But the others turned down the request and gave that year's Pulitzer Prize in music to Jacob Druckman for his orchestral work *Windows*.

The last important venture Bernstein would undertake before his break was a new *Carmen*, with a new management at the Met. By the time of *Mass*, Schuyler Chapin had left Bernstein to serve as assistant manager to Göran Gentele in his new post replacing Rudolf Bing as general manager of the Met. Krawitz was leaving with Bing. A meeting took place in Lucerne, Switzerland, which was attended by the outgoing and incoming managers. According to Krawitz, Gentele set the tone of the meeting: "He laid out all the ground rules and in doing so was critical of everything that Bing had done. 'If you do a new production in one season,' he said, 'then it must be repeated the next season with the same conductor and the same cast.' I explained that one could lay out such principles easily, but that when it came to implementing them any number of things could go wrong. Of course, exactly that happened. Lenny agreed to do only five or six *Carmen*s for Gentele and immediately they made an exception of him. Lenny also insisted, as he did now about everything he did, that the production be tied to a recording. The Met chorus refused to make it and that became the Met's fight. When the opera was recorded it was with the Thomas Pyle Chorus."

Bernstein's *Carmen* was to have been the opening production under Gentele's management. If Bernstein could not open the Met when it first opened its doors at Lincoln Center, at least he would be in the pit for the first production of the new regime. But Gentele was killed in Europe in an automobile accident just before coming to New York.

His death left Bernstein in total control of the production. Schonberg wrote that it was "daring, provocative and a brilliant conception." Still, whatever problems there had been in the mounting of the piece escalated now when it came to the recording. Not only did that make trouble for the Met, CBS Records wanted no part of it. By this time the classical divisions of the record companies were in deep financial trouble. The Beatles, other rock groups, and novelties like *Switched-On Bach* were reaping huge profits, while classical performers who were kept on were retained for prestige, not money. Bernstein was the company's biggest-selling conductor, so he had been treated with care. But by now even he was not treated with the attention to which he was accustomed. By 1970 Clive Davis was running CBS Records. In a book, *Clive: Inside the Record Business*, Davis writes of an afternoon when he visited Bernstein. John McClure and Schuyler Chapin were there. The conversation concentrated on Bernstein's wish to make recordings of opera. Davis articulated CBS's reluctance because of the costs involved. Davis says that CBS, at first unwilling to accede to Bernstein's demand to record *Falstaff and Rosenkavalier*, finally did give in. Its concession cost the company $100,000 for each opera.

"Monetary considerations," Davis writes, "were not as boring to us as to Bernstein ... and he was said to be miffed that he was getting any flack *at all* from the company."

The strained relations between Bernstein and CBS reached a crisis during a summer conference in London. Bernstein demanded the company record his new *Carmen* in New York, a venture that, according to Davis, would have cost more than $200,000. Other executives report he also asked for a large promotion budget and a junket to Spain. "We decided to pass," Davis writes. Bernstein was given a release from CBS to take his *Carmen* to Deutsche Grammophon, a company that was pursuing him.

McClure says, "Bernstein's relations with Deutsche Grammophon have been lucrative, prestigious and good. We did his repertoire once at CBS. At this point he wanted to do everything in concert, everything live, and that is no fun for any record company. For him it is infinitely easier and far more profitable. He maximizes his returns on every square centimeter."

Peter Munves, an executive who is still with CBS, goes further. "Bernstein," he says, "took a career that was on a plateau and opened up a whole new world in his career with Deutsche Grammophon. He became an international star, eclipsing every other living conductor."

Although Bernstein had made more than two hundred records with the New York Philharmonic and, by the late 1960s, was the most successful conductor in the United States, Herbert von Karajan still prevailed abroad. Similar in looks, the two conductors approach music in strikingly dissimilar ways. Karajan

December 1952
Bernstein and Jennie Tourel at a fundraising dinner for the Weizmann Institute.
Five women, not all of whom readily tolerated each other, played major roles
in Bernstein's life: Jennie, his mother; Shirley, his sister; Felicia, his wife;
Helen Coates, his strong right arm; and Jennie Tourel, his first professional artistic
collaborator. Tourel was the first to die. In 1973 Bernstein spoke at her
funeral. He said he was talking as "one who loved her deeply, and knew her,
perhaps, a little better than most."

delivers gleaming, polished performances without many surprises. Bernstein, on the other hand, is often attacked by purists for erring in one way or another. Faithful, of course, to the notes, he preserves creative freedom for himself in the manner of interpretation. Probing what lies beneath a work, Bernstein often brings to it qualities that make for fiery, intense performances. Still, in the mid-1960s, he was not a major conductor on the European scene.

At the time Columbia wanted to change that, to make inroads on Karajan sales abroad. To that end the New York Philharmonic persuaded the State Department and Trans World Airlines to underwrite a tour of Europe that included Israel. Before leaving, Bernstein led the Philharmonic in Berlioz's *Symphonie Fantastique* and he was so pleased with what they did that he tried to persuade Columbia to record the work even though he had recorded it with the orchestra some time before. Comfortable with the earlier recording, Columbia at first refused. In the end Bernstein got his way and the effort paid off handsomely.

In addition to adding a first-rate performance of the Berlioz to the catalog, Columbia published program notes in both German and English, produced a striking record jacket with Bernstein's face in silhouette, enclosed a Bernstein discography, and, with Trans World Airlines' support, offered the record at half price. The package succeeded in doing what no other Bernstein record had: It pushed Karajan out of record store windows in the cities where Bernstein and the orchestra performed. Bernstein's *Symphonic Fantastique* was listed week after week as the number one seller on the list published by *Der Spiegel*, Germany's leading weekly.

Trans World Airlines had put up posters, ordered large batches of records, and held news conferences in all the cities where the promotion took place. Bernstein was genuinely impressed by the difference this kind of treatment could make. He knew that if all of this was needed to make him an international star, Columbia was not the company to help him reach that goal. It was natural for him to look to Deutsche Grammophon. Why Deutsche Grammophon would have sought out Bernstein when it had Karajan on its roster is more difficult to understand.

In the late 1960s, when Bernstein was feeling increasingly dissatisfied with Columbia, Deutsche Grammophon was trying to gain a foothold in the United States. The signing of Bernstein, America's star conductor, would help the company do better in the American marketplace. Hans Hirsch, a Bavarian Catholic and a conservative in both manner and dress, joined Deutsche Grammophon in 1969. Even then he was a passionate admirer of Bernstein. Hirsch was to Bernstein at the German company what Chapin had been to him at Columbia, someone who would spare no effort in getting Bernstein whatever he wanted when he wanted it. In 1970 Hirsch signed Deutsche Grammophon's first American contract, with the Boston Symphony. At that time he let his colleagues know that he saw in Bernstein an American who understood all there was to understand about the German tradition. He wanted Bernstein for his company.

The signing of the contract for *Carmen* took place in May 1972, in Washington. Among those who were present were Hirsch and Thomas Mowrey, the artistic director for Deutsche Grammophon's American Artists and Repertoire department; Abe Friedman, Bernstein's lawyer; and Harry Kraut, who had by then replaced Schuyler Chapin as the head of Bernstein's Amberson Productions in New York when Chapin went to work under Gentele at the Met. Unlike Chapin, who is an aristocrat, Kraut is, like Bernstein, from the middle class. Both Kraut and Bernstein were educated at Harvard. Kraut emphasizes their compatibility by noting that both had parents who fought bitterly throughout their lives. Most important, Kraut possessed skills as a negotiator that Chapin never enjoyed. Smart, tough, with a background as assistant manager of the Boston Symphony, Kraut was clearly the man for the job. He has protected Bernstein's interests ever since the *Carmen* days. To his colleagues and friends Bernstein appears a man absolutely incapable of saying no. Kraut says no for him.

The meetings between the Germans and Americans were held in the Watergate Hotel just before the break-in at the Democratic National Headquarters in the adjacent office building. This was also the time that the Met was giving Bing a gala send-off. While opera stars from all over the world contributed their services, Bernstein absented himself and made plans to herald the new non-Bing regime by being the conductor and overseer of its first production. He was in the process of cutting out virtually every institution that had been a part of his life, first the New York Philharmonic, then Columbia, then the Bing regime at the Met. If Felicia had succeeded in cutting all the comfortable middle-class Jews out of the family's social circle in the 1950s and 1960s, Bernstein, in the 1970s, succeeded in cutting out all the American institutions and replacing them with organizations German or Viennese. Deutsche Grammophon's *Carmen* took ten sessions to record and cost the company $275,000, then a great deal of money for a classical recording.

Through that experience, Bernstein learned that the company could accomplish in the marketing of opera what Columbia had not—with either *Falstaff* or *Rosenkavalier.* The next work Bernstein recorded for Deutsche Grammophon was Liszt's *Faust* Symphony, the same piece he had insisted on doing early in his days with Columbia. It had sold poorly then. In 1975, in a passionately conceived and vigorously directed performance, Bernstein conducted the work, this time with the Boston Symphony. This musical treatment of a man who sells his soul to the devil in return for youth, young love, and wealth still attracted Bernstein.

Carmen sold more than one hundred thousand copies within the first few years and went on to become Deutsche Grammophon's best-selling opera. The *Faust* Symphony, while it may not have fully earned its keep, was anything but a financial disaster.

In 1976 the first exclusive contract between Bernstein and Deutsche Grammophon was drawn. It provided a handsome guarantee and an attractive repertory. "It was clear," Mowrey says, "that DG was not simply trying to catch a big name and then give him obscure works to record." The contract held that Bernstein would do the central repertory—Mozart, Haydn, Mahler, and Stravinsky—and some American works—Copland and Schuman—as well as his own compositions. Several operas written into the original agreement— *Tales of Hoffmann, Eugene Onegin*, and *Madame Butterfly*—did not materialize but virtually everything else did.

In 1980 DG let Hirsch go. Bernstein and Kraut let their unhappiness be known. Still Bernstein has remained with DG. The results have been beneficial both to him and to the company. The orchestras he has led include the Vienna Philharmonic, the Israel Philharmonic, the Concertgebouw, the London Symphony, the Bavarian State Chorus

and Orchestra, the BBC Symphony, the English Bach Festival Chorus
and Orchestra, the Orchestra of the Academy of Saint Cecilia, the
Orchestre National de France, and such American orchestras as the
Boston Symphony, the National Symphony, and the New York
Philharmonic. The performances, recorded by DG and, for the most
part, filmed by Unitel-Munich, have made Bernstein an amount of
money that would have stunned his father.

With tremendous financial acumen, Bernstein has increasingly
insisted on controlling every fight he could negotiate, present and
future. The consequences are twofold. First, because of the diversity of
the vehicles, his music is presented in many different forms. Second, he
appears to have conquered time. Bernstein's performance income will
surpass immeasurably that of any other composer or conductor, for he
has virtually everything he performs recorded on film or tape. All that
he owns survives technological progress because in his own time there
has been the move from monophonic to stereo to audiocassette to com-
pact disc to videocassette, with Bernstein's masters still being used and
still producing revenue for him. Amberson Productions employs about
a dozen people full time, including several accountants. In fact, when
Bernstein left CBS (as the classical record division came to be known)
and made the move to DG, John McClure also left CBS and joined
Amberson. Since then, as Amberson's representative, he has been working with his former colleagues to reissue Bernstein's Columbia press-
ings with the result that Bernstein's new DG recordings compete with
the old ones from Columbia. The comparison makes for interesting listening. The new ones do not contradict the basic conceptions of the old
versions. But while the DG recordings show a Bernstein who often
sounds surer, warmer, even more Germanic, the old Columbia discs,
not surprisingly, seduce with a youthful aspect, an instinctual energy
generally lacking in the recent recordings.

Bernstein and DG both have profited from their relationship.
Bernstein has rerecorded his repertory under the best of all possible
arrangements. DG not only has gone on to build a powerful American
base but also has acquired a star with international box office appeal and
has consolidated its position as the IBM of the classical recording industry. Bernstein's signing with DG also meant that he and Karajan were
recording for the same company.

Whatever competition now exists between Karajan and Bernstein has its own history. After the war Bernstein was scheduled to conduct the Vienna Symphony. He had conducted Bartók's *Music for Strings, Percussion, and Celesta* in Budapest. Word of the enormously successful performance traveled to Vienna. Meanwhile Karajan had conducted the same work with the Vienna Philharmonic apparently with disastrous results. In Bernstein's version, even before he got off the train in the station in Vienna, three men in tall black hats who were representing the Vienna Symphony called out to him that he must conduct the Bartók to compete with Karajan. Bernstein refused, but says the incident left such a bitter taste that to avoid such "infighting," he did not return to Vienna for years.

Nor did Karajan visit the United States for years, but for entirely different reasons. Karajan had been a member of the Nazi party as early as 1933, and he had conducted frequently for Hitler. Yet, in 1958, the first year Bernstein took over the New York Philharmonic, he paved the way for Karajan to come as a guest conductor. In telling the story, Bernstein adds that when he went backstage to greet Karajan at Carnegie Hall, the visitor turned away from him.

Today an outwardly civil relationship prevails between these two great conductors. But their personalities and temperaments differ so much that they not only come forth with altogether different interpretations of the same works, they pursue strikingly different careers.

Thomas Mowrey says that "Karajan enjoys one advantage Bernstein does not: a single great orchestra, the Berlin Philharmonic. Bernstein has done wonderful things all over the place but that is like having a bunch of great mistresses instead of one wife. It can be a lot of fun but it gets exhausting. On the other hand, Karajan gets his way artistically. He has a stranglehold on his orchestra. If you have that you can pretty well do exactly what you want to do. Since leaving the Philharmonic, Bernstein has had no base."

While it is true that Karajan appears to prefer only one orchestra under his control and does not spread his attentions much beyond that, Bernstein thrives on a different approach. Michael Tilson Thomas speaks of Bernstein's "sheer energy and drive. Nobody I've ever met comes close to him. It's always on to the next script, the next project, the next piece. As for his guest conducting, it is apocalyptic. There are always situational roadblocks. Then Lenny comes in. 'I'm here to make this music great,' he says, and he makes that happen. The contract disputes disappear. There is a coalescing. Everyone recommits himself to music."

Mowrey has a point, however, in seeing a distinct advantage in Karajan's method. When Bernstein has great or even very good orchestras to conduct, he gets his way with them. But, for example, in 1985 he conducted eleven orchestras and several were less than very good. Those performances were far removed from the ones in Vienna in the 1970s or the ones he had achieved with the New York Philharmonic in the 1960s. Although Bernstein had thought the title laureate conductor would ensure his having the New York orchestra to conduct whenever he chose to, that turned out not to be true. The management of the New York Philharmonic did not want to threaten the almost immediately troubled tenure of Pierre Boulez, Bernstein's successor, with too great a dose of his predecessor. Bernstein thought that the death of George Szell, the musical adviser to the New York Philharmonic and a man very much behind Boulez's appointment, would open the doors for him to conduct Brahms, Schubert, and Beethoven. This would have seemed natural. In the original plan Szell was to have conducted the classic repertory while Boulez concentrated on the particular twentieth-century repertory with which he was closely identified. But Szell's death opened up no such doors to Bernstein. In public Bernstein would refer to this "other person," meaning Boulez, who was not open to the arrangement Bernstein desired.

Once the whole situation got out of control. On April 10, 1975, after a guest appearance in New York, Bernstein addressed the audience in an improvised talk. He had not told management he was going to say anything at all. After the performance he said, "Somehow and in some way I'm going to come back to the Philharmonic." The remark was carried in the New York papers, prompting Harold Lawrence, manager of the New York Philharmonic, to remark, "It came as a surprise to me and to everybody backstage." The explanation was that Bernstein was in such an emotional state, coming back after more than a year away to conduct his musicians in front of his beloved audiences, that he was simply carried away.

Still the incident underlined the fact that throughout the 1970s,

Bernstein had no American orchestra of his own. In Europe the orchestra closest to him was the Vienna Philharmonic. He has conducted it in Beethoven, Brahms, and Mahler cycles and in symphonies by Mozart, Haydn, and Robert Schumann among many other performances. Gunther Schuller, whose parents were born in Germany and who has had a long-standing, close professional relationship to the country, speaks of Bernstein's curious liaison: "The Vienna Philharmonic can be an undisciplined, nasty orchestra, yet there is a great love affair between the musicians and Lenny. They play well for him. It is perverse that Lenny should have this love affair with the most anti-Semitic of cities. There is no city where anti-Semitism is as ardent as in Vienna. For Lenny to go back to that city and make believe these are wonderful people is hard for me to comprehend. The first thing most Viennese musicians do when someone new arrives is find out if he is a Jew. One of the most ardent Nazis was Karl Boehm, who conducted the Vienna Philharmonic much of his life."

On the one hand, Bernstein clearly enjoys a situation in which one hundred Viennese musicians watch every gesture be makes and thousands of Viennese listeners exult in the music they hear. On the other hand, Bernstein knows there is another side to the story, the side that Schuller articulates. Chapin tells of an incident when Bernstein's *Fidelio* was being moved from one house to another and needed additional rehearsal time. Bernstein told the members of the orchestra that they would have to stay longer than they thought. While the Vienna orchestra is known to be more pliable with Bernstein's requests for more time than orchestras in the United States, one musician made a highly audible anti-Semitic remark. According to Chapin, Bernstein left the podium very pale, very silent.

That the most profound cultural anti-Semitism can exist hand in hand with a reverence for Bernstein's talent is illustrated by another story, an incident that took place in 1985. When the orchestra was playing in New York, Erich Binder, one of the concertmasters, spoke of his experience playing the Schumann Fourth Symphony with Bernstein. "The rubato was so great, so natural. It was my first Schumann with Bernstein and it was a truly great performance. I have played under Boehm, under Karajan, under any number of others, but I never played anything as great as that Schumann under Bernstein."

When asked what he thought of *Kaddish*, which the orchestra had played a few years before on tour, Binder winked: "It is *jüdische Musik*, so I cannot have a good feeling about it."

How one interprets Bernstein's "love affair" with Vienna depends not only on one's perception of Bernstein but also on one's sense of values concerning very complicated issues.

Bernstein's friends and business associates see his activities in Vienna as an assertion of the cultural supremacy of the Jew. To them Bernstein rises phoenix-like in this heartland of anti-Semitism. This thesis finds support in the way Bernstein describes his postwar experience in Germany, emphasizing that one hundred Nazis actually knelt at his feet. The argument gains strength when one considers that a Bernstein festival mounted by the Israel Philharmonic in Tel Aviv during a three-week period in April 1977, the first major retrospective of his work as a composer, was transported several months later to the Carinthian Festival. In this southern Austrian setting, Bernstein not only conducted *Kaddish*, which was the central work of the celebration, but explained its meaning to this Austrian audience. There are other ways Bernstein prevails; for one thing, he got Deutsche Grammophon to record the Israel Philharmonic not only in his own compositions but in other repertory. For another, Deutsche Grammophon executives report that when Bernstein is in Vienna, on the High Holy Days he steadfastly remains behind closed doors in his hotel room, frustrating Germans and Viennese who frenetically seek him out.

More cynical observers commenting on the Viennese liaison see not so much a heroic man as an opportunistic one, a man who, angered by the problems he encountered in New York, simply turned to what looked like a better deal in every way. This theory is given credence by Bernstein's continued refusal ever to enter the Reagan White House, while he continues to conduct in Austria, even after the election of Kurt Waldheim, who lied about his Nazi past. Bernstein says he will "go back, because the musicians are my brothers—my *Brüderlein*—I love them. Not to go would be abandoning them."

Finally there are those even less enchanted with Bernstein who see him as the token Jew, the court Jew, the Jew the Viennese are willing to "make the exception of." In this scenario, Bernstein, in the whipped-cream world that is Vienna, has become the candy-coated symbol of a national catharsis. If the Viennese can say, "We love this man," it would follow, this particular argument holds, that they cannot be as bad as their critics say they are.

In addition to the moral complexities, there are aesthetic considerations not to be dismissed when one evaluates Bernstein and Vienna. The Viennese are good musicians, good listeners, good administrators in the arts, so they and Bernstein have much to give one another.

Still, Artur Rubinstein and Isaac Stern managed great careers without ever stepping into Germany or Austria after World War II. And Shirley Bernstein, altogether loyal to her brother, passes up traveling with him whenever his concert schedule takes him to Austria or Germany.

The more one knows about Bernstein, the more complicated the portrait is of him as a Jew. Capable of working productively with anti-Semites, he still holds a soft spot in his heart for his fellow Jews, whom he says he finds superior to all others. "He is so adamant about music being Jewish," Schuller says. "It is important to him that a composer is a Jew, that a performer is a Jew. He told me that *Triplum*, my composition, has a Jewish soul. That is meant as a compliment. I am not a Jew. When Lenny says, 'You can almost be Jewish,' that is considered by him to be the most supreme of compliments." McClure echoes this: "Lenny used to tell me that I had a Yiddish head. That was always meant as great praise." Charles Turner, Samuel Barber's longtime friend, says, "Lenny likes to tease his WASP friends about being *goy*. I was called Charles Epworth Turner and he said I was as *goy* as Schrafft's. Sam, he pretended, was Jewish because of his name. Once, when Sam's name appeared in a book on Jewish artists, Lenny sent him a copy inscribed, 'I always knew you were Jewish, Sam.'"

Virtually everyone who knows Bernstein agrees that Jews have a better chance to connect with him artistically than Gentiles. The major collaborators for *West Side Story* were Jews, but although Bernstein made several efforts to develop new shows with one or more of the *West Side Story* collaborators after 1957, nothing happened. The first collaborative attempt that did prove fruitful was *The Dybbuk* with Jerome Robbins, who says he had been thinking of the idea since 1944. In 1964 Robbins had choreographed *Fiddler on the Roof*, a Broadway musical by Jerry Bock and Sheldon Harnick. Robbins wanted his new ballet to spring from the same Jewish background as *Fiddler*. Bernstein worked on the piece during the fall of 1973.

A benefit performance of *The Dybbuk* opened the New York City Ballet's spring 1974 season with seats at $250 a pair. Bernstein and Robbins together again seemed likely to make a commercial success. The score is immensely complicated; Ned Rorem thinks it is Bernstein's best piece to date. But the ballet failed, and the company rarely programs it these days.

The work in final form lasts forty minutes, though it ran longer in earlier versions. As usual Bernstein deferred to Robbins and cut what he was told to cut. The next year Bernstein transformed it into a suite he conducted with the New York Philharmonic, along with the Tchaikovsky Fourth Symphony. Based on eleven dances, all having to do with ritual and hallucination, *The Dybbuk* is based on a Yiddish play by S. Ansky that was given its world premiere in 1920 in Poland. A *dybbuk*—the word is Hebrew—is a disembodied spirit, a demon from a dead person that enters the body of a living being. According to the program notes, the work was not to be thought of as Jewish. The play on which it was based was used, the notes claimed, "only as a point of departure."

After all that, according to Arthur Laurents, there was nothing Jewish about the piece at all. A finger-snapping scene, he says, came directly out of *West Side Story*. The play had to do with the mystical numerology of the Cabala, so Bernstein based his score on a convoluted numerical system. Before the first performance Bernstein said, "Every note in the ballet was arrived at by cabalistic or analytic manipulations of numbers. These include numerology, conversions, anagrams." One of the main elements came from the fact that every one of the twenty-two letters of the Hebrew alphabet is also a number. "The cabalistic numbers," Bernstein said, "adapt almost naturally to the basic components of the twelve-tone system." Yet the only times Bernstein uses the twelve-tone technique in *The Dybbuk* are when he wants to convey a sense of the devil. When, on the other hand, he wants to express the purity of the young woman he does so with passages that are unerringly tonal.

In 1972 Bernstein called on Thomas Cothran, the man who had

worked for Bernstein during the composition of *Mass*, to help him prepare the Norton Lectures at Harvard. Bernstein had remained close to Cothran, a relationship that was out of character for him. With Cothran something was different enough for Bernstein to send him to Paris, telling his friends that New York wasn't big enough for Tommy and Felicia. Bernstein had decided to use the Norton Lectures to prove that his preference for tonality over twelve-tone music was not just a personal quirk of a sentimental man, but the expression of a universal truth. He gave the first of the Norton talks in the fall of 1973 in the Harvard Square Theater, a squalid building but the only one in Cambridge large enough to accommodate the crowds that came to see Bernstein.

While he and Cothran were working on the lectures, Bernstein was as usual occupied with a number of other projects. One was the European premiere of *Mass*. Produced by the Yale School of Music and Drama and televised by the BBC, it was recorded in Vienna's Konzerthaus by DG. The performance, conducted by John Mauceri, apparently went very well. At the end Bernstein rose in his box to acknowledge the applause, which was reported to have run ten minutes. Asked his opinion of the production, he pressed a bunch of roses to his lips and said, "You expect me to talk also. They did it. I just wrote it."

Such sentiment appears out of character for a holder of the Charles Eliot Norton lectureship, among the most distinguished in the U.S. academic establishment. But then, none of Bernstein's predecessors came with an entourage carting audio and visual recording equipment. He dedicated the talks to the late David Prall, the professor of philosophy who had opened his quarters to the students of Eliot House when Bernstein was a Harvard undergraduate.

Bernstein's use of Thomas Cothran for these talks recalls Stravinsky's use of Pierre Souvchinsky for the same series of lectures in 1939. Stravinsky then, and Bernstein thirty-five years later, apparently believed it was not enough to be a talented composer or, for that matter, a remarkably intelligent and fiercely perceptive man. Both went to a good deal of trouble, making use of outside resources, to convey the impression that they were also literary heavyweights.

Felicia and Burton Bernstein often complained to their friends about Leonard's spending his free time with show business people. But the fact is that intellectuals do not seem interested in spending time with Bernstein. For one thing he always wants to play word games and he plays them relentlessly. For another, he allows no dialogue: Bernstein always holds the floor. Most important, a number of cognoscenti have gone on record as saying that Bernstein offers no new ideas and generally disseminates middlebrow pap. They see his great success as a lecturer coming from his ability to popularize and simplify complex notions in an invariably fresh way and from his remarkable showmanship.

Bernstein's title for the series was "The Unanswered Question," an homage to Charles Ives, who had composed a work with that title in 1908. Bernstein explained that its meaning now was "Whither music?" and he remarked that to answer this question he would draw on linguistics, "mankind's newest key to self-awareness," and would explore the viability of constructing musicolinguistics according to Noam Chomsky's model of psycholinguistics. His purpose was to apply the principles of transformational grammar to musical analysis.

Bernstein's first lecture was on phonology, sound itself. The second was on syntax, the structures based on these sounds. The remaining four dealt with semantics, the meaning—musical and extramusical—of these sounds. In all of these explications, Bernstein's love of music came through. This enthusiasm was remarked on with some cynicism by Michael Steinberg, music critic of the *Boston Globe*, in an article harshly critical of the lectures.

Steinberg was not alone. Composers who had been nourished by the twelve-tone method were enraged that all this verbal virtuosity and production equipment were being placed in the service of illustrating that tonality was the language of the gods, the only true condition for a poetic music. One writer claimed that Bernstein had presented Schoenberg as the villain, Stravinsky as the hero—that is, until he made the shift to the serial idea; and Bernstein had added that Stravinsky had to die for composers to feel free to rediscover their innate sense of tonality. Bernstein ended the sixth and last lecture with the articulation of his credo: I believe in tonality.

Many intellectuals attacked the talks but a few did rally to Bernstein's side. Ray Jackendoff, a music theoretician and composer, wrote a letter that was published in *The New York Times* claiming that the "value of Bernstein's lectures lay in his attempt to juxtapose linguistic theory and musical analysis, putting a new range of possible interpretations on well known techniques.... Anyone would have groped with this topic, it is an area where so little is known that simply to impose interesting questions is a significant advance." Five years later Allan Keiler, a scholar with credentials in both music and linguistics, wrote an essay that was published in *The Musical Quarterly* in which he expressed the notion that linguistic theory may one day play a crucial role in the study of music's language. If that proves to be true, he said, Bernstein may have led the way.

As Bernstein began his Harvard lectures, Jennie Tourel died. Some who were close to her say that she had been in love with him from the day they met.

That relationship had its vicissitudes. In 1946, after she had introduced *Jeremiah* in Pittsburgh and sung it in Boston and New York, she was replaced for the Victor recording by the mezzo-soprano Nan Merriman. The record was made when Bernstein and Felicia were engaged. Whether Felicia had the power with Bernstein to rule out Tourel, or whether Tourel withdrew because of Felicia, is impossible to say. But Friede Rothe, Tourel's press representative, says her client was devastated by the replacement. Rothe says Tourel was devastated again, about twenty years later, when Bernstein bypassed her with Dietrich Fischer-Dieskau for a recording of Mahler's *Das Lied von der Erde*.

During her last years Tourel had difficulty with her voice. Nevertheless, in 1968, Bernstein called on her to sing in the Mahler *Resurrection* Symphony. To commemorate the reuniting of Jerusalem after the Six-Day War, they performed in a now-legendary concert with the Israel Philharmonic on the top of Mount Scopus. It was the first time Tourel had sung the work in Hebrew and she learned the text on the flight over. The following year Tourel sang under Bernstein again, this time in performances of *Jeremiah* with the New York Philharmonic that honored the memory of Samuel Bernstein. Those performances in May 1969 took place a little more than twenty-five years after the work's world premiere in Pittsburgh.

Between the New York Philharmonic performances and her death, Tourel saw little of Bernstein. She remarked on this with regret to friends. By then his career was in Europe and he was leading a fundamentally different life, which left little room for women friends.

On hearing of Tourel's death, Bernstein, in Cambridge, Massachusetts, sank into a depression. At first he refused to go to New York to attend her funeral, but then he responded to pressure and even agreed to speak. He told the mourners he was talking as "one who loved her deeply, and knew her, perhaps, a little better than most."

blacks talking about the real danger of being shipped back to Africa. In compiling a list of all the reasons for the fiasco, *Time* listed as one the fact that "the show was racist."

Bernstein may be sympathetic to blacks in his pronouncements, but his actions have spoken differently. Harry Smyles, an oboist, came to New York in 1947 from Cleveland on a Julius Rosenwald Fellowship, the same kind of fellowship that gave James Baldwin his first break. Smyles played under Bernstein in the student orchestra at Tanglewood. "Bernstein," Smyles said in 1985, "talked to me about jazz, nothing else, and although I like jazz, I had training exclusively in classical music. Later he would talk to me about a work he was doing for Woody Herman, or how saxes were going around in his head. That was when I was playing in the pit of *Candide*. There was nothing genuine about this. In fact there was a profound falseness. By then I had studied with Harold Gomberg, the first oboist in the New York Philharmonic, but because I was black, Bernstein talked to me about jazz. His party for the Panthers was an effort on his part to dispel what many blacks had thought about his behavior at the hearings of the Commission on Human Rights, when he kept saying he had to maintain artistic discretion and refused to accept behind-the-screen auditions."

Despite Bernstein's seeming generosity to blacks—giving them tickets for performances, being seen in jazz clubs with them—his attitude has not changed in forty years. Recently black chauffeurs from his limousine service have been subjected to Bernstein's mimicking of an uneducated black locution when he gives them directions. And in November 1986, after a memorial tribute to songwriter Harold Arlen at the Majestic Theatre in New York, he mimicked that same uneducated black locution when socializing with Lena Horne backstage.

In 1972, while he was recording *Carmen*, Bernstein spoke of a flutist in the orchestra whom he called a terrible mess. He said the man had been in psychiatric treatment for years and "look at all the good it did him." By this time he may well have concluded that the years of treatment he himself had gone through had not transformed him into the man he had hoped he would become.

The Bernstein's moved out of their apartment on the East Side and into a cavernous one in the Dakota, a historic building on the West

Side, in the early 1970s. Michael Tilson Thomas remarked on the difference in the apartments that was reflected in the difference in the family: "The walls," he says, "of the Park Avenue apartment seemed to keep things in certain balance. After that everything was different."

When *1600 Pennsylvania Avenue* opened in New York, a photograph of Felicia smiling, with Leonard in his black cape at her side, appeared in *People* magazine. The smile apparently was more a symptom of the "stiff upper lip" her children describe than a sign of happiness. A few months later, on October 28, 1976, on her way to school, Nina read a headline in the New York *Daily News*: WEST SIDE STORY '76: BERNSTEIN & WIFE SPLIT! Stunned with disbelief, she pointed it out to the friend who was with her on the bus. Nina said bitterly in 1985 that the friend had just looked at the news and giggled.

Bernstein left for Berkeley, California, to be with Cothran. Jamie and Alex were away at school. Most of Nina's classmates were talking about going out of town to boarding school, for the following year was the beginning of high school and the traditional time to make such a change. "But I knew I wouldn't go," Nina says, "I would never leave Mummy alone in the city with only the maids."

When Bernstein returned to New York, he and Cothran moved into the Navarro Hotel. He told the press there comes a time in life when a man must be what he really is. His decision coincided with the height of the gay liberation movement.

Felicia tried to reconstitute her life and appeared in a play. *Poor Murderer.* Her husband was not there on opening night or on the nights that followed. Anytime Felicia spoke to the press, she said she hoped for a reconciliation. The fact is that she was distraught. During a guest-conducting engagement at the New York Philharmonic, Bernstein would be told of calls coming into that office from Felicia, who was looking for him. In August 1977, at Tanglewood, when Alex was celebrating his twenty-second birthday, Felicia went to Stockbridge but most of the time was seen alone, for Bernstein was always surrounded by the crowds of young homosexual men who devoted themselves to serving him.

Felicia became seriously ill with lung cancer. In the last year of her life, she told her husband, who had moved back into the house, in front of others that she probably had gotten sick to pay him back for the anguish he had caused her. At least one person close to the family says that Felicia often cursed Bernstein with these words: "May you live on and on—absolutely alone."

Felicia died on June 17, 1978. *The New York Times* said that "although she was a mainstay in the acclaimed dramas on television and won critical praise in the theater, she attained far wider fame as the elegant wife of the conductor and composer, and as a New York hostess."

In 1953, two years after the Bernsteins married, Marian Seldes, an actress and the daughter of a famous journalist, married Julian Claman, who had worked with the Revuers. In 1955, Claman wrote a play about a composer and wanted to use "A Quiet Place," a song from *Trouble in Tahiti*, Bernstein's 1952 opera. Bernstein not only let Claman use the song, he even coached Tyrone Power, who played the composer. Claman's play, entitled *A Quiet Place*, opened in New Haven on November 23, 1955, and closed on December 31 in New York.

Seldes has said that Leonard and Felicia were to her generation what Scott and Zelda Fitzgerald had been to her parents'. "They were a golden couple," she recalls. "During the 1950s, at the Osborne, there was good talk, music, food, and wine. All of it was wonderful, everything one could have wished for with friends. Felicia and Leonard would sit at the two pianos and play. It was perfection. People who were alone found their way there late at night knowing they would receive friendship. Felicia was a magnificent actress, a delicious, helpful, serious person. She was very gifted, in the most subtle and refined way."

Felicia probably was everything Seldes says she was. Yet Bernstein saw another side. For, in the 1970s, he showed some of his colleagues a book for a show based on Evita Perón that he was thinking of treating. He said he saw things in common between his own wife and the dictator's consort, who had been so effective in her political efforts on his behalf.

In a letter dated June 19, 1945, mailed from the Hotel Lincoln in Mexico City, Tennessee Williams wrote to Donald Windham that Bernstein had arrived in the city and invited him to lunch with "some friends in the International Set." In describing Bernstein, Williams wrote that "he is nice, but oh, what an egoist! When not getting all the attention, he sits in a chair with closed eyes, pretending to be asleep."

Bernstein was never able to tolerate anyone else's getting the spotlight. A friend who was in Felicia's room after the diagnosis had been made says that when the doctor arrived, Bernstein intercepted him on his walk to her bed, pointing out what he thought was a small growth on his own nose. After Felicia died Bernstein did grieve, but he spoke only about *his* terrible and obsessive guilt.

Bernstein then began to lash out against others even more than he had when his wife had been alive. When Sam Barber was first hospitalized, Bernstein called Barber to tell him that he knew what his illness was: "My wife died from it." His behavior at funerals was worse. At the one for Renée Longy Miquelle, his lifelong friend, he read a harsh private letter he had received from her son detailing what he saw as his mother's grave flaws. At the funeral for Steven Kyle, Betty Comden's husband, Bernstein recalled how when he had first seen the couple together, they looked so beautiful that he "didn't know which one I preferred." In a symposium that took place in Milwaukee in the fall of 1986, in which he and Lukas Foss were onstage, Bernstein described for a large audience Foss's circumcision, performed when Foss was twenty years old. Arthur Laurents has a compassionate explanation for what seems to be inordinately cruel behavior: "Lenny is so riddled with unhappiness. That is why he strikes out. It is getting back at his sadness."

Striking out characterized Bernstein's professional behavior as well. Bill Fertik, a film writer and director, was hired in 1981 to work on the Bernstein-Beethoven series. Fertik prefaces his story with the fact that the very business of filming music is fraught with risk, and adds that if three percent of the television public in the United States watches a serious music show, it is considered a tremendous success. Fertik says that his pursuit of this career was entirely because of Bernstein: "In the 1950s, when I was a little kid in Brooklyn, I watched the *Omnibus* shows and was completely knocked out by the dramatic approach to music."

Fertik's professional career began in 1974. He filmed Zubin Mehta conducting the Los Angeles Philharmonic in Ravel's *Boléro*. Shot with one camera, the production cost $160,000, won an Academy Award, and reportedly even turned a profit. The Bernstein project was nothing like that.

"Lenny had signed a contract with Unitel," Fertik said in 1985, "for a tremendous amount of symphony work. The company shoots it on thirty-five-millimeter motion picture stock, which is the most expensive way. There are lots of cameras, lights, action. There is an Italian television crew and sometimes BBC and NET are involved. It is a major worldwide development and the company never makes back what it spends. Unlike performances put on videotape in the United States—such as the old Horowitz concerts, which look ancient today— the Bernstein films will survive forever."

Fertik says that CBS-TV was casting around for classical music, "and wanted only the most outstanding program. It seemed to them that Beethoven and Bernstein were the emperors of music and they considered the Vienna Philharmonic to be on the same level. I was called in to coordinate everything.

"We received a catalog of information. I was to accomplish twelve hours of broadcasting and we were two hours and forty minutes short. When we found we had to fill in the time with other pieces and some narration, it was decided to ask Maximilian Schell to do it. He agreed to carry the show from one place to another. It was a big commitment for Schell and did not bring with it the big money he can command.

"Max is exceedingly talented. We were scheduled to meet one day with Lenny in New York—Max, Lenny, Harry Kraut, and myself. This was early in the project. Max was coming to town to publicize something and we all went to the Dakota. I noticed Max seemed nervous, apprehensive.

"We waited an hour for Lenny. Max seemed happy to wait. Finally Lenny came in. 'So sorry' and 'darling' all over the place. He called me *boychik*. Then we all went into his office and he sat down and said he wanted a drink. He started drinking—enormous glasses of scotch. Suddenly he said he had to call Israel. Then he called Daniel Barenboim. In Hebrew and English he kept telling Barenboim how much he loved him. With tears in his eyes he got off the phone and said, 'I love that boy. He's having such a hard time in Israel. I really have to help him. I've got to go over there at such and such a time and help him out there.' Kraut interceded: 'You can't. You're booked.' To which Lenny replied, 'OK.'

"Then Bernstein and Max started to talk about the *Egmont* Overture. Max said, 'I've been meaning to tell you that I've never agreed with the tempo you took,' this about a recording Bernstein had done about a decade before. Schell continued, 'I think it went too slow.'

"Now these two guys had to work together over the next year. Schell didn't know what he had done. Bernstein started to give him a lesson, instructing him on the meaning of the *'ma non troppo'* written on the first page of this allegro score. By this time he was drinking heavily and dishing out one nasty quip after another. Harry looked nervous. We had gotten around to absolutely no business at all and when I started to bring the subject up, Lenny terminated the meetings. Max was reduced to the position of a supplicant. Outside I said, "I'm embarrassed. This is shit.' Max answered, 'Wasn't he marvelous? That is Lenny.' "

The principals got together again in Vienna. "The director," Fertik says, "usually gets the final cut. Not so in this instance. After I signed the contract, I found that Lenny got the final cut. I cautioned Schell that he might kill him with that, but Schell replied, 'Lenny is a true artist. Lenny is a genius.' We put tremendous effort into this. Max played Beethoven on the piano. He played Rossini. He rewrote scripts with me. By the time we had finished, we had done enough research to have uncovered a lot of material and to have discovered and dealt with what was myth and what was real."

Fertik says that when they finished they had ten hours of Bernstein and one hour and twenty minutes of Schell. "We edited and reconstructed it for about six months. We kept sending material to Bernstein but heard only from Harry. And that was always social stuff, nothing real about the material. Seventy-five thousand dollars went into the editing.

"We finished it, spending Unitel's money, and wanted Lenny to look at it. There was a screening set for eight o'clock one evening in a New York studio; the screening time cost five hundred dollars an hour. We thought Lenny would simply scan the twelve hours. He arrived at eleven-thirty with twelve or thirteen people in tow and plenty of bottles of scotch. During the first two programs, he kept saying, 'I love it. I love it.'

"By the third he was raving mad about Schell's presence. He shouted out, *'Schauspieler,'* the German word for actor, with a pejorative tone. Then he began to call out, 'This is my show, my show! This is not Max's show.' He proceeded to cut the heart out of every segment that had been provided by Max. Max was horrified but decided not to do anything about it. After demolishing Max in this way, Bernstein inserted a new preface in which there was all this 'my good friend Max Schell, my dear friend Max Schell...' He also put back into the film many scenes which I had edited out—including the one we called the butterfly speech, which he delivered at the end of the Ninth Symphony. There was Bernstein, with his hands clasped, extending in front of him. He opened them and told the audience that here, in this very room, a butterfly had flown in. What was it? The soul of Beethoven. The butterfly had come back as the soul of Beethoven and was with us here right in this room."

The extra editing time cost an additional $100,000.*

Like Schuller, Fertik finds it difficult to comprehend Bernstein's loving relationship with a city as anti-Semitic as Vienna. Fertik's wife, Greta, a psychiatrist, ascribes the Austrian city's fascination with him not to guilt over its past treatment of the Jews, as Bernstein himself does, but to "an Aryan narcissism, a homosexual sensibility that is pervasive there." If that homosexual sensibility played a role in attracting the Viennese to Bernstein, it certainly also worked the other way around.

Bernstein shares with his father a quest for money and need to control people. He also shares Sam's contempt for women, remarked on in Burton Bernstein's book. In *Family Matters*, Sam is quoted comparing his female colleagues to "two-bit whores" and his rough treatment of his wife is documented in some detail. Bernstein's commitment to a homosexual life in recent years may echo his father's real disgust with women, but it does not follow that he is capable of romantic feeling or love for men.

Bernstein has never been known to have expressed a dream of a shared intimacy with someone, of enjoying the fantasy of a nice cottage for two with one doing the shopping and the other the cooking, like Chester Kallman and W. H. Auden, among other renowned homosexual couples. In *Philharmonic*, the novel based on Bernstein's life, Lourand, the Bernstein character, says, "What put me off Peter was the fact that he wanted—closeness. Not just the sex thing, but closeness. An attachment. I didn't want that at all."

---

* *Schell has proven himself a talented filmmaker, with his biographical documentary* Marlene, *released in 1984.*

Not only did Bernstein choose to stay clear of any long-standing attachment with another man, he despised the stereotypical homosexual. In his memoir, Tennessee Williams writes of a day in 1945 when Bernstein and he were invited to lunch "by a pair of very effete American queens. Bernstein was very hard on them and I was embarrassed by the way he insulted them." Williams claims that Bernstein told them that when the revolution came, they would be stood up against a wall and shot.

In the late years of his career, Bernstein started to turn to Wagner, conducting parts of *Götterdämmerung*, *Siegfried*, and *Die Walküre*. He also conducted all of *Tristan und Isolde*, with Hildegard Behrens and the Bavarian State Orchestra. Broadcast on German radio and transmitted via European TV, this *Tristan* was taped simultaneously by Philips Records. For this remarkable achievement, Bernstein did not hold back on the use of powerful voices, something he could be faulted for in the past. Bernstein's *Tristan* was released in September 1983, only months after *A Quiet Place*, his new opera, had received its world premiere.

A Quiet Place was the result of a commission from the Houston Grand Opera, the Kennedy Center, and La Scala. Bernstein started to work on the opera at Indiana University when he was a composer in residence for six weeks during the winter of 1982. While there he lived in an apartment where he and Stephen Wadsworth, his twenty-nine-year-old librettist, worked. They wrote the first act, as well as parts of the second and third acts.

Bernstein's apartment was twelve miles from campus. A young musician who was there reports that "Bernstein got on the telephone to make certain that people would be with him there, and they did come all that distance in the ice. Then they stayed over. The last week or ten days there was a student party every night and Bernstein went to all of them. He would sit in a corner with a group of people surrounding him."

For the last party, Bernstein wrote a parody to be sung to the tune "A Bicycle Built for Two." Dedicated to the dean of the School of Music of Indiana University, Bernstein sang it to him at the party. The words went this way:

BERNSTEIN

Deany, weeny, show me your penie, do!
I'm all steamy, all for the love of you!
You want to see mine? It's teeny!
But that's 'cause I'm a sheeny—
But you're a goy,
And boy oh boy!
I'll just betcha it's built for two!

BERNSTEIN

35

Bernstein composed several thoroughly professional
and appealing works between the Bicentennial musical and *A
Quiet Place*. They included *Songfest*, a cycle of American poems for six
singers and orchestra; *Divertimento for Orchestra*, written for the hundredth anniversary of the Boston Symphony Orchestra; *A Musical*

August 1982
*Bernstein embracing exhilarated conducting fellows of the Los Angeles Philharmonic
Institute Orchestra, Eigi Oue, Leonid Grin, and Jah-ja Ling. "The totality of
admiration, adulation, and love that have been poured onto him is unparalleled, outside
of the superstars of popular culture."*

Toast, composed in memory of André Kostelanetz; *Touches,* a piano piece for the 1981 Van Cliburn International Piano Competition; and *Halil: Nocturne for Solo Flute, Strings, and Percussion.* But the opera was the most ambitious work of the years 1975 to 1985. Completed in 1983, *A Quiet Place* picks up the lives of the principal characters in *Trouble in Tahiti* after Sam and Dinah set out for a movie rather than face each other in the living room. In a taped conversation after the dress rehearsal, Bernstein said, "I always wanted to know what happened to these people. How did they get through the next ten years? Did they go home and fuck? Is that where Dede came from?" Now its thirty years later. Dinah has died, and the first act takes place in a funeral home. Here the musical language is twelve-tone. Junior, who has evaded the draft, is bisexual. He suffers psychotic moments in which he cannot control what he says. These passages are scored in bebop style.

Apart from this idiosyncratic American sound, the primary influence in the opera is Wagner, an influence that had been nowhere apparent in Bernstein up to the late 1970s. In fact, in a filmed interview for the United States Information Agency, when Bernstein listed the many influences on him throughout the years, Wagner was not one of them.

By the early 1980s, things had changed. John Dunlop, one of many of the beautiful young friends Bernstein had made, tells of an evening in the Dakota when someone called saying she was a medium. At first Bernstein kept asking her how she had found his number. But he stopped when she told him he was a reincarnation of Mahler and Wagner. After hanging up, Bernstein repeated what she had said to the men around him. When Dunlop disagreed about Wagner, Bernstein became angry and said he thought he *could* have been a reincarnation of Wagner.

In *The New Yorker,* Andrew Porter, likened *A Quiet Place* to

an American "Ring" ... Wotan-Fricka, Wotan-Brünnhilde, and Wotan-Siegfried encounters find clear vernacular reflections here. And the "moral" is essentially that proclaimed by Brünnhilde at the close of Wagner's cycle... "Not goods, not gold, or godly magnificence; not house, not hall, or lordly splendor; not astutely drawn-up legal contracts, or hypocritical observance of the conventions; but only *Love* can bring happiness in weal or woe."

As he started work on *A Quiet Place*, Bernstein had his sights on opera rather than Broadway. After Felicia's death, he did begin to work on a musical, but after six months he let it go. Arthur Laurents recalls: "I had an idea for a musical. Lenny wanted it to be an opera. He canceled conducting engagements to work on it. I'd go up to the Dakota flying, then come home with the heaviest shoes in New York. The work was about being free in all senses of the word. It was to be a fable set in a fantastic country with no time. It was called *Alarums and Excursions*, and we worked on it for five or six months. We even went with his kids to Jamaica to concentrate on it."

Stephen Wadsworth says that when he first met Bernstein, "he was recovering from a falling-out on a creative project with Laurents, finding it too Broadway. He felt that the creative choices were going to be controlled by producers and the Broadway formula. He had paid his dues to Broadway and was now looking for ways in which he could press ahead in a daring manner in regard to form and content."

Wadsworth got through to Bernstein with the help of Jamie, whom he had known at Harvard. He speaks of Bernstein with admiration and warmth: "Lenny is the most generous-spirited man I have ever known. Here he met a young man of twenty-seven and gave this person his absolute respect. I was never condescended to. He would always say, 'When are we going to have our first fight?' But that never happened. To work all night with him is a ticket to intellectual and emotional Nirvana. Those hours we spent defeating the night were so great. Sometimes there was a lot of pain because the people we were dealing with were taken from our lives."

Bernstein had recently lost his wife, and Wadsworth had recently lost his sister. "There was an air of trauma around everything," he says. "Just before the opening, Sheri Greenawald [the lead mezzo-soprano] learned that her father died. There was a lot of crying, a lot of getting angry, a lot of firing. We were most unhappy with the direction. Some day I'll write about my experience with Lenny. It was an indescribable growth period for me. Winning the lottery couldn't have been better."

At the premiere on June 18, 1983, one day after the fifth anniversary of Felicia's death, Jamie and Nina, in Houston with their father, were wearing their mother's dresses, just as Dede, the daughter in the opera, did on stage. In fact the clothes in the closet on stage belonging to the mother who had died were actually clothes taken from Felicia's closet, which had been kept in perfect condition over the years since her death. The opening funeral scene was modeled on Felicia's funeral. Bernstein was playing a game, watching to see who could pick up the fact that there was autobiography here.

Autobiography was everywhere. One of the characters, Mrs. Doc, represented Lillian Hellman, who had lived on the island of Martha's Vineyard when the Bernsteins were there and who had become attached to Felicia. While Mrs. Doc admits that she was "in love" with Dinah, there is never any suggestion of a lesbian relationship between them.

There was real tension between Hellman and Bernstein. Among friends Bernstein had always referred to her as "Uncle Lillian." For her part, Hellman had enraged the Amberson staff when, on Bernstein's sixtieth birthday, two months after Felicia's death, during a nationwide telecast from Wolf Trap in Virginia, she walked up to her microphone, threw her script away, and said she was there to talk of Felicia. Nor did Hellman ever forgive Bernstein for changing her version of *Candide*. On her deathbed she said that the only good news she had had for days was that the New York City Opera production of *Candide* got bad reviews.

If Mrs. Doc was an echo of Hellman, Sam represented Sam, Junior represented Leonard, and Dede represented Shirley in ways even less ambiguous. When Junior faces his father after a long absence, he shifts into his bebop style and sings of the Sam we know through Bernstein:

> *Hey, Big Daddy, you driving me batty.*
> *You big bizness, you ratty boo.*
> *You some cat, you so fat,*
> *You a rich city Daddy-boo.*
> *Hey, Big Daddy, then why you blue?*
> *Cuz you Lady's dead,*
> *and you drove her to drivin' 'round the bend,*
> *and it's on you head.*
> *You a winnin' cat, but that's that, Big Daddy.*

> *Look out, here comes Bow-wow-wow.*
> *Look out. You a loser now. Wow!**

Later Junior recalls an early trauma, of Sam finding him in bed with Dede and shooting him in the shoulder. It parallels the story Bernstein told Harvey Probber, his friend of the late 1940s. Bernstein said that when he was a child, his mother had found him and his sister engaged in sex play. "She kept shouting and screaming at him," Probber says, "and then went for a broom to sweep him out from under the bed where he had hidden. Lenny remembers calling, 'Mother, Mother, Mother.'"

However traumatic that incident may have been, brother and sister made no effort to conceal the closeness of their connection. During Bernstein's Harvard years, friends frequently saw the two kissing in a parked car on a popular lover's lane, and through the years, Shirley easily confided that Lenny had given her her "first French kiss." Though all of this is hearsay, it is worth mentioning because of the way it fits the libretto of *A Quiet Place*. Here Junior not only tells François, as Bernstein had told Probber, of sister and brother being discovered by an enraged parent. He goes on to detail the several incidents of incest between Dede and himself:

> *You and your Didi, well she and we, she and...*
> *used to do it all the time...*
> *all the time, all the time, all the...*
> *I know we're not suppose' to me and Dede bed.*
> *Oh sure, I lied, I scared, I lied and um... um...*
> *and anyway I never dared to come inside her.**

The last line is the only one in this confession by Junior that is grammatically correct and that the protagonist has no difficulty articulating. In this opera Bernstein tries to go beyond *Mass* in revealing himself, but even here he comes to the brink, then stops short with a disclaimer. After Junior describes the origins and the development of the incestuous relationship with Dede, Dede's husband says, "*Encore des fantaisies.*" While Bernstein appears to be torn here, his wish seems to be to tell it all, for Junior's explicit description is in English, while François's three-word repudiation is in French.

JALNI Publications, Inc.

According to Wadsworth: "Because Junior is having an episode when he tells of the incest, we don't know if what he is saying is the truth. At first, when Lenny and I wrote the scene, we considered it something that had happened, then something that might have happened, and finally something that did not happen." Bernstein indulges in a rite of purification without ever quite confessing to the sin itself. He behaves like the penitent in a confessional booth who, after asking for forgiveness, then says, "But, in all truth, father, I may have just imagined this." The phantasmagoric quality of Junior's and François's words have the nebulous texture of a half-remembered dream in which the pendulum of memory swings tantalizingly back and forth from reverie to revelation to rebuttal.

However intense these passages are, there is another that moves Bernstein still more. "I cry," he has said, "when Junior says 'I love you Daddy,' and obviously something has built up to that. This psychotic working out of something he has never been able to say before ... it's an unbelievable spiritual orgasm."

By July 1984, the time of the Kennedy Center production, some changes in the form of the opera had been made. Most of them were the decisions of John Mauceri, the conductor in Washington and a Bernstein protégé. The most crucial of these changes was the moving of *Trouble in Tahiti* from its position as the opening opera to the middle of *A Quiet Place*, where it serves as a flashback.

Still the work provoked negative reviews. In a "Critic's Notebook" column in *The New York Times*, Bernard Holland wrote that he could not understand why "this immensely talented man has allowed himself to squander his fury and intensity on characters like Sam, his grown children, and the children's bisexual lover. Their sufferings repel rather than move." There is no reason why Holland should have known that the libretto, in the main, was based on Bernstein's own life.

However dark the inner life of Bernstein remains, the outer life reached something of an apotheosis during a fortnight in the summer of 1986. Twice his photograph appeared on page one of *The New York Times*. The precipitating event on July 25 was a concert at Tanglewood where his soloist, a fourteen-year-old Japanese girl, broke strings on two violins. The event on August 5 was his first concert in ten years in New York's Central Park. For both concerts Bernstein conducted the

Candide Overture, his *Serenade,* and Tchaikovsky's Symphony No. 6. The park performance even moved the *Times* to publish an editorial on August 6. The attacks by Harold Schonberg seemed light years away. "Some 200,000 spectators," the editorial said,

> did not simply recline at ease as Mr. Bernstein leaped high to stress a sforzando here or twisted erotically to coax a melody there. They participated. They hummed, applauded at every opportunity and when "Stars and Stripes Forever" and the closing fireworks exploded together, they jumped to their feet and, cheering and waving, gave Mr. Bernstein ten thousand co-conductors.

The editorial echoed the review of the day before. "He is Chaplinesque in his pantomime," wrote Tim Page,

> and can convey the essence of a particular measure with such acuity and grace that watching him is like reading a map of the score. He wiggles and dances like an orgiastic surfer, carried aloft on waves of sound. But his gestures are not merely histrionic. He seems a personification of music—in all its complexity, pain, and exaltation.

Twice, in recent years, Bernstein has fallen off the podium just after the completion of a work. Some say it happened because he is too vain to wear glasses when he turns to the audience. Others attribute the falls to all the alcohol, although his staff maintains he does not drink before rehearsal or performance. Nevertheless the two falls frightened some of Bernstein's fans, who thought he had had fatal attacks.

Bernstein himself appears to have no fear of dying on the podium. He says he wants to go in an apocalyptic way, perhaps in a "rickety plane" that falls apart. He fears he will die like Dinah, his grandmother, lying quietly in bed.

Such an exit would not suit this man of remarkable temperament who longs for mesmerizing, upbeat finales. Although he has told outsiders that he liked his brother's memoir, he confided to friends that he did not. Most particularly he deplored the ending of the first section, with the listing of all those members of the Bernstein family who were dead by the end of World War II. He found it too severe. He was also disappointed in Stephen Wadsworth's failure to come up with a spectacular ending for *A Quiet Place* and in Alan Jay Lerner for letting him down with the ending to *1600 Pennsylvania Avenue*. Bernstein loves the ending to his own *Divertimento*, a particularly rousing one, which always draws huge applause. But some part of him must know that there are few simple happy endings in life, for in his most ambitious works, the final tonic chord is infiltrated by a far more restless one, a chord that is highly ambiguous.

The music reveals the man. Bernstein said something like this during a television show he made for the BBC devoted to an exploration of Mahler. His point was that while Mahler converted from Judaism to Christianity to further his career, he revealed his profound Jewish identity in every measure he composed.

As the ambiguous final chord reflects Bernstein's own assessment of the outcome of the highly complicated race he has run, so his most frequently used interval may well reflect his real view of his character. The interval is the tritone, made up of three whole tones; it is also known as an augmented fourth. The first two notes of "Ma-ri-a!" (C to F sharp) will bring it to mind. This was the interval to which executives at Columbia Records objected when they first heard it throughout the *West Side Story* score. The augmented fourth has always been known as the "devil in music." While Bernstein is certainly both angel and devil, in his later years the devil may have the upper hand. It usually takes Valium and two sleeping pills to put Bernstein to sleep as the dawn comes up. Even when he has a rehearsal at 10 A.M., Bernstein rarely dozes off before 6 A.M.

If the seminal gene in Bernstein had been political rather than musical, he would probably have become one of the most controversial figures in history, more like the czar in *Boris Godunov* than Alexander the Great or Ivan the Terrible. There would have been great and cruel things. "Off with his head" would have been a common command. At a recording session in 1983 Bernstein fired everyone on the spot and had to rehire the participants the next day so the recording could be made. Hotels where Bernstein stays report it takes their cleaning staffs several days to repair the damage. Far more terrifying is

Bernstein's recent habit of giving wet kisses to virtually everyone, then telling those who are homosexual, "Some say AIDS can be spread by saliva. Then if you or I have it, the other one now will."

Poet, lyricist, political activist, possessor of wide-ranging interests, Bernstein is to many the Renaissance man his mother claims him to be. And because he understands how to use the media, he has brought music to more people than anyone else. The qualities that made him a natural for television would have worked against him in an earlier time. In the 1930s, the decade of Toscanini, Stokowski, and Koussevitzky, it would have been unthinkable for a conductor of classical music to talk to his audience at a concert. Similarly, a serious composer could never have put his private life on display in the particular way Bernstein has. Aaron Copland, by comparison, has been a model of discretion.

In 1985, Deutsche Grammophon prevailed on Bernstein to take four days out of his crowded summer schedule to go into a New York studio to record *West Side Story*. With a first-rate pickup orchestra, and operatic stars of the highest caliber, Bernstein's score shone as it never had before. While the original cast album possesses an American vitality lacking in this treatment, the 1985 recording not only became the best-selling record that Deutsche Grammophon ever made, it moved Will Crutchfield to write in *The New York Times* that Bernstein was in a class with Verdi.

During a film made at the recording of the album, Kiri Te Kanawa, the soprano who sang the role of Maria, said that this was the music she had grown up on in New Zealand. In fact, she said, a boyfriend sang Tony and she sang Maria. She added, "The funniest thing of all was when he [Bernstein] suddenly stopped conducting and said, 'That's the tempo, that's it.' And I laughed, because it was like having Mozart with you; you were getting it from the master himself." She was talking about *West Side Story*, a Broadway show, not *The Age of Anxiety* or *Mass*.

Today *West Side Story* is still the single piece for which Bernstein is most renowned. As in *A Quiet Place*, life goes on. Thirty years have passed. Some dreams have been fulfilled, others have not. Some lives have ended. The remaining family is united by an underlying love. But someone has missed a cue; the final curtain has not come down. The actors stand around uncertainly, then finally drift off into the wings.

The audience files out. Only the composer is left on the stage. The instinct is to do something, fill the time, not let them know. The mixture is as before only everything is bigger: more applause, more money, more adulation, more sensation, enough to distract the audience. But what has gone wrong?

Bernstein had hoped they would accept his answer but they left without even having heard the question. In *Mass* the underlying theme was "Fuck you!" In *A Quiet Place* the underlying theme is "Love me." The ultimate test of love for Bernstein is that the giver feel it for him, knowing who and what Bernstein really is. But the figure in the opera does not elicit love. Junior is not only charmless, he doesn't make art. Allowances will be made even for Wagner but not for Bernstein's fictional counterpart of his own self.

The irony is that allowances are always being made for Bernstein by those who love him and see at least some of what he is. Still that never gets through to him. The totality of admiration, adulation, and love that have poured onto him is unparalleled, outside of the superstars of popular culture. But none of it will penetrate. Of love there is not enough, and finally love is not enough. It is not enough to stop the pain, and the only thing that can explain this man, with his chain smoking, pills, liquor, insomnia, and need for crowds, is incredible pain. In *A Quiet Place* Bernstein tried to vomit his soul to get rid of the poisons that are causing the pain.

Stephen Wadsworth says that after *A Quiet Place*, Bernstein and he began another opera. "Lenny said it was to be about the tragic nature of history," Wadsworth explains, "as it relates to this century, like war as a fact of life, and how dangerous it is that man needs to express himself and socialize himself in this way.

"I worked very hard," Wadsworth goes on. "I did a sprawling first draft and actually wrote the first two scenes. But after a few sessions together I withdrew. I walked out. I said to myself, 'We've done this opera before.'"

Afterword

In the fall of 1980, *The New Grove Dictionary of Music and Musicians* (TNG), the most trusted reference work in the field in English, was appearing in a sixth edition. The fifth edition had been published in 1955 and Stanley Sadie, its current editor, was claiming that 97% of the sixth was new. A 20-volume work, with

August 1983
With biographer Joan Peyser. "The late Heinz Weissenstein had been photographing Bernstein since 1940. Bernstein pulled me in for one of the shots...."

more than 2500 contributors, costing $2,000, it was awaited with great eagerness by the international community of scholars and musicians.

Macmillan of London, its publisher, was hosting a party at New York's Waldorf Astoria Hotel with Sir Harold Macmillan, former prime minister of England, representing the publisher. As the editor of *The Musical Quarterly* (*MQ*), which is to academic music journals what *TNG* is to music dictionaries, I was on the guest list. I planned to devote an entire issue—almost 300 editorial pages—to a review and had begun to commission specialists to write essays on how specific fields met their own standards.

The invitation had Bernstein as a primary speaker. But when he addressed the audience, he did not come forth with traditional remarks. Instead he said a button on his shirt had popped and that he was wearing a white silk scarf to hide his otherwise visible "big belly." Bernstein then admonished the publisher for holding its party on November 22, the anniversary of John F. Kennedy's death. He asked everyone to stand for a moment of silence in memory of America's slain president.

Some stood, some remained seated. A man at my table who identified himself as a former editor of *The Wall Street Journal*, attacked Bernstein for always calling attention to himself and away from the matter at hand. Bernstein did always call attention to himself but something led me to believe that night that, in addition to the U.K.'s disregard of an American trauma, another factor may have been involved. I received my set of *TNG* late that afternoon, and, immediately after the festivities, I looked to see how *TNG* had dealt editorially with the man whom they expected would give their evening a special panache.

TNG had not treated him well. Including a photograph, the entry occupied less than one page while the one on Pierre Boulez, to cite only one example, extended to more than eight pages. In addition, *TNG* made an egregious error. American musicians have November 14, 1943, virtually engraved on their brains—for that was the date on which the 25-year-old Bernstein, in business suit and bow tie, stepped in for Bruno Walter and launched what went on to become the greatest career in American music. *TNG* gave that date as November 13, 1944. That not only made Bernstein a year older; it annihilated the magical significance of November 14 for anyone assessing his interior life. (Six years before the Walter event, he met Aaron Copland on November 14, which was also Copland's birthday, and eleven years later, in 1954, Bernstein dazzled a nation of television viewers with his first *Omnibus* show, again on November 14.)

It took two years for the *TNG* reviews to come in. Most of my authors delivered encomia on the various specialties of historical musicology. But I wrote an editorial taking *TNG* to task for problems that, admittedly, lie outside the realm of traditional scholarship. One was the whitewashing of several German musicians' careers when they were working with the Nazis. The second was the unambiguously contemptuous attitude towards the American musical theater, or what we know as Broadway. In addition to my own remarks on this, Paul Wittke, senior editor at G. Schirmer for more than forty years and *MQ*'s musical theater expert for this issue, wrote that "Bernstein and Sondheim have greatly enlarged the harmonic, rhythmic and structural arsenal of our theater. But you would never know this from these tepid entries."

My review issue was scheduled for April 1982. Before its distribution, Sadie telephoned me to say my criticisms had been leaked to him and made him very unhappy. Turning his attention to Bernstein, Sadie said that no important critic or scholar had been willing to write that particular piece and that it was unfair of me, therefore, to single Bernstein out. That surprised me. I replied that he had not asked me. If he had, I would have been happy to do it. It was then that Sadie commissioned me to write an essay on Bernstein for a set of volumes then in preparation that would be called *The New Grove Dictionary of American Music*. (The story of my contribution does not end there. *TNG*'s edited version of my article so distorted its tone, making the content virtually indistinguishable from the original entry, that I sent a wire threatening legal action.)

When Bernstein learned I was writing a piece on him, he was delighted. We arranged to meet at Tanglewood after a morning rehearsal with the Boston Symphony Orchestra. In the Green Room he was surrounded by his usual entourage. When I told him I wanted to see him alone, he smiled, and with great charm dismissed everyone present saying, "She wants me alone." We lunched together at Saranak—the house in which Koussevitzky had lived—shopped for a going-away present for his cook, had his hair cut in a Lenox salon, and went to a photoshoot at Whitestone Studio; the late Heinz Weissenstein had been photographing Bernstein since 1940. Bernstein pulled me in for one of the shots which is reproduced here.

It was during the lunch, when he described his fit of uncontrollable coughing as an "emotional reaction" to my question about Gershwin, that I began to think of Bernstein as the perfect vehicle through which to tell the story of music in the United States over the last 50 years, particularly in reference to musicians who had turned their backs on their vernacular heritage in favor of a connection with European culture. Before 1977, when I assumed the post of editor of *MQ*, I had written two books tracing serious music in Europe during the twentieth century. The first, published in 1971, and entitled *The New Music: the Sense behind the Sound*, charted the lives and works of Schoenberg, Stravinsky and Varèse. The second, concentrating on Pierre Boulez, appeared in 1976.

Even before my contretemps with Stanley Sadie, I sent my entry for the American *Grove* to Bernstein to check for accuracy. He inserted the name of a work I had inadvertently neglected and forgave me with "Brava, Joan!" written on the manuscript. Some time later I sent Bernstein a letter saying I wanted to write his biography. Kraut replied on Bernstein's letterhead noting that Bernstein was "pleased" and that he and Amberson would give me any help I needed. Still, the reader may well wonder why I felt qualified to be Bernstein's first bone fide biographer.

The more points of identification a biographer and a subject have the more insightful the biography is bound to be.

I felt particularly suited to write about Leonard Bernstein. He and I are American Jews, raised in Boston and New York, two major cities in the American northeast. He did his undergraduate work at Harvard University, I at Smith and Barnard Colleges, all first-rate academic institutions concentrating on the humanities. Both of us spent our lives in music, playing the piano seriously as children, and following college with graduate work in the field, he at the Curtis Institute of Music, and I at Columbia University. Bernstein, of course, went on to become a composer, conductor and teacher of international fame, I a musicologist and writer in the field.

Bernstein and I had fathers who were successful businessmen, his in the beauty supply industry, mine as an importer of laces. Both mens' first-born children were sons—relentlessly rebellious—with younger, adoring sisters—Shirley and me. Bernstein and I married only once and had three children in the same order—girl, boy, girl—who, remarkably, are the same ages.

In addition to all of this, Bernstein and I have subscribed to psychoanalytic psychology as the particular prism through which to understand ourselves. Bernstein was in and out of treatment much of his adult life with two New York psychoanalysts. I was married for 25 years to a psychiatrist grounded in psychoanalytic psychology. Having profited from rich conversation with my husband and his colleagues and ready access to an immense library, I continue to find this intellectual discipline the most useful tool I have in deciphering the person at the center of my study as well as those figures surrounding him.

There is one point of identification Bernstein and I do not share. I am not a homosexual man. Much of the uproar that followed the publication of my book focused on that particular point, with some critics going as far as to suggest that I am a homophobe. That is not true. For more than 20 years—from the mid-1960s to the mid-1980s—my writing appeared regularly on the music page of the Arts and Leisure section of the Sunday *New York Times*. The pieces could be described as very small biographies of composers whose newest works were to be performed the following week. Each centered on an interview with the artist. The world of contemporary composition includes many homosexual men—Bernstein and his associates were not alone in this regard—and I could not have written as I did without the trust of those to whom I spoke.

While I was at work on the book, Bernstein is reported to have told friends that he believed nobody could do the job better than I. Harry Kraut spoke of an incident to me that took place when he, Bernstein and Carlos Moseley, former music director of the New York Philharmonic, were lunching on Central Park South. According to Kraut, Moseley said he could not understand why Bernstein was cooperating as he was with me when "she did what she did to Boulez." Bernstein answered: "What she did to Boulez! She was on target in every detail. Not a nuance was off in any way."

In any event Bernstein accorded me trust. He always returned my occasional phone call, replied to my occasional letter. Often when we met at a party or as listeners at a concert, he talked about his sexual life. I did not ask for more than that, for I do not write authorized biography. Authorized biography implies the subject or his representatives gives the author material—letters, diaries, professional fees and so on—and in return the author gives those persons the manuscript before it goes to press. This allows them to make additions and deletions and set the tone for the portrait. That is hack work. I do not ever do that. Nor do I write opposed biographies. If I approach someone and that person says he or she prefers I not write about them, they will never hear from me again.

Still, to be comfortable with the accuracy of detail, I needed someone who had been a long-time friend and colleague of Bernstein to read the finished manuscript. I chose Arthur Laurents, who had known my subject since *Fancy Free*, had written the book for *West Side Story*, and continued to remain in touch with him. Laurents gave me his word that he would not show the book to Bernstein or those people surrounding him. At the time the playwright was staying in his house in Quogue, New York. I sent him the work via overnight mail, and in a short time he called. He said he had not slept but read straight through. As to the question of errors: Mr. Laurents told me a theater I put on West 46th Street was, in fact, on West 45th.

In sum Bernstein did not think that because of my gender I would be incapable of writing a fair biography of him. He told me he thought a gay, male biographer would be too limiting. I think he was right about this. Not only did my biography become an immediate national bestseller, but within a few years it moved into nine foreign editions. Meanwhile Bernstein, the man, escalated in popularity. Record sales, prizes, public frenzy at his every appearance, multiplied exponentially.

When, in the spring of 1987, I received the first two copies of *Bernstein: A Biography*, I inscribed one of them and left it with the doorman at the Dakota who told me Bernstein was at home. Soon after Bernstein went to a party in New York. Joseph Machlis, musicologist, author, professor of music at the Juilliard School and Queens College, and a famous Manhattan host, was present as a guest. According to Machlis, as soon as Bernstein arrived, the other guests besieged him with questions about his reaction to the book. Raising his palms towards the ceiling, shrugging his shoulders, Bernstein smiled and responded: "What can I say? Now my mother knows everything."

Despite the agitated response by Bernstein's acolytes, despite several anonymous death threats to me, no lawyer or publicist attached to Bernstein made a single call or sent a single letter to my literary agent, my lawyer, my publisher, or me.

The following February I received a letter from Nicolas Slonimsky, composer, conductor, associate to Koussevitzky, and author of the famous *Lexicon of Musical Invective: Critical Assaults on Composers Since Beethoven's Time*, and the valuable, immensely useful one-volume work, *Baker's Biographical Dictionary of Musicians*. In it he wrote that my biography of Bernstein would result in my being "glorified in languages that neither you nor I can even read." As for its effect on Bernstein, Slonimsky predicted that "the book may increase the public curiosity about him so much that he will be getting even more engagements than he can accept and more money for his appearances than he can possibly use." Moving into the arena that had generated so much controversy, Slonimsky gave this assessment: "Whether he and his family will enjoy reading about his sexual aberrations is something else again. But, after all, history is history and biography is biography and we have gone in the direction of glasnost (hardly a word suitable to the subject) far enough to justify candor in reporting."

In July of 1988, Ballantine Books, a division of Random House, published a mass market paperback of *Bernstein*. A small, fat book, it was sold in drugstores and airports. I went on a second publicity tour.

Just after I returned, I received a call from Tim Page, then the chief music critic for *Newsday*. Page was preparing a major story on Bernstein for the ASCAP magazine. He said he had been in the bookstore at Tanglewood and that customers were unable to find my biography. When the sales clerks were asked for it, they answered that executives at Tanglewood had forbidden its appearance there. Then they reached below the counter and retrieved copies from the stacks kept out of view.

Halfway through my book I wrote: "One of Bernstein's least apparent characteristics is that despite his seemingly aggressive ways he is, at heart, a passive man.... He allows himself to be bullied." Even in his advanced years, that passivity remained intact. Despite his great gifts and international fame, he ran from confrontation with tough people, particularly those who appeared to be acting on his behalf. To that end, to satisfy the demands of his numerous handlers, Bernstein agreed to tell the press that he had never read the book, that he had promised his children—sometimes on bended knees—that he would never read it.

But read it he did.

In August of that same summer, virtually everyone who was ever connected to Bernstein contributed their talents to a four-day celebration commemorating his 70th birthday. Events covered the spectrum of his career, ranging from Dawn Upshaw singing "I Hate Music," to the student orchestra playing his most beloved works, to Christa Ludwig singing an aria from *Candide*, to Rostropovich flying in from Sicily to conduct the epilogue from Strauss's *Don Quixote*, a memento from Bernstein's New York Philharmonic debut, to lighter material from his children and Stephen Sondheim, all attended by, reports claimed, more than eight thousand people. Beverly Sills hosted the event. Videotaped messages from orchestras throughout Europe were played and princes and princesses appeared to be everywhere on the Tanglewood lawn.

Throughout the musical tributes and elaborate parties, Bernstein graciously greeted people and appeared to be overwhelmed with joy—at least during those moments that my particular sources described. But once the last guest had departed, and Bernstein was finally alone in his rented house, the dichotomy between the huge adoring crowds and the loneliness at the end of the day struck him as close to unbearable.

Only one month after the festivities, Bernstein sent a poem he wrote to his friend John Malcolm Brinnin. In it he revealed the paradoxical effect such hyperbolic expressions of love and awe can generate:

> (*The Birthday Continues...*)
> *I am celebrated beyond bearing.*
> *The adjectives become intolerable*
> *As they hump upon one another, Two-Dogs Fucking;*
> *Double-descriptives, á la Time:*
> *Masterful/loving, peacemaker/igniter*
> *Und so weiter,*
> *Ass-licking, ego-rimming, soul sucking.*

> *On the other hand, what right do I have to complain?*

How dare I envy the young, so driven, so confused,
Ambitious up the hall? And yet I do.
They lust, they penetrate, they get it up.
They flock about me, linger in my arms;
But I withdraw (if they've not done so first)
And I am left to write these lines, alone,
Alone, and safe from ultimate exposure,
Or foolish rash commitment. (That was a close one.)

The contrasts out-sonata Beethoven:
Bright gala! (empty bed); the blare! (The blues)
Encomia! (sinusitis, prostatism,
and all the spooks of swift-advancing age.)
Today is my free day; What shall I do?
I do not want another thousand kisses,
Na, Ja, Vielleicht fahre ich in den Prater
And kiss at length one pure and total stranger.

Brinnin was not the only recipient of what many would consider the communication of private miseries. In July of 1990, with Michael Tilson Thomas and the London Symphony Orchestra, Bernstein embarked on a music festival in Sapporo, Japan, that was to move onto performances in Tokyo, Yokohama, Kyoto and Osaka. Bernstein told a reporter with the English paper *The Sunday Telegraph* that "it starts with a force called gravity. Somehow things start falling and drooping that never did. And your fingers dry up, like your tears. I have to put drops in my eyes at night. To turn pages, I must lick my fingers; that's an old man's habit. Other things dry up, other fluids...." Despite his public unhappiness about his sexual abilities, Bernstein continued to have romances. One was with a six-foot-five, 28-year-old man, an aspiring novelist from Alabama. Mark Adams Taylor was a speechwriter for Jay Oliva, president of New York University. Apparently the position provided a flexible schedule because, when Amberson called on him to come to Tokyo, believing he would elevate Bernstein's mood, Taylor flew there right away. The maestro's cruelty to those who loved him had not, however, diminished over the years. When after a long, hard trip, Taylor arrived, he found Bernstein flagrantly demonstrative with a young, gay Japanese liaison. Taylor returned to New York.

As it happened, soon after that, Bernstein suffered a genuine physical collapse and was forced to return home too. There he recovered sufficiently to make plans to go to Tanglewood to celebrate the festival's 50th season and to conduct the Koussevitzky Memorial Concert on Sunday, August 19, 1990.

From the start things seemed ominous in the Berkshires. For years Bernstein had been renting a house in Great Barrington that was owned by Michael Ugo Stille, a New York correspondent for 40 years for the *Corriere della Sera*, and, from 1987, its editor-in-chief. Bernstein told Elizabeth, Stille's wife, that she decorated the house and tended the garden exactly how Felicia had cared for their various country homes. In addition, he looked forward to the highly intellectual, multi-lingual library there. By 1990, conditions had changed in the Stille family and the house was not available. Bernstein moved into a damp rental in Lenox which his entourage called "The Mildew Palace."

When he was there he was unhappy. When he went to work it was not much better. Bottles of oxygen greeted him in his dressing room. Suffering from emphysema, a lung tumor and pulmonary infections, Bernstein was physically spent. Despite all his maladies, he continued to smoke, drink, and take drugs.

The Koussevitzky concert was to proceed in this way. First Britten's *Four Sea Interludes*. Next the Beethoven Seventh. After intermission *Arias and Barcarolles*, a suite of seven songs for soprano, baritone and piano he had written in 1988 for a fund-raising event for AIDS. Because Bernstein wanted to present something at this Tanglewood concert that he himself had composed, he had Bright Sheng, a young, talented composer, orchestrate the work for him.

When August 19th arrived, Bernstein knew he was not capable of conducting the concert as planned. After Bernstein conducted the *Four Sea Interludes*, Carl St. Clair, the assistant resident conductor of the Boston Symphony Orchestra, substituted for Bernstein for *Arias and Barcarolles*. During that performance Bernstein rested backstage, being massaged. After intermission Bernstein walked slowly onto the stage. For the first movement of the Beethoven symphony, he barely lifted his arms. The second, an Allegretto, was played adagio. In the third he coughed ferociously, much as he did in our first interview. But he recovered and led the fourth movement with such intensity that he seemed to know it would be his last time on a podium. Jenny Bernstein knew it too. "I saw," she later said, "he couldn't do more after that."

Throughout the period before that Koussevitzky concert, Bernstein pursued a schedule crowded with travel and performances. The most celebrated events were two concerts in Berlin, one in the West, the other in the East, commemorating the reunification of Germany. That was in December 1989. With an international roster of soloists, telecast to millions via satellite, Bernstein conducted the Beethoven Ninth, changing a word of Schiller's text. Instead of "Freude," (Joy), the chorus sang "Freiheit" (Freedom). Other performances during these last years included a festival at Prague, concerts with the Vienna Philharmonic, the Israel Philharmonic, the Santa Cecilia Orchestra of Rome, the New York Philharmonic and the Boston Symphony Orchestra.

Often Bernstein would talk about his fear that his legacy would be that of a conductor, not a composer in the tradition of those whom he held in awe—Beethoven, Brahms, Mahler and Wagner. He failed in his efforts to write his Holocaust opera, the work that his librettist Stephen Wadsworth had abandoned some time before. Bernstein approached Peter Shaffer and John Guare, both prominent playwrights, to collaborate with him, but they turned him down.

Here is a story that is revelatory about the kind of animus that has been invading the environment for music throughout most of this century.

The climax of Bernstein's 70th birthday tribute at Tanglewood was the Sunday afternoon concert, the result of a Boston Symphony Orchestra commission to eight composers to write a work based on a theme by Bernstein. There was no fee attached. It was understood the honor sufficed. The theme was "New York, New York," from the Bernstein show *On the Town*. Those composers named in the publicity releases who were reported to have accepted the challenge were Luciano Berio, John Corigliano, Leon Kirchner, Jacob Druckman, Lukas Foss, John Williams, Tōru Takemitsu and William Schuman. The event was widely heralded as a demonstration of the affection and respect in which Bernstein was held by his compositional peers.

In preparing this afterword, I started to move down the list of composers to see how they reacted. Berio did not remember the request but is certain he contributed nothing to the event. John Corigliano, one of the United States' most successful serious composers, chose as his melody not the Bernstein tune from *On the Town*, but the song by John Kander and Fred Ebb recorded so successfully by Frank Sinatra. From time to time the theme we associate with the Bernstein show appears but when it does, it lies below the Kander and Ebb melody, and whenever *that* tune reappears, it crushes the Bernstein motive. Corigliano, who speaks with great affection for Bernstein, did this, he says, in the tradition of a roast, to puncture the absurd, worshipful tribute to a living musician that was going on in high gear that long weekend at Tangelwood.

I next called Leon Kirchner, Professor Emeritus at Harvard and a man with a long career of highly distinguished work. When I spoke to him, in February of 1998, Kirchner could not remember if he had incorporated the tune in question into the score he delivered. Kirchner eventually expanded the piece to a major work of more than twenty minutes. What Kirchner did know was that he quoted music from Schoenberg, Stravinsky and Bruckner. When Bernstein later asked him why, in light of his own deep ties to Mahler, the composer had used Bruckner, Kirchner said he told the maestro, "Well, you *should* hear more Bruckner."

If all of this sounds less than generous on the part of Bernstein's most gifted colleagues, let us look at a concert that took place only a few months earlier, in which roles were reversed. On May 11th, 1988, Carnegie Hall hosted a centenary tribute to Irving Berlin. Bernstein was invited to compose something in honor of the great American songwriter, probably the most prolific melodist this country has ever produced. What Bernstein delivered was a dour, mean little piece he entitled "My 12-Tone Melody." The Berlin family expressed its outrage.

What is one to say about this? That each gesture by these late-twentieth-century masters is a shot fired in a battle that is difficult to comprehend but is at one with the temper of our time.

Two years after the birthday festival, in the summer of 1990, Bernstein returned from Tanglewood to New York and entered Lenox Hill Hospital. He spent the better part of a week surrounding his 72nd birthday there. During that time the family called Dr. Samuel Klagsbrun who described himself to me as a psychiatrist who specializes in managing the dying. By then Bernstein and those close to him knew he was dying. But the press releases that went out suggested something entirely different. Bernstein was exhausted, they claimed. He needed to be freed from the arduous task of conducting. He would continue to compose and work on his various educational projects.

The last six weeks proved very harsh. Bernstein had to use a wheel-chair. He had difficulty sleeping and, when he did, he occasionally awakened gasping desperately for breath because his respirator had accidentally become disconnected. Bernstein definitely did not die as he had said he wanted—dramatically, in a rickety airplane. Nor did he die as his grandmother did—peacefully, in her sleep. Apart from Harry Kraut, who was in Europe on his behalf, all those close to him remained nearby; his friends Mendy Wager, Betty Comden, Adolph Green and Phyllis Newman; his associates Phillip Allen and Craig Urquhart; his family, most particularly Alex, whom Bernstein characterized to me as a saint.

Even at the moment of death, Bernstein participated actively. On October 14, a little after 6 P.M., Kevin Cahill, his physician since 1979, prepared to give him a shot. While Cahill's son and Mendy Wager were carrying Bernstein from his chair to the bed, Cahill inserted the needle into his upper leg. Bolting upright Bernstein asked "What's this?" and then slumped lifeless. He could not have been referring to the injection which was routine. What he saw or heard we can never know. The time of death was 6:15.

There was a private funeral in the Dakota apartment. The casket, with a tallith on it, stood in the living room. Jamie and Alex spoke. Nina tried but choked up so audibly that nobody could hear what she said. Shirley remained silent, Jennie dry-eyed. Later Bernstein's mother said that no matter where her son was or what he was doing on Friday nights, he called to wish her a good Sabbath.

During the next three months, three memorials took place. One, at Carnegie Hall, celebrated Bernstein the conductor. The second, at the Majestic Theater, focused on Bernstein the Broadway man. The third, at the Cathedral of St. John the Divine, concentrated on Bernstein the teacher.

Bernstein was buried at Greenwood, a non-sectarian cemetery in Brooklyn. He was placed next to his wife, Felicia, who had died a Catholic with a priest's blessing.

Situated very near the Bernstein plot on a road called Battle Path lies the Skarvelis family gravesite. Regina Skarvelis visits frequently. She says that every time she goes, there are pairs of young men visiting the Bernstein grounds, and that there are stones on Bernstein's grave, the Jewish symbol of respect for the dead.

George Gershwin and Leonard Bernstein each became the best cross-over artist of his generation. Each achieved his greatest renown with a work he composed before he was 40. Each of those works received its first performance not at the Met, but on Broadway.

Porgy and Bess opened when Gershwin was 37, *West Side Story* when Bernstein was 39. Gershwin died less than two years after his magnum opus appeared; ever since journalists, scholars and music lovers have asked what he would have done had he lived another 30 years. Bernstein did live another thirty years. He knew very well what he had done and was gravely disappointed at his short list of works. Measuring himself against those composers he held in awe, the German and Viennese symphonists of the eighteenth and nineteenth centuries, he considered himself to have failed.

I think Bernstein was too hard on himself when he judged what he *should* have done to achieve the immortality he craved.

I would like the reader to call to mind those acknowledged by today's arbiters of taste to be the finest composers of serious music. Try to name even five winners of the Pulitzer Prize during the last few decades. Bernstein deeply coveted that award but it eluded him. The reason it is difficult to call up the names or conjure up the music of these respected figures lies not in the absence of talent, even genius. It lies in the matter of musical language which has posed a problem for the majority of listeners throughout the better part of this century.

Now think of Bernstein as a conductor, a profession he considered less worthy. Virtually everyone would agree that he was the greatest American conductor of his time, and, along with Herbert von Karajan, the greatest international conductors of their time. Even more than Karajan, Bernstein was always aware of the value of technology. In the

1950s and 1960s, he embraced television with his *Omnibus* programs and *Young People's Concerts*. In the 1970s and 1980s, he used the most sophisticated technology to make superb CDs and videos of his innumerable live performances.

Bernstein's name will ultimately be better known than that of Toscanini, Stokowsky, Walter, Reiner and Koussevitzky, those maestros who are icons to many listeners over 60 today. Bernstein's name will be more widely known in the future because the technology of several generations ago could not accomplish for these conductors what current technology has achieved for Bernstein.

Because Bernstein left behind remarkably interpreted, brilliantly executed performances of Western civilization's most beloved music—music that is beautiful, moving and profound—his legacy is immense and assured.

Index

C O L O P H O N

The designer of this book is Derek Bacchus
who composed this volume in the Janson typeface by Linotype AG
on an 11 point body, with 3 points of leading.
Janson is a beautiful script closely modeled after a seventeenth-century Dutch typeface,
which was thought to have been designed and punchcut into metal by Anton Janson,
but in fact was designed and cut by Nicholas Kis.
The Dutch settlement of New Amsterdam was granted legal autonomy in 1653 and
later became known as New York City — the site of Leonard Bernstein's
greatest professional triumphs.
The display type is Phaistos Roman by The Font Bureau.

———————

The half-title page, title page, and colophon page illustration is a graphic translation
from a photograph by Robert P. Millard.

———————